TELECOMMUNICATIONS AND BUSINESS STRATEGY

With today's communications industry experiencing major changes on an almost daily basis, media managers must have a clear understanding of the different delivery platforms, as well as a grasp of critical management, planning, and economic factors in order to stay current and move their organizations forward.

Telecommunications and Business Strategy helps current and future media professionals understand the relationship and convergence patterns between the broadcast, cable television, telephony, and Internet communication industries. Author Richard A. Gershon examines telecommunications industry structures and the management practices and business strategies affecting the delivery of information and entertainment services to consumers. He brings in specialists to present the finer points of management and planning responsibilities. Case studies from the International Radio and Television Society (IRTS) competition supplement the main text and offer an invaluable perspective on management issues.

Developed for students in telecommunications management, electronic media management, and telecommunication economics, this volume also serves as a practical reference for the professional manager.

Richard A. Gershon, Ph.D. (Ohio University), is Professor and co-founder of the Telecommunications and Information Management program at Western Michigan University, where he teaches courses in Telecommunications Management and Communication Technology and Innovation. Dr. Gershon is the author of *The Transnational Media Corporation: Global Messages and Free Market Competition*, winner of the 1998 Book of the Year sponsored by the National Cable Television Center in association with the University of Denver. Dr. Gershon has twice been selected for teaching honors at the national level, including the Steven H. Coltrin Professor of the Year Award (2000) by the International Radio and Television Society (IRTS) and the Barry Sherman Award for Teaching Excellence (2001) by the Management and Economics division of the Association for Education in Journalism and Mass Communication (AEJMC). In 2007, he was the recipient of the Distinguished Teaching Award at Western Michigan University. Dr. Gershon is a founding member of the International Telecommunications Education and Research Association (ITERA) and served as the organization's first President.

TELECOMMUNICATIONS
A Series of Volumes Edited by
Christopher H. Sterling

Selected titles include:

THE ELECTRONIC GRAPEVINE: RUMOR,
REPUTATION, AND REPORTING IN THE NEW
ON-LINE ENVIRONMENT
Borden/Harvey

MAKING UNIVERSAL SERVICE POLICY:
ENHANCING THE PROCESS THROUGH
MULTIDISCIPLINARY EVALUATION
Cherry/Wildman/Hammond

THE INTERNET AS A DIVERSE COMMUNITY: CULTURAL,
ORGANIZATIONAL, AND POLITICAL ISSUES
Gattiker

COMPETITION, REGULATION, AND CONVERGENCE:
CURRENT TRENDS IN TELECOMMUNICATION
POLICY RESEARCH
Gillett/Vogelsang

FROM RURAL VILLAGE TO GLOBAL VILLAGE:
TELECOMMUNICATIONS FOR DEVELOPMENT
IN THE INFORMATION AGE
Hudson

COMMUNICATIONS SATELLITES:
GLOBAL CHANGE AGENTS
Pelton/Oslund/Marshall

SHAPING AMERICAN TELECOMMUNICATIONS:
A HISTORY OF TECHNOLOGY, POLICY, AND ECONOMICS
Sterling/Bernt/Weiss

Congruence – walk the talk
Reliability - do what you say you will do
Acceptance – people want to be accepted for who they are
Openness – who will not hide anything?
4 A's – anywhere, anytime, anything, on any device

Marketing mix – price, product, place , promotion

SWOT – strengths, weaknesses, opportunities, threats

Horizontal integration – growth strategy that allows a business to spread its
influence by expanding into different geographic markets while maintaining a
commitment to its primary business .. example – McDonalds

Vertical - Vertically integrated companies are united through a hierarchy with a
common owner. Usually each member of the hierarchy produces a different product
or service, and the products combine to satisfy a common need

Diversification – a growth strategy that recognizes the value of owning a variety of
related and unrelated businesses.

Industries – TV, Newspaper, Telecoms, radio, internet, cable, wireless and satellite.

Market - market is any one of a variety of different systems, institutions, procedures,
social relations and infrastructures whereby persons trade, and goods and services
are exchanged, forming part of the economy

Broadband – penetration rural markets because nothing exists besides agriculture.

Broadband in telecommunications refers to a signaling method that includes or
handles a relatively wide range of frequencies, which may be divided into channels
or frequency bins. The wider the bandwidth, the greater the information-carrying
capacity.

TELECOMMUNICATIONS AND BUSINESS STRATEGY

Richard A. Gershon

Routledge
Taylor & Francis Group

NEW YORK AND LONDON

First published 2009
by Routledge
270 Madison Ave, New York, NY 10016

Simultaneously published in the UK
by Routledge
2 Park Square, Milton Park, Abingdon, Oxon OX14 4RN

Routledge is an imprint of the Taylor & Francis Group, an informa business

© 2009 Taylor & Francis

Typeset in Garamond 3 by
RefineCatch Limited, Bungay, Suffolk
Printed and bound in the United States of America
on acid-free paper by Edwards Brothers, Inc

Library of Congress Cataloging in Publication Data
Gershon, Richard A.
Telecommunications and business strategy / by Richard A. Gershon.
p.cm.
1. Telecommunication–Management. 2. Strategic planning. I. Title.
HE7661.G46 2008
384.068—dc22
2008013736

ISBN10: 0–8058–6248–X (hbk)
ISBN10: 0–415–99353–9 (pbk)
ISBN10: 1–4106–1641–X (ebk)

ISBN13: 978–0–8058–6248–5 (hbk)
ISBN13: 978–0–415–99353–1 (pbk)
ISBN13: 978–1–4106–1641–8 (ebk)

CONTENTS

List of Figures	ix
List of Tables	xi
Foreword	xv
Preface	xvii
Acknowledgments	xxi

PART 1
The Telecommunications Industry Structure — 1

1 Telecommunications Economics I: Principles of Market Structure, Supply and Pricing and Business Conduct — 3

2 Telecommunications and Strategic Planning — 24

3 Broadcast Television — 51

4 Cable Television — 90

5 Telecommunications Economics II: Principles of Public Utilities, Common Carriers and Information Carriage — 122

6 Telephony — 138

7 Satellite Communication — 173

8 Cellular and Wireless Communication — 193

9 The Internet and Electronic Commerce — 216

10 Transnational Media and Telecommunications — 242

CONTENTS

PART 2
Management and Planning Strategies   267

11 Telecommunications Management   269

12 Telecommunications and Financial Management   296
    RON RIZZUTO, UNIVERSITY OF DENVER, AND
    MIKE WIRTH, UNIVERSITY OF TENNESSEE

13 Telecommunications Marketing   321
    HEIDI HENNINK-KAMINSKI,
    UNIVERSITY OF NORTH CAROLINA AT CHAPEL HILL

14 Leadership and Change Management   340
    ROD RIGHTMIRE, INDIANA UNIVERSITY, AND
    RICHARD GERSHON, WESTERN MICHIGAN UNIVERSITY

15 Innovation and Technology Management   358

    Notes   377
    People Index   403
    Company Index   407
    Subject Index   411

FIGURES

1.1	International Broadcast Rights Fees, Summer Olympics, 1980–2008	15
1.2	Evolution of Broadcast Rights Fees as a Percentage of Total Rights	16
4.1	Cable Television Network Architecture	93
4.2	Coaxial Cable as a Transmission Medium	94
4.3	Cable Modem Penetration Rate: Number of Customers, 2001–2006	103
4.4	Residential Telephone Customers, 2001–2006	104
6.1	Dual-Tone Multifrequency (Touchtone) Display	141
6.2	The LEC and Local Loop	142
6.3	Twisted Copper Pair to the Home	142
6.4	The LEC and Local Loop	143
6.5	The U.S. Telephone Switching Hierarchy (pre-1984)	145
6.6	Consolidating Switching Centers: Three-Layer Network Hierarchy	146
6.7	Signaling System No. 7 (SS7) Network Design	147
6.8	Packet Switching Overview	148
6.9	Fiber Optics Transmission Path	151
6.10	Comparison of Single-Mode and Multimode Fiber	152
6.11	Verizon: Broadband Bundling Strategy	168
7.1	Satellite Transmission Link	174
7.2	Satellite Communication Footprint	176
7.3	Intelsat Communication Satellite Footprint	177
7.4	Parabolic Dish and Signal Concentration	178
7.5	Satellite Primary Design Formats	178
7.6	Global Positioning Satellite System	183
7.7	International Satellite Revenue: Four Area Segments, 2001–2006	185
8.1	Cell Site Coverage Areas	196
8.2	Honeycomb Cell Structure	197
8.3	Seven-Cell Cluster Configuration	198

8.4	Cell Splitting	199
8.5	Cellular Telephone Base Tower and Transmitter	199
8.6	MTSO and BS Dedicated Landline Links	200
8.7	Frequency Channel Handoff	201
8.8	Comparison of Multiple Access Design Approaches	204
8.9	Top Ten Leaders in Cellular Communication (2006)	207
8.10	International Market Share: Cellular Telephone Manufacturers, 2007	208
9.1	ARPANet Distributed Network Architecture	217
12.1	The Walt Disney Company: Revenue and Net Income, 2003–2006	311
12.2	The Walt Disney Company: Revenue by Major Division, 2003–2006	312
12.3	Comcast Corporation: Percentage Contributions to Overall Revenue by Major Division, 2006	313
12.4	Sony Corporation: Percentage of Sales and Operating Revenue by Major Division, 2006	314
15.1	Dell's Inventory and Production Management System	365
15.2	The Innovator's Dilemma and Product Life Cycle	369

TABLES

1.1   U.S. Electronic Media Organizations   4
1.2   Select Sampling of U.S. Telecommunications Carriers   5
1.3   Most-Watched U.S. Television Series Finales   17
2.1   Strengths, Weaknesses, Opportunities and
        Threats (SWOT) Model   25
2.2   Michael Porter's Value Chain: Improving
        Organizational Performance   34
2.3   General Electric Corporation's 11 Primary
        Divisions (2007)   36
2.4   Strategy Implementation Problem Areas   43
2.5   Pixar Studios: Major Animated Films   46
2.6   The Walt Disney Company: Revenues by Major
        Divisions (2006)   47
3.1   Radio and Television Stations in the United States
        (2008)   52
3.2   U.S. Major Broadcast Television Networks   53
3.3   Select U.S. Minor Broadcast Television Networks   54
3.4   CBS Television O&O Stations   58
3.5   Sources of Funding for U.S. Public Broadcasting (2008)   62
3.6   Anatomy of a Television Program Idea   67
3.7   Television Day Parts Program Schedule   67
3.8   Standard Program Syndication Contract   76
3.9   News Corporation Ltd.'s Purchase of Seven
        Metromedia Stations (1986)   82
4.1   Top 15 U.S. Cable Multiple System Operators (2007)   95
4.2   Cable Television Development in the U.S. (2007)   96
4.3   Cable Television Network Services in the U.S. (2007)   97
4.4   Basic and Pay Cable Subscriber Revenue, 1985–2007   105
4.5   Cable Television Programming: Program and
        Service Tier Options   107
4.6   The Future of Entertainment and Information-
        Based Cable Service   121

5.1   Public Utilities: Rights and Responsibilities   124
5.2   AT&T: Organizational Structure (Prior to
      Divestiture Agreement, 1984)   131
5.3   The Seven Regional Holding Companies post
      Divestiture (1984)   136
6.1   Telephone Communication in the United States   139
6.2   North American Digital Transmission Hierarchy   154
6.3   SONET Optical Carrier Level and Transmission Speeds   154
6.4   General Categories of Telephone Service Requests   155
6.5   LEC Enhanced Information Services   156
6.6   The Business Communication Planning Model   161
6.7   Communication Features and Applications   162
6.8   Business Communication Planning Model: A
      Checklist for Small Business and the Professional User   164
6.9   Telecommunications Consulting: Seven Criteria
      for Presentation Analysis   165
7.1   Satellite Frequency Bands   174
7.2   U.S. Direct Broadcast Satellite Services   181
7.3   International and Regional Satellite Carriers   185
7.4   Satellite Launch Services: U.S. and International   189
8.1   Cellular Telephony Industry Estimates, 1987–2007:
      U.S. Subscriber Patterns and Annual
      Wireless Revenues   206
8.2   Mobile Wireless Communication Standards   212
9.1   Top 20 Internet Usage by Country and
      Penetration Rate as a Percentage of Population Base   219
9.2   Internet Penetration Rate as a Percentage of
      Continental/Regional Population Base   220
9.3   Top 15 Most Widely Visited Websites in the U.S.   222
10.1 The Transnational Media Corporation   245
10.2 Major Mergers and Acquisitions: Media and
      Telecommunication Companies (1997–2007)   251
10.3 The Transnational Media Corporation: Select
      Examples of Feature Products and Services   255
11.1 Fayol's 14 Principles of Management (Adapted)   278
11.2 Maslow's Hierarchy of Needs   281
12.1 KWLX-TV: Income Statement for Year Ending
      December 31, 200X   299
12.2 Verizon: Consolidated Income Statement   301
12.3 KWLX-TV: Balance Sheet for Year Ending
      December 31, 200X   303
12.4 Microsoft: Consolidated Balance Statement   306
12.5 KWLX-TV: Statement of Cash Flows for Year
      Ending December 31, 200X   307

12.6 Sample Stock Quotations for Selected
       Telecommunication Firms Listed on NYSE
       and NASDAQ   316
12.7 Moody's and Standard & Poor's Ratings   318
13.1 PRIZM-NE Urban Uptown Social Group   325
13.2 The 30 Most Valued Global Brands of 2006   329
13.3 Elements of the Promotional Mix   332
15.1 Select Examples of Media and Telecommunications
       Product Innovation   361
15.2 Select Examples of Media and Telecommunications
       Process Innovation   363
15.3 Select Examples of Media and Telecommunications
       Business Model Innovation   366

FOREWORD

When an author today takes on the formidable task of writing a text in our Internet driven world where credible content on almost any subject is readily intertwined with raw opinion, the risks of timeliness, content erosion as well as credibility are significant. This is especially true in the highly dynamic fields of media and telecommunications where entire companies are here today and gone tomorrow. Due to convergence, entire areas of technology can change or be threatened with a single breakthrough in research or major policy shift.

I have had a small hand in pioneering in these fields for over thirty years and know first hand the difficulties in writing about an area as dynamic and ever changing as media and telecommunications. And yet Rick Gershon and his fellow authors have tried to do exactly that in this book. They provide an outline for understanding where we have been, where we are at a given time, and what that may mean for our future.

Having had the pleasure of working with Professor Gershon over a period of years I can believe that the same persistence, optimism and integrity which led him to pursue the creation of the International Telecommunication Education and Research Association were his guiding tools in creating this book.

Everyone is an expert or a critic of business strategy, until they have to apply it themselves and make something work. The author of this text has had to translate concepts into working plans. He understands both the joys of success and the disappointments when even good plans in changing times do not get the desired results.

Like all written works, this book has its strengths and its limitations. Nevertheless, it is a highly credible effort written by an experienced and determined author who has dared to stand in the river of change and try to add some meaning for the rest of us as we struggle to make sense of the complexities that surround this field.

What makes this book important now is not the technologies which it helps readers to better understand but the business and marketplace context in which they are presented. Professor Gershon understands the dynamism of a digitized marketplace and the challenges of disruptive change brought to those who must somehow manage a future built on convergence and innovation.

It is the kind of book which will energize many, disturb some, and contribute a little more meaning to our world. I, for one, am grateful for the help!

Ray L. Steele, Ph.D.
Distinguished Professor,
Center for Information and Communication Sciences
Ball State University;
Founder and Executive Director, International Digital
Media and Arts Association;
Chair Emeritus, International Telecommunication
Education Research Association.

PREFACE

The fields of media and telecommunications are at an historic crossroads in their evolution and development. Changes in technology, most notably the Internet and digital media arts, are changing many of our basic assumptions regarding information, news and entertainment content. The combination of a rapidly changing global economy coupled with advancements in new media and information technology is having a profound effect on higher education and those academic disciplines that specialize in media, telecommunications and IT management.

The difficulty of writing a book on telecommunications management is that no sooner have you completed the text than the information begins to erode owing to the steady changes taking place in all areas of the field. In 2001, I published a book entitled *Telecommunications Management: Industry Structures and Planning Strategies*. Two years ago, I set out to write the second edition for that book and it became quickly apparent that I was effectively engaged in an entirely new project. So much had changed in the course of a few years. Thus my publisher Linda Bathgate and I have decided to launch the present text as an altogether new book.

Changes across Time

In the field of broadcasting, we are witnessing the nation's television broadcasters transitioning to an all-digital environment. The Federal Communications Commission has mandated that the switch from analog to digital broadcast television will take place by February 17, 2009. After that date, all full-powered U.S. television stations will broadcast in digital only. Inclusive in these changes is the implementation of high-definition television, which most observers consider the most significant development in television technology since color television because of its remarkably improved picture quality as well the ability to feature Dolby Digital sound. Also on the technology front, the development of digital video recorders (DVRs) is steadily transforming the business of television broadcasting by allowing users to manage and record their favorite television programs. DVRs allow users to fast-forward through the various recorded advertisements. As DVRs become more widely diffused in the marketplace, they will challenge the very under-pinnings of advertiser-supported television as we know it.

In the field of telephony, AT&T, once the largest corporation in the world, has undergone a major transformation. In 2001, AT&T sold its broadband division to Comcast Corporation for $54 billion, thus making Comcast the largest cable operator in the world. In January 2005, SBC Communications, then the second largest Regional Bell Operating Company in the U.S., acquired AT&T's business and residential services for more than $16 billion. Instead of witnessing what appeared to be the final chapter in AT&T's long and storied history, the newly combined AT&T has risen from the ashes to take its place as one of today's most formidable telecommunications companies. We now have telephone companies like AT&T and Verizon offering video services to the home using an Internet Protocol Television platform in direct competition with the nation's cable television industry. Conversely, we have cable companies like Comcast and Cox offering cable telephone service as part of a triple play of communication services, including multichannel television, high-speed Internet access and wired and wireless telephony.

Perhaps the biggest change in the intervening years has been in the area of Internet communications and electronic commerce. In 2001, the Internet was a relatively new and emerging communication technology. Today, the Internet has become steadily woven into all aspects of work and leisure. The Internet has created a new business model that maximizes the potential for instantaneous communication to a worldwide customer base. Companies like Google, Amazon and eBay have given breadth and depth to the principles of electronic commerce. On the technology front, Steve Jobs and the team from Apple Computer unveiled the Apple iPod in 2001. The combination of the Apple iPod and iTunes media store has created the first sustainable on-line music distribution model of its kind. It qualifies as both a new business model innovation and a business process innovation since it successfully takes advantage of MP3 software distribution technology. In July 2007, the iPhone was introduced, which is the quintessential example of media and IT convergence. The success of iTunes, Amazon and Netflix has set into motion the era of personalization and personalized services.

About this Book

This book is intended for the advanced undergraduate and graduate student who is working in the fields of media and telecommunications management. It is also intended for the professional manager, who can utilize this as a useful reference guide. What distinguishes this book from the current set of textbook offerings in the field of media and telecommunications management is the commitment towards understanding the relationship and convergence patterns between the broadcast, cable, telephone and Internet communication industries. It is incumbent upon today's manager to understand both the program software and the different delivery platforms. In my view, the student of telecommunications management should be equally conversant whether it's negotiating intellectual property rights, understanding the technical parameters of Voice Over Internet Protocol or recognizing the business implications of satellite-delivered radio and what it means to the principles of localism. This same student needs to understand that a communication satellite that transmits voice, data and video communication is equal to the task whether it's televising the Olympic Games from Beijing, China, facilitating an MP3 music file transfer via the Internet, or engaging in an electronic funds transfer on the London stock market. The main driving force behind such convergence is the digitalization of media and information technology. The twenty-first century promises a very different set of industry players than was the case in past years. The future will allow for the full integration of voice data and video services and give new meaning to the term "programming."

Inventing the Future: A Word about Curriculum Development

Designing curriculum is very similar to what a software engineer does. The information contained in a telecommunications course can become quickly dated (or worse irrelevant) when educators and the materials they use become static. The best software designers (and companies) routinely challenge themselves and ask whether they are making the kinds of products and services that their customers will want in the future. It's an exciting time to be in the field. It's also a very difficult time to be a practitioner of the discipline given the rapid changes taking place on a daily basis. As educators, we need to routinely ask ourselves the same kinds of questions as the software designer. Are we giving our students the kinds of information and experiential learning that are both timely and relevant?

Anyone who purports to teach in the fields of media, telecommunications and information technology has to be comfortable with change. It is not a subject area that allows us to teach the same course in the same way using the same notes, as is the case in other disciplines. Therein lies the challenge and dynamism of what we do. Yesterday's state-of-the-art technology can soon find itself relegated to the dustbin of history; think floppy disks and traditional long-distance telephone service. Such ongoing changes have to be reflected in the curriculum design and specific courses we teach, and we have to realize that some curriculum models are no longer sustainable.

As we look to the future, it is my belief that we are reaching a point in higher education where departments can no longer afford to go it alone. Rather, reaching out within colleges and across the university at large becomes important in ensuring that various kinds of core knowledge areas and skill sets are made available to our students. As Microsoft's Bill Gates shrewdly observes, "Companies fail when they become complacent and imagine that they will always be successful." That imperative is every bit as true in the field of higher education. The long-term success of any academic program will ultimately depend on the proper blending of its core strengths with a view towards the future in terms of innovative curriculum design. We have a unique and special obligation to prepare our students for the future world of work.

Richard A. Gershon, Ph.D.
School of Communication
Western Michigan University

ACKNOWLEDGMENTS

This book was largely completed during the 2006–2008 time period. There are several people whose comments and suggestions have made this book immeasurably better. My thanks to Mike Wirth, University of Tennessee, Rod Rightmire, Indiana University, Andy Snow, Ohio University, Heidi Kaminski, University of North Carolina and Steve Wildman, Michigan State University. I also want to take a moment to acknowledge the past contributions of Sylvia Chan-Olmsted, University of Florida and Joseph Kayany, Western Michigan University to an earlier version of this book in 2001.

I want to thank Ray Steele, Ball State University, James Gantt, Murray State University and my colleagues on the Executive board of ITERA for their remarkable insight and experience in helping to make me a better educator. A special thank you goes to Steve Rhodes, Mike Tarn and my colleagues at Western Michigan University for their continuous support and friendship. They allow me to do what I love doing best – teaching.

I am indebted to the editorial staff at Routledge (and Taylor & Francis) for helping to make this project possible. In particular I want to thank Linda Bathgate (my editor) who was instrumental in helping me navigate the sometimes rough and varying waters of this project. My partnership with Linda spans more than a decade and three books from the time that I first met her at an AEJMC conference in Chicago. Linda is truly excellent at what she does and I deeply appreciate her friendship and continued support. Special thanks also goes to Kerry Breen, Senior Editorial Assistant who was critical to the project's success. I also want to take a moment to thank the Routledge London staff for their invaluable assistance in the production of this work, and Colin Morgan of Swales & Willis who served as the book's project manager. Colin was responsible for keeping the book on schedule; he possesses a special talent for knowing how to decipher and coordinate my cryptic comments and last-minute insertions into legible form. A special thank you to Dr. Richard Willis, Sarah Phillips and Helen Moss for their important contributions to the development of this book as well.

In addition, a number of people listened to me talk through the ideas contained in this book or provided friendship and support in a variety of ways: Rod and Nancy Rightmire, Tom Kent, Bassam Harik, Alex Enyedi, Bernie Han, Joe and Gracie Kayany, Carol Levin, Leigh Ford, Peter Gershon, Marilyn Kritzman, Steve and Susan Wildman, David Gershon and Gail Straub and the entire Brown family, Janet and; John, Tony and Margie, Jim and Betsy, and Sam and Dina. My special thanks to all of them.

Finally, a special thank you to my wife Casey for her unwavering love and support. From bicycling adventures to a glass of wine over dinner, I so appreciate her grace, wisdom and sense of humor. She is my north star. . . And to my son, Matthew; I wish you the very best as you look to the future.

Richard A. Gershon

Part 1

THE
TELECOMMUNICATIONS
INDUSTRY STRUCTURE

1

TELECOMMUNICATIONS ECONOMICS I

Principles of Market Structure, Supply and Pricing and Business Conduct

The Telecommunications Industry Structure

The word "telecommunications" refers to those organizations (both commercial and noncommercial) involved in the production and distribution of information and entertainment via electronic communications media. It is derived from the Greek word *tele*, which means far away or transmission over a long distance. The prefix "tele" can be found in such words as "telephone," "television," "teleconferencing" and "teleport," to name only a few. In this book, we will address two very different types of telecommunications players, including media organizations and common carriers.

Media Organizations

The media organization is in the business of creating information and entertainment content. According to media business scholar Joseph Turow, "Mass communication is the industrialized production, reproduction, and multiple distribution of messages through technological devices."[1] To that end, the media organization routinely makes creative and editorial decisions that affect content. Their business depends primarily on the sale and distribution of their product or service. In principle, there are two ways that media organizations make money, including advertising and/or subscription fees. Table 1.1 provides a brief sampling of the different kinds of electronic media organizations that will be examined in this book.

Production Cycles

The nature of information and entertainment product requires that media organizations produce new product in regular production cycles. Some production cycles are daily, as in the case of newspapers or television news broadcasts. Other production cycles can be weekly or monthly, as is the case

3

Table 1.1 U.S. Electronic Media Organizations

U.S. television networks	ABC, CBS, NBC, Fox (major), CW, Univision (minor)
Network affiliate stations	Select examples: —WBBM: CBS affiliate, Chicago, IL —WOOD: NBC affiliate, Grand Rapids, MI —KABC: ABC affiliate, Los Angeles, CA —KSAZ: Fox affiliate, Phoenix, AZ
Independent broadcast stations	Select examples: —WPIX: New York City, NY —KTLA: Los Angeles —KMSP: Minneapolis/St. Paul, MN
Television and film production	Select examples: —Universal Studios —Paramount —20th Century Fox —Sony Pictures, MGM —DreamWorks —Walt Disney Studios
Cable program services	Select examples: —ESPN —CNN —MTV —HBO —Fox News —Discovery Channel
Multiple system operators (MSOs) cable television	Select examples: —Comcast —Time Warner Cable —Cox Cable Communication —Charter Communication
Internet portals	Select examples: —Google —Yahoo —WebMD —Ask.com
Direct broadcast satellite	DirecTV EchoStar
Satellite radio	Sirius XM

with magazines. Still other production cycles can be seasonal in nature, such as the premiere of a new television program or film release.

Some media products, including newspapers, magazines and television sports, are highly perishable commodities. In short, such media products as yesterday's newspaper and televised sporting events lose their commercial value once the intended message reaches its audience. The combination of regular production cycles coupled with the highly perishable nature of media product requires journalists, writers and producers to be fast and creative while simultaneously adhering to strict deadline pressures.[2]

Alternatively, some media products, including films, syndicated television programs, copyrighted music and computer software, retain much of their intrinsic value well after their initial release. The economics of television, film and music are built on the assumption that such products build value over time. Once the cost of production has been realized, the same software product can be sold over and over again in different venues. The objective, therefore, is to maximize audience reach and to favor those distribution media (or windows) that can accomplish this.

Common Carriers

Common carriers are in the message delivery business. Common carriers transmit (or carry) messages to anyone who is willing to pay for it. The message can include a telephone conversation, a fax message, an Internet data transmission, a videoconference, a satellite transmission and a cellular telephone call. In principle, a common carrier must offer its services on a nondiscriminatory basis; that is, the service provider cannot interfere with the content of a message nor can it pick and choose its users. In short, if the user pays for the telephone call (or affixes the right amount of postage to a letter), the common carrier by law must send the message as sent without interference.[3] In this book, the reference to common carriers will typically refer to those businesses principally engaged in the delivery of voice, data and video communication messages to business and residential customers.[4] Table 1.2 provides a select sampling of the different kinds of telecommunications carriers that we will discuss and analyze.

Table 1.2 Select Sampling of U.S. Telecommunications Carriers

Telephony (wireline)	Select examples: —Verizon; —AT&T; —Qwest.
Cellular telephony	Select examples: —Verizon Wireless; —AT&T; —Sprint Nextel; —T-Mobile; —Alltel.
Satellite carrier	Select examples: —Intelsat; —SES Global (SES Americom); —Eutelsat.

Telecommunications and Economic Performance

Economics provides an important lens through which to understand the important structures and interplay of forces that occur in the marketplace. Most of the definitions and problems posed in this chapter help us to clarify why certain business organizations adopt the business strategies that they do. It is my intention to apply relevant economic terms and examples to the fields of media and telecommunications.

Microeconomics

The term *microeconomics* refers to the behavior of decision makers in the economy. As Robert Picard points out, business organizations and governments are decision makers. So too are individual citizens in their role as workers and consumers. The field of microeconomic study is built around three basic types of choices that must be made in any economy:

1 What products and services should be produced?
2 How shall the products and services be produced, including method, location and time frame?
3 Who is the intended audience for the various products and services being produced?[5]

A central tenet of this book is that different market structures give rise to different patterns of behavior by the firms that operate in them. The term *competition* can be used to describe the degree of rivalry among sellers or buyers in the marketplace. It can also be used to describe the degree of openness that may exist in a market with respect to the availability of certain products and services.

Elements of Market Structure

Elements of market structure refer to the interaction of buyers and sellers in the marketplace and the structural features which affect the behavior of firms in the marketplace. They include:

1 seller concentration;
2 product differentiation;
3 barriers to entry;
4 buyer concentration;
5 demand growth.

6

Seller Concentration

Seller concentration refers to the number of sellers of a given product or service in the marketplace. Seller concentration takes into consideration the degree of competition in the marketplace and its effect on the quality and cost of service. The level of competition can be subdivided into three categories of players: monopolies, oligopolies and a fully competitive marketplace (i.e., the neoclassic model of market organization).[6]

Monopoly

At one end of the marketplace spectrum is the pure monopoly, where there is a single seller who controls the product or service. In a telecommunications context, a monopoly refers to a single service provider in a given marketplace. A good example from the past was local cable television. Until the late 1990s, cable television tended to be a one-of-a-kind service provider in most small to medium-sized communities. This is no longer the case with the advent of direct broadcast satellite (DBS) television as well as telephone-based Internet Protocol Television (IPTV). The monopoly, owing to the lack of competition, exercises strong control over prices and product quality since consumers presumably cannot go elsewhere. Monopolies, by their very nature, have little incentive to be innovative. The lack of competition causes them to be satisfied with the status quo. And while they may ensure adequate levels of service, they are by no means willing to promote the development of new products and services. As noted earlier, DBS has forced cable television to become more customer oriented in terms of program offerings and enhanced information services.

Oligopoly

An oligopoly is a situation where a few sellers are dominant within an industry. Perhaps the simplest example would be the four major U.S. television networks, ABC, CBS, NBC and FOX. Together, they account for 40–45 percent of prime-time television viewing. Oligopolies can be seen in other telecommunications fields as well, such as cellular telephony, where such companies as Verizon, AT&T, Sprint Nextel and T-Mobile dominate the industry. It is common among oligopolies for a certain amount of "interdependent" price setting. If one firm raises or lowers its prices (or engages in a unique marketing strategy), the others are likely to follow suit. As an example, the decision by AT&T (formerly Cingular) to eliminate receiving charges from placed cellular phone calls prompted their competitors to follow suit.

Pure Competition

Pure competition suggests that there are multiple players providing service within the marketplace. There is a constant entering and exiting of the field among product and service providers. Pure competition can be seen in cable television programming, where there are multiple program services vying for the viewers' attention. Similarly, pure competition can be seen among the manufacturers of consumer electronics like DVD players and television sets. In the latter case, the cost of entering the market is low, with few barriers to entry.

In principle, a highly competitive marketplace leads to the greatest control of prices by the consumer. Computer and DVD manufacturing, for example, exhibit highly elastic demand qualities, since consumers presumably have access to a wide variety of product offerings. This, in turn, allows consumers to exercise greater discretionary choice (elasticity) when it comes to selection.

Product Differentiation

Product differentiation is the degree to which an industry's product differs from one producer to another. In principle, products and services that provide utilitarian value (e.g., local telephone, gas and electric service) tend to be undifferentiated. In the field of media entertainment, however, product differentiation is a critical element of any marketing strategy. Cable programmers like HBO, MTV, Disney and ESPN, for example, go to great lengths to differentiate their product from the competition.[7] To that end, program marketers emphasize the importance of brand identity or *branding* as a way to distinguish one's program service. Similarly, radio broadcasting is a highly competitive environment where so much depends on a radio station's ability to differentiate its program format from the competition.

Barriers to Entry

We begin by asking: what are the market limitations that restrict new companies from getting into select areas of business? Barriers to entry are the extent to which competition from new companies is controlled or restricted within an industry. There are several kinds of barriers to entry.[8]

Absolute Cost Barriers

Some businesses are highly capital intensive and require significant capitalization and/or commitment to sophisticated equipment. This serves as a significant barrier to entry for many would-be players owing to the high start-up costs involved. As an example, the design and manufacture of LCD chips is highly specialized to the extent that most companies would not venture into that area unless they have the proper financing and requisite expertise to successfully compete in this business. In the field of media and telecommunications, venture capital firms have proven especially important over the years by providing the necessary funding in allowing many high-tech as well as small Internet start-up firms to develop and expand. It is not surprising, therefore, that numerous venture capital firms are located in high-tech industrial centers like Silicon Valley in California and Bangalore, India.

Scale Economy Barriers

Some business ventures require a significant amount of time before the newly established business or project venture becomes profitable. This requires significant patience on the part of the investor and a willingness to sustain financial losses for several years before the company sees a return on investment. This is particularly true in the field of telecommunications, where high start-up costs often preclude an immediate return on investment. Consider, for example, the start-up of News Corporation's BSkyB direct broadcast satellite service in the United Kingdom. It took five years and an estimated $1.2 billion in losses before the company achieved eventual profitability.[9]

Cable television is another example of a business that requires high start-up costs and may require five to seven years before the operator sees a return on investment. The issue of scale economy barriers is an issue that factors very heavily into the granting of a cable television franchise. There is an implicit understanding that, in granting a 10- to 12-year cable franchise, the municipality recognizes that the successful development of a cable operating system may require several years before the operator sees a return on investment.

Established Leaders

The question may be rightfully asked: what's in a name? Everything's in a name, especially when it comes to such telecommunications giants as Microsoft, Comcast, Disney, Intel and NBC, to name only a few. Highly successful firms often have an established reputation and dominant market presence that make it difficult for new firms to compete against them, particularly in the early stages of development. Most successful entrants develop a niche strategy rather than trying to go head to head with established leaders.

The issue of established leaders becomes especially important when it comes to the purchasing of new equipment. Consider for a moment the following scenario. As the newly appointed managing director of telecommunications for your organization, you have the responsibility to purchase a new videoconferencing system. In your analysis, you recognize that the future system has to interface with the company's five international location sites, must be expandable, must provide excellent audio and video capability, must offer good customer support and must be competitively priced. As you attend the NXTcomm industry trade show you have a chance to inspect a variety of equipment. The question very simply is whether you will go with an established leader or take a calculated risk on a lesser-known brand (or start-up) that may indeed provide a better system. Bear in mind that your decision will affect thousands of your colleagues, not to mention your own professional standing within the company.

Buyer Concentration

Buyer concentration refers to the number of potential buyers available to purchase a company's products or services. Buyer concentration is a critical element in any proposed business plan. In principle, the fewer the number of potential buyers, the lower the profits for the industry and the more difficult it is to sustain an ongoing business venture. Consider for a moment a different scenario. As the director of business planning for 21st Century Cable Inc., you are considering the feasibility of building a new cable system in the city of Kalamazoo, Michigan, in direct competition with the existing operator, Charter Communications. In your market analysis, you determine that greater Kalamazoo has a population base of 220,000 residents. Approximately 80 percent of the community's residents take the existing cable service. First, you need to determine whether there are a sufficient number of cable subscribers to support a second cable system. In addition, you must also consider whether you can compete for at least half of the existing customer base and possibly obtain new subscribers who currently don't take cable. A second consideration is the impact that DBS services are having on the community, which for purposes of this discussion have a penetration rate of 11 percent. The scale economy barriers, coupled with the level of buyer concentration, are two critical factors that you will need to address before committing your company to enter the market.

Demand Growth

In addition to buyer concentration, demand growth asks us to consider the level of consumer demand for an industry's products or services. Do consumers see real value in the product or service being proposed? And more importantly, are they willing to spend their discretionary income in order to have it? The history of telecommunications is replete with examples of products that looked good in principle but were too costly and/or technically complex to implement in practice. Such notable examples as the Sony Betamax (a VCR playback device), Time Warner's Full Service Network (an interactive cable television system prototype, Orlando, FL) and the Apple

Newton (an electronic portable notebook) remind us of the difficulty in making good ideas work. The real test for these products and other such examples is the marketplace and whether people are willing to spend their hard-earned money in order to have them. As the saying goes, this is where the rubber meets the road.

Another aspect of demand growth has to do with elasticity of demand. The elasticity of demand refers to the level and/or need for a product or service. It measures the level of demand response to a change in price. The more responsive the demand is to a change in price, the more elastic is that product or service. As an example, the demand for a second-tier pay television service would be considered "highly elastic" since presumably a significant change in price might prompt the consumer to cancel since it is more of an added-value service than a necessity. Conversely, the less responsive the demand to a change in price, the less elastic ("inelastic") is that product or service. For example, the demand for gasoline is highly inelastic due to the necessity of driving. No matter how volatile the politics of the Middle East and/or fluctuations in gas production, consumers still need to drive even if it means paying higher prices. Similarly, the demand for phone service can be considered inelastic since voice communication service is also something of a necessity. Demand growth and pricing, of course, also depend on the availability of good substitutes.

Principles of Supply and Pricing

Supply is the products and services that a manufacturer or service provider is willing and able to sell to the consumer for a select period of time. The classic supply-and-demand relationship describes the ratio between the availability of a product or service and its corresponding cost.[10] Throughout the 1990s and early twenty-first century, the deployment of optical fiber communication has led to an oversupply of telephone circuits. The passage of the Telecommunications Act of 1996 hastened the speed of deployment for fiber optic cable, since many local exchange carriers saw the value of upgrading their networks while simultaneously positioning themselves to offer both local and long-distance telephone service. The success of the Internet also led business strategists to think that Internet traffic would exponentially grow well into the twenty-first century. In the end, so much fiber was placed below ground as well as on the ocean floor that the telephone industry unintentionally created an enormous surplus (or overcapacity) of telephone transmission capability. The result has been a continuing decrease in price for long-distance telephone calls and Internet data traffic between the USA, Europe and Asia. All things being equal, an over-supply of a product, service or resource can lead to a decrease in cost.

In contrast, the electromagnetic spectrum is considered a scarce resource which is in high demand for both the television and the wireless communication industries. This, in turn, makes the cost of acquiring spectrum space exceedingly high. In 2000, Europe's wireless carriers found themselves in a bidding war, having to spend large sums of money to purchase spectrum space in pursuit of so-called Third Generation ("3G") wireless capability. In the U.K. alone, the Blair government was able to generate $33 billion from spectrum auction sales. Other European finance ministers soon followed. Germany was able to raise $45 billion from the sale of spectrum space. While the auction system may have propped national coffers, it proved to be an enormous challenge for Europe's various wireless carriers which found themselves having to overcome numerous technical challenges as well as absorbing the high cost of spectrum space.

In the U.S., the issue is a little different. The Federal Communications Commission (FCC) has mandated that by February 17, 2009 all broadcast television services in the U.S. will be fully digital in format and signaling capability. In principle, the current allocation of broadcast assignments in the VHF band of frequencies will be returned to the government. The presumption is that the same spectrum space will be reallocated (and auctioned off) to various wireless carriers and Internet companies to support cellular and other forms of wireless telecommunications. Both the European and U.S. examples point to the fact that the electromagnetic spectrum is considered a scarce resource and therefore can command a high price. All things being equal, an under-supply of a product, service or resource can lead to an increase in cost. Let us consider four factors that can influence supply and its corresponding cost. They include:

1   a change in technology;
2   a change in the method of product distribution;
3   the availability of good substitutes;
4   the expectations of product manufacturers and service providers.

A Change in Technology

A change in the technology can directly affect the supply of a product or service and its corresponding cost. Consider, for example, that music recording technology has never been cheaper or more readily accessible. The speed and efficiency of producing audio compact discs (CDs) or Internet-delivered music using MP3 file-sharing software has fundamentally changed the cost structure of music recording and distribution on a worldwide basis. The development of iTunes by Apple Computer is an e-commerce (EC) service designed to play, organize and sell music files. iTunes permits users to download music directly to a desktop PC, laptop or MP3 portable music player. More importantly, Apple has created the first sustainable EC business model for the delivery of music to a worldwide customer base. MP3 file sharing is here to stay. There is no going backwards.

12

Economies of Scale

A company is said to realize an economy of scale when the long-term average cost for producing something declines as output increases. Let us consider for a moment the economics which support the music industry. The production of a music album, for example, presupposes some initial first copy costs, including music licensing, recording time, marketing and distribution. Once the costs of production are realized, there are clear advantages to those who operate at high volume. In short, music producers hope to realize an economy of scale, whereby, as production increases, the cost per individual CD unit decreases.[11] For the music industry, in particular, the economies of scale increase over time, since many music albums retain their value.

Economies of scale can also be seen in the technology of satellite delivery. The communication satellite is a microwave relay operating at 22,300 miles above the earth's equator. It receives microwave signals in a given frequency and retransmits them at a different frequency. The satellite footprint (or area of coverage) permits multiple earth stations to simultaneously receive the same signal. In short, it doesn't matter whether one earth station or a thousand earth stations fall within the same footprint, since the cost of transmission is still the same. Moreover, the satellite feed allows for certain efficiencies by overcoming both distance and terrain factors. An economy of scale is realized, since the cost of transmission bears no relationship to the number of users and/or the distance involved. The value of satellite delivery and its inherent economies of scale are of particular benefit to the DBS television and satellite radio industries.

A Change in the Method of Product Distribution

Distribution is the series of steps involved in the transfer of a product or service from producer to consumer. As noted earlier, satellite distribution represents a highly efficient way to convey television or radio signals on a point-to-multipoint basis. In short, we begin by asking: what is the most efficient way to distribute the product or service to the consumer? Marketers recognize the importance of exchange efficiency, that is, setting up the optimum conditions for consumers to purchase the said product. Exchange efficiency can be seen in today's superstores, where a premium is placed on one-stop shopping. Superstores like Wal-Mart and Meijer provide customers with a complete product line ranging from grocery items to clothes to home and garden equipment. Today's superstores use dedicated speed lanes, optical scanning and self-checkout to get customers in and out of the store as quickly as possible.

Distribution also means providing enhanced value to the customer in order to facilitate the exchange of goods and services. A good example of this can be seen in the use of mail order catalogues, the signature approach used by such companies as L.L. Bean and Lands' End. Both companies use an 800 toll-free telephone number or Internet e-mail ordering system that allows customers to purchase clothing. They provide a convenient no-questions-asked return policy that has enabled such companies to successfully develop a retail clothing business.

In the field of telecommunications, the principle of exchange efficiency can be seen in the use of video-on-demand services.[12] Video-on-demand clearly provides the consumer with exchange efficiency and enhanced value when compared to the traditional DVD rental industry. Similarly, the advent of Netflix has created an altogether different approach to exchange efficiency by allowing customers to order up movies by telephone or the Internet and have them delivered by mail in three business days. There are no late fees and no due dates, and shipping is free both ways.

The Availability of Good Substitutes

There is no such thing as a static market. Advancements in new technology as well as product innovation can have a corresponding effect on supply and pricing. Consider, for example, that advancements in direct broadcast satellite have challenged the one-time unassailable position of the cable industry by giving consumers the availability of a good substitute. Competition has forced the cable industry to become more responsive to customer needs in terms of program offerings, quality of service and pricing structure.

The availability of good substitutes is particularly evident in the area of electronic commerce (EC). The Internet provides consumers with immediate access to a whole host of goods and services, including the ability to comparison-shop. As an example, a website like Kelley Blue Book (http://www.kbb.com/) gives consumers the ability to comparison-shop when it comes to the purchase or sale of an automobile in terms of knowing the manufacturer's suggested list price as well as the general selling price of a particular make and model of automobile. Secondly, the Internet has fundamentally changed how retail trade is conducted in terms of information gathering, production and distribution. Today's consumer can interact directly with a manufacturer or service provider and, thereby, eliminate the so-called middleman, whether it be travel agencies, department stores or music retail outlets.

The Expectations of Product Manufacturers and Service Providers

The expectations of product manufacturers and service providers refers to the idea that a highly publicized product introduction or special event can have a significant effect on product supply and pricing. Consider, for example, the expectations generated by television coverage of the Olympic Games. In

2000, an estimated 3.7 billion viewers from 220 countries watched the summer Olympic Games from Sydney, Australia, making it the most watched sporting event in history. For advertisers and marketers, the Olympic Games represent a unique opportunity to showcase one's products and services as well as being associated with a highly prestigious event.

The Olympic Games have seen tremendous growth in broadcast coverage since 1980. From 1984 until 2008, the International Olympic Committee (IOC) has concluded broadcast agreements with the major U.S. television networks worth more than $10 billion. This can be seen in Figure 1.1. The expectation going forward is that audience size will continue to get bigger over time. This, in turn, becomes a critical factor in determining what to charge advertisers for commercial time.

In addition, television viewership patterns have increased internationally as well. The IOC has realized increased international television revenue, thereby reducing the Olympic movement's dependency on U.S. broadcast revenue alone—the primary funding source in 1980. This can be seen in Figure 1.2.[13]

The expectation of product manufacturers can be seen in other program venues as well. Special event television programs can generate similar expectations on the part of program producers. Consider, for example, the final episode of America's much-loved television comedy *Friends*, which aired on May 6, 2004. The program finale commanded more than $2 million per 30-second spot commercial, making it the near-equal rival of the 2004 NFL Super Bowl. For NBC, setting the expectation (in terms of advertising sales) before the fact translated into a sizeable financial win.[14] In its last season, a

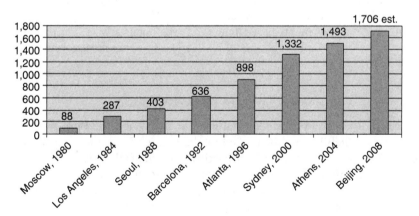

Figure 1.1 International Broadcast Rights Fees, Summer Olympics, 1980–2008 (in $U.S. millions).

Source: IOC, "International Broadcast Rights Fees," Available at: http://www.olympic.org/uk/organisation/facts/revenue/broadcast_uk.asp (retrieved August 17, 2005).

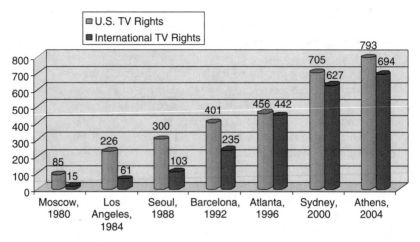

Figure 1.2 Evolution of Broadcast Rights Fees as a Percentage of Total Rights (in $U.S. millions).

30-second regular spot commercial on *Friends* cost advertisers $473,000. NBC's last major television program finale was in 1998 when the comedy series *Seinfeld* ended. A 30-second spot commercial then went for about $1.7 million. In sum, when a highly successful television series goes off the air with a well-planned and heavily promoted finale, it can produce a significant jump in ratings at two to three times the asking price in advertising dollars. In terms of actual ratings, the final episode of *Friends* was seen by an estimated 52.4 million people and achieved a rating of 29.8, placing it sixth on the all-time list of top-rated series finales. It should be remembered that programs like M*A*S*H and *The Fugitive* aired at a time when broadcast television was not nearly as competitive as it is today. A complete listing of the top-rated series finales can be seen in Table 1.3.

Principles of Market Conduct

In a market economy, the principal goal for both public and private corporations is profitability and increasing market share.[15] For some companies, the goal of profitability is shared with other important objectives, including a commitment to product quality and customer service. A company's overt or behind-the-scenes behavior towards its professional rivals says a lot about its professional conduct in the marketplace. In this section, we will consider the issue of market conduct in terms of three kinds of market conduct behaviors. They include:

1   attitudes toward product quality;

Table 1.3 Most-Watched U.S. Television Series Finales

Rank	Series Finale	Number of Viewers (in millions)	Percentage of Households	Date	Network
1	*M*A*S*H*	105.9	60.2%	Feb. 28, 1983	CBS
2	*Cheers*	80.4	45.5%	May 20, 1993	NBC
3	*Seinfeld*	76.3	41.3%	May 14, 1998	NBC
4	*Friends*	52.5	29.8%	May 6, 2004	NBC
5	*Magnum PI*	50.7	32.0%	May 1, 1988	CBS
6	*Tonight Show*	50.0	?	May 22, 1992	NBC
7	*The Cosby Show*	44.4	28.0%	Apr. 30, 1992	NBC
8	*All in the Family*	40.2	?	Apr. 8, 1979	CBS
9	*Family Ties*	36.3	20.8%	May 14, 1989	NBC
10	*Home Improvement*	35.5	21.6%	May 25, 1999	ABC

Sources: USA Today, Reuters, AOL Television.

2 legislating against the competition;
3 engaging in anticompetitive behavior.

Attitudes Toward Product Quality

Since the early 1950s, different management theorists have discussed the importance of product quality. In the aftermath of WWII, writers W. Edwards Deming and Joseph Juran began developing a series of principles that in later years has come to be known as Total Quality Management (TQM). They were instrumental in helping Japan rebuild its war-torn economy.[16] TQM presupposes a systemic approach to product quality and customer satisfaction. It is a philosophy where business and organizations are committed to improving product quality and customer satisfaction at every level.[17] According to researcher G.T. Fairhurst:

> [Total quality] is an approach to management that seeks to improve product quality and increase customer satisfaction largely through strong quality oriented leadership, a more efficient use of resources, participation in team based structures, and statistical monitoring of work processes.[18]

In their highly successful 1982 work *In Search of Excellence: Lessons from America's Best Run Companies*, authors Thomas Peters and Robert Waterman write that what characterizes America's premier companies is a passion for excellence. More specifically, such companies exhibit a corporate-wide commitment to exceed customer expectations.[19] Jim Collins in his 2001 book *Good to Great* makes the argument that great companies promote a culture of

17

discipline.[20] "When you combine a culture of discipline with an ethic of entrepreneurship, you get the magical alchemy of great performance."[21] Collins also makes the point that good companies seldom achieve greatness in one fell swoop. Rather, greatness is achieved over time through a steadiness in approach in what he calls the "flywheel and the doom loop."[22]

In today's media and telecommunications environment, there are numerous companies that emphasize the importance of product quality and customer satisfaction as part of their corporate mission. The Walt Disney Company is highly illustrative of one such company that adheres to the principles of TQM and product excellence.

The Walt Disney Company

Creating the Disney experience is largely dependent upon the 57,000 Walt Disney staff members. They are responsible for translating Disney's commitment to customer satisfaction into action. The Walt Disney Company employs one of the most sophisticated employee training programs in the world. To ensure that employees at all levels are guided by a common sense of purpose, founder Walt Disney established a formal training program that has come to be known as Disney University.[23]

Training begins with an appreciation for the fact that appearance is everything. It is not surprising, therefore, that Disney employees are referred to as cast members. The presentation includes everything from the way in which Disney employees interact with the public to the clothes they wear. In creating the right appearance, cast members are taught to be polite. They are taught to understand that park attendees are to be treated as guests and that helping a guest often means going the extra mile. In addition, Disney employees are expected to follow a dress code and are not permitted to eat, drink, smoke or chew gum in front of guests. At all levels, Walt Disney World is about creating an impression that the park is safe, accessible and fun.[24]

Legislating Against the Competition

Most companies in the field of telecommunications will make the claim that they are big supporters of free market competition. They will often resort to such euphemistic phrases as "All we're really asking for is a level playing field." In point of fact, such companies are routinely jockeying for position in order to achieve some type of home court advantage, albeit a regulatory one. One of the ways to tilt the playing field is for the company (or its respective trade lobby group) to engage federal and state government to pass regulation designed to limit (or punish) the competition. In short, such companies are trying to legislate against the competition.

The historical relationship between broadcasters and cable television provides a good example. Between the years 1952 and 1977, U.S. broadcasters and television/film producers supported a number of regulatory measures designed to limit the growth of cable television. In principle, broadcasters were concerned about program siphoning, that is, the ability of the cable industry to siphon programming intended for broadcast use. Broadcasters were concerned that cable programmers would feature the said programming on cable and thereby fragment the viewing audience as well as inflate the cost of program acquisition.

HBO v. FCC

In 1973, after a considerable lobbying effort by the National Association of Broadcasters (NAB), the FCC introduced a highly controversial set of rules called the pay cable television rules. The rules were designed to limit prospective cable programmers from distributing select forms of programming entertainment, including feature-length films and sporting events.[25] More to the point, the rules were designed to protect the interests of broadcasters. The rules prevented cable systems from showing feature-length films which had a general release in the U.S. and were more than two years old. In addition, the rules prevented cable systems from featuring television series-type programs with ongoing characters.

HBO and several motion picture distributors challenged the FCC in the U.S. District Court in Washington. The Court was asked to consider two questions. First, did the FCC exceed its legal authority by issuing the pay cable television rules? And second, did the rules violate the petitioner's First Amendment rights? The rules were eventually overturned in Home Box Office v. Federal Communications Commission.[26] The U.S. District Court concluded that the FCC had not established regulatory jurisdiction over pay cable television and that the rules were in direct violation of the petitioner's First Amendment rights. The Court noted:

> The purpose of the Commission's pay cable rules is to prevent "siphoning" of feature films and sports materials from conventional broadcast television to pay cable. Although there is dispute over the effectiveness of the rules, it is clear that their thrust is to prevent competition by pay cable entrepreneurs for film or sports material that either has been shown on conventional television or is likely to be shown there. How such an effect furthers any legitimate goals of the Communications Act is not clear.[27]

The court reminded the FCC and the broadcast industry that prior restraints on speech are heavily disfavored and can be sustained only where the proponents of the restraint can convincingly demonstrate a need. In the end, the cable television industry prevailed despite such efforts to establish regulatory barriers to entry. The outcome of this case made it possible for the newly emerging cable television industry to access all forms of television programming.[28] The rest, as they say, is history.

Engaging in Anticompetitive Behavior

An industry may be openly competitive and/or it may be coercive; that is, it takes steps to weaken the competition. When companies find ways to limit competition in the marketplace, the public interest is at risk. Today's anti-trust laws are direct descendents of common law actions intended to limit restraint on trade (i.e. agreements between firms that have the effect of reducing competition in the marketplace). In 1890, the U.S. Congress passed the Sherman Antitrust Act, which was intended to ensure a competitive economy.[29] In large measure, the bill's passage was a direct response to the enormous market power wielded by the Standard Oil Trust.[30] Section 1 of the Act states that "society's welfare is harmed if rival firms are permitted to join in an agreement that consolidates their market power or otherwise restrains competition." In 1914, Congress attempted to strengthen federal antitrust laws by enacting the Clayton Act.[31] The Clayton Act was aimed at specific anticompetitive behaviors not covered by the Sherman Act, including inter-locking directorates, that is, the practice of having individuals serve as directors on the board of two or more competing companies.

In past years, the U.S. courts have traditionally applied the rule of reason in their examination of corporate misconduct. The rule of reason suggests that simply being a monopoly with substantial control over a market is not against the law. It is when market dominance is used to limit (or restrict) competition that such companies can find themselves in violation of the Sherman Antitrust Act. There are several ways that a company can engage in anticompetitive behavior, including 1) price fixing and collusion, 2) predatory pricing and 3) exclusive dealing and tying arrangements.

Price Fixing and Collusion

One type of anticompetitive behavior is price fixing and collusion. Price fixing is an agreement among competitors to fix prices and, thereby, control what consumers pay for a product or service. Collusion is a collective agreement among product manufacturers or service providers to limit output in order to charge high prices.[32] Collusion can also occur when the same manufacturers or service providers agree to pay a predetermined amount for product or labor supply. Such efforts to engage in price fixing and collusion are typically accomplished behind closed doors. While price fixing is illegal in the U.S., there is nothing to prevent such practices at the international level. Consider, for example, the Organization of the Petroleum Exporting Countries (OPEC). Formed in 1960 at Baghdad, OPEC today is composed of

11 major oil exporting countries (Venezuela, Algeria, Nigeria, Libya, Saudi Arabia, Qatar, the United Arab Emirates, Kuwait, Iraq, Iran and Indonesia).

Officially, "OPEC seeks to ensure the stabilization of oil prices in international oil markets with a view to eliminating harmful and unnecessary fluctuations" and to ensure a fair return "to those investing in the petroleum industry."[33] What this means in practical terms is that a cartel of oil producing countries establish production quotas for member countries with a goal of keeping oil production steady and prices reasonably high. So when prices are low the member countries cut their production to boost the oil price, and when prices are high they boost production to bring them down, as was the case in the 1991 Gulf War. But not always. What is important to remember is that collusion (and price fixing) is difficult to sustain over time and has a distorting effect on the marketplace. The challenge for OPEC is that not all of its member states have equal reserves, and hence the quotas aren't equal.[34] Thus cuts in production aren't uniform, hurting some countries more than others. This inability to share the pain equally has led some of the smaller members of OPEC to cheat on their quotas. Worse still, many non-OPEC oil producing countries such as Mexico, Russia and Norway have benefited from increased world demand for oil since they fall outside the rules and production quotas set by OPEC.

Predatory Pricing

Another form of anticompetitive behavior is predatory pricing, which involves restricting competition by offering a product or service at a price too low to compete against. Predatory pricing often occurs when a national or international company floods the market with products that are priced too low to compete against. The intention is to weaken the competition by driving them out of the marketplace. Consider, for example, the controversy surrounding companies like Wal-Mart. The company has become America's preeminent retail superstore by selling clothes and appliances at lower cost than its competitors. The company's motto is, after all, "Always low prices." Wal-Mart's low prices are a function of its ability to extract low prices from its national and international suppliers as well as imposing strict internal controls on staff and operations. Yet some communities are fighting back to keep the retail giant out of their neighborhoods, claiming that Wal-Mart's low prices damage small businesses, particularly the "mom and pop" stores that they say make their community unique. This criticism has become even more vocal since Wal-Mart began moving into additional areas of retailing, such as groceries, opticals and flowers.

21

Exclusive Dealing and Tying Arrangements

Another way to limit competition is for a company to engage in exclusive dealing and tying arrangements. An exclusive dealing arrangement exists when a firm obtains the product of a certain supplier on the condition that it will not buy the products of competing suppliers. Often the buying firm that enters into such an arrangement will receive in return the exclusive right to handle the seller's product in a particular market. Tying arrangements are often found to be more illegal than are exclusive dealings. A tying arrangement is one that forces a customer to buy one product in order to get another. When companies are found to be engaged in the kinds of anticompetitive behaviors thus described, it may result in government intervention. Such government intervention can take the form of an antitrust lawsuit and includes all the legislative and judicial actions necessary in order to restore competition in the marketplace.

U.S. v. Microsoft: A Case Study

In 1994, Netscape Communications began marketing Navigator, the first popular Internet browser. Navigator worked with Java, a technology software developed by Sun Microsystems that enabled applications to run on a number of operating system platforms, which meant that users did not need Windows. For its part, Microsoft perceived Netscape Navigator as a threat to its dominance in the business software market and, therefore, developed a competing browser, Internet Explorer. Microsoft then began to require computer makers who wanted to install the company's Windows operating system to also install Microsoft's Internet Explorer and exclude Netscape Navigator. In addition, Microsoft intermixed browser code (and other proprietary code) so that deleting files containing Explorer would disable a user's operating system.

In 1995, the U.S. Justice Department began the first phase of an investigation alleging that Microsoft was engaged in a form of tying, whereby it was requiring personal computer manufacturers that ship Windows on their PCs to include Microsoft's Internet Explorer software as well. The Justice Department also alleged anticompetitive behavior on the part of Microsoft in terms of its corrupting the Java code and making users dependent on Microsoft's proprietary operating system. What's important about this case, however, is how Microsoft's actions affected the development of the Internet web browser market.

In 1997, Netscape was the premier Internet web browser, claiming an estimated 60 percent of the U.S. software market. The Justice Department took the position that, if Microsoft was able to require PC makers to ship Explorer with every Windows-based machine, the company would obtain an unfair advantage and thereby limit competition.[35] Starting in 1998, Microsoft fully merged its Internet Explorer web browser with its Windows 98 operating system. The company justified its actions on the basis that the two software products are mutually supportive and should be integrated. Microsoft's action, in combination with other events, prompted the Justice Department to initiate a massive antitrust lawsuit against Microsoft, claiming that such exclusive dealing and tying arrangements were a direct violation of the Sherman Antitrust Act, resulting in the case U.S. v. Microsoft, Inc.[36]

At issue was whether Microsoft had used its monopoly power and position to stifle competition.[37] On November 5, 1999, Judge Thomas Penfield Jackson issued his ruling stating that Microsoft had in fact engaged in a variety of anticompetitive behaviors, including a well-orchestrated campaign to limit Netscape's access to the market. In his written opinion, Judge Jackson ordered that Microsoft pay reparations and that the company be subject to a forced separation of its Internet services division from its PC Windows division. The case was later appealed to the U.S. Circuit Court of Appeals, which affirmed the part of the lower court's ruling holding that Microsoft did possess and maintain monopoly power in the market for Intel-compatible operating systems. The Appellate Court, however, reversed that part of the lower court's ruling pertaining to how the problem should be remedied (i.e., the forced divestiture). The Court was dissatisfied with Judge Jackson's handling of the case, feeling that his personal comments about the case (off the record) impeded his professional and legal judgment. The Court also felt that Judge Jackson's decision to impose a break-up on Microsoft was arbitrary and not necessarily in the best interest of the company. The Appellate Court remanded the case for reconsideration of a more appropriate remedy.

2

TELECOMMUNICATIONS AND STRATEGIC PLANNING

As today's media and telecommunication companies continue to grow and expand, the challenges of staying globally competitive become increasingly more difficult. Such competition has engendered a new competitive spirit characterized by a belief that size (and complementary strengths) is crucial to business survival. The need to be profitable and the fear of failure have made such companies vigilant in their attempts to rightsize, reorganize and re-engineer their business operations. Thus no company, large or small, can afford to be casual in its approach to business.[1]

Strategic Planning

Strategic planning is the set of managerial decisions and actions that determine the long-term performance of a company or organization. The main role of strategy is to plan for the future as well as to react to changes in the marketplace. A competitive strategy is the master plan, including specific product lines and approaches, to be used by the organization in order to reach a stated set of goals and objectives. In principle, there are four steps involved in the strategic planning process. They include:

1   environmental scanning;
2   strategy formulation;
3   strategy implementation;
4   evaluation and control.[2]

Environmental Scanning

The first step in any strategic planning process is environmental scanning, the purpose of which is to monitor, evaluate and disseminate information from both the internal and the external business environment to the key decision makers within the organization. Environmental scanning requires assessing the internal strengths and weaknesses of the organization as well as the external opportunities and threats to the organization.[3] Accordingly, the strengths, weaknesses, opportunities and threats (SWOT) model serves as a way to illustrate the environmental scanning process (Table 2.1).

Triggering Events

Researchers Wheelen and Hunger suggest that the need for strategic planning is sometimes caused by triggering events. A triggering event can be caused by changes in the competitive marketplace or changes in the management structure of an organization as well as changes associated with internal performance and operations.[4] Author Henry Mintzberg suggests that for some organizations developing a strategic response is neither a regular nor a consistent process. Instead, strategy formulation is "an irregular, discontinuous process proceeding in fits and starts. There are periods of stability in strategy development, but also there are periods of flux, groping, of piecemeal change, and of global change."[5]

A strategic plan, regardless of whether it's deliberate or reactive, should demonstrate a clear understanding of an otherwise rapidly changing business environment. The strategic plan should clearly articulate a vision for the future. In doing so, it has the overriding objective of attaining a natural fit between internal capabilities and external opportunities.[6]

The External Environment

The external environment can include a number of different forces that can impact the financial performance and operations of an organization, including:

1   competitive factors;
2   political/legal factors;
3   the economic environment;
4   technological factors;
5   sociocultural factors.

Competitive Factors

There is no such thing as a static business environment. The actions of one's competitors can force a change in one's current business strategy. Until the

Table 2.1 Strengths, Weaknesses, Opportunities and Threats (SWOT) Model

Internal	External
1 Strengths of the organization	3 Opportunities for the organization
2 Weaknesses of the organization	4 Threats to the organization

start of the 1990s, the cable television industry enjoyed a near de facto monopoly in the delivery of multichannel television service to the home. The advent of satellite television, most notably DirecTV and the Dish Network, has forced the U.S. cable industry to become more responsive in terms of programming and customer services, as well as the addition of new and enhanced service offerings. Today, both direct broadcast satellite (DBS) providers have achieved a combined penetration rate of 15 percent of all U.S. television homes. Similarly, telephone companies like Verizon and AT&T have made major commitments to enter the business of broadband television delivery using a systems delivery approach known as Internet Protocol Television (IPTV). Such efforts represent major competitive threats to the U.S. cable television industry. Both Verizon and AT&T are marketing their ability to deliver multichannel television as part of a so-called "triple play of services" consisting of Internet Protocol Television, high-speed Internet access and full-service telephone communication.

Political/Legal Factors

Political/legal factors represent changes in the political and regulatory environments that can significantly influence the business operations of a company or organization. This can occur both domestically and internationally. The passage of the Telecommunications Act of 1996, for example, represented a watershed event in the development of U.S. telecommunications policy.[7] The Telecommunications Act was the first comprehensive rewrite of the Communications Act of 1934 and dramatically changed the ground rules for competition and regulation in virtually all sectors of the communications industry. Prior to the Act, large segments of the U.S. telecommunications marketplace adhered to strict marketplace regulation, thus creating protected markets (or de facto monopolies).[8] As a consequence of the 1996 Telecommunications Act, merger and concentration rules were relaxed and cross-market entry rules eliminated altogether. The latter provision was especially important for local exchange carriers like Verizon and SBC (now AT&T), which saw opportunities to enter the field of long-distance telephony. Today, Verizon and AT&T offer long-distance service as part of a standard package of telephone service offerings. Similarly, cable operators like Cox Cable and Comcast were free to enter the business of telephone communication as well by offering cable-based telephone services.

The Economic Environment

The economic environment represents the general economic conditions that can either help or hurt one's business operations. Such economic factors as the investment climate, interest rates, exchange rates, inflation and/or economic recession can dramatically affect the financial performance of a media or telecommunications company. Consider, for a moment, the effect of a change in exchange rates on the expected value of a firm's operating cash flow. The foreign exchange system is the method by which the currency of one country is converted into another. An exchange rate is simply the rate (or exchange value) at which one currency is converted into another.[9]

Telefónica, for example, is the leading telephone common carrier in Spain and Portugal and one of the world's top telecommunications companies. Its activities are centered mainly on the provision of fixed and mobile telephone services, having broadband as a key tool for the development of both businesses. Telefónica has a significant presence in 15 countries around the world and has access to more than 550 million potential clients. Telefónica negotiates international contracts with companies like Nokia (Finland), Motorola (U.S.A.) and Sony Ericsson (Sweden) for the provision of cellular telephone equipment.

Service and equipment contracts can run for periods of two to three years. The time lag between placing an order and making a final payment can pose a financial challenge for companies like Telefónica. As a European company, Telefónica has revenues designated in euros. When purchasing Motorola products, Telefónica must convert its currency into dollars to pay Motorola. Likewise, it must do the same and convert its currency into Swedish kronor in order to pay Sony Ericsson. The company has no conversion issues when working with Nokia since both countries use the euro as their main currency. During the interval between placing the order and making the final payment, the value of the currency may change. Telefónica could find itself paying 15 percent more (or less) for the same set of products and services based upon the terms of the original contract.

Technological Factors

Technological factors represent advancements in new technologies that can help or adversely affect one's business operations. Consider, for example, the business and technological implications of Voice Over Internet Protocol (VOIP), that is, using the Internet to send and receive basic voice communication. The ability to switch and route telephone calls via the Internet is much less expensive when compared to basic circuit-switched telephone calls. As service quality continues to improve, more and more businesses and government organizations are making the switch to VOIP telephony. This, in turn, has huge implications for traditional telephone service providers, which must grapple with the fact that part of their basic business model is dramatically shifting. As VOIP technology steadily improves, some analysts predict that the VOIP penetration rate will increase by as much as 30 percent in the U.S. by 2010. Last, VOIP also offers new opportunities for both cable and Internet companies that may want to offer voice telephony services.

Sociocultural Factors

Sociocultural factors are social and cultural changes in the marketplace that can affect consumer buying habits. A telling example is the use of tobacco products. Throughout the 1990s and early twenty-first century, the U.S. tobacco industry has experienced a negative backlash by state and federal government as well as consumer groups. This, in turn, has had a direct effect on the sale of tobacco products in the U.S. as well as the creation of strict rules concerning the smoking of cigarettes and pipes in public places.

A telecommunications example of this can be seen with public attitudes involving information piracy and the illegal downloading of music and video via the Internet. The illegal downloading of music has become a worldwide phenomenon. The Recording Industry Association of America (RIAA) estimates that the music industry loses an estimated $4.2 billion worldwide on a yearly basis owing to the illegal downloading of music and other forms of music piracy. As the RIAA notes:

> No black flags with skull and crossbones, no cutlasses, cannons, or daggers identify today's pirates. You can't see them coming; there's no warning shot across your bow. Yet rest assured the pirates are out there because today there is plenty of gold (and platinum and diamonds) to be had. Today's pirates operate not on the high seas but on the Internet, in illegal CD factories, distribution centers, and on the street.[10]

At issue is the fact that many people consider the illegal downloading of music and video to be a lesser crime when compared to other forms of theft. After all, the thinking goes, the music companies can afford it; everyone's doing it and no one is really getting hurt. Nothing beats free. . . . Suffice to say, the music and films industries are faced with an enormous sociocultural challenge of educating the public that the illegal downloading of music is no different than any other form of theft.

> Many do not understand the significant negative impact of piracy on the music industry. Though it would appear that record companies are still making their money and that artists are still getting rich, these impressions are mere fallacies. Each sale by a pirate represents a lost legitimate sale, thereby depriving not only the record company of profits, but also the artist, producer, songwriter, publisher, retailer . . . and the list goes on. The consumer is the ultimate victim, as pirated product is generally poorly manufactured and does not include the superior sound quality, art work, and insert information included in legitimate product.[11]

The external challenge for today's music companies (and recording labels) is how to adapt to a changing technology and develop solutions that will change consumer thinking and make the business of music recording profitable once again. As the RIAA has learned, developing a strategic response to a triggering event requires both formal and informal solutions.

The Internal Environment

The internal environment can include a number of different factors that can affect organizational performance, including:

1   core competency;
2   organizational decision making;
3   organizational culture;
4   management–labor relationships;
5   operational issues;
6   management–subsidiary relationships.

Core Competency

The principle of core competency suggests that a highly successful company is one that possesses a specialized production process, brand recognition or ownership of talent that enables it to achieve higher revenues and market dominance relative to its competitors. A good example of core competency can be seen with Cisco Systems, which specializes in the design and installation of Internet routers. Today, more than 80 percent of the world's Internet routers are made by Cisco Systems. Core competency can be measured in many ways, including brand identity (Disney, Apple, ESPN), technological leadership (Cisco, Intel, Microsoft), innovation (Apple, Google), superior research and development (Sony, Philips), and customer service (Dell, American Express, Amazon.com). In sum, a company's core competency is something the organization does especially well in comparison to its competitors.[12]

There are several things that can challenge a company's ability to maintain its core competency in the production of a certain product or service, including:

1   *Imitation by competitors:* Is the company making a product that has been highly saturated with imitators? This can be seen in the field of consumer electronics with low-end margin products such as CD and DVD players, television sets, etc.
2   *Technological obsolescence:* Is the company producing equipment or a service that is becoming technologically obsolete? Consider, for example, the problem faced by Blockbuster Video, which at one time dominated the business of video rentals and sales. Advancements in pay-per-view

29

television and Netflix' overnight DVD delivery service have challenged Blockbuster to rethink its business strategy in light of such business and technology changes. Similarly, videogame manufacturers like Sega and the Nintendo Corporation used to design their game consoles using a cartridge format. The Sony Corporation, for its part, challenged both companies by introducing PlayStation with its CD Rom format. In response, both Sega and Nintendo were forced to redesign their systems using a CD Rom format as well.

3   *Problems associated with product life cycle:* Is the company making outdated products and equipment that have less consumer appeal? A good example can be seen with the sale of traditional wireline telephone sets. Increasingly, the public prefers highly portable cell phones with enhanced information and entertainment features. Part of the challenge for any successful company is to know when in the course of a product life cycle to phase out an existing product line in favor of an untested, but highly promising, technology that may help to advance the company's future. We call this the innovator's dilemma (see Chapter 15).[13]

Organizational Decision Making

There is a noticeable difference between some organizations and others in terms of their ability to make decisions, as well as the skill to implement them quickly and efficiently. The importance of organizational decision making can be seen in such things as 1) developing new project initiatives, 2) meeting product delivery deadlines, 3) providing the proper managerial and technical support in order to make projects succeed, and 4) coordinating successful supply chain management operations and troubleshooting organizational problems when they occur. In summary, does the organization foster an entrepreneurial spirit that encourages innovation and new ideas or does it adhere to a rigid bureaucracy that kills initiative and creative thinking?

BERTELSMANN AG

Bertelsmann AG is a transnational media corporation that is the largest in Europe and ranks in the top seven worldwide. The company's central headquarters is based in Gütersloh, Germany. Bertelsmann is a transnational media corporation (TNMC) that reflects the business philosophy and media insight of its founder, Reinhard Mohn, who believed in the importance of decentralization and long-range strategic planning. It was a legacy that Mohn instilled in the company before his retirement in 1981.[14] Today, Bertelsmann AG is arguably the most transnational of the world's leading media companies. The company's management style is highly decentralized. Two-thirds of its business is done outside Germany. That philosophy is captured in the company charter, which stresses:

30

- entrepreneurial leadership and decentralization of operations;
- creativity and innovation at every level of the corporation;
- commitment to being a valued corporate citizen of the communities in which Bertelsmann companies operate.[15]

Organizational Culture

Organizational culture (or corporate culture) is the collection of beliefs, expectations and values shared by an organization's members and transmitted from one generation of employees to another. In short, does the organizational culture enhance (or take away from) the effectiveness of the company's business operations? Does senior management promote a culture that is highly supportive of its employees or does it create a climate of fear and intimidation?

In 1982, researchers Deal and Kennedy suggested that the more highly successful companies are those that exhibit a strong organizational culture. Deal and Kennedy identify four component parts to a strong business culture, including: values, heroes, rites and cultural network.[16]

Accordingly, values are the intrinsic beliefs that members hold for an organization. As an example, the Walt Disney Company places a high premium on the value of customer service. It's central to the mission of creating the Disney experience when one visits the theme parks at Walt Disney World.

Heroes are the individuals who come to represent the organization at its best. Often, the heroes are the founders of the company who either established the business and/or were responsible for its successful development. Examples include William Paley (CBS), Walt Disney (the Walt Disney Company), Ted Turner (Turner Broadcasting) and Masaru Ibuka and Akio Morita (Sony Corporation), to name only a few.

Rites and rituals are the traditions through which an organization celebrates its values. Bertelsmann, for example, offers its employees a unique nonvoting profit-sharing plan. It's one of the principal reasons that unions have traditionally proven unsuccessful at Bertelsmann.

Finally, the cultural network is the communication system through which organizational values are transmitted and reinforced. The cultural network can be both formal and informal. This can include everything from formal orientation programs of new employees to informal mentoring by senior-level staff members.

SONY INC.

The Sony Corporation is a company that was largely shaped and developed by its founders, Masaru Ibuka and Akio Morita. Together, they formed a unique partnership that has left an indelible imprint on Sony's worldwide business operations.[17] As a company, Sony was decidedly Japanese in its business values. Senior managers operating in the company's Tokyo headquarters identified themselves as Japanese first and entrepreneurs second. According to Morita, Shimomura and Reingold, "The most important mission for a Japanese manager is to develop a healthy relationship with his employees, to create a family-like feeling with the corporation, a feeling that employees and managers share the same fate."[18]

Today, Sony is no longer the same company. The challenges of staying globally competitive have had a profound effect on Sony's organizational culture. The once family-like atmosphere of the past is no more. The vast majority of Sony's worldwide employees are not Japanese. They are not part of the company's cultural network and history. The new Sony is steadily transforming itself into a transnational media corporation where more and more emphasis is being given to the value of local autonomy and individual performance. Sony has moved to a position where local management means finding the best person regardless of nationality. One indication of this was the April 2005 appointment of Howard Stringer as the company's new CEO. Howard Stringer is a native of Wales, UK, but has had extensive experience in the U.S., having served as chairman and CEO of Sony Corporation of America.

Management–Labor Relations

Management–labor relations involve the working relationship between managers and the people who work for the said business or organization. One important consideration is whether the organization is unionized or not. Although union membership in the U.S. has dropped considerably from the 1970s, unions still represent over 20 percent of the U.S. workforce. The importance of good management–labor relations cannot be underestimated. The real question is whether the company enjoys a good working relationship with its employees or whether it fosters a hostile (or indifferent) climate. There are several issues that have become especially important for today's unions. They include:

1   the loss of jobs to foreign manufacturing sites;
2   the threat of pay-cut demands from employers who threaten to eliminate or export jobs;
3   outsourcing and the hiring of temporary workers;
4   professional skills training;
5   companies that build advanced factories in low-wage countries, making those employees more competitive (and productive) than U.S. employees at home.

Operational Issues

Operations management is the area of management that focuses on the production of goods and services. What is important to remember is that a serious flaw in the manufacturing process (or breakdown in routine service operations) can seriously destabilize the organization as a whole. A design flaw in the manufacturing process, for example, can prove costly to a company that must engage in a product recall in order to remedy the problem. Worse still, a product recall (or temporary shutdown) undermines consumer confidence in the company's product or service.

VALUE CHAIN

The importance of value is central to any discussion concerning an organization's internal capabilities and resources. Value chain analysis represents a template (or set of criteria) that an organization can use to promote strengths and efficiencies in the production and distribution of goods and services.[19] The ability to purchase desktop or laptop computers via the Internet with direct home (or business) delivery is one such example of value creation. Let us consider some of the different ways that a firm can create value to the business–customer relationship. Michael Porter's (1999) value chain model suggests that a firm's business activities can be subdivided into two parts: 1) primary activities—those that are directly involved in the manufacture, sale and delivery of a product or service to the customer; and 2) support activities, which improve organizational performance as a whole (e.g. human resource management).[20] (See Table 2.2.)

Management–Subsidiary Relationships

One of the difficult challenges for an international company is the ability to properly coordinate and oversee projects and goals throughout a company's multiple worldwide subsidiaries. Most international companies are highly complex organizations that require a system-wide method for tracking and evaluating the performance of a company's subsidiaries and foreign operations. The term "organizational control" is used to describe the parent company's ability to track, communicate, allocate resources and take corrective action when and if a subsidiary's performance becomes problematic.

A telling example of what can go wrong in terms of managing a company from afar can be seen with Sony Corporation's 1989 purchase of Columbia Pictures Entertainment for $3.4 billion. The idea was to leverage software as a way to increase sales of its hardware products. The idea, while correct in principle, proved hard to implement in practice. Throughout the early 1990s, Sony sustained repeated losses. In 1994, Sony was forced to take corrective action, but not before writing off an estimated $2.7 billion of its

Table 2.2 Michael Porter's Value Chain: Improving Organizational Performance

Primary	
Inbound logistics	Concerns those activities involved with receiving and storing externally sourced materials.
Operations	Concern the manufacture of products and services. Specifically, operations look at the ways in which inputs (e.g. materials) are converted to outputs (e.g. products).
Outbound logistics	Concerns those activities involving the distribution of products and services to the consumer.
Marketing and sales	Concerns the information methods used to inform the buying public about the availability of goods and services, including benefits, price, features, etc.
Service	Concerns those activities involving product maintenance, training and repair after the product has been sold and delivered.
Secondary	
Procurement	Concerns how material suppliers (and product sourcing) are acquired for a business. This involves contract negotiation, establishing terms of agreement, etc.
Human resource management	Concerns those activities involving the recruitment, placement, training and dismissal of the business workforce.
Technology development	Concerns those activities central to improving a firm's research and development capability, product manufacturing, B-to-B and B-to-C information activities, etc.
Infrastructure	Concerns general activities such as management, planning, finance, accounting, legal support and government relations that fully support the primary business and value chain.

Source: Adapted from Michael E. Porter, *Competitive Advantage: Creating and Sustaining Superior Performance* (New York: Free Press, 1985).

foreign investment in Columbia Pictures. In the end, it came down to bad management oversight and poor communication between Sony and its Hollywood subsidiary.[21] Today, Sony Pictures is one of the preeminent film production companies in the world. Nevertheless, the company was forced to undergo a steep learning curve in terms of managing a foreign subsidiary during the mid-1990s.

Strategy Formulation

The success of any business is dependent on its ability to plan for the future. Strategy formulation can be a response to a triggering event (i.e., a competitive threat in the marketplace) or it can involve a change in direction for the company as a whole. Corporate strategy is every bit as essential for the small organization as it is for the transnational corporation. Strategy formulation requires an ongoing commitment to enlarge and improve the flow of a company's products and services.

There are different kinds of strategy, depending on the organization and its goals. There are mergers and acquisitions strategy that looks at methods for achieving complementary strengths through the combining of corporate, managerial and technical resources. There are also foreign direct investment strategies that consider the kinds of foreign markets a company is prepared to serve and where the said firm wants to locate its managerial and technical resources (see Chapter 10). For purposes of this discussion, we will focus our attention on two kinds of strategy: 1) planning and growth strategies and 2) competitive business strategy.

Planning and Growth Strategies

The success of any business is dependent upon its ability to plan for the future. This presupposes an ongoing willingness to enlarge and improve the flow of its products and services. Media and telecommunications companies will typically adopt one or more of the following three growth strategies: 1) horizontal integration, 2) diversification and 3) vertical integration.

Horizontal Integration

Horizontal integration is a growth strategy that allows a business to spread its influence by expanding into different geographic markets while maintaining a commitment to its primary business. The classic example is McDonald's, which essentially replicates its business in different markets. In terms of granting a franchise, there is an obvious efficiency that allows McDonald's to replicate its business in terms of product design, operations, marketing and research. The primary advantage is the public's familiarity with McDonald's and the expectation of consistency in the product offering. The major disadvantage is the fundamental reliance on and commitment to one product offering.

The cable television multiple system operator (MSO) provides a good example of a telecommunications industry that operates on the basis of horizontal integration. The cable MSO, like its McDonald's counterpart, has learned the strategic advantage of being able to replicate its business in different geographic markets while adhering to a consistent business plan. The MSO achieves certain efficiencies when it comes to franchise negotiations, programming, system design and operation, program acquisition and marketing.

Diversification

Diversification is a growth strategy that recognizes the value of owning a variety of related and unrelated businesses. In principle, a company that owns a diverse portfolio of businesses is spreading the risk of its investments. Thus a downturn in any one business during a fiscal year is more than offset

Table 2.3 General Electric Corporation's 11 Primary Divisions (2007)

GE Advanced Materials	Providing material solutions through engineering thermoplastics, silicone-based products and technology.
GE Commercial Finance	Major financial and investment company offering financial products worldwide.
GE Consumer Finance	A leading provider of financial services to consumers and retailers in countries around the world.
GE Consumer and Industrial	A major leader in appliance, lighting and integrated industrial equipment.
GE Energy	A leading supplier of technology to various energy producing companies.
GE Equipment Services	Helps businesses manage, finance and operate a variety of business equipment.
GE Healthcare	Medical technologies, and expertise in medical imaging and medical diagnostics.
GE Infrastructure	A high-technology platform composed of some of the fastest-growing businesses within GE.
GE Insurance	Provides commercial insurance and reinsurance products and services to Fortune 1000 companies.
NBC Universal	Owns and operates a major US television network, a Spanish-language cable network, a portfolio of news and entertainment programs, a major film company and a theme park.
GE Transportation	Composed of aircraft engines and rail business units.

by the company's successful performance in other areas. The disadvantage, however, is that some companies can become too large and unwieldy in order to be properly managed. Such companies can under-manage a specific division by failing to provide the proper oversight, management expertise and/ or financial investment in order to be successful. It is the principal reason why former General Electric CEO Jack Welch once stated that GE would not operate a business where it could not be one or two in its respective market. Said Welch, "We will be number one or two in every business we're in, or we will fix it, close it or sell it."[22]

General Electric is the quintessential example of a highly diverse company whose products range from medical imaging equipment to the NBC Universal television network. GE is consistently ranked as one of the top three corporations in the U.S. Table 2.3 provides an overview of GE Corporation in terms of its 11 major divisions.

Vertical Integration

Vertical integration is a growth strategy that emphasizes the importance of owning most or all of a company's operational phases. The goal is to create internal synergy and efficiencies between a company's various operating divisions. In principle, a media company can control an idea from its appearance in a book to its conversion to film, as well as later distribution via cable, direct broadcast satellite and/or DVD. TNMCs like the Walt Disney Company, Time Warner and News Corporation have taken the philosophy of vertical integration to a whole new level in terms of strategic planning and operations (see Chapter 10). Many of today's TNMCs engage in cross-media ownership, that is, owning a combination of news, entertainment and enhanced information services. Cross-media ownership allows for a variety of efficiencies, such as:

1 cross-licensing and marketing opportunities between company-owned media properties;
2 sharing of newsgathering, printing and distribution facilities between company-owned media properties;
3 negotiating licensing and sales agreements across different media platforms;
4 offering clients package discounts in advertising that cut across different media platforms. TNMCs like Time Warner, Viacom and News Corporation routinely offer clients package discounts.

Competitive Business Strategy

A competitive business strategy is the master plan (including specific approaches) to be used by the organization in order to reach a stated set of goals and objectives. There are any number of competitive strategies employed by today's media and telecommunications companies, including:

1 the introduction of a new product or service;
2 initiating a new marketing and promotion strategy;
3 implementing the acquisition of a company;
4 a commitment to reorganize the company and its existing reporting structure;
5 the decision to enter a new foreign market.

Defining the Business Mission

Strategy formulation starts by defining the business mission. An organization's business mission is the reason (or purpose) for the organization's existence. A well-conceived mission statement defines the fundamental unique purpose that sets the company apart from other firms of its type and defines where it wants to be in the next five to ten years.

Goals and Objectives

Strategy formulation involves establishing long-range goals and objectives for the company or organization. Goals and objectives are the end result of a planned set of activities. They state what is to be accomplished and when. The achievement of goals and objectives should be measurable. Such examples might include:

1   to achieve at least 10 percent annual growth in revenues
2   to achieve at least 40 percent market share in the area of ____
3   to achieve greater productivity and efficiency in ____
4   to achieve technological leadership in ____
5   to achieve improved customer service in ____

The Importance of Competitive Scope

Good strategic planning requires an ongoing commitment to enlarge and improve the flow of a company's products and services. Michael Porter argues that an organization's competitive business strategy needs to be understood in terms of scope, that is, the breadth of the company's product line as well as the markets it is prepared to serve.[23] In short, will the company adopt a mass market strategy as evidenced by the U.S. broadcast television networks or will it adopt a niche strategy illustrated by many of today's cable television networks? According to Porter, competitive scope breaks down into three general categories. They include: cost leadership, differentiation and focus.[24]

Cost Leadership

Cost leadership is the ability to produce a product or service at lower cost and more efficiently than one's competitors. Examples include: Wal-Mart superstores, Alamo car rental and Southwest Airlines discount fares.

Differentiation

Differentiation strategy is the ability to provide unique or superior value to the consumer in terms of product quality, special features, etc. Select examples include HBO and ESPN. Both HBO and ESPN are highly differentiated from their competitors in terms of program content as well as value perception on the part of the public.

Focus

Focus (or narrow niche) strategy involves targeting a particular demographic or consumer group. Select examples include: MTV (teenagers and young adults, 12–25); Black entertainment television (African American youth and adults) and the Disney Channel (children and family entertainment).

Strategy Implementation

Strategies often fail because they aren't executed well. Strategy implementation is the process by which strategies are effectively put into practice. The implementation of strategy needs to occur at all levels of the organization, including marketing, engineering, manufacturing and operations, corporate and distribution. For that reason, senior-level managers (and strategy planners) should take the time to fully explain (and seek comments where appropriate) regarding the overriding goals and objectives. According to management consultants Larry Bossidy and Ram Charran:

> [Strategy implementation] is a systematic process of rigorously discussing hows and whats, questioning, tenaciously following through and ensuring accountability. It includes making assumptions about the business environment, assessing the organization's capabilities, linking strategy to operations and the people who are going to implement the strategy, synchronizing those people and their various disciplines, and linking the rewards to outcomes.[25]

Successful strategy implementation presupposes three important core processes:

- properly communicating the goals and objectives of the proposed strategy;
- assembling the project team in order to carry out the strategy;
- working through the operational details necessary in order to get the job done.

Setting Strategy into Motion: Explaining the Goals and Objectives of the Strategic Plan

Strategy implementation starts at the top. An organization can only implement a proposed strategy if the executive leadership is involved in the three core processes. It is the responsibility of the executive leader (and the leadership team) to set strategy into motion by establishing realistic goals and objectives. The stated goals and objectives should be clear to everyone within the organization. In the best sense, middle-level managers and professional staff should be given some opportunity to help shape goals and objectives, including time lines for completion, etc. It is the middle-level manager (or line supervisor) who is often the most familiar with the challenges and operational details necessary in order to successfully implement the proposed strategy.

Management by Objectives

Management by objectives (MBO) represents a structured and organized approach that allows management to focus on achievable goals and to attain the best possible results from available resources. The principle of MBO was first outlined by Peter Drucker in 1954 in his seminal book *The Practice of Management*.[26] The goal of MBO is to increase organizational performance by aligning goals and subordinate objectives throughout the organization. To that end, strategy planners determine both short-term and long-term objectives and compare actual outcomes against the originally stated objectives. MBO presupposes an ongoing tracking and feedback mechanism that allows for periodic self-assessment. MBO features the SMART system, a set of criteria for checking the appropriateness and validity of the stated objectives. According to the SMART system, objectives should be: 1) Specific, 2) Measurable, 3) Achievable, 4) Realistic and 5) Time-related.

Who Carries Out the Strategic Plan?

The senior executive leader is responsible for choosing the right people in order to successfully implement the strategy. Nothing is more fundamental to successful outcomes than having the right management team in place. In his book *Good to Great*, author Jim Collins makes the argument that great leaders start by getting the right people on the bus and the wrong people off the bus. It is only then that you can determine where to drive the vehicle.[27] The challenge for the executive leader is to find the right people capable of carrying out strategy. This requires a level of rigor and paying attention to detail in assessing the strengths and limitations of a successful management team. Collins refers to this as getting the right people into the right seats. Yet often there is a mismatch between people and the jobs they are asked to perform. What accounts for this? The executive leadership team will sometimes pick people with whom they are comfortable rather than select people who have better skills for the job. Or sometimes, given immediate and pressing deadlines, the executive leader will select someone to head up a major project assignment and simply not know enough about the person's qualifications and skill level. In sum, the long-term success of any company is its people. As Collins concludes:

> Those who build great companies understand that the ultimate throttle on growth for any great company is not markets, or technology, or competition, or products. It is one thing above all others: the ability to get and keep enough of the right people.[28]

Working through the Operational Details

One of the difficult challenges of strategy implementation is that everyone agrees to the plan but no one is responsible (or accountable) for results. As mentioned earlier, it is the project manager and/or middle-level manager (who may not have been part of the original strategy formulation) who must execute on the details. He/she will be responsible for follow-through, that is, making sure that the job gets done. All strategies regardless of size and scope have a common set of operational requirements that need to be coordinated.

Project Team

The project team is the group of individuals responsible for implementing the strategy. Project teams cut across various divisions and represent the best people to do the job. Equally important, they bring to the project a diverse set of core expertise that advances the best interests of proposed strategy. The project team will determine the procedural steps necessary for implementing the strategy.

Budgeting

Budgeting is the managerial document in which the costs associated with carrying out the proposed strategy are estimated. The budget should include such things as costs for professional staff internal to the organization as well as external consultants (i.e., legal, financial, managerial, etc.), data analysis and presentation equipment (computers, software, photocopying, etc.), communication costs (telephone, mail, fax, videoconferencing, etc.), travel and lodging (site visits, presentations, etc.), and marketing (advertising, promotion and sales presentations, etc.). In sum, a budget is a financial blueprint that identifies the anticipated cost allocations and expenses necessary for implementing the proposed strategy as well as related programs.

Setting Target Dates

Successful strategy implementation presupposes a set of target dates by which to achieve different stages of project completion. Consider, for example, the construction of a new research and development building. The building's construction should have a corresponding set of completion dates. To that end, the project will undergo periodic review points in order to assess the different stages of project development with a view toward a final target date for completion.

Operational Support

Good strategy implementation requires that the project team have the right kinds of people resources and technical support equipment (computers, data analysis equipment, etc.) to successfully carry out the strategy. In a mergers and acquisitions strategy, for example, the legal and financial expertise necessary may not be entirely available in-house. The organization may require the outside expertise of a law firm that specializes in mergers and acquisitions activities.

Policies and Procedures

Policies and procedures are broad guidelines used by the organization designed to support strategy implementation. As an example, monthly sales and marketing meetings will require that each member of the team have relevant information and data prepared in a certain format for purposes of reporting to the group. Alternatively, the organization may have certain prescribed ways that marketing and the research group work together in promoting design features for new project development.

Evaluation and Control

Evaluation and control are critical to the success of any strategic planning process. This is the point in the process where management (and the leadership team) takes a strong, hard look at the numbers in order to determine whether the organization has indeed met its goals and objectives. Evaluation and control can sometimes point out flaws in the original strategy or identify changing external conditions that may require an adjustment in the next phase of the planning process. In order for evaluation and control to work, the manager (or management team) must establish appropriate performance standards. The performance standards are the baseline measurements that indicate whether the original goals and objectives have been met. The resulting information can then be used to make adjustments or take corrective action as needed.

Measuring Performance

The first step is to measure the performance of the business (or department) against the stated objectives. As mentioned earlier, the original statement of goals and objectives should be clear and measurable (e.g., a 10 percent increase in revenues, a 20 percent increase in market share, etc.). Many organizations rely upon various kinds of quantitative measurements (e.g., monthly or quarterly sales figures, revenue by product line, revenue by client or geographic location, quality control data, etc.). Most businesses will use some form of comparative data analysis that includes both the targeted goals and the actual performance figures. Moreover, the manager may use additional qualitative measurements such as talking with customers or hosting informal conversations with staff and employees in order to determine the relative progress of an applied strategy.

Assessing Actual Performance

Assessing actual performance requires that the manager (or management team) exercise powers of analysis when and if performance fails to achieve the stated objectives. Under such circumstances, the senior manager is expected to look at all aspects of the problem. If the said performance falls outside an acceptable tolerance range, the senior manager (or management team) needs to consider several questions.

1   Was the outcome(s) a chance fluctuation?
2   Was there some intervening set of variables that caused the outcome to fail?
3   Was the strategy itself flawed in some unforeseen way?
4   Are corrective actions necessary?
5   If so, what actions are to be taken?

What are some of the kinds of problems that can undermine the successful implementation of strategy? Table 2.4 provides a brief listing of why strategic plans can sometimes fail or not meet organizational expectations.

Table 2.4 Strategy Implementation Problem Areas

1 Goals and/or key implementation tasks were unrealistic or poorly defined.

2 Implementation took more time than was originally planned.

3 Competing activities and crises took time away from the implementation.

4 Unanticipated major problems arose:
—major competitive threat emerged;
—union strike;
—natural disaster.

5 There was no buy-in from the middle- and lower-level managers who would ultimately have to implement the plan.

6 Strategy implementation was ineffectively coordinated.

7 Corporate and/or departmental managers provided inadequate leadership.

8 The employees needed to implement the strategy were poorly trained or lacked the appropriate skills to carry out the plan.

Taking Corrective Actions if Needed

The project manager's investigation may reveal that the original set of goals and objectives was unrealistic. The analysis may reveal that the original goals couldn't be accomplished without sacrificing quality or increasing costs. The investigation may reveal that there is a changing set of external conditions that precludes the strategy from succeeding no matter what the effort. Or it may be that the sales staff or project team simply didn't meet their objectives. In the final analysis, the project manager is responsible for taking whatever corrective actions are necessary in order to meet future goals and objectives. It is the project manager who must ask the tough questions that need to be asked and direct departmental heads who must provide answers to those questions. Author Jim Collins calls it "confronting the brutal facts."

> All good- to-great companies began the process of finding a path to greatness by confronting the brutal facts of their current reality. When you start with an honest and diligent effort to determine the truth of your situation, the right decisions often become self-evident. It is impossible to make good decisions without infusing the entire process with an honest confrontation of the brutal facts.[29]

Finally, a strategic plan is never fully realized. Rather, it is an evolving process that combines successful practices of the past with fresh and innovative approaches to the future.

The Walt Disney Company: A Case Study in Vertical Integration and Complementary Assets

In the world of media entertainment, Walt Disney (WD) is a brand name that is clearly differentiated from all other entertainment products and services. Through the years, the Disney name has become synonymous with family entertainment. The result has been an ongoing relationship with the public that has spanned over 80 years. Less visible to the public, however, is that the Walt Disney Company is a highly successful transnational media corporation that has successfully applied vertical integration throughout its worldwide business operations. Since its 1996 acquisition of Capital Cities/ABC, the Walt Disney Company has focused on four primary areas of entertainment, including 1) Disney theme parks and resorts, 2) media networks, 3) studio entertainment and 4) consumer products.

Disney Theme Parks and Resorts

The Disney theme parks and resorts division is responsible for the operation of the company's theme parks and corresponding venues. The two primary theme parks are Disneyland and Walt Disney World. The Disneyland theme park is located on 250 acres in Anaheim, California. It features the original Magic Kingdom as well as numerous rides and attractions. The WD Company also owns and operates Walt Disney World located in Lake Buena Vista, Florida. The Walt Disney World resort features four major theme parks: the Magic Kingdom, Epcot Center, MGM Studios and Animal Kingdom. Walt Disney Attractions is an equity investor in Disneyland Paris (formerly Euro Disney) located in the suburbs of Paris, France, as well as Hong Kong Disneyland located on Lantau Island, 30 minutes from downtown Hong Kong. The company also has a licensing agreement with the Oriental Land company that operates Tokyo Disneyland located in Tokyo, Japan. Also included in the theme parks and resorts division are the Disney Vacation Club, Disney Cruises and the ESPN Zone sports theme restaurant chain.

Disney Media Networks

Disney's media networks division is divided into broadcasting and cable television. On February 9, 1996, the Walt Disney Company acquired Capital Cities/ABC for $19 billion, which at the time was the second largest merger in U.S. corporate history. The merging of both companies transformed the WD Company into a transnational media giant. For Disney, the purchase of ABC represented an opportunity to obtain a well-respected and highly profitable television network. ABC features some of the most successful television programs in the industry as well as a highly respected news operation, including *World News Tonight* and *20/20*.

The Disney-ABC Television Group manages all of the WD Company U.S. and global entertainment and news television properties. The group includes the ABC television network as well as ABC Studios (formerly Touchstone Television). ABC Studios is responsible for producing a number of prime-time programs that appear on the ABC television network, including *Grey's Anatomy, Desperate Housewives, Lost* and *Ugly Betty*.

The WD Company also owns ten local television stations and 26 local radio stations. The 1996 acquisition of Capital Cities/ABC brought with it the ESPN cable network, which at that time was a subsidiary of ABC Television. Today, ESPN is one of the most watched cable television networks on TV. ESPN currently hosts four major sports channels, including: ESPN (92 million households), ESPN2 (91 million households), ESPN Classic (62 million households) and ESPNEWS (51 million households). ESPN has become the branded franchise for all sports entertainment at the WD Company and is one of its most prized assets.[30]

Disney Studio Entertainment

Disney's studio entertainment division is responsible for the production of television and film programs. The WD Motion Pictures Group comprises four separate film production companies, including Walt Disney Pictures, Touchstone Pictures, Hollywood Pictures and Miramax. The Walt Disney Motion Pictures Group produces live action films for distribution to theatrical, television and home video markets. More recently, Walt Disney Pictures has been responsible for several box office hits, including *Pirates of the Caribbean*, *National Treasure* and *The Chronicles of Narnia*.

In addition, Disney Studio Entertainment is home to two major animation groups, including Walt Disney Animation Studios and Pixar Animation Studios. WD Animation Studios is the oldest surviving animation studio in the world. This studio has produced numerous animation classics through the years, ranging from *Snow White and the Seven Dwarfs* (1934) to *The Lion King* 60 years later (1994). In May 2006, the Walt Disney Company acquired its former production partner, Pixar Animation Studios, for $7.4 billion in an all-stock transaction. Starting in 1995, Pixar Studios has produced a number of digital animation hits, as can be seen in Table 2.5.

Table 2.5 Pixar Studios: Major Animated Films

Film	Year	Worldwide Gross
Toy Story	1995	$361,958,736
A Bug's Life	1998	$363,398,565
Toy Story 2	1999	$485,015,179
Monsters, Inc.	2001	$525,366,597
Finding Nemo	2003	$864,625,978
The Incredibles	2004	$631,442,092
Cars	2006	$461,981,604
Ratatouille	2007	$615,258,053

Source: Nash Information Services, "Box Office History for Pixar Movies," Available at: http://www.the-numbers.com/movies/series/Pixar.php (retrieved December 10, 2007).

Disney Consumer Products

Disney's consumer products division is responsible for licensing the Walt Disney name and its literary and film properties, animated characters and music to various manufacturers, retailers and publishers worldwide. Most of these products are distributed through a variety of Disney venues, including the company's theme parks and catalogues, as well as Disney stores located throughout North America, Europe and Asia/Pacific. Disney Consumer Products creates Disney-branded merchandise inspired by characters from *The Lion King* (Simba the Lion), *Aladdin* and *Pocahontas*, as well as Pixar's *Finding Nemo* and *Cars*. WD is the world's largest licensor, with global retail sales of $23 billion for 2006.

In FY 2006, the Walt Disney Company generated revenues of $34.2 billion, with a net income of $5.4 billion. Table 2.6 provides an illustration of contributed revenues by the company's four major divisions.

Vertical Integration and Cross-Promotion Strategy

The Walt Disney Company has a history and a product name that is one of the mostly easily identifiable in the world. Disney takes full advantage of its name and is able to leverage it throughout the entertainment field. Disney's major divisions are able to engage in a variety of cross-promotion strategies. As a starting point, consider the commercial value of a good film product. Starting in the mid-1980s, Walt Disney Animation Studios was responsible for producing an ongoing series of animated film hits, including: *The Little Mermaid, Beauty and the Beast, Aladdin, The Lion King, Pocahontas, The Hunchback of Notre Dame* and *Tarzan*, to name only a few. Several of Disney's more notable animated

Table 2.6 The Walt Disney Company:
Revenues by Major Divisions (2006)

Division	Revenues ($ million)
Media Networks	14,638
Parks and Resorts	9,925
Studio Entertainment	7,529
Consumer Products	2,193
Total revenue	34,285

Source: Walt Disney Company, 2006 Annual Report, Available at: http://corporate.disney.go.com/investors/annual_reports/2006/index.html (retrieved December 10, 2007).

film characters have become regularly featured attractions in the company's theme parks. Once the films have been successfully debuted in the theaters, they are then converted to DVD for purchase and rental. But that's only the beginning.

In June 1994, Walt Disney Studios premiered *The Lion King*, considered to be one of the company's most successful films ever. It cost the company $55 million to produce. In its first year alone, *The Lion King* earned $313 million in the U.S. and $454 million internationally. After a successful run in the theaters, the film was converted to VCR tape and DVD for sale and rental. The film's music sound track was produced by Walt Disney's Hollywood Records subsidiary and sold 11 million copies.[31]

In addition to the film and music sound track, the character of Simba the Lion and others were cross-licensed by the consumer products division to merchandisers who subsequently created Simba the Lion stuffed animals, tote bags, T-shirts and other products that are sold and distributed throughout Disney's multiple theme parks as well as the company's retail stores worldwide. It has been estimated that the public has spent in excess of $3.8 billion on Lion King merchandise alone. In the meantime, interest in *The Lion King* continues, evidenced by the Broadway debut of *The Lion King* in November 1997, with continuing productions throughout the U.S., Canada and Europe in order to meet the overwhelming demand.

Discussion

Strategic planning is the set of managerial decisions and actions that determine the long-term performance of a company or organization. In principle, there are four steps involved in the strategic management process. They include 1) environmental scanning, 2) strategy formulation, 3) strategy implementation and 4) evaluation and control.

The first step in any strategic planning process is environmental scanning, the purpose of which is to monitor, evaluate and disseminate information from both the internal and the external business environment to the key decision makers within the organization. This chapter introduced the strengths, weaknesses, opportunities and threats (SWOT) model as a way to illustrate the environmental scanning process. Environmental scanning requires assessing the internal strengths and weaknesses of the organization as well as the external opportunities and threats to the organization. The external challenges and issues include: 1) competitive factors, 2) political/legal factors, 3) the economic environment, 4) technological factors and 5) sociocultural factors. The internal challenges and issues, include: 1) core competency, 2) organizational decision making, 3) organizational culture, 4) management–labor relationships, 5) operational issues and 6) management–subsidiary relationships.

The second step in the strategic planning process is strategy formulation. Strategy formulation can be a response to a triggering event and/or it can involve a change in direction for the company as a whole. There are different kinds of strategy, depending on the organization and its goals. This chapter looked at two kinds of strategies: growth and development strategies and competitive business strategies. The success of any business is dependent upon its ability to plan for the future. Media and telecommunications companies will typically adopt one or more of the following three growth strategies: 1) horizontal integration, 2) diversification and 3) vertical integration. A competitive business strategy is the master plan (including specific approaches) to be used by the organization in order to reach a stated set of goals and objectives. There are any number of competitive strategies employed by today's media and telecommunications companies. Such examples include: 1) the introduction of a new product or service, 2) initiating a new marketing and promotion strategy and 3) implementing a mergers and acquisitions strategy.

The third step in the strategic planning process is strategy implementation, the process by which strategies are put into practice. One of the difficult challenges of strategy implementation is that everyone agrees to the plan but no one is responsible (or accountable) for results. It is the project manager and/or middle-level manager who must execute on the details. He/she will be responsible for making sure that the job gets done. All strategies regardless of size and scope have a common set of operational requirements that need to be coordinated and worked through. They include the selection of a project team, budgeting, setting target dates for project completion, designing good operational support and establishing the proper organizational policies and procedures.

The fourth step in the strategic planning process is evaluation and control. Evaluation and control is the process of evaluating performance against the stated objectives. The information is then used to make minor adjustments or take corrective action when necessary. Evaluation and control essentially breaks down into three stages: 1) measuring performance, 2) assessing actual performance and 3) taking corrective action if needed. If the strategy implementation fails to achieve an acceptable outcome, the project manager needs to consider several questions:

1   Was the outcome(s) a chance fluctuation?
2   Was there some intervening set of variables that caused the outcome to fail?
3   Was the strategy itself flawed in some unforeseen way?

There are any number of reasons for failed strategy, including the fact that the project goals (and key implementation tasks) were unrealistic or poorly defined, the implementation took more time than was originally planned, and competing activities and crises took time away from the implementation. In the end, the project manager is responsible for taking whatever corrective actions are necessary in order to meet future goals and objectives.

3

BROADCAST TELEVISION

The Business of Broadcasting

Television is an entertainment and information medium that pervades our lives. Approximately 98.2 percent of all U.S. homes have one or more television sets.[1] Moreover, 95.7 percent of those same homes have a DVD playback device.[2] The number of available digital-based cable or satellite channels has increased exponentially from an estimated 113 channels in 1994 to well over 300 channels today.[3] According to Nielsen Media Research, the average American home has the television set on more than seven hours per day.[4] For many such viewers, television is a source of entertainment and news, while for others television provides a general backdrop to one's day-to-day activities. Television and the Internet are the two principal leisure activities for most Americans.

Broadcast television is first and foremost a business. Television stations are in the business of producing audiences. As media economists Bruce Owen and Steven Wildman point out:

> The first and most serious mistake that an analyst of the television industry can make is to assume that [advertiser-supported broadcasters] are in the business to produce programs. They are not. Broadcasters are in the business of producing audiences. These audiences (or means of access to them) are sold to advertisers. The product of a television station is measured in dimensions of people and time. The price of the product is quoted in dollars per thousand viewers per unit of commercial time, typically 20 or 30 seconds.[5]

Demographic Considerations

Advertisers are interested not merely in the size of an audience, but in its composition. The term *demographics* refers to the age, sex, income and other quantifiable characteristics of the audience. Programming decisions, in terms of general content and scheduling, are based on the composition and size of the audience. Television programs such as *CSI, Desperate Housewives* and *60 Minutes* elicit different types of audience composition. It is the very composition and size of an audience that allow a television network, affiliate or independent station to charge more depending on the number and composition of people watching a particular program—hence the phrase "selling audiences to advertisers."

Television Organizational Structure

Television stations can be divided into two categories, *commercial* and *noncommercial*. The primary distinction between the two is the funding mechanism by which each station is able to operate. Commercial television (and radio) stations make their money by selling air time to advertisers. Noncommercial stations are funded through a variety of methods, including federal and state appropriations, business and foundation grants, and direct viewer contributions. Some critics have observed that over the years noncommercial underwriting has reached the point where it has begun to resemble commercial sponsorship.

Table 3.1 provides a look at the organization of radio and television stations in the United States.

Table 3.1 Radio and Television Stations in the United States (2008)

Television stations—total	1,780
PBS TV stations—noncommercial	355
FM radio stations	10,520
AM radio stations	5,095
Noncommercial radio stations	860
Low-power TV and FMs	5,269

Sources: National Association of Broadcasters, PBS, NPR.

The Broadcast Industry Structure

The broadcast industry structure refers to the principal players involved in the production, distribution and financing of television programs to the U.S. public. Let us consider the following six players:

1 the television networks;
2 program producers and distributors;
3 the network affiliates;
4 independent television stations;
5 public broadcasting;
6 the advertisers.

The Television Networks

The television network provides the organizational structure for many of the television stations in the United States. The networks function as brokers (or agents) between the program producer (i.e., Paramount, Disney, 20th Century Fox, etc.) and the local affiliated station (i.e., WBNS, WCBS, KRON, KABC, etc.) in the acquisition and distribution of programming. The networks sell advertising spots to major advertising accounts as a way to finance the cost of programming. In the U.S., there are four major television networks: NBC, CBS, ABC and Fox. In addition, there is the CW network, which functions as a minor network. The CW network is a joint venture between the former Warner Brothers and United Paramount Network(s). There is also a host of Spanish-language minor networks as well, including Univision, Telemundo and TeleFutura. Many of the major and minor television networks are the subsidiaries of larger transnational media corporations (TNMCs). This can be seen in Tables 3.2 (major) and 3.3 (minor).

Achieving Profitability

The networks achieve profitability through the sale of national advertising, less the cost of programming. If the networks obtain programming from a program producer, then the network provides seed capital but will not assume the major costs for production. If the production is internal, as in the case of a news and public affairs show (e.g., *60 Minutes, Dateline, 20/20*, etc.)

Table 3.2 U.S. Major Broadcast Television Networks

	Television Network	Parent Company
	CBS	Viacom
	NBC	General Electric (NBC Universal Group)
	ABC	Walt Disney Company
	Fox	News Corporation Ltd.

Table 3.3 Select U.S. Minor Broadcast Television Networks

	Television Network	Parent Company
CW	CW	Viacom and Time Warner (Warner Brothers)
UNIVISION	Univision	Investment partners: Haim Saban, TPG Capital and Thomas H. Lee
TELEMUNDO	Telemundo	General Electric (NBC Universal Group)
TELEFUTURA	TeleFutura	Univision Communications: Haim Saban, TPG Capital and Thomas H. Lee

or reality TV shows (e.g., *Survivor, The Apprentice, Amazing Race*, etc.), then the network assumes all costs for production. One reason for producing television internally has to do with cost. In principle, it costs less to produce a news and public affairs program or reality show when compared to prime-time comedy and drama.

In 1970, the Federal Communications Commission (FCC) implemented a set of rulings called Financial Interest and Syndication Rules (Fin-Syn Rules).[6] The goal was to increase program diversity and limit the market control of the three major television networks over the major television studios that produced television programming. The rules prohibited network participation in two related arenas: the financial interest of the television programs they aired beyond first-run exhibition, and the creation of in-house syndication arms, especially in the domestic market. Throughout the 1980s, the major television networks lobbied hard to eliminate the Fin-Syn Rules, arguing that such rules were unfair given the changing nature of the television industry. And by 1995 the rules were all but eliminated. As a result, more than 70 percent of the prime-time television that appears on network television is produced and owned by the networks themselves. The more successful prime-time dramas and comedies will later be sold into the syndication market. In addition, in-house production offers increased opportunities for vertical integration by owning the entire creative development process.

Network Clearance

Network television has the ability to reach the largest number of people when compared to other kinds of advertising media. This is accomplished through a clearance arrangement, that is, a contractual agreement whereby the affiliate agrees to rebroadcast the said programming and advertisements as scheduled. This, in turn, enables the network to deliver a cleared schedule to national advertisers on all 210-plus affiliates' sites. Consider, for example, NBC's telecast of the 2006 Winter Olympics from Turin, Italy. NBC paid $613 million for the right to broadcast the two-week event. NBC televised an estimated 418 hours of Olympic coverage both on its NBC broadcast network and on several of its broadcast services, including Telemundo, its Spanish-language network as well as its MSNBC cable network. Television network ads for the Olympics then cost an average of $700,000 for 30 seconds. Overall, NBC sold an estimated $950 million worth of combined advertising on both its broadcast and cable network services.[7] Similarly NBC televised the Summer Olympics in Beijing, China, and spent an estimated $900 million for the U.S. television rights.

Program Producers and Distributors

Program producers are the studios and production houses that make the television programs and films that are leased to both broadcast and cable networks for viewing. They include such production companies as 20th Century Fox, Paramount, Universal Studios and Walt Disney, to name only a few. In addition, there are various independent producers or executive writers like Steven Bochco, producer of *Hill Street Blues, L.A. Law* and *NYPD Blue*, Dick Wolf, producer of *Law and Order*, and Stephen J. Cannell, producer of *The Rockford Files, 21 Jump Street* and *The A-Team*, to name only a few.

The program producers contract with the networks to supply a certain number of program episodes for a broadcast season. The number of episodes will vary depending on the program and length of time it has been in production. The standard contract allows the network to show newly produced episodes twice during a regular season. Although the networks will provide seed capital, most of the production costs are assumed by the program producer. Thus, during the early stages of development, the cost of leasing seldom pays for the cost of production. Once the program has proven successful, the cost structure can change dramatically, with the network assuming a much higher percentage of the production costs. As television programs become more successful over time, the writers and actors of the said program demand more money.

Achieving Profitability

Why are program producers willing to assume the risk and costs associated with television production? The program producer achieves profitability when that same program can be sold as part of a syndication package, that is, reruns that are made available to local stations on an exclusive basis. In addition, the program producer retains the right to sell the same series to cable programmers as well as to consumers directly as part of DVD box set collections (e.g., *Friends, Seinfeld, M*A*S*H*, etc.). Program producers through their distributing agents try to maximize the sale of television and film products by carefully planning the selection of distribution media and release times.

There are two basic economic assumptions that characterize the production and sale of television and film products. The first is that television and film products are examples of a public good. That means that the cost of production is independent of the number of people who consume it. If a viewer watches television, this action does not prevent others from watching. A second important assumption is that the cost of television and film production is fixed. Once the cost of production has been realized, the cost per viewer declines as the size of the audience increases. The objective, therefore, is to maximize audience reach and to favor those distribution media which can accomplish this goal. Media economists Owen and Wildman refer to this as *windowing*, the method by which television and film programs are sold and distributed using different distribution media.[8]

Program Distribution

In recent years, the number of distribution windows has increased significantly, and now includes broadcast syndication (both domestic and foreign), basic and pay cable television, direct broadcast satellite, DVD sales and rentals and Internet sales. All television program producers have designated groups responsible for distributing television programming, including syndicated programs, films and ongoing television series. A major media company such as the Walt Disney Company, for example, will operate several distribution subsidiaries responsible for different kinds of software products such as international television and film distribution, off-network syndication, DVD prime-time rental and sales distribution, film library, music distribution, etc. As an example, Disney-ABC International Television is responsible for the Walt Disney Company's branded and non-branded television and filmed entertainment, providing more than 30,000 hours of program content to over 1,300 broadcasters across 240 territories worldwide. Disney-ABC International Television distributes programming from the ABC Television Network (and ABC Studios), including reality and scripted TV formats. The international film distribution arm licenses movies from producers including Walt Disney Pictures, Touchstone Pictures and Miramax Films.

Network Affiliates

Affiliates are the local stations that make up the network. It is the local station that provides the network with access to viewers. In practice, a local station enters into an affiliation agreement (or contract) with a parent network to carry the network's programs in accordance with the parent network's schedule. The networks are responsible for approximately 60–70 percent of their affiliates' schedules depending upon the network. During that time, the affiliate receives a select number of advertising slots and can sell local or national spot advertising. The other 30–40 percent of the affiliate's schedule is made up of local programming, most notably news and sports as well as syndicated programming. During those time periods, the affiliate station derives 100 percent of the revenue from the sale of local and spot advertising.

The Network–Affiliate Relationship

The network–affiliate relationship can trace its origins back to the early 1930s when the radio networks (and later television networks in the 1950s) needed a technical means of transmitting broadcast signals to different parts of the continental U.S. The networks would send their programming via leased telephone (and cable) lines to affiliate stations located across the U.S. The affiliate station, in turn, would receive the transmitted signal and rebroadcast it over the air to radio (and later television) sets located within a specified broadcast range. Leased cable lines gave way to satellite communication starting in the late 1970s.

Station Groups (Group Broadcasters)

Broadcasters have long understood the value of owning multiple AM, FM and television properties. The ownership of multiple television stations creates certain efficiencies when it comes to negotiating the cost of programming, purchasing equipment and supplies, selling advertising and conducting market research. The term *station group* (or *group broadcaster*) refers to a company or organization that owns multiple AM, FM or television stations. The ownership pattern can be exclusive to television or a combination of radio and television. A group broadcaster can own stations that are affiliates of one network or several. Some of the better-known station groups include Hearst Argyle, Scripps Howard, Tribune and Cox, to name only a few.

Owned and Operated (O & Os)

The term *owned and operated* (or O&O) refers to the ownership of an affiliate station by the parent network. CBS Television, for example, owns 13 affiliate stations as part of its general operations. O&O stations tend to be stations located in the major markets. As an example, WCBS, New York, is both an affiliate of the CBS Television network and also owned by the parent network. The principal advantages to the network in being an O&O are the efficiencies to be derived in terms of programming, scheduling and general operations. The major networks, CBS, ABC, NBC and Fox, are also considered station group owners because they own and operate multiple stations that make up their specific network. Table 3.4 provides a listing of the 16 O&O stations that make up the CBS Television network. According to FCC regulation, the total number of television stations that can be owned by a station group (including a television network) cannot exceed a reach of 39.5 percent of the potential viewing audience in the U.S.

Achieving Profitability

The network–affiliate relationship is truly a partnership. The networks benefit since they are able to achieve national reach and charge advertisers accordingly. The networks are able to guarantee a national advertiser that the said advertisement will be seen in its proper time and place. It's a win–win for the affiliates as well. The affiliates benefit since 60–70 percent of their program schedule is accounted for by the parent network and such programming is made available for free. Equally important, the affiliate benefits from the professional association with the parent network and the programming brand that it represents. This, in turn, helps to build station identity.

In achieving profitability, the affiliate station has two important revenue

Table 3.4 CBS Television O&O Stations

Television Market	Station	Channel
New York City	WCBS-TV	Ch. 2
Los Angeles	KCBS-TV	Ch. 2
Chicago	WBBM-TV	Ch. 2
Philadelphia	KYW-TV	Ch. 3
San Francisco	KPIX-TV	Ch. 5
Dallas–Fort Worth	KTVT	Ch. 11
Boston	WBZ-TV	Ch. 4
Detroit	WWJ-TV	Ch. 62
Minneapolis–St. Paul	WCCO-TV	Ch. 4
Miami	WFOR-TV	Ch. 4
Denver	KCNC-TV	Ch. 4
Sacramento	KOVR	Ch. 13
Pittsburgh	KDKA-TV	Ch. 2
Baltimore	WJZ-TV	Ch. 13
Salt Lake City	KUTV	Ch. 2
Austin	KEYE-TV	Ch. 42

streams, including the sale of local and national spot advertising and network compensation. Affiliate stations generate approximately 70 percent of their income during the 40 percent of their broadcast day that is not committed to the network when they carry locally originated and syndicated programming. The term *network compensation* refers to payment from the parent network to the affiliate for carrying the said programming (and advertising). In the past, network compensation amounted to approximately 8 percent of the network affiliate's revenues. The actual rate is based on the program and the station's effectiveness in its local market. Today, providing network compensation is becoming less and less of a factor for affiliate stations. The major networks are steadily moving away from compensation to affiliates, especially during the airing of highly successful prime-time comedies, dramas and reality programs. Last, affiliate stations can also make money by hosting a station website (inclusive of the sale of local advertising) and from local television ad production as well as a variety of barter arrangements, such as trading out hotel space for advertising time.

Independent Stations

Independent stations are not aligned with the traditional networks. The independent station may be owned and operated as a separate entity within a local market or it may be owned as one of several independent and/or affiliate stations by a television station group. In the beginning years of television, a station rarely became independent by choice. Rather, a station was independent because it could not get an affiliation with a major network. Starting with the advent of the Fox television network (late 1980s) and the minor networks (1990s), many independent stations today have become either full- or part-time affiliates to a network. Some of the better-known independent stations include WGN in Chicago and WPIX-TV in New York. Both WGN and WPIX-TV are highly recognized stations within their respective markets. The success of independent stations (particularly UHF television stations) has been greatly aided by cable television, which has leveled the electronic playing field by making it easier for viewers to access small and large stations alike.

Achieving Profitability

Being an independent station has its advantages and disadvantages. The primary advantage is that the station has a greater opportunity to sell local and national spot advertising and that all advertising dollars go directly to the station. An independent station can be highly profitable in some medium- to major-size markets. In the past, the lack of a direct steady supply of programming forced the independent station to position itself as the home of local sports entertainment. As an example, WGN in Chicago is a highly profitable independent station largely owing to its association with Chicago Bulls basketball and Cubs baseball. Similarly, WPIX-TV is home to the New York Mets baseball team. It's also a part-time affiliate station of the CW network.

The audience demographics are very appealing for advertisers wanting to reach sports enthusiasts. In addition, both stations have a strong news operation as well as a good assortment of syndicated programming. The primary disadvantage of being an independent station is that the station must come up with an entire slate of programming on its own. This costs money. As mentioned earlier, one solution is to become a part-time affiliate of a minor network such as WPIX and the CW network. But for the many stations that are not able to affiliate with a minor network, the challenges are significant. Independent stations will typically program a combination of syndicated programming, sports and news.

Public Broadcasting

In 1967, the FCC put forth a series of recommendations that resulted in Congress passing the Public Broadcasting Act of 1967 for the purpose of establishing noncommercial radio and television in the U.S.[9] The Public Broadcasting Service (PBS) was founded in 1969 and provides a bottom-line guarantee that select forms of broadcast programming (regardless of commercial viability) will have a place on the American radio and television landscape. Thus, programming such as *All Things Considered* (radio), *Masterpiece Theatre, Nova* and *Sesame Street* (television), to name only a few, are made available to those listeners and viewers who might want to avail themselves of higher-end cultural, educational and public affairs programming.

Corporation for Public Broadcasting

The Public Broadcasting Act of 1967 established the Corporation for Public Broadcasting (CPB), which serves as the principal funding agent for the 1,000-plus noncommercial radio and television stations in the U.S. Although CPB is not a government agency, it does function as a liaison organization between the federal government and the various public broadcasting services. Most CPB-funded television programs are distributed through the Public Broadcasting Service (PBS), which was established in 1969. Most CPB-funded radio programs are distributed through National Public Radio, which was created in 1970.

Public Broadcasting Service

The Public Broadcasting Service is a private, nonprofit corporation owned and operated by the nation's public television stations. PBS provides quality educational, cultural, public affairs and children's programming to 355 noncommercial television stations located in the U.S., Puerto Rico, the Virgin Islands, Guam and American Samoa. PBS, unlike the commercial television networks, produces no programs of its own. Instead, PBS provides an interconnection and distribution network for television programs produced by others. It relies on the production capability of a handful of PBS stations such as WGBH, Boston; KQED, San Francisco; WQED, Pittsburgh; WNET, New York; WTTW, Chicago; WETA, Washington, D.C.; and KCET, Los Angeles. In addition, there are other production entities that produce programs for PBS.

Member stations sign contracts with PBS for the right to be part of the PBS programming and distribution network. Member stations provide nearly half of PBS's operating budget through the payment of annual dues in order to receive national programming and various support services. The payment of dues is based on a sliding scale which is determined by the station's budget and market size. PBS does not impose a master program schedule on its affiliate members. However, it does try to encourage its member stations to carry the same program schedule from 8 to 10 P.M. Sunday–Friday. Thus, PBS television schedules vary somewhat from market to market.

PBS Programming and Scheduling

Program selection is largely determined by the affiliates, who must pay for the programs they receive. PBS offers its affiliates a list of proposed programs for the upcoming season. Some programs are fully underwritten by business or foundation grants, whereas other programs are partially funded or have no financial support. In the latter case, PBS will carry such programs when and if there are a sufficient number of stations willing to pay for it. This is accomplished through a series of voting rounds during which time stations must commit their programming dollars. PBS affiliates make such commitments based on the level of program appeal to local audiences, attractiveness to local underwriters and program affordability.[10]

PBS Organization and Financing

The PBS system of organization consists of 168 noncommercial, educational licensees that operate 355 member stations.[11] Today's public broadcasting stations are licensed to four administrative entities: state and municipalities (40 percent), colleges and universities (25 percent), community nonprofit foundations (33 percent) and public school boards (less than 3 percent).[12] PBS's operating revenue in fiscal year 2006 was approximately $573 million.[13] Both PBS and NPR are financed through a combination of different funding methods that can be seen in Table 3.5.

Table 3.5 Sources of Funding for U.S. Public Broadcasting (2008)

PBS station membership
State government
Business (underwriting and direct contribution)
CPB appropriation
University/college support
Foundation support
Local government
Contracts
Retail sale of PBS programming and merchandise
Direct viewer contributions

Source: Corporation for Public Broadcasting.

PBS stations' membership provides nearly half of PBS's operating budget through the payment of annual dues in order to receive national programming and various other services. Other important contributing sources include CPB allocation, foundation grants and direct viewer contributions. PBS member stations will typically hold biannual pledge drives as the basis for generating local station revenue.

The Advertisers

Advertising is the principal engine that enables U.S. radio and television to occur. The goal of advertising simply stated is to inform and/or to persuade potential consumers to purchase products and services in the marketplace. Advertising is a dynamic field, with advertisers constantly looking for new ways to achieve those goals. The advertising process begins with the client, that is, the company that wishes to sell its products and services to the public at large. It is the client that must decide how much money is to be allocated for the purpose of advertising. A company's advertising budget is usually calculated as a fixed percentage of its projected sales. Clients will typically spend between 10 and 15 percent of their general revenues on advertising.

The Advertising Agency

The advertising agency performs three major roles. First, the agency services the client by providing it with an account executive (or set of executives) responsible for understanding the client's needs and helping to develop an appropriate advertising strategy. Second, the agency is responsible for developing an advertising campaign in terms of the concept and design as well as overseeing the production of print, display and/or video ads. Third, the agency works closely with the client in terms of deciding the best ways to promote the client's products and services. The agency is responsible for media selection and ad placement.

In the past, clients paid advertising agencies on a commission basis. The agency would bill the client for the full price of a placed ad. The traditional broadcast or print media, in turn, would provide it to the agency at a discounted rate of 15 percent. For example: A TV station would bill the agency $1,000 for the time purchased and the agency would pass that bill on to the advertiser. When the bill was paid, the agency would retain $150 (its commission) and the station would receive $850 (the remaining 85 percent). The agency would charge the client the full prices of the ad less the 15 percent which became the agency's commission rate. In more recent years, however, advertisers have evolved different kinds of payment systems, which might include a direct service fee for designing and producing an advertisement. Some companies use a performance-based compensation approach, whereby the agency will accept a lower fee but be rewarded with special incentives if the clients' sales objectives are met or exceeded.[14] Some agencies function as full-service agencies where the cost of advertising is factored into a much larger system-wide marketing effort that may include public relations, market research, direct marketing, trade show displays, interactive services, etc.

Understanding the Media Mix

Advertisers think in terms of a media mix, that is, a combined strategy for advertising products and services. While broadcasting is an essential part of any advertising strategy, it represents only one part of a much larger array of media choices. Thus the actual mix will depend largely on the nature of the product or service and the best way to advertise it. Consider, for example, the media mix employed by American Express Co. as compared to Anheuser-Busch in the selection of media and the total advertising dollars spent by each company. American Express is perceived as a high-end consumer product, while the beer products of Anheuser-Busch are generally seen as a mainstream, middle-of-the-road product. What is interesting to note is the selection of media type and how it reflects the perceived value of the brand and the audience for whom it is intended. As an example, Anheuser-Busch may spend nearly twice as much money on television advertising as compared to American Express. This is based on the audience it's trying to reach. In contrast, American Express may divide its advertising budget amongst multiple platforms including the Internet, high-end magazines and newspapers.[15]

Broadcast Advertising

Television revenues are derived from the sale of advertising time to potential sponsors. The amount of money that a network or television station can charge is dependent upon several factors, including:

1   the number of people expected to watch a given program;
2   the time period in which the advertisement would appear;
3   the size of the television market;
4   the number of advertisements the commercial sponsor wishes to purchase with the network or station (i.e., volume discount);
5   the demographic make-up of the audience.

Advertising Time and Cost

During a regular 30-minute television program, approximately six to eight minutes are devoted to advertising. The amount of advertising time varies according to the program. The cost of advertising time is based on the estimated number of people expected to watch a given program during a given time period. In the case of established programs, that estimate is based upon past performance (i.e., ratings and shares). In short, the higher the ratings, the more a network or station can charge for advertising time. Broadcast advertising falls into three categories. They include: network, national spot and local.

National and Regional Spot Advertising

National and regional spot advertising refers to the purchase and placement of advertisements in select markets. A national spot advertiser would be a company like Coca-Cola or Toyota. A regional spot advertiser might be a Midwest supermarket chain like Meijer or Kroger. The assumption is that certain products are more regionally or geographically dependent. The sale and marketing of ski equipment, for example, would do better to place spot ads in those regions of the U.S. where people live in close proximity to the mountains with good snow conditions. In order to accomplish this, the national or regional advertiser will purchase time from individual local stations. The obvious problem, of course, is the sheer number of stations that need to be contacted and the level of coordination. Thus, the purchase of a spot ad is typically handled though a local station's national representative (or rep firm). The national rep firm makes it easier for local stations to sell national advertising by serving as a central contact point between local stations and national advertisers In order to avoid a potential conflict of interest, a national rep will only represent one station in a given market. The rep makes its money based on a percentage of advertising sales.

Local Advertising

Local advertising refers to the sale of advertising time to local merchants. The local merchants, including banks, car dealerships and appliance stores, to name only a few, are highly dependent on local customers for the vast majority of their business. Local television advertising represents an important marketing strategy for such businesses. Oftentimes, the local television station is involved in both the production and the advertisement of the said product or service.

Broadcast Programming

Commercial television stations have two sets of customers. The first set of customers are the viewers. Their primary motivation is in watching television programs. They make it possible for the second set of customers, which are the advertisers. The advertisers purchase air time based on the belief that the said program will attract the right kind of viewers to see their commercials. According to Susan Tyler Eastman and Doug Ferguson:

> Programming is both a skill and an art. The primary goal in programming advertiser supported media is to maximize the size of an audience targeted by advertisers. The only way to accomplish this goal is to satisfy the needs and wants of that audience.[16]

Program Development

Programming that appears on a major television network represents a blend of creative content combined with long-term commercial viability. Any television program that makes it on network television goes through a development process. Ideas for a possible television series can come from a variety of sources, including writers, actors and producers. The television networks designate a series of individuals to serve as program development specialists. Their job is to review the multiple television proposals (or pitches) between the months of September and December. On average, a major network may review upwards of 400–600 pitches during the fall months. The pitches can range from a simple story idea to a full script. After reviewing the multiple pitches the development specialists will ask the writer to refine his/her proposal (or script) into working script before making a presentation to a network executive team. In all, a set of 50-plus scripts will be reviewed in the months of December and January.

Do the network development teams sometimes get it wrong? Absolutely. There are numerous examples across the board of how a network development specialist passed on a proposed idea only later to have it become a blockbuster hit on another network. As an example, the program development teams at both ABC and NBC passed on a proposed television series called *Crime Scene Investigation* only later to have it debut on CBS as *CSI*. The rest, as they say, is history.

In December, the network executive team will meet and review the best ideas and determine that 10–15 of the proposed series ideas should be commissioned into a pilot episode. In late December or early January, the respective writer or producer is notified of the network's interest and he/she is then charged with putting together a cast and production crew for shooting in the months of February and March. It can be said that television is a writer's medium. A successful television program starts with good storytelling and strong character development. A lot is at stake in the development of the pilot episode since it will ultimately determine whether the series will be picked up by the network. An important person throughout the entire development process is the program producer. It is his/her job to serve as an advocate on behalf of the television program series. The producer is ultimately responsible for all aspects of the production and serves as the chief liaison person between the production unit and the network. The producer must know everyone's job and responsibility.

The finished pilots are typically reviewed by a network executive team in the month of April. The discussion takes into account a number of factors, including story line (and the potential for successful episodes), budgetary considerations in terms of production costs (writers, actors and actresses, etc.) and whether the said series will have strong advertising appeal. After the review process is complete, a decision will be made to support eight to ten of the pilot presentations. The networks, in turn, commit to support the production of six episodes per new television series going into the summer. Now the pressure starts to mount up. The good news is that the proposed television series has been given the green light. The bad news is that the production team now has less than four months to develop six episodes prior to the start of the fall season. Throughout the production process the writers are being given notes (or feedback) from the producer and network executives in terms of ways to refine and improve the television series.

Starting in May and June, the network's marketing department starts the process of putting together a publicity strategy to help advance the introduction of the new series. The debut of the new television series occurs sometime in the second or third week of September. For purposes of better understanding the development process we have put together a table entitled Anatomy of a Television Program Idea (Table 3.6).[17]

Program Scheduling

Program scheduling is not an exact science. When and where you locate a television program requires a combination of showmanship skills and a clear understanding of audience research and analysis. Add to it a little bit of gut instinct, and the network's "Rubik's Cube" schedule seems to take shape and form. The network television schedule is broken into day parts, starting with early morning and ending with overnight. The complete set of television day parts can be seen in Table 3.7. Throughout the day, affiliate stations will

Table 3.6 Anatomy of a Television Program Idea

Story idea/pitching	September–November
Review submitted scripts	December–January
Ordering up a set of pilot episodes	January
Production of pilot episode	January–March
Pilots reviewed—final series selection made	April
Series selection—six episodes put into production	May–August
Program marketing begins	June–September
Series airs on network television	September

Table 3.7 Television Day Parts Program Schedule

Early morning	5 A.M.–9 A.M.
Daytime	9 A.M.–4 P.M.
Early fringe	4 P.M.–6 P.M.
News	6 P.M.–7 P.M.
Prime access	7 P.M.–8 P.M.
Prime time	8 P.M.–11 P.M.
Late news	11 P.M.–11:30 P.M.
Late fringe	11:30 P.M.–2 A.M.
Overnight	2 A.M.–5 A.M.

block out certain portions of the broadcast day for their own internal programming, such as local news at 6 and 11 P.M. and syndicated programming during the early fringe period from 4 to 6 P.M.

Prime Time

We start with the fact that prime time, that is, 8–11 P.M. is the most valuable piece of television real estate. Prime time garners the most audience viewership, and advertising rates are at their highest. The 18–54 age demographic is especially valued during this time period. Therefore, a lot is at stake in terms of what programs are aired and on what day and time they are located. While programming is not an exact science, there are certain truisms about programming.

The Compatibility Principle

Scheduling strategies take advantage of the fact that programming should coincide with what people do throughout the course of their day. The compatibility principle presupposes that broadcast programmers have only one channel at their disposal and must therefore plan programs based on a so-called typical lifestyle of their audience. Day parts such as early morning feature soft news and lifestyle programs such as *Good Morning America* on ABC and the *Today Show* on NBC. In contrast, a day part such as late fringe features more adult comedy/variety programming like CBS's David Letterman and NBC's Jay Leno.

Audience Flow

Programmers realize that a good program encourages a natural audience flow (or transference) from the completion of one program into the beginning of another. The networks, as a general rule, try to grow the audience during the course of an evening by building on programs that are similar in nature. On Thursday evenings, for example, NBC might build strong audience flow by programming an entire evening devoted to comedy. At 10 P.M., NBC is likely to shift gears by programming a dramatic series like *ER* or a similar-type program. NBC helps contribute to the audience flow concept by designing promotions that tell the viewer where he/she is in the sequence of the evening's programs. As a concept, audience flow has become less of a factor given the widespread availability of the remote control tuner. The ease of switching channels offsets many of the potential benefits of program blocs.

Stripping

Stripping is a strategy employed by the networks and local stations. Stripping involves scheduling the same program in the same time slot every day. In the case of local stations, syndicated programs are often stripped five days a week during the late afternoon Monday to Friday. Similarly, local news is stripped seven evenings a week at 5:30 or 6:00 P.M. The value of stripping is to build audience awareness for a certain program in a given time slot. Habit formation becomes an essential part of building audience loyalty. The difficulty with stripping occurs when a certain program does not work. A failing program is associated with a certain time slot.

Seeding

Television programming is subject to a natural life cycle, not unlike other types of products in the market. The evolution of a television program tends to follow a natural bell curve, with strong performance in the first three years, established maturity during years 4–6, and a decline phase during years 7–9. As mentioned, successful programs engender strong audience loyalty (i.e., habit formation). Sometimes when programs have peaked and are in the decline phase, the television networks will take a highly successful

68

program and schedule it on another evening as the foundation for growing another evening's worth of programming, hence the term "seeding." The risk with seeding is that it sometimes doesn't work. The audience sometimes fails to make the jump to another evening, thus eroding viewership even further.

Special Event Programming (or Stunting)

Special event programs are unique, one-of-a-kind programs designed to create large (or specialized) audiences. Special event programming will often draw audiences away from the competition. The special event program also generates strong advertising interest. Examples of special event programs include the World Series (baseball), the Super Bowl (football), NCAA College Basketball Playoffs and the Olympics. Special event programs can also include the Country Music Awards or a television mini-series.

Counterprogramming (A Defensive Strategy)

Most programming strategies are proactive, whereas counterprogramming is a defensive strategy. In principle, the network programs according to what the competition is doing. Counterprogramming often involves targeting an unserved audience segment during a given time period. As an example, a typical counterprogramming strategy may involve programming movies and comedies against Sunday afternoon football with the goal of reaching those members of the audience who do not like football. A counterprogramming strategy can include special event programming as well.

Program Positioning and Profitability

While every network would like to be number one in each and every time slot, that goal is unattainable. Therefore, the real question is whether the said program is profitable in its time period. More to the point, it's not whether you're number one in your time slot but whether you're profitable. Consider three weekly news magazines, *Time, Newsweek* and *U.S. News and World Reports*. If the metric for success is readership, *Time* would be number one, closely followed by *Newsweek*. But what if you're the publisher of *U.S. News and World Reports*? Do you discontinue the magazine given the fact that it ranks third in readership? The answer is no. *U.S. News and World Reports* is still a highly profitable publication and therefore continues to be a viable business. The same can be said for the television network that ranks second or third in the ratings during a given time period. So long as the program remains profitable, the argument can be made for its continuation.

Opportunity Cost

At the same time, network planners continually ask themselves whether a substitute program might do better in a given time slot if the said program is lagging in comparison to the competition. Opportunity cost refers to the value of what you are currently doing as compared to the value of doing something else (i.e., the next best alternative). Opportunity cost becomes the basic reason why certain television programs get canceled. In the world of television programming, there is an underlying assumption that a new substitute program will garner better ratings and is therefore worthy of being introduced in place of a less successful television program.

Broadcast Station Management and Operations

The organization of a radio or television station can be influenced by a variety of factors, including the market size and geographical location, whether the station is an affiliate or independent and whether the station is group-owned or not. In addition, the management style of the general manager can be very important in the way the station is organized and run. In general, there are seven departments that are common to most broadcast stations. They include:

- sales;
- programming;
- news;
- engineering;
- business;
- marketing and promotion;
- traffic.

Sales

Advertising represents the principal source of revenue for commercial radio and television stations. The sales department, under the direction of the vice president of sales (or senior sales manager), is responsible for the sale of advertising on a local, regional and national basis.

Programming

Programming, under the direction of the program director or manager, is responsible for program selection, acquisition and scheduling. The program schedule must maintain continuity between network feeds (if affiliate), locally produced programs and syndicated programs that have been purchased. For station groups, a lot of the decision making involving syndicated program selection occurs at the corporate level.

70

News

The news department, under the direction of the news director or managing editor, is responsible for regularly scheduled newscasts, sports specials, public affairs programming, etc. The news director will assign news stories to be covered locally. Local television news is not only an important profit center for the station, but through its on-air talent provides much of the identity for the station within the local market.

Engineering

The engineering department, under the direction of the chief engineer, operates and maintains studio and control room equipment. The engineering staff are also responsible for technical monitoring and staying in accordance with FCC technical requirements.

Business

The business department (or administrative area) carries out the business and support tasks necessary to the functioning of the station, including secretarial, bookkeeping, billing/accounting and payroll.

Marketing and Promotion

The marketing and promotion group is responsible for promoting and enhancing the visibility of the station. Marketing and promotion increase public awareness of the station and the opportunities for purchasing advertising time. Marketing and promotion work closely with the sales department.

Traffic

The traffic group is responsible for maintaining a schedule (or log) of the programs and advertisements aired. In addition, traffic is responsible for maintaining an availability list showing times that are available for purchase by advertisers, and monitors advertisements in order to ensure that contracts have been fulfilled.

Responsibilities of the General Manager

The responsibilities of the general manager can be divided into two areas, including strategic planning and basic operations. Strategic planning involves the formulation of plans for achieving long-range organizational goals. One such strategic goal is increased profitability (i.e., television sales). In a broadcast television environment, however, strategic planning also refers to other organizational goals such as improving the quality and visibility of the station's news and public affairs programming. Strategic planning can also refer to a station's commitment to be more technologically innovative. This issue becomes especially important as today's broadcast stations continue the process of becoming fully digital, as well as enhancing the station's marketing and news capability via the Internet. The general manager is also responsible for operations management, which refers to the day-to-day management of the station. This can include many of the following tasks:

1 Providing support and coordinating goals with the sales and marketing staff, the programming department and the news department.
2 Planning and overseeing the station's operating budget. This typically involves working closely with the station's business department.
3 Personnel management, which can include helping to determine the staffing requirements for the station. Depending on the size of the station, the general manager can and will get involved in hiring decisions as well as taking disciplinary actions when necessary.
4 Negotiating contracts and approving major programming and equipment purchases.
5 External relations, that is, representing the station in a variety of community affairs, ranging from meeting with community officials to handling consumer complaints.
6 Serving as the station's primary representative to corporate management when and if that station is an affiliate and/or a group-owned station.

Program Selection and Scheduling

The constant demand for television programming by affiliate and independent stations requires that they have direct access to both new and old sources of programming. The programming department of any station is responsible for making sure that the station offers viewers good product inventory. We will examine some of the strategies employed by broadcast managers in the selection, negotiation and scheduling of programs that are seen on both affiliate and independent stations.

As mentioned, the networks fill approximately 60–70 percent of an affiliate's schedule with programming. That means the affiliate is responsible for filling the remaining 30–40 percent of the schedule. Independent stations, by comparison, have the more formidable task of trying to fill their entire schedule with different sources of programming. In addition to locally originated programming (i.e., news and public affairs), one of the important sources of programming for the local station market is through the purchase of syndicated programming.

Syndication

Syndication is the licensing of a television or film product by a program distributor to an affiliate or independent broadcast station on an exclusive basis, that is, one station per market. A syndicator like King World Productions (CBS) will lease a program such as *Oprah Winfrey* and have the same program appear on an NBC affiliate in San Francisco, an ABC affiliate in New York and an independent station in Atlanta. Each station buys the exclusive rights to that program in its market. In the case of a major station group, the decision about program selection is often made at the corporate level on behalf of the company's multiple station outlets. In general, there are three types of syndicated programming: 1) first run, 2) off-network and 3) feature films.

- *First run:* First run syndication refers to programs that are made for the syndication market. Such programs include talk shows (*Oprah Winfrey, Dr. Phil*), game shows (*Wheel of Fortune, Jeopardy*), entertainment shows (*Entertainment Tonight, Inside Edition*) and made-for-television dramatic series (*Star Trek Voyager*, etc.).
- *Off-network (reruns):* Off-network syndication refers to programs that have appeared previously on the networks (i.e., reruns such as *Friends, Home Improvement, Seinfeld, M*A*S*H, Cheers, The Bill Cosby Show*, etc.).
- *Feature films:* Feature films are movies that were originally made for theatrical exhibition that are now available for television.

Syndicated programming is typically purchased to fill the hours of non-network feeds (typically late afternoons) or the entire schedule in the case of independent stations. Syndicators such as Buena Vista (Disney-ABC), Paramount (Viacom), Universal (NBC Universal), to name only a few, license the exclusive rights to a program in that station's market. The syndicated program is usually sold as an entire package and specifies a set number of plays through the life of the contract. This does not include the current year if the program is still in production. The purchase price for syndicated programming will vary according to the program offering, the television market size, and the expected returns during select day parts (e.g., the early fringe period, 5–6 P.M, will be worth more than regular daytime or late night).

For most television stations, the purchase of syndicated programming represents the single largest expense for a station on a year-to-year basis. It should not be surprising, therefore, that program acquisition and negotiation are areas that occupy a considerable amount of time for station management. The challenge, of course, is to purchase the right program at the right price. For a station manager (and program director), the right program has to achieve the objective of attracting a large number of people with the right demographics. Depending on the time slot, the right program has to provide a possible segue into the local evening news at 5:30 or 6:00 P.M. Clearly, the station that makes the mistake of purchasing a syndicated program that underperforms (or where too much was spent on the licensing fee) can seriously destabilize the station's financial performance.

The program distributor (syndicator) will typically negotiate contracts with the station's general manager or the group station program director. Throughout the year, both sets of managers will routinely meet with syndicators, listening to sales pitches, reviewing research reports and watching DVDs of program excerpts or actual pilots. Oftentimes, the meeting takes place at industry conferences such as the National Association of Television Program Executives (NATPE). That said, most of the important contracts are written in advance of the convention. In the pitch, the syndicator tries to convince station management of the program's merits, pointing out the potential upside for improved station ratings.

The Station Representative (Rep)

Station management also utilizes the support services of national representation (or rep) firms. Rep firms are companies hired by television stations to sell advertising outside the station's local market. The air time is called a *national spot* because it can be placed in any market (or combination of markets) in the country. Spot advertising time is typically sold to advertising agencies or dedicated media buyers representing a select set of clients.

In addition, the rep firm (and its sales personnel) acts as an outside consultant to the station in matters of market research, programming and sales trend analysis. The national rep firms have research and programming staffs that work closely with client stations in order to assist in the selection and scheduling of programs in order to maximize advertising performance. One of the rep firms' most important functions is to regularly disseminate ongoing market research reports to client stations. Typically, no additional fee is charged to the station for these kinds of support services. The information is included in the rep firm's sales commission.

Most syndicators maintain a close working relationship with the national rep firms and their sales personnel. They inform station reps of ratings successes, changes in sales strategies, and purchases of the program by leading stations or station groups. Syndicators will sometimes try to enlist the station rep's support for a particular show. While the station rep does not actually purchase the program, a rep's positive recommendation to the station can help pave the way for the syndicator when he/she contacts the station or the group programming head. At the same time, station reps must consider the programming philosophy (and strategy) of the individual stations they represent. If a rep dislikes a certain program (or does not feel it suits a station's needs), the rep's advice to the station can damage the syndicator's efforts. Many stations will refuse to buy syndicated shows largely because their reps do not endorse them.[18]

Program Negotiation

Too often, local station programmers play it safe and rely on past performance as the sole basis for decision making. This can lead to a conservative (or the proven track record) method of programming, which may be the right approach in some circumstances—but not always. According to Carroll and Davis:

> A programmer's job is to determine what the target audience wants regardless of personal preference. Thus she or he must have the flexibility to recognize the circumstances of the market and adapt and innovate in order to attract the audience that is available.[19]

In short, a highly successful run on network television does not guarantee automatic success in syndication. The real art to programming is the ability to foresee the potential of an unknown program (or a program that has specialized audience appeal) and to include it in the station's mix of program offerings.

A second important skill is the ability to have good negotiation skills. Program negotiation is the ability to obtain the right program at the right cost. The one thing that station managers all agree on is that everything is negotiable. Getting it right is the all-important essential to broadcast station management since so much depends on offering viewers good product at a price that is cost-effective. To that end, the general manager has to consider several important questions:

1 Does the said program have clear audience appeal?
2 Who is the program targeted to? In short, what is the audience composition?
3 Does the program have a proven track record? If so, in what kind of markets?
4 How does this program fit into the station's overall program lineup? As an example, does this program contribute to good audience flow in the late-afternoon program bloc?
5 What is the competition doing? Programming decisions are sometimes based on not wanting the competition to get a particular program.
6 What is the station's bottom line in terms of cost? How much can the station afford to spend given the cost of local advertising in that specific market?

After that, it is pure negotiation plain and simple. Syndicated programming is subject to the laws of supply and demand. The syndicator's degree of pricing flexibility will largely depend on the past and present success of the program in question. As an example, a highly successful game show (or off-network program) enables the syndicator to more or less set the asking price. The syndicator knows full well that there are other stations in the market that would be willing to bid on the same program. Station management, for its part, must assign a dollar value to the program, with a clear ceiling price on how much the station is willing to spend. This is where the station rep can be of invaluable assistance to the station management by being able to provide market research to support a potential purchase. In the end, the only real price is the price agreed to by the syndicator and local station management. Acquiring the rights to a syndicated television program involves entering into a contract between the station and the program syndicator. The standard contract usually contains eight principal features, which can be seen in Table 3.8. It should be noted that, in the case of a group broadcaster, the purchase of syndicated programming does not always take into account the unique requirements of the individual station. In such cases,

Table 3.8 Standard Program Syndication Contract

Title	Some syndicated programs that are off-network will acquire a new title in order to differentiate it from a program series that may be currently airing.
Description of the program	Describes the program format and whether the program is first run or off-network.
Duration	Describes the length of the program, typically 30–60 minutes in length.
Number of episodes	Identifies the number of episodes in the package as well as specifying the number of repeats.
Starting and ending dates	Identify the length of the contract, which can typically range from one year to three years.
Commercial format	Specifies a fixed number of commercial spots that can be formatted into the program. As an example, a typical half-hour program is formatted to allow six and a half commercial minutes per episode.
Program schedule	Specifies, depending on the program, when during the broadcast day the program will be aired. This will vary according to the syndicated program and the nature of the contract.
Method of payment	Specifies the method in which the station will finance the said program. Syndicated programs are sold for cash, for barter, or for cash-plus-barter.*
Down payment and layout	Specifies the method in which the station will pay for the syndicated program over time, starting with a possible down payment of 10–20 percent. It also specifies the terms of installed payments through the life of the contract.

* Starting in the mid-1980s, syndicators began asking for the right to barter portions of their syndicated material, that is, the right to sell parts of the adjoining advertising spots within the program in exchange for the station getting the program and/or a reduction in the cost of acquisition. This is known as a cash-plus-barter arrangement.

the station that did not want the program has to adjust its schedule in order to make room for it.

Broadcast Television Sales

Successful television programs provide an efficient means for advertisers to promote their products and services. The selling of air time (both before and during a television program) can be thought of as advertising inventory. Broadcasters place a predetermined dollar amount on the selling of commercial ads based on the ratings and perceived demographics of each program. The station's ability to command the best dollar value for a 30- or 60-second commercial is dependent upon successful programming. As Carroll and Davis note:

> A programmer's function is to develop and implement strategies to attract and maintain audiences that can be delivered to advertisers. It is virtually impossible to separate programming decisions from sales objectives. . . . Advertising [sales] are always the other half of programming considerations.[20]

Broadcast Sales Team

All television stations have a sales team of account executives. It is the responsibility of the account executive to seek out new customer prospects as well as to service existing ones. A good account executive will help the business (or organization) to plan an advertising strategy that tries to achieve the client's objectives while factoring in the amount of money the client has to spend. In smaller markets, the account executive can and often does get involved in the creative development of the advertisements as well. The account executive is paid a commission based on a percentage of sales.

Pre-buy "Up-front" Arrangements

Advertising is something that has to be sold in advance of the air date since it can never be recouped after the fact. At the same time, there is a fixed limit on the number of advertising spots that can be sold by a network (or station) during a given broadcast day. To that end, the networks provide their major advertisers with a so-called pre-buy arrangement, whereby they can purchase a large segment of the network advertising inventory (typically in June and July) in advance of the fall season. Larger clients are typically given advertising discounts based on the volume of ads purchased. The pre-buy arrangement takes the pressure off both the networks and advertisers in terms of ensuring consistency and reliability of ad sales and placement.

Approximately 70 percent of the network's advertising inventory is sold using the pre-buy arrangement.

Rate Cards

The account executive relies on two important pieces of information when making a presentation to a client. The first information tool is the rate card, which provides a list of prices for advertising. The rate card lists the prices for advertising during various parts of the broadcast day. There are a number of factors that can influence the cost for a 30- or 60-second advertisement, including:

- the current or projected ratings of a television program during which the advertisement will appear;
- whether the advertisement is a single ad purchase or part of a volume discount;
- the day part (or time period) in which the ad is scheduled to run;
- the size of the television market.

Both the broadcast and cable industries are highly dynamic industries. In larger markets, the traditional printed rate card has given way to flexible rate cards where the cost of advertising can change on weekly basis and/or according to special event programming. As mentioned earlier, pre-buy arrangements also factor heavily in the sale of advertising inventory.

Ratings and Market Analysis

The second information tool is a ratings book, which provides comparative data analysis in terms of audience viewership between the station and its competition. While programmers need to be mindful of ratings information, ratings data is of primary importance to the sales person in the field. As the late Barry Sherman once wrote:

> A popular misconception about the use of audience research is that ratings are of primary interest to programmers. The fact is, however, that while program directors, producers and writers follow the ratings assiduously, the main motive for conducting audience research is advertising sales.[21]

The basic measures of evaluating audience size in broadcasting are rating and share. The ratings book also provides information pertaining to the demographic make-up of that audience.

Two ratings firms, Nielsen Media Research and Arbitron, dominate the field of audience research and are the principal sources of ratings analysis used by electronic media as well as the advertising community. Nielsen provides ratings analysis primarily in the area of broadcast and cable television. Arbitron focuses primarily on radio communication, having discontinued its television research in 1994.

Local Market Ratings

Local television stations depend on local ratings reports as their primary tool in selling air time to advertisers as well as evaluating how their programming stacks up against the competition. Nielsen gathers and publishes television data for some 219 television markets across the U.S. Nielsen refers to its market delineation as "designated market area" (DMA). Nielsen generates an ongoing series of published reports called the Nielsen Station Index (NSI).

The cost of gathering such data for local television is enormous. Nielsen surveys all local television markets at least four times a year. These quarterly surveys are known in the television industry as *sweeps* or *sweep periods*. Each sweep period lasts one month. The NSI survey reflects the relative position of each station among its competitors and estimates the size of the local audience for various types of programming regardless of whether it is network originated, syndicated or locally produced.

National Television Ratings

The major television networks and cable programmers require faster and more frequent reporting than do local stations. Nielsen also generates a separate set of ratings every two weeks. These ratings are based on a national sample of 1,100 people-metered homes and are referred to as the Nielsen Television Index (or NTI).[22] At the national level, the NTI ratings books include the major television networks as well as major cable program services. A single rating point is the equivalent of 1.1 million homes. Each of the Nielsen households is equipped with a people meter, which is an electronic device that attaches to the household TV sets. Each person's viewing habits are recorded electronically at the touch of a button. Television ratings are not an exact science, but they are a powerful force in helping to shape programming and advertising decisions where millions of dollars are at stake.

Overnight Ratings

Nielsen also uses people meters in seven cities throughout the U.S. to produce overnight ratings or overnights. These seven cities can, at any given time, provide a representative sample of what the nation is viewing. Overnights give an indication of how select programs are performing at a given time. In addition, Nielsen performs a variety of other surveys, as well as publishing supplementary reports based on its analysis of specialized audience groups or program formats.

Measuring Audience Size

The basic measures of audience size in broadcasting are rating and share. A rating refers to the percentage of people in a given market (or population) who are tuned to a radio or television station during a given time period. As advertisers for a local car dealership, we are interested in knowing how many people were watching the program *CSI* on the CBS affiliate station WFRV in Green Bay, Wisconsin, on Thursday night between 9:00 P.M. and 9:30 P.M. In order to calculate a rating, we simply divide station viewers by television households or:

$$\frac{\text{Station viewers (number of households watching a particular program)}}{\text{Television households (number of households in a population with a TV set)}} = \text{Rating}$$

Let's assume that the city of Green Bay, Wisconsin, which is located in the Green Bay–Appleton, Wisconsin, market, has 400,000 television households and supports six television stations. In a Nielsen sample of the Green Bay–Appleton, Wisconsin, market, it has been determined that 80,000 people are watching CBS affiliate station WFRV between 9:00 and 9:30 P.M. on Thursday night. Therefore:

$$\frac{\text{Station viewers}}{\text{Television households}} \quad \frac{80,000}{400,000} = \text{Rating of 20\%}$$

We know that 20 percent of the population was watching station WFRV on Thursday night between 9:00 and 9:30 P.M. The advertiser, however, also wants to know how station WFRV compares with the other stations in terms of actual viewership during the same time period. In other words, what percentage (or share) of the viewing market did station WFRV capture during the 9:00 to 9:30 P.M. time period? Share is the number of station viewers divided by the number of households' sets in use during a given time period. Using the same example, the Nielsen sample revealed that only 320,000 television households had their sets on. That said, we divide 80,000 by 320,000 in order to obtain share or:

$$\frac{\text{Station viewers}}{\text{Television households with sets in use}} \quad \frac{80,000}{320,000} = \text{Share of 25\%}$$

Another way to understand share is to consider it as part of the viewing pie. For example, station WFRV claimed 25 percent of the viewing pie for that time period and the other five stations accounted for the remaining 75 percent. For ease of reporting, a Nielsen ratings book will drop the percentage sign and report station WFRV's viewership figures as:

Rating / Share or 20/25

Cost per Thousand

For advertisers, commercial air time is only valuable if it's reaching the right audience. In order to measure the cost-effectiveness of an advertisement, advertisers use *cost per thousand* or CPM (*M* is Latin for "thousand") as a way to represent the cost of reaching 1,000 households. In order to calculate CPM, you divide the cost of the advertisement by the size of the audience in thousands. For example, if an advertiser pays $400 for a television spot commercial and the ratings show that the spot is reaching 20,000 households, then you calculate:

CPM: $400 / 20 = $20

The advertiser is paying $20 for each 1,000 households. CPM becomes a baseline measurement for comparing the effectiveness of different advertising media (e.g., newspapers vs. television) to reach 1,000 households, as well as station and program performance within the same market.

The Fox Television Network: A Case Study

In 1985, Australian media magnate Rupert Murdoch entered the U.S. market with the purchase of seven television stations from Metromedia Inc. for $2 billion. The purchase of seven Metromedia stations allowed News Corporation Ltd. the ability to lay the foundation for what would become the future Fox television network. These television stations were all highly ranked stations in seven of the top 11 U.S. markets. Table 3.9 identifies the seven stations that were purchased from Metromedia, including their market rank and competitive position.

A year later, News Corporation Ltd. bought 20th Century Fox for $1.55 billion. From the very beginning, Murdoch understood the importance of vertical integration as the basis for launching a new business. In two short years, Murdoch had ensured himself a steady supply of programming with ready-made distribution outlets. In April 1987, Murdoch launched the Fox television network with 106 affiliates. Barry Diller was hired as the new chair and CEO of the Fox network.[23]

Under Diller's direction, the Fox network was conceived as a more highly differentiated service from the other three U.S. networks. The

---

81

Table 3.9 News Corporation Ltd.'s Purchase of Seven Metromedia Stations (1986)

Station	City	Market Percentage of U.S.	Market Rank in U.S.	Competitive Position and Rank in Market
WNEW	New York	7.7	1	4
KTTV	Los Angeles	5.1	2	3
WFID	Chicago	3.5	3	5
WCVB	Boston	2.3	6	1
WTTG	Washington, D.C.	1.8	8	3
KNBN	Dallas	1.7	9	7
KRIV	Houston	1.6	11	4

Source: Nielsen Media Research.

programming was directed at a younger, more urban set of viewers. Fox programming was decidedly counterculture and irreverent. There were three distinguishing program formats that characterized the Fox network, including: 1) reality-based programming (*America's Most Wanted*); 2) counterculture (*The Simpsons, Married with Children*); and 3) tabloid television (*Current Affair*). According to Sandy Grushow, then president of 20th Century Fox: "Finding the irreverent shows was half the battle: letting folks know what they were and when they aired was the other."[24]

In 1988, News Corporation purchased Triangle Publications, publishers of *TV Guide*, the *Daily Racing Form* and *Seventeen* magazine for $3 billion. The purchase of *TV Guide* was especially important given the fact that it was America's largest-selling weekly magazine, with a circulation of 17 million copies. Equally important was the fact that *TV Guide* would provide an important vehicle for promoting the Fox television network and its new lineup of programs.[25] By 1988, Fox had also increased its distribution to 121 stations, covering 86 percent of the U.S.

Rupert Murdoch and News Corporation Ltd.

In appreciate the development of Fox Broadcasting, one has to have some appreciation of Fox Broadcasting's parent company, News Corporation Ltd., and its president and CEO, Rupert Murdoch. Murdoch is the consummate business opportunist. He is also the quintessential risk taker.[26] As early as 1964, Murdoch defied the conventional wisdom of newspaper publishing in Australia by launching the *Australian*, the country's first national newspaper. That effort, in combination with his other newspaper holdings, gave News Corporation Ltd. some

60 percent of Australia's metropolitan newspaper sales.[27] Similarly, the start-up of the Fox television network came at a time when the conventional wisdom said that starting a fourth U.S. network was impossible. Equally significant was the start-up of the British Sky Broadcasting (BSkyB) direct broadcast satellite network, which was launched well before the technology had proven itself in the marketplace.

News Corporation experienced sizeable financial losses during the early start-up years at both Fox and BSkyB. News Corporation suffered an estimated $1.2 billion loss on BSkyB between the years 1989 and 1993. Similarly, Fox Broadcasting sustained significant losses, including a $95 million loss in 1988. The losses sustained at both Fox and BSkyB almost cost Murdoch the company. By 1990, however, the Fox network was able to reach 91 percent of the U.S. through a combination of VHF and low-powered UHF stations. In addition, the network moved from three nights of programming to five. In June 1991, Fox earned an impressive $550 million from the sale of advertising.

Rupert Murdoch is a shrewd businessman who knows how to maximize his operations. Murdoch's politics are very pragmatic, as are his expectations regarding the work of his editors. When it comes to management and editorial control, Murdoch is very hands-on and displays little or no sentimentality. The makeover and start-up of several of his newspapers and broadcast services, including the *Sun*, the *New York Post* and Fox television, seem to follow a similar pattern. The publications (and broadcast services) begin as tabloids and are often quite irreverent toward the establishment. They appear somewhat radical at first. But, over time, most of the senior managers (editors and producers) who were first involved in the start-up phase are slowly replaced by a more conservative management team. The start-up of the Fox television network, for example, is highly illustrative of this pattern. Once the Fox network became stable, Murdoch became more directly involved in the company's day-to-day operation. This was the principal reason that prompted Barry Diller, Fox president and CEO, to resign his position rather than face the prospect of co-managing the Fox network.

Fox Broadcasting Makes the Transition

From the beginning, the plan was to move Fox beyond its image as a counterculture network in order to become a more fully diverse television network. Starting in 1992, Fox premiered some highly successful and innovative programs including *Melrose Place* (1992), *Fox Night at the Movies* (1993) and *The X-Files* (1993). In addition, Fox began airing programming seven nights a week. The company's rite of passage, however, occurred in December 1993 when Fox acquired the television rights to the National Football League (NFL) by outbidding rival network CBS at a cost of $1.6 billion. The successful debut of the National Football League firmly established Fox as a legitimate network contender. In 1998, the Fox network retained its right to televise the NFL by paying an estimated $4.1 billion for broadcast rights through the year 2005.

The debut of *American Idol* on June 11, 2002, has created a television phenomenon that has become one of the top-rated programs in the U.S. *American Idol* is the creation of Simon Fuller and is based on the British reality program *Pop Idol*. The program seeks to discover the best young singer in the country, through a series of nationwide auditions. The outcomes of the latter stages of this competition are determined by public voting by phone. The winners from this series have gone on to become highly successful music stars in their own right, including Kelly Clarkson, Ruben Studdard and Carrie Underwood. In 2007, *American Idol*'s two-hour finale attracted 36.4 million viewers, Fox's highest-ever number of total viewers for a night of entertainment programming.

Simultaneously to its programming efforts, Fox also strengthened the quality of its affiliate stations. In May 1994, Fox improved its affiliate position by paying New World Communications $500 million to break its 12-station affiliation agreement with the three major U.S. networks and to join with Fox Broadcasting instead. In exchange, Fox received 20 percent of New World's stock as well as improving its market position in 12 key cities. The purchase of New World Communications caused a ripple effect that was felt throughout the entire broadcast industry. The three major networks (CBS in particular) were now forced to renegotiate their affiliation contracts with several important stations given the possibility that they would break their existing affiliate contracts. In July 1996, News Corporation purchased the remaining 80 percent of New World's stock at an estimated cost of $2.5 billion. Today, the Fox Television Station group includes 35 owned and operated stations located throughout the U.S.

Strategic Challenges: Discussion

The U.S. broadcast industry is at an important crossroads in its history and development. The four major U.S. television networks (ABC, CBS, NBC and Fox) are faced with a level of competition never before seen in their history. The success of cable television and the growth of the Internet have irrevocably changed the business of broadcasting. This coupled with continuing advancement in DVR technology poses a significant challenge to the traditional broadcast model going forward.

Cable Television

Historically, the relationship between broadcasters and cable can be characterized as antagonistic. Before cable television became an accepted medium in the late 1970s, it was often looked upon by broadcasters as a technology that was ancillary to the function of broadcasting.[28] All this began to change with the successful debut of HBO in 1972 and the judicial outcome of HBO v. FCC where the U.S. District Court affirmed HBO's right to seek programming from the same sources as traditional television. The success of program services like HBO, CNN, ESPN and MTV (to name only a few) underscored the fact that cable television was well positioned to offer viewers a more highly differentiated television service. During the mid-1970s the three major television networks (CBS, NBC and ABC) accounted for 92 percent of what viewers watched. Today, the four major networks account for about 40 percent of what viewers watch on television.

Broadcast/Cable Cross-Ownership

Cable television provides a classic example of a new communication medium and its efforts to successfully compete with an established medium of communication. As Ithiel de Sola Pool writes: "The first defensive tactic by the owners of an old medium against competition by a new one is to have the new one prohibited. If this does not work, the next defensive tactic is to buy into the attacker."[29] As Pool correctly forecasted, the four major television networks have slowly bought into the attacker. All of the major television networks (and their parent companies) are heavily invested in cable television. Viacom, parent company to CBS, also owns MTV, BET, Spike TV and Nickelodeon. Similarly, Walt Disney, parent company to ABC, owns ESPN and the Disney Channel. In the case of Disney, ESPN has become the brand name that deliberately blends both broadcast and cable sports entertainment under one corporate banner.

The Internet

The public's growing interest in and use of the Internet have had a major impact on the way we spend our leisure time. The Internet has had a significant impact on how consumers choose to use their leisure time. For broadcasters, this means time not being spent watching television. The challenge going forward is how to align television viewing with the numerous ways in which the Internet can be used to generate increased viewer interest. One telling example can be seen with ABC's *Lost*. The producers and writers of *Lost* have placed a number of clues in each episode for the express purpose of generating interest beyond the program itself. The series has leveraged the Internet to promote a number of *Lost*-related websites (e.g., http://www.lost-tv.com/, http://www.losttvshow.org/) to spin off books such as *Bad Twin*, a novel written by Oceanic Flight 815 fictional passenger Gary Troup (http://www.amazon.com/BAD-TWIN-Hyperion-Gary-Troup/dp/1401302769).

Walt Disney president and CEO Robert Iger considers the Internet to be part of the company's three major strategies going forward. Disney-ABC has made a strong commitment to advance multimedia and digital platforms. In 2006, Apple Computer and Disney announced a landmark deal that would allow television programs such as ABC's *Desperate Housewives* and *Lost* to be available for purchase the day after their initial airing. Apple's video iPod creates an altogether new distribution window for commercial broadcasters.

The Apple–Disney partnership represents the first time that commercial television programming is being made available for purchase via the Internet. Under the terms of the deal, the Apple's iTunes store will sell commercial-free episodes of ABC's *Desperate Housewives, Lost* and three other shows for $1.99 each. Users of iTunes will be able to view a preview of each episode for free. For consumers, the video iPod provides a stable and legal method for downloading original television programming. Equally important, the Apple–Disney arrangement will shorten the distribution window for popular television programs by making them immediately available for purchase.[30] Disney's Robert Iger believes that video downloading via the Internet is the way of the future: "This is the first giant step to making more content available to more people online. It is the future, as far as I'm concerned."[31]

Digital Video Recorders

The development of Digital Video Recorders (DVRs) is poised to dramatically alter the television viewing experience. The DVR or personal video recorder (PVR) is a device that records television programming onto a computer hard drive for later viewing. A DVR is essentially made up of two elements: the hardware device that stores programming and the subscription service that provides programming information and the ability to encode the various data streams.[32] Two of the better-known DVR services are TiVo and ReplayTV. DVRs offer many of the same functions as a traditional VCR, including recording, playback, fast forwarding, etc. Moreover, the DVR offers the added feature of being able to instantly jump to any part of the program as well as the ability to skip over commercials. It is the latter issue that has broadcasters seriously concerned. Advertisers, for their part, are now having to reconsider the value of advertising on broadcast (and cable) television if and when viewers can easily skip over the commercials.

At issue is the future of the advertiser-supported television model. In 2007, DVRs have achieved a penetration rate of 18 percent of America's TV households. That figure is expected to climb to 50 percent by 2010. In the meantime, cable television operators are incorporating DVR technology as part of their set-top box offerings. The continued deployment of DVRs will have a major impact on traditional programming and advertising strategy. Instead of television being one-directional (i.e., programmer to consumer), today's consumer can and will be more proactive in terms of program selection, recording and viewing. This, in turn, will force the networks and advertisers to find news ways to keep the consumer interested in television ads. While product placement ads offer some opportunity, it is by no means a long-term solution. The real solution lies in changing technology. As TV sets and computers become more fully integrated, we can expect to see a variety of icons (and select pop-ups) appear on TV screens allowing viewers to link to an ad display during the course of a program.

Digital Television

Digital television (DTV) represents the next generation of television capable of delivering significantly improved television pictures. DTV involves the transmission of television signals using digital rather than conventional analog signaling methods. A digital picture is more detailed and stable, offering the viewer ten times more pixels on the screen. Digital television comes in two basic formats: 1) standard-definition television (SDTV) and 2) high-definition television (HDTV). Digital television offers certain obvious advantages when compared to analog television, including:

- *Improved picture quality:* The picture you now receive is based on an analog transmission standard that is over 50 years old. In a digital system, images and sound are captured using the same digital code found in computers—ones and zeros.
- *Improved sound quality:* DTV offers better sound quality featuring Dolby Digital Audio. Dolby Digital is used with DVDs, HDTV and digital cable and satellite transmissions. It has been selected as the audio standard for digital television.[33]
- *More computer friendly:* DTV will become more computer friendly; that is, future TV monitors will be able to display television pictures as well as computer graphics and data such as picture-in-picture websites.
- *More spectrum efficient:* The future of DTV presupposes that broadcasters can squeeze increased picture detail and higher-quality surround sound into the same 6 MHz (or similar amount) of bandwidth used by analog television. DTV allows for digital video compression, thus enabling television pictures to be processed, stored and distributed with greater flexibility and ease.
- *Multicasting:* DTV allows a broadcaster to offer multiple programs (multicasting) or a single program of high-definition digital TV.

High-Definition Television (HDTV)

HDTV is a television display technology that provides picture quality approaching that of 35-mm film. HDTV is considered the most significant development in television technology since color television because of its remarkably improved picture quality as well the ability to feature Dolby Digital sound. HDTV set design is wider than a traditional television set and more closely resembles a wide screen in a movie theater. HDTV would move the current aspect ratio (i.e., screen width to height) from 4:3 to 16:9. HDTV sets generally come in two formats: plasma and LCD.[34]

Transitioning to Digital Television and HDTV

The transition to an all-digital television world is ongoing, and the FCC has mandated that by February 18, 2009, all broadcast, cable and DBS services in the U.S. will be fully digital in format and signaling capability. At that time, U.S. broadcasters will be required to give back the spectrum space that they once occupied for their analog transmissions. The newly returned spectrum space will be sold (or auctioned off) for other wireless use applications, most notably cellular telephony and WIMAX.[35]

Switching from analog to digital broadcast means that local broadcasters have to update their studio equipment and transmitting antennas to DTV and HDTV. By 2009, all broadcasters will be transmitting their signals exclusively on channels assigned for digital television use. As a consequence, traditional analog television will be discontinued. A key issue in the transition to digital television is that millions of analog televisions that rely on over-the-air broadcast signals will no longer work once the analog TV signal is turned off. Viewers with conventional analog TV sets will lose their picture unless they install a set-top converter box to convert digital signals to analog, purchased a new digital television set or subscribe to a cable or satellite service that can accommodate both technologies. There is a general concern that consumers are not going to have the necessary information in time to make the decision that best fits their own viewing and financial situation. The FCC estimates that 15 percent of the viewing public relies on traditional over-the-air analog television sets. The challenge for today's broadcasters is to leverage that transition by educating local audiences regarding the impending changes that are about to take place.

Concluding Remarks

In an era of multichannel television, television viewers have become far less loyal to a specific network or channel. The remote control keypad enables the average viewer to surf the dial for better or more highly differentiated program fare. Today's viewers have a far greater number of media and entertainment choices than ever before. This is especially true for the under-30 generation of viewers, who have grown up in an era where it's just television. Broadcasting, cable—it's all the same to them. According to Frank Biondi, former chairman of Universal Studios: "If there's a way to have too many choices, that's what we have. Finding a way to bring the consumer to us instead of the other guy is the toughest thing we do."[36]

4

CABLE TELEVISION

Historical Overview

Cable television is wired communication to the home. Cable television (also called community antenna television or CATV) was first developed in the late 1940s in communities unable to receive conventional broadcast television signals owing to distance or geographic factors. Cable systems located their antennas in areas having poor reception, picked up broadcast signals and then distributed them by means of coaxial cable to subscribers for a fee. The cities of Mahanoy City, Pennsylvania, and Astoria, Oregon, are credited with having been the first two communities in the U.S. to offer CATV service to their residents.[1]

One of the first CATV systems was started in 1948 in Mahanoy City, Pennsylvania, to cope with the problem of poor television reception. In Mahanoy City, a coal-mining town of 10,000 people in the Appalachians, reception from the three TV networks 86 miles away in Philadelphia was all but nonexistent. An appliance store owner by the name of John Walson could not sell any TV sets to local residents. The lack of reception prevented Walson from demonstrating his TV sets.

During the summer of 1947, Walson erected an antenna on a high ridge of a nearby mountain. Later that year, Walson strung electrical ribbon wire from the mountain antenna down to his appliance warehouse, which was a few blocks from his store. He was then able to demonstrate for visitors a dim video image and a weak audio signal. In the spring of 1948, he erected a larger antenna on top of the mountain and replaced the ribbon wire with a more efficient army surplus twin lead wire. Walson placed three TV sets in the window of his store. The display caused a local sensation. People gathered outside the store window to watch the programs being brought in from Philadelphia.[2]

Walson next arranged to run leads (wires) for a fee between his warehouse and store to the homes of several residents living along the route. Many of them were neighbors to whom he had sold television sets with the promise that they would be connected to his service. The demand for television sets and for inclusion in the system jumped substantially in Mahanoy City. The service was soon established as an ongoing business.[3]

Another early CATV system was developed in Astoria, Oregon, by L.E. (Ed) Parsons, who began experimenting with distant reception of television signals after attending the National Association of Broadcasters convention in Chicago in 1948. Parsons ran the local Astoria radio station, KAST, and had some training in electrical engineering. Parsons was deeply impressed with the possibilities of TV. The most immediate problem was television reception. The nearest TV station was KRSC in Seattle, 125 miles away. Parsons rigged an antenna on the roof of the Astoria Hotel and then ran a line to his apartment, which was a short distance away. According to Parsons and Frieden:

> the frequent visits by friends who wanted to see the only operating TV set within one hundred miles and even by strangers who stopped by unexpectedly, prompted Parsons to drop an extension line into the lobby of the Astoria Hotel. When the lobby became too crowded with eager [viewers] for the hotel manager, the antenna line was moved down the street to Cliff Pool's Music Store, where it was connected to a television set in the window.[4]

The public responded enthusiastically, and the wire was extended to several bars in town and then eventually to private customers. What is important about the Mahanoy City, Astoria, Oregon (and later Lansford, Pennsylvania) examples is that such early CATV systems provide a basic blueprint of how cable television started in the U.S. The origins of early cable television in the U.S. began as a practical solution to the problem of poor television reception. All three CATV systems would later evolve into successful business ventures. The same basic pattern would repeat itself in community after community during the next several years to follow.

Cable Network Services

The real move to modern cable television began on November 8, 1972, when a fledgling company named Home Box Office (HBO) began supplying movies to 365 subscribers on the Service Electric Cable TV system in Wilkes-Barre, Pennsylvania.[5] That night, Jerry Levin, then vice-president for programming (and future CEO of Time Warner), introduced viewers to the debut of HBO. The feature programming for that inaugural night was a hockey game between New York and Vancouver and a film prophetically entitled *Sometimes a Great Notion*. Seven years later, Jerry Levin recalled that first night and said:

It wasn't that we had a startling new idea, or even that it hadn't been tried before, but we became the first to make it work; maybe because we believed in what we were doing, maybe because we were too naive to realize what an impossible dream it was.[6]

From the beginning, HBO developed two important strategies that helped promote its rapid growth and development. First, HBO introduced the principle of premium television. Specifically, HBO achieved what no other television program provider had accomplished up until that point, namely, getting people to pay for television. The principle of advertiser-supported "free" television was firmly engrained in the minds of the American public. What HBO did was change public perception about the nature of television entertainment. HBO offered a uniquely innovative service emphasizing recently released movies and other specialized entertainment that could not be found elsewhere on the general airwaves. While HBO was not the first company to introduce a monthly per-channel fee service, it was the first to make it work successfully. This marked the beginning of premium television entertainment.[7]

Second, as Gershon and Wirth point out, HBO utilized microwave and later satellite communications for the transmission of programming, rather than distribution by videotape. Prior to HBO, there was no precedent for the extensive use of satellite-delivered programming in the U.S. HBO's 1975 decision to use satellite communications was significant in two ways. First, it demonstrated the feasibility of using satellite communication for long-haul television distribution. As a consequence, HBO was able to create an efficient distribution network for the delivery of its programming to cable operators. Second, the development of the satellite–cable interface would usher in a whole new era of cable programmers that were equally capable of leasing satellite time and delivering their programs directly to cable operating systems, including: WTBS, 1976; ESPN, 1979; CNN, 1980; and MTV, 1981. This set into motion the principle of cable networking, that is, television programming designed exclusively for cable operating systems (and later direct broadcast satellite systems).[8] As cable analyst Paul Kagan once remarked:

Rarely does a simple business decision by one company affect so many. In deciding to provide on the beaming of satellite TV channels, Time Inc. took the one catalytic step needed for the creation of a new television network designed to provide pay TV programs.[9]

Cable Television: Standard Features

A cable television system is a communication system that distributes broadcast and satellite-delivered programming by means of coaxial and/or fiber optic cable to people's homes. The standard cable television system consists of three parts, including: the head-end point, the distribution network and the receiving equipment. The cable distribution network is patterned after a tree-and-branch architecture using a combination of fiber optic and coaxial cable. The head-end point is the cable system's master receiving site for all incoming broadcast and satellite-fed programming. The cable operator uses both over-the-air television antennas and satellite earth stations to receive, downconvert and process all incoming signals.

The signals from the head-end point are distributed to population centers (or neighborhoods) on heavy-duty cable called trunk lines. The trunk lines are generally attached to utility poles. Since the start of the 1990s, the technical capabilities of cable operating systems have been greatly enhanced with the integration of fiber optic cable. The physical design of today's cable operating systems has evolved into hybrid fiber–coax (HFC) structure. In a modern HFC cable plant, the trunk cables and amplifiers are replaced by fiber optic cable that runs directly from the head-end point to an optical node in a neighborhood. The node converts the optical signal into an RF signal, which is then passed on to the end user's home via coaxial cable. Optical nodes are spaced to serve a neighborhood with 500 to 1,000 homes. Another important benefit of the HFC architecture is that it enables the user to engage in reliable two-way interactive communication with the cable head-end point, thus making possible high-speed Internet access, enhanced video on demand, etc.[10] This can be seen in Figure 4.1.

Today's cable television systems use coaxial cable as the primary transmission medium (or conduit) for television signals to the home. Coaxial cable's principal conductor is either a pure copper or a copper-coated wire. The single conductor (wire) is protected by surrounding insulation. The cable is

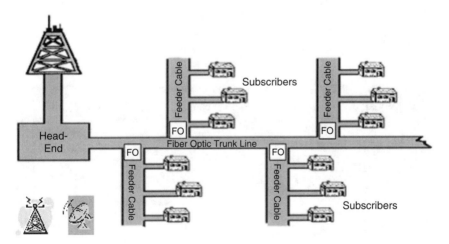

Figure 4.1 Cable Television Network Architecture.
Illustration: Chan, Chin Bong.

encased in a heavy protective sheath of plastic or vinyl. This can be seen in Figure 4.2.

In a typical cable system, the drop line coming into the subscriber's home connects to a digital converter box or directly to the user's television set. Most television sets are equipped with a converter unit that has been built into the television set, thus making it "cable ready." The digital converter box performs several important functions:

1   It receives the incoming signal and reassigns that signal to a predetermined set of carrier frequencies.
2   It allows television users to access their cable television system (i.e., channel selection).
3   It manages internal security to the system (i.e., making sure that the viewer has access only to those program services that have been requested from the cable operator).
4   It is capable of providing smart-feature elements, including digital video recording capability, and providing access to video-on-demand programming.

The Business of Cable Television

The business of cable television consists of two primary sets of players, including: the cable television operator and the cable program supplier. The cable operator is responsible for providing cable television service to the community. The cable operator packages a diverse set of program services and charges subscribers a fee accordingly. Comcast, Time Warner Cable, Cox Cable and Charter are all examples of multiple system operators (MSOs), that is, cable companies that own multiple systems nationwide. Table 4.1 provides a listing of the nation's top 15 cable MSOs for 2007 based on the total number of cable subscribers per company.

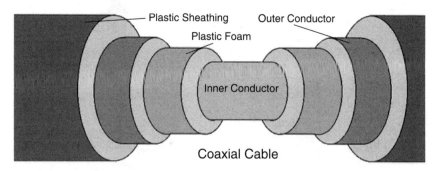

Figure 4.2 Coaxial Cable as a Transmission Medium.
Illustration: Chan, Chin Bong.

Table 4.1 Top 15 U.S. Cable Multiple System Operators (2007)

1	Comcast Cable Communications	24,236,000
2	Time Warner Cable	13,448,000
3	Cox Communications	5,451,900
4	Charter Communications	5,415,400
5	Cablevision Systems Corporation	3,139,000
6	Bright House Networks	2,321,000
7	Suddenlink Communications	1,370,000
8	Mediacom Communications Corporation	1,362,000
9	Insight Communications	1,344,000
10	Cable One	703,200
11	WideOpenWest	363,400
12	RCN Corporation	354,000
13	Bresnan Communications	296,600
14	Service Electric	290,400
15	Atlantic Broadband	288,700

Source: National Cable and Telecommunications Association, "Top 25 Cable MSOs," Available at: http://www.ncta.com/ContentView.aspx?contentId=73 (retrieved September 18, 2007).

The cable programmer is responsible for delivering program services to the cable operator. A program supplier can include both broadcast television suppliers (ABC, CBS, NBC, Fox, PBS, etc.) and cable network suppliers (ESPN, CNN, MTV, History Channel USA, etc.). Program suppliers break down into two major categories, including advertiser-supported services (CBS, NBC, ESPN, CNN, etc.) and pay-supported services (HBO, Showtime, Starz, etc.). In principle, the cable operator will pay advertiser-supported cable networks such as ESPN and CNN a license fee in order to receive the cable network service, whereas the cable operator has not traditionally paid for broadcast television services. This has changed in light of retransmission consent.[11] In principle, the broadcast station (or parent company) is given financial compensation in the form of extra channel assignments to support various kinds of broadcast and cable television programming.

Deregulation and the Advancement of Cable Television

Beginning in the early 1980s, the U.S. under the Reagan administration actively promoted the cause of economic deregulation. The policy was designed to foster greater economic competition by allowing the marketplace to establish priorities and professional standards of business conduct rather than needless government intervention. Perhaps no one championed the cause of deregulation more than the Federal Communications Commission (FCC) under the leadership of its former chairman Mark Fowler. It was during Fowler's tenure at the FCC that telecommunications in the U.S. experienced the most dramatic effects of deregulation put into practice, including the passage of the Cable Communications Policy Act of 1984.[12]

The passage of the Cable Act of 1984 was a watershed event in helping to advance the cause of cable television in the U.S. Cable operators were now given the ability to adjust service and rates more flexibly in response to market conditions. In a few short years, the cable industry experienced dramatic growth in terms both of subscribers and of the number of operating systems. In 1978, there were 13,391,910 basic cable subscribers (households) on 3,875 cable systems. In 2007, there were an estimated 65,600,000 basic cable subscribers (households) on 7,090 cable systems.[13] It should be noted that the number of cable operating systems has declined in recent years. Consider that as recently as 1994 there were 11,200 cable operating systems in the U.S. The reason for the decline is largely the consolidation of systems by the major cable MSOs.

In the U.S. today, cable TV is the primary means of delivering multichannel television service to the home. Cable television is available in approximately 58.8 percent of all U.S. homes. Table 4.2. provides an overview of cable television in the U.S.

Changing the American Television Landscape

Cable television has fundamentally changed the American television landscape in four important ways. They include: 1) increasing the level of consumer choice; 2) the development of narrowcasted television services; 3) leveling the electronic playing field; and 4) exercising a critical gatekeeping function. Cable's most enduring contribution to the field of television programming is that it has given subscribers a greater selection of choice. In 1986, there were 60-plus cable network services as compared to the 530-plus cable network services of today. Much of that programming is narrowcasted; that is, the programming is targeted to a more narrowly defined audience. Examples of narrowcasted programming can be seen in such program services as CNN (news), ESPN (sports), the Disney Channel (children's entertainment),

Table 4.2 Cable Television Development in the U.S. (2007)

U.S. basic cable subscribers	65,600,000
Cable penetration of TV households	58.8%
Cable systems	7,090
Digital cable subscribers	35,255,000
Cable high-speed Internet services	119,100,000
Cable telephony (residential customers)	12,136,000

Source: National Cable and Telecommunications Association, "Industry Statistics," Available at: http://www.ncta.com/ContentView.aspx?contentId=66 (retrieved September 5, 2007).

BET (African American entertainment and news) and the History Channel (history and news information), to name only a few. Table 4.3 provides a listing of the top 20 cable network services in the U.S. based on subscribers.

Cable television has leveled the electronic playing field in terms of distribution. Cable can be considered the great equalizer in terms of providing equal access to a variety of broadcast and cable programmers. Cable television allows VHF, UHF and cable network services equal access to prospective viewers. The principle of equal access becomes especially important for smaller VHF and UHF television stations that have a long history of not being seen due to poor reception and/or their channel positioning on UHF rotary dials.

In today's television market, the cable operator exercises a critical gate-keeping function in the selection and channel positioning of television program services. The quality and diversity of program services are largely determined by the actual size of the cable system and its channel capacity. To that end, not being carried on a cable system can mean virtual obscurity for large and small stations alike. The problem becomes especially acute in those communities where a cable operator has a penetration rate of 70 to 80 percent. The situation becomes all the more problematic as the cable industry steadily transitions from analog to digital cable, adhering to retransmission consent obligations and dual carriage obligations as well as offering high-definition television capability. This means the allocation of channel space becomes very important to the cable operator in terms of cost-effectiveness, programming diversity and regulatory obligations.

Table 4.3 Cable Television Network Services in the U.S. (2007)

Rank	Network	Subscribers
1	Discovery	92,500,000
2	ESPN	92,300,000
2	CNN (Cable News Network)	92,300,000
4	TNT (Turner Network Television)	92,100,000
4	Lifetime Television	92,100,000
4	USA Network	92,100,000
7	Weather Channel	92,000,000
8	Nickelodeon	91,900,000
8	History Channel	91,900,000
10	ESPN 2	91,800,000
10	A&E Networks	91,800,000
12	TBS	91,700,000
12	The Learning Channel	91,700,000
12	Spike TV	91,700,000
15	CNN Headline News	91,500,000

Source: National Cable and Telecommunications Association, "Top 20 Cable Program Networks," Available at: http://www.ncta.com/ContentView.aspx?contentId=74 (retrieved September 5, 2007).

Cable System Management

The size and scope of a cable television system can be influenced by a variety of factors, including community size, location and whether the system is individually owned or part of a multiple system operator (MSO). In general, there are five departments (or staff responsibilities) that are common to most cable television systems. They include:

1   sales and marketing;
2   customer service;
3   programming;
4   service repair;
5   customer billing.

Sales and Marketing

Sales and marketing, under the direction of the sales or marketing manager, is responsible for increasing new subscribers and retaining old ones. The basic objective of this department (or staff) is to persuade consumers to purchase cable television and to promote higher-end premium services.

Customer Service

The customer service division (or staff) is responsible for dealing with the public in a variety of ways, including: taking orders, scheduling installation and service repair work and answering questions about billing. In addition, customer service can be involved in the direct selling or upgrading of cable television services to the customers. To that end, they work closely with the sales and marketing staff.

Programming

Programming, under the direction of the program manager, is responsible for program selection, organization and packaging of cable television services. The challenge for the manager is to program 75–150 channels of television (depending on the size of the cable system) factoring in licensing fees, retransmission service obligations, digital and HDTV channel accommodation, etc. The program manager must also consider the importance of creating a highly diverse set of services. To that end, the program manager works closely with marketing and sales in order to optimize customer subscribership.

Engineering and Service Repair

Service repair refers to those activities that support the physical plant and operation of the cable system. The service repair division (or staff) is responsible for the direct installation of service, upgrading or downgrading program service options and fixing a possible degradation in signal strength and/or a break in the cable lines.

Customer Billing

Customer billing is responsible for organizing and sending out customer bills, involving monthly subscriber fees and specialized charges associated with the service. It is also expected to address customer complaints concerning potential billing inaccuracies or the handling of partial or late payments. Information that is sent to the billing department can take the form of phone calls, letters or returned bills with enclosed messages.

Responsibilities of the Cable System General Manager

The cable manager oversees all of the departments and areas of the operation described thus far. The cable manager reports directly to the system owners or senior management if it is an MSO. For those systems that are part of an MSO, the cable manager works very closely with corporate management in terms of coordinating marketing, engineering and public affairs support. Programming decisions in particular are closely coordinated between the individual cable system and corporate management.

In terms of local system operation, the cable manager is directly involved in local sales and marketing decisions. The cable manager also works with the engineering staff during the construction phase of the system or when the system requires a major technical upgrade. In addition, the cable manager is closely involved in community affairs, working with local government and/or its franchising authority.

In general, the cable manager is responsible for:

1   Planning and overseeing the cable system's operating budget. This typically involves working closely with the system's business department.
2   Providing support and coordinating goals with:

the sales and marketing staff;
the programming department;
the customer service department;
engineering and service repair.

3   Interfacing with local government and its franchising authority.

4 Personnel management, which can include overseeing and evaluating staffing requirements for the cable operating system.

5 Approving programming decisions and equipment purchases. The cable manager will coordinate programming decisions with corporate management.

Cable Television Programming

Programming for a cable operating system differs significantly from broadcasting. In principle, a broadcaster is responsible for programming one channel (or set of subchannels), whereas a cable operator must program a multichannel television service that can include hundreds of channels and a host of information services. The very word "channel," itself, is undergoing a major redefinition as to its term and purpose. Cable television is a customer-driven business. The cable operator's success is dependent on whether customers are willing to renew their subscription at the end of a billing cycle. All this presupposes that subscribers perceive value in the product they are purchasing. In short, the cable television operator is selling a service, not an individual channel.

Building Brand Equity

Cable television programming represents a highly differentiated set of brands ranging from sports entertainment (ESPN) to news (CNN) to African American entertainment (BET). Cable television can be likened to the magazine industry. Most readers do not read all of the articles contained in a magazine issue. So, too, the average cable viewer watches only a partial fraction of what is available on the cable system. The FCC estimates that the average viewer watches between 15 and 17 channels of the available cable service offerings.

The cable programmer's challenge, therefore, is to package a diverse set of program and information services that appeal to the largest set of possible users. A typical cable television system will usually contain the following kinds of program and service offerings. They include: 1) basic cable, 2) expanded basic, 3) pay cable television, 4) pay-per-view television, 5) high-definition television, and 6) information services

Basic Cable

Basic cable is the gateway service that all subscribers must take in order to obtain expanded basic and/or premium services. Basic cable consists of approximately 20–25 services. It typically includes the four major broadcast networks, PBS, minor broadcast networks including the CB network, a Spanish-language channel (Univision, Telemundo, etc.), a few independent stations, a few select cable services, C-Span, public access channels and one or more religious channels.

Expanded Basic

Expanded Basic is the foundation of cable television programming and consists of 60–90 channels of programming. Expanded basic represents the highly recognized cable program services such as ESPN, CNN, MTV, the Discovery Channel, USA Networks, etc. Most cable operators do not distinguish between basic and expanded basic and sell the two as an integrated package. Expanded basic cable services are mostly advertiser supported, with the exception of PBS, C-Span and public access channels.

Pay Cable Television

Pay cable television is charging the customer an additional fee for the right to receive a premium television channel or service. Pay cable television comes in two forms, including monthly services like Home Box Office, Showtime and Starz as well as pay-per-view (PPV) events which involve charging the customer by the program rather than by the service (or channel). In principle, pay cable services add a premium value to the traditional television viewing experience by offering subscribers programming that they wouldn't normally be able to get on basic cable, such as recently released films, made-for-cable specials, specialized concerts, sporting events, adult entertainment, etc. In principle, the cable operator splits the programming fee in a 60/40 split, with the programmer like HBO or Showtime receiving the 60 percent.

Pay-per-View Television (Video on Demand)

Pay-per-view (PPV) television represents a distinct category of pay television services. PPV involves charging the customer by the program rather than by the service (or channel). PPV represents the consummate form of interactive television and has proven an excellent strategy for promoting special event programs like feature films, professional boxing and wrestling, music concerts and adult entertainment. PPV television is not a new idea. Early attempts at marketing PPV can be traced back to the 1950s and the early subscription television systems involving traditional broadcast television. Companies like Skiatron and International Telemeter experimented with plastic punch cards and coin boxes attached to TV sets.[14] Pay-per-view television has steadily evolved over the years. By the mid-1990s, PPV had begun to fulfill its long-overdue promise given improvements in delivery capability and interactivity. In 2007, the number of homes accessing PPV programming totaled 51.6 million units.[15]

Video on Demand

Video on demand represents a subset category of PPV services capable of downloading feature films and concerts on request. Video on demand is well positioned to become the most important strategy that cable system operators have in competing and eventually surpassing the DVD rental industry. The future success of video on demand presupposes an interactive system that is capable of downloading a virtual library of television and film products. Also important to this discussion are the steady improvements being made in the area of HDTV and digital video recording. Both are critical elements to the future success of pay-per-view television.

Another technology that is poised to redefine video on demand is the work being done by companies like Apple Computer and the concept of downloadable television programs on to a computer or its iPod playback device. The new video iPod can support up 150 hours of video on a 2.5-inch QVGA color display. What is significant is the fact that increasingly desktop and laptop computers represent a viable option for watching television.

High-Definition Television (HDTV)

HDTV program tiers are fast becoming an important new revenue source for today's cable television operators. HDTV is considered the most significant development in television technology since color television because of its remarkably improved picture quality as well as the ability to feature Dolby Digital sound. HDTV set design is wider than that of a traditional television set and more closely resembles a wide screen in a movie theater. HDTV changes the traditional television aspect ratio (i.e., screen width to height) from 4:3 to 16:9. HDTV sets generally come in two formats: plasma and LCD.[16]

HDTV when combined with HDTV DVD playback devices represents a logical progression in terms of advancing the home theater experience. There are presently two HDTV DVD television formats vying for consumer attention. The first is the Blu-ray standard backed by Sony Pictures Home Entertainment, the Walt Disney Company, 20th Century Fox, Apple Computer and Dell Computers. The second standard is HD DVD, backed by such companies as Toshiba, Paramount Studios, Microsoft and Dream Works

Information Services

The principle of two-way interactive cable has captivated the imagination of television entrepreneurs since the late 1960s. Early supporters of interactive television realized that two-way capability would allow a cable system to offer its customers a whole host of entertainment and value-added services, including pay-per-view television, home shopping and on-line database services. The joining together of television and applied utility services has fundamentally changed the way people regard the business of cable television, telephony and electronic media programming.

Cable Modems

Cable television systems were originally designed as one-way, analog transmission systems utilizing coaxial cable. However, the demand for high-speed Internet access and other two-way services prompted cable operators to upgrade their systems using a combination of fiber optic and coaxial delivery systems. These hybrid fiber–coaxial, or HFC, networks have greatly enhanced the speed and reliability of cable information services. The cable modem is an external peripheral device (or slide-in card) that provides high-speed access to the Internet for personal computers. Developed in the early 1990s, the cable modem provides access and downloading capability that is faster than comparable transmission media.[17] A cable modem connects over the cable plant to equipment in the cable head-end known as a cable modem termination system.[18] The number of U.S. homes that subscribe to a cable modem service is estimated to be 28.9 million customers.[19] Figure 4.3 illustrates cable modem penetration rates for the years spanning 2001–2006.

Cable Telephony

Cable companies, both large and small, are steadily positioning themselves to offer telephone services to residential customers. The provision of telephone

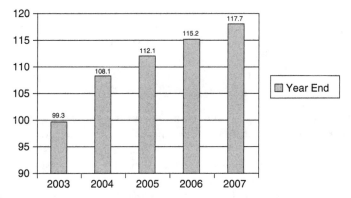

Figure 4.3 Cable Modem Penetration Rate: Number of Customers (in millions), 2001–2006.

Source: National Cable and Telecommunications Association and Paul Kagan Associates, Inc., "Residential Cable High Speed Data Subscribers," Available at: http://www.ncta.com/ ContentView.aspx?contentId=59 (retrieved September 10, 2007).

communication services via one's cable system represents a natural add-on service for many of today's cable television operators. The cable industry offers consumers both traditional telephone service and Voice Over Internet Protocol (VOIP), which represents the ability to conduct a telephone call via the Internet. VOIP relies on packet switching technology.[20] The number of cable telephone VOIP subscribers has greatly increased in recent years, giving cable operators a good reason to be optimistic about the future of telephony. Today, there are about 9.5 million U.S. cable telephone subscribers (Figure 4.4). Companies like Comcast, Time Warner and Cox Communications are aggressively moving forward in the delivery of telephone communication service. Both large and small cable television companies recognize that telephone communications represent an untapped market.

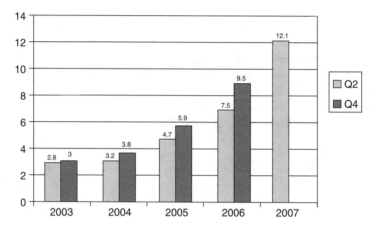

Figure 4.4 Residential Telephone Customers (in millions), 2001–2006.

Source: National Cable and Telecommunications Association, "Residential Cable Telephone Customers," Available at: http://www.ncta.com/Statistic/Statistic/ResidentialTelephony Customers.aspx (retrieved February 18, 2008).

Home Shopping

The successful launching of the Home Shopping Network (HSN) in the mid-1980s demonstrated the market potential for interactive shopping. The HSN was launched by Lowell "Bud" Paxson and Roy Speer in 1982 as the Home Shopping Club, a local cable channel seen on Vision Cable and Group W Cable in Pinellas County, Florida. The shopping club steadily expanded into the first national shopping network three years later on July 1, 1985. During its early years, the HSN mostly sold high-volume, low-budget catalogue products. The HSN became enormously successful and was soon followed by a host of imitators, which resulted in a major market shakeout. The second major shopping channel was established by Joseph Segal in

West Chester, Pennsylvania, in 1986 and was called QVC. By 1993, QVC (the quality, value and convenience network) had become the number one televised shopping service, reaching over 80 percent of all U.S. cable homes and 3 million satellite dishes.

Throughout the decade of the 1990s, the HSN and QVC became the two most profitable home shopping services in the U.S. Both HSN and QVC are carried to people's homes via their local cable operator and use an 800 telephone number (or Internet on-line shopping capability) as the principal method for ordering merchandise. HSN offers over 25,000 unique products in the categories of home and entertainment, electronics, health and beauty, fashion and jewelry. QVC broadcasts 24 hours a day, 364 days a year, to 87 million households in the U.S. and an additional 15.4 million households in the UK and the Republic of Ireland.[21] In exchange for cable carriage, HSN and QVC pay the cable operator a 3–5 percent commission based on sales in each operator's franchised area.

Programming and Cable Revenues

Table 4.4 provides a listing of cable revenue derived from both basic and premium revenues for the years spanning 1985–2005. Total cable revenue includes basic plus premium, which includes high-speed Internet access, cable telephony, HDTV premium channels and other enhanced information services.

Table 4.4 Basic and Pay Cable Subscriber Revenue (in millions), 1985–2007

Year	Basic Revenue	Premium Revenue	Total Revenue
2007	$33,608	$6,467	$74,716
2005	$31,025	$6,389	$62,267
2003	$28,960	$5,190	$51,300
2001	$27,031	$5,259	$43,518
1999	$23,146	$4,930	$36,919
1997	$20,405	$4,823	$30,493
1995	$16,860	$4,607	$25,421
1993	$13,528	$4,810	$22,843
1991	$11,418	$4,968	$19,426
1989	$8,671	$4,663	$15,378
1987	$6,016	$3,959	$11,563
1985	$4,138	$3,610	$8,331

Source: Kagan Research, "Revenue from Customers 1986–2007," *Broadband Cable Financial Databook*, 2007, Available at: http://www.ncta.com/ContentView.aspx?contentId=69 (retrieved September 10, 2007).

Cable Television Marketing

The first challenge facing the cable manager and marketer is how to balance the need for creating a diverse set of program services with the cost of acquiring such programming. In short, how many program services are enough to satisfy the customer and to give perceived value to the product? In the end, offering more program services does not guarantee an automatic increase in subscribership. In fact, just the opposite can start to occur. Cable customers will sometimes resent having to pay for packaged tier services that they don't watch.

Program Tier and Service Levels

In designing a program service, it is incumbent upon the cable operator to offer programming choices and options to meet the various levels of consumer demand and budget constraints. To that end, cable operators will offer their services according to different program tiers. A program tier refers to the packaging (or clustering) of programs according to service levels. The selection of program services is guided by a number of factors, including program popularity (i.e., the broadcast networks, ESPN, CNN, etc.), retransmission consent obligations, franchise obligations (community access channels), the opportunity to market new program services (i.e., premium services, HDTV channels, etc.) and channel capacity issues.

Program tiers are structured according to foundation services (basic, expanded basic) followed by thematic packages (i.e., a sports package, premium services package, HDTV package, etc.). Table 4.5 provides a sample menu of program offerings made available by a typical cable system operator.

Subscriber Growth and Retention

A second important task of cable marketing is how to maximize long-term subscriber growth and profits. There are several questions that need to be taken into consideration. What are the best methods for attracting new subscribers? What are the reasons that contribute to viewers' decisions to disconnect the service? What can be done to offset that effect? In principle, there are two ways to increase long-term subscribership: attract new subscribers to the service and retain old subscribers by avoiding churn.

Attract New Subscribers

Marketing new subscribers to a service is typically achieved through a combination of mass media, including television, radio, Internet and newspapers, as well as direct sales efforts. In addition, some national pay television services such as HBO and Showtime will assist the cable system operator in

106

Table 4.5 Cable Television Programming: Program and Service Tier Options

Basic:

2 WGN	12 C-Span
3 CBC (local affiliate)	13 C-Span 2
4 NBC (local affiliate)	14 Independent station
5 Fox (local affiliate)	15 Telemundo (Spanish)
6 Independent station	16 UPN (local station)
7 ABC (local affiliate)	17 Public access
8 Home Shopping Network	18 Public access
9 PBS (local station)	19 Public access
10 CW (local station)	20 Public access
11 TV Guide Channel	21–24

Expanded basic:

25 Lifetime	46 National Geographic
26 The Disney Channel	47 Sci-Fi Channel
27 ABC Family	48 USA
28 Cartoon Network	49 HGTV
29 Nickelodeon	50 CNN
30 Game Show Network	51 CNN Headline
31 Food Network	52 The Weather Channel
32 Gameshow Network	53 Fox News
33 Hallmark Channel	54 CNBC
34 Fox Sports Network	55 Court TV
35 ESPN	56 MSNBC
36 ESPN 2	57 TNT
37 ESPN Classic	58 Spike TV
38 Golf Channel	59 BET
39 The Learning Channel	60 MTV
40 The Discovery Channel	61 MTV 2
41 Biography	62 VH1
42 Arts and Entertainment	63 Oxygen
43 Bravo	64 CMT
44 The History Channel	65 Turner Classic Movies
45 Animal Planet	

Digital family tier 200–299:

200 BBC America	*Digital sports tier 300–399:*
205 Biography	300 Fox College Sports
210 Science Channel	310 Fox Soccer Channel
215 CNN International	320 Outdoor Life Network
220 ESPN Classic	330 Fit TV
225 The Military Channel	340 NFL Network
230 American Life	
235 Sundance	*Digital pay-per-view 400–499:*
240 Lifetime Movie Network	400 Pay-per-view previews
245 History International	410 PPV concerts
250 CMT Pure Country	420 PPV wrestling events
255 Discovery Health	430 PPV movies
	440 PPV sporting events
	450 Playboy Channel

Premium:

500 HBO	*HDTV 700–799:*
	770 HDNet

(Continued Overleaf)

Table 4.5 Continued

501 HBO 2	771 HD Movies
503 HBO Latino	772 ESPN 2 HDTV
504 Cinemax	773 ESPN HD
505 Cinemax West	774 TNT HD
506 Showtime	775 Discovery HD
507 Starz	777 HBO HD
508 Starz Kids and Family	778 Showtime
509 Starz Cinema	780 ABC (affiliate) HDTV
510 Encore	782 CBS (affiliate) HDTV
511 Encore Mystery	787 Fox (affiliate) HDTV
512 Encore Action	788 NBC (affiliate) HDTV

presenting information about the service to prospective customers or provide free trial offers. At the system level, each cable operator approaches marketing in slightly different ways based on an understanding of the local audience.

Retain Old Subscribers

The cable operator must also ensure that current subscribers will continue to renew their subscription. Each monthly fee represents the magazine equivalent of renewed subscribership. Retention marketing has to do with understanding the reasons why subscribers cancel their service and the steps necessary in order to keep the operator's customers satisfied. Cable operators use the term *churn* to describe audience turnover or cancellation of service. While a certain amount of disconnect activity is unavoidable (i.e., consumers move, etc.), there are four basic reasons that contribute to churn activity. They include general dissatisfaction with the service, perceived duplication of programs (repetition), cost of service and poor customer service.

GENERAL DISSATISFACTION WITH THE SERVICE

Cable subscribers will disconnect if they feel the service provider is not providing good value. Good value can include everything from program quality and diversity to cost. One strategy employed by MSOs such as Cox, Time Warner and Comcast is to provide their customers with special giveaways or discounts as a way to thank them for being loyal customers.

PERCEIVED DUPLICATION OF PROGRAMS (REPETITION)

Many cable television programs (and pay services in particular) run the risk of alienating customers if the programming seems repetitive. The solution lies in designing a highly differentiated basic program service as well as offering a good variety of premium service options including the possible bundling (with discount) of high-speed Internet access coupled with two or more pay services at the upper levels. Such bundling efforts are often referred to as "value packages."

COST OF SERVICE

As the cost of cable goes up, some customers are not willing to continue to pay for television. This is especially true for premium services. An important role for the customer service representative is to work closely with a prospective customer in order to select a program tier (or service level) that objectively meets the customer's programming interests and budget. The proper design and format of program tiers become an essential element in promoting the importance of program value to the customer. As an example, some cable operators have designed so-called lifeline cable services that include a core set of basic channels in order to make cable television available to those who cannot afford cable or who are concerned about cost.

POOR CUSTOMER SERVICE

Some subscribers will disconnect if they feel the cable operator is slow or not responsive to customer complaints. The problem becomes especially pro-nounced when the service goes out just prior to or during an important special event or sports program. In past years, the cable industry earned a reputation for poor customer service. This has dramatically changed given increased choices in the marketplace (i.e., DBS and telephone-based IPTV for broadband entertainment and DSL for high-speed Internet access).

The Value of Customer Service

Cable television is not a presold business, but requires a constant effort to maintain good relations with one's customers. To that end, customer service is a critical element in all growth and retention strategies. The customer service representative (CSR) is the person who provides the point of contact between the cable operator and the customer. The CSR is responsible for orders and installation as well as service repair. The CSR may also handle customer billing questions and scheduling of repair work in the event of a disruption in service. The importance of customer service cannot be overestimated.

Orders and Installation

The CSR is first and foremost the person responsible for taking the order. Taking orders requires product knowledge and a basic understanding of sales-manship. Often, the CSR will adhere to a scripted conversation (or manual) for the purpose of ensuring consistency. At the same time, being a CSR is more than just signing up prospective customers to the service. The CSR is also responsible for selling the customer additional (or premium) services where possible. As an example, the CSR may offer the customer a special incentive for taking a premium service in lieu of routine installation costs.

Service Repair

When a CSR receives a customer complaint concerning the cable system's operation and performance, the CSR will ask the customer a series of questions in order to isolate the problem. Sometimes talking the customer through a series of questions can address the problem without having to send a repair person to service or fix a relatively easy problem such as an adjustment on one's television set or tightening a cable connection. When a service repair person is required, the CSR will schedule the repair work and perform a follow-up telephone call to make sure that the work was performed satisfactorily.

Cable Management and the Franchise Agreement

A cable television system operates under the auspices of a franchise agreement. A cable television franchise is a contractual agreement between the cable operator and local government which defines the rights and responsibilities of both parties in the construction and operation of the cable system. One of the important responsibilities of the cable manager is to ensure that the cable system is adhering to the rules and requirements stated in the cable franchise agreement. It is also the responsibility of the cable manager to represent the interests of the cable system owner or MSO when the franchise agreement comes up for renewal.

A typical franchise agreement gives the cable operator a nonexclusive right to provide cable service for a period typically between 10 and 12 years. The length of time is based on the assumption that a new cable system (or rebuilt one) will require a minimum of seven years in order for the operator to see a return on investment. The franchise obligates the cable operator to work with the community in order to achieve an appropriate level of service,

The franchise agreement is the principal document against which the performance of the cable operator is judged at the time of renewal. Any major changes in the provision of service must be approved by the local community or its designated franchising authority. The subsequent modifications are then written into the franchise agreement. It is understood by both parties that certain changes are inevitable in the life of a franchise agreement.

A cable operator has certain rights and responsibilities. Two of the cable operator's important rights include: 1) the right to make a reasonable return on investment and 2) the right to make all programming decisions that affect the business operation of the cable system. The Cable Communications Policy Act of 1984 protects the cable operator from communities that seek to impose unreasonable programmatic or service obligations that would adversely affect the financial or technical performance of the cable operator.

Franchise Fee

The cable operator has certain obligations as well. One of the operator's key obligations includes the requirement to pay a franchise fee to the local community in which it operates. The franchise fee cannot exceed 5 percent of the cable operator's gross annual revenues.[22] It is understood by both parties that franchise fees can be used to support a variety of local community projects, including education and community access channels.

Cable Television Franchise Renewal

A cable television franchise comes up for renewal approximately every 10 to 12 years. At that time, the cable operator and the said community are both obligated to negotiate a new franchise agreement that will outline the requirements and expectations of both parties. The franchise renewal process is both formal and informal. According to attorney Nicholas P. Miller, there are four basic steps that a community (or franchising authority) should expect to follow:

1   evaluate the past performance of the cable operator;
2   determine the future cable-related needs of the community;
3   evaluate the incumbent cable operator's proposal;
4   make the decision to renew (or not renew) the franchise agreement.[23]

Evaluate the Past Performance of the Incumbent Cable Operator

Typically, the local municipality will assign a task force to examine whether the cable operator has fulfilled its obligations to the community and to its subscribers. The evaluation of past performance will include, but is not limited to, a franchise compliance audit, performance review, franchise fee audit (if applicable), customer satisfaction survey, and technical compliance audit.[24]

FRANCHISE COMPLIANCE AUDIT

The franchise compliance audit is a detailed review of the specific contractual and legal requirements imposed on the cable operator during the term of the existing franchise. This information will typically contain the franchise agreement, the cable operator's original proposal, any amendments to the operator's franchise and all letters sent to the operator by the franchising authority outlining shortcomings in compliance.

PERFORMANCE REVIEW

The performance review is an investigation of the operator's performance during the term of the franchise. Franchising authorities will typically use two techniques to evaluate the past performance of a cable operator: staff inquiries and public hearings.

FRANCHISE FEE AUDIT (IF APPLICABLE)

The franchise fee audit is a specific review to audit whether franchise fee payments have complied with the terms of the franchise agreement. The franchise fee audit is usually conducted by the cable operator. If there are discrepancies between what was paid and what is owed, the two parties should be able to reach a settlement.

CUSTOMER SATISFACTION SURVEY

The customer satisfaction survey evaluates the past and present performance of the cable operator. It can indicate the kinds of services that subscribers want as well as providing customer reaction to the services currently offered by the cable operator.

TECHNICAL COMPLIANCE AUDIT

The technical compliance audit is an engineering field survey of the cable system in terms of its physical design and performance capability. The technical compliance audit will reveal the operational strengths and limitations of the system, the operational quality of the transmitted signals and whether they meet FCC and franchise requirement guidelines, and cost estimates regarding possible upgrades and/or maintenance of the system. Each part of the performance review should conclude with a written analysis detailing the relevant facts and resulting conclusions. The overriding goal is to develop a comprehensive review that will demonstrate a gathering of reasonable evidence that can withstand a legal challenge should the community decide not to renew the cable operator's franchise.

Determine the Future Cable Needs of the Community

The second phase in the renewal process is making some preliminary determinations as to what the community will need in the future. The local community and its franchising authority are asked to consider some of the following questions:

1 What are the community's future cable-related needs and interests?
2 What are the cost requirements in order to meet those needs?
3 Is this a reasonable burden to impose on the cable operator?
4 Will the cable operator's proposal reasonably meet those needs?

The best tool for answering these questions is to perform a community needs assessment. There are several ways that a community can get at this information. They include surveys, interviews with community leaders, and interviews with public officials. The needs assessment begins with a review of the current cable system. Then it extends into a series of "what if" scenarios to see what future demands for services may exist. Finally it attempts to estimate the costs of those various future scenarios and to assign priorities. The primary goal is to assemble a list of priorities in terms of:

1 programming, in terms of number of program channels and/or diversity of programs;
2 enhanced information services, including education channels, high-speed Internet access, DVD recording capability, security systems, etc.;
3 conditions for service provision, which cover such activities' responsiveness to customer complaints, billing procedures, etc.

The aforementioned list of priorities is subject to negotiation with the cable system operator.

Evaluate the Incumbent Cable Operator's Proposal

The task here is to evaluate the incumbent operator's proposal for a new franchise taking into consideration the operator's financial, technical and legal qualifications to fulfill its proposal. In the U.S., the operator can submit a proposal for renewal at any time during the life of the franchise agreement or in response to a request for a renewal proposal issued by the franchising authority.

Make the Decision to Renew (or Not Renew) the Franchise Agreement

After conducting the community assessment and establishing priorities (as well as reviewing the operator's proposal), it is then time to begin serious negotiations between the cable operator and the franchising authority. The decision to renew or not renew is usually the result of extensive negotiations (or failed negotiations) with the operator.

Afterward, a decision is made whether or not to renew the existing cable operator's franchise and, if so, under what terms and conditions. The decision should be based on analyzing the strengths of the facts, including the data obtained from parts one, two and three. If the franchising authority decides not to renew the franchise, it is standard to provide a written justification using the same support data from parts one, two and three.

It should be noted that the cable television franchising process is not without some real limitations. While the Cable Act of 1984 gives communities the right to deny a cable franchise, in practice this a rare occurrence. To start with, few government officials are willing to justify the inconvenience and public relations fallout that would result should the community's franchising authority actually deny a cable franchise and shut down the system altogether. Secondly, most small to medium-sized communities are not prepared to face the probable lawsuit that would occur should a cable franchise be denied. In short, the threat of costly litigation is a powerful disincentive for those communities that may want to challenge the business practices of the local cable operator. The goal for the local community should be to upgrade (or significantly improve) the cable television system rather than looking for ways to deny the cable television franchise. It should be further noted that the franchise renewal process itself is under serious review given the interest by the telephone industry to move toward a national franchising system approach. (See "Strategic Challenges: Discussion" at the end of this chapter).

Music Television (MTV): A Case Study

The Music Television channel is an advertiser-supported music entertainment cable channel that began as a joint venture between American Express and Warner Amex Communications, then a subsidiary of Warner Communications. It was conceived in 1980 by John A. Lack, who was then vice president of Warner Amex. Lack envisioned programming three- to five-minute commercials for recorded albums in the same manner that a radio station programs recordings. His goal was to reach television viewers aged 12–35. Lack was able to secure $20 million in start-up capital from both Warner Communications and American Express.[25] Lack recruited Robert Pittman (who would later oversee the AOL–Time Warner merger) to assemble a team responsible for developing the MTV concept. MTV was launched on August 1, 1981. MTV's originator, John Lack, left the network in 1984. Robert Pittman rose to the position of president and CEO of MTV before leaving in 1986. By the mid-1980s, the music video had become a highly desirable program format for programmers, advertisers and audiences.[26] What made MTV especially attractive from a business standpoint was the fact that the music video (i.e., programming software) was made available for free by the various music companies which saw the MTV platform as a great way to promote their respective music and recording artists.

In March 1986, MTV, VH1 and Nickelodeon were sold to Viacom for $513 million. Soon thereafter, Viacom CEO Sumner Redstone appointed Tom Freston as president of MTV. Freston was the last remaining member of Pittman's original development team. MTV's global success is in part due to the innovative management and programming strategies that Freston implemented early on in his tenure. In 1987, MTV launched its first overseas channel in Europe, which was a single feed consisting of American music programming hosted by English-speaking artists. MTV soon discovered that, while American music was popular in Europe, it could not offset differences in language and culture and an obvious preference for local artists. European broadcasters, however, understood the importance of MTV as an engaging programming concept. They soon adapted the MTV programming format and began broadcasting music videos in various languages throughout the whole of Europe. This, in turn, severely affected MTV's financial performance in Europe.

In 1995, MTV was able to harness the power of digital satellite in order to create regional and localized programming. MTV's international programming drew upon the talent, cultural themes and language from select parts of the world, and it was then satellite fed into that particular geographical location. Approximately 70 percent of MTV's content is generated locally, with an attempt to offer continuously new program offerings. This has made it easier and more profitable for MTV to sell advertising air time overseas, given that most advertising needs and budgets of companies tend to be more local than international.[27] MTV airs more than 22 different feeds around the world, all tailored to their respective markets. They comprise a mixture of licensing agreements, joint ventures and wholly owned operations, with MTV International still holding the creative control of these programs.

Presently MTV has a huge market share in Asia, Europe, China, Japan and Russia. In all, MTV airs more than 22 different feeds around the world, all tailored to their respective markets. MTV International is organized into six major divisions: MTV Asia (Hindi, Mandarin), MTV Australia, MTV Brazil (Portuguese), MTV Europe, MTV Latin America (Spanish) and MTV Russia.[28] The management of MTV's international operations is highly decentralized, which allows local managers the ability to develop programming and marketing strategies to fit the needs of each individual market.

Strategic Challenge

Today, MTV is no longer the brash upstart service that it was in the early 1980s. The challenge is to keep MTV (and the host of its spin-off networks) as cool and fresh as it once was. At issue is the fact that growth of MTV's target audience (12–34) has leveled off at approximately 5 percent from 2002 to 2005. MTV's CEO, Judy McGrath, believes that MTV has to be delivered across the full spectrum of communication technology platforms, including cell phones, videogames and MP3 music downloads.[29] In 2005, Viacom split the company into two major parts, consisting of CBS and the television broadcast group, and MTV Networks. MTV has become the flagship cable service for all of Viacom's cable network services, including Spike TV, Nickelodeon, CMT and Comedy Central, to name only a few. One reason for the organizational separation is for each division to realize its full potential and offer separate tracking stocks.

Strategic Challenges: Discussion

National Cable Franchise Policy

The current system of local cable franchising is undergoing a major change. The U.S. House Energy and Commerce Committee supports replacing the nation's existing system of local cable TV franchising with a national scheme, an approach supported by the U.S. telephone companies AT&T and Verizon.[30] The proposed changes would help telephone companies more easily secure video franchises, which according to the FCC would help spur broadband delivery while offering greater choice to consumers and increased competition to the cable television industry. In principle, telephone companies would be granted ten-year national video franchises with automatic renewal.[31] The National Cable and Telecommunications Association (NCTA), for its part, is lobbying hard to ensure that a national franchising policy would include cable service providers as well. According to NCTA president Kyle McSlarrow:

> While our policy recommendation would be to reform and streamline the franchising process to ensure speedy entry by new competitors, we are pleased that the national franchising scheme proposed in the House bill seeks to ensure that all providers compete on a level playing field.[32]

The current legislation, as it is presently constituted, would allow new video providers to get a ten-year franchise within 30 days of filing the requisite application. It also allows cable operators to get a franchise under the same national franchise terms if a competitor enters the market with a national franchise or when their current franchise expires. The national franchise can be revoked for "repeated and willful violations," including discrimination in terms of service (i.e., "redlining"), violating rights-of-way laws, or making false statements about service.[33]

À La Carte Pricing

Today, the average consumer can see upwards of 75 channels of television service. Most viewers, however, typically watch only 15 to 17 channels per month, according to FCC estimates. In the meantime, the cost of expanded basic cable has jumped more than 40 percent in five years.[34] At issue is the fact that consumers do not want to pay for a whole host of television services that they don't watch. Part of the problem is related to a tying arrangement, whereby cable programmers will sometimes make cable systems take less popular program services (or new channels) in order to get the more high-profile services.[35] In other words, the price for getting ESPN is having to take ESPN 2, ESPN Classic, etc. Broadcasters will sometimes do the same thing by leveraging retransmission consent obligations as a way to promote new services. The price for getting CBS on the local cable system is to take additional broadcast or cable services owned by CBS's parent company, Viacom. Expanded basic (and the extra channels that go with it) adds more cost to the consumer's bill. The alternative is an à la carte approach that would allow consumers to customize their viewing options and pay for only those services that they watch with regularity. The a la carte approach is endorsed by Kevin Martin, chairman of the Federal Communications Commission. In a 2005 released study, the FCC found that consumers could realize a savings of up to 13 percent on their cable TV bills using an à la carte system approach.[36]

The cable industry, for its part, is adamantly opposed to an à la carte approach. The NCTA makes the argument that the "expanded basic" package of channels that most viewers choose is a bargain. For about $41 a month, they note, a viewer can see numerous cable channels including CNN, ESPN and MTV. The problem with an à la carte approach is that it would quickly eliminate the lesser-known cable channels and provide less opportunity for viewers to experiment with new program services. Nor does an à la carte approach address the problem of high licensing fees, as well as retransmission consent obligations.

Competitive Business Challenges

Direct Broadcast Satellites

Direct broadcast satellites represent a new generation of highly powered satellites capable of delivering television programs to users equipped with small earth stations (parabolic dishes) approximately 18 inches in diameter. Today's generation of DBS satellites are much larger in size and utilize digital compression techniques that allow them to offer 250–400 channels of service. The two principal competitors to the cable industry are DirecTV, owned by News Corporation Ltd., and the Dish Network, owned by EchoStar Communications. These services began in June 1994 and December 1995 respectively.

DBS is well positioned to challenge the cable television industry by offering digital television services comparable in number of channels and quality to, and at less cost than, cable television. Both DirecTV and EchoStar have seen a steady increase in subscribership since their initial start in the mid-1990s. While the original target audience for DBS service was people living in rural areas, both companies have seen an increase in subscribership among people living in medium to larger-size communities. The market for multichannel television programming continues to grow according to a 2006 FCC report on video competition. While cable television remains the largest distributor of multichannel television service, there has been a noticeable decline in cable subscribership numbers since 2004. According to that same FCC report, cable's share of the multichannel television market is 69.4 percent, down from 71.6 percent a year earlier. DBS represents the second largest purveyor of multichannel television, serving almost 27.7 percent of the U.S. market compared to approximately 25.1 percent in 2004.[37]

IPTV

A second player poised to challenge the incumbent cable operator is the major U.S. telephone companies offering a broadband video service known as Internet Protocol Television (IPTV). IPTV is a method for transporting television over the Internet using packet switching technology. Companies like Verizon and AT&T are investing heavily in IPTV as the basis for entering the broadband video market of the future. IPTV is fast becoming the all important battleground between telecom operators and cable companies.[38]

Verizon has made a multibillion-dollar investment in deploying fiber directly to consumers' homes in a project known as FIOS. The goal is to deliver multichannel, broadband capability with a delivery speed approaching 100 megabits per second. Similarly, AT&T is rolling out IPTV broadband capability in a project dubbed "Lightspeed." Microsoft and a half-dozen other vendors are collaborating on the Lightspeed project by developing set-top boxes and software capability. They hope to achieve a global presence in the nascent IPTV market. Time is a critical element in advancing the cause of IPTV service. The cable industry has a 30-year head start and is the established player of record. As Comcast CEO Brian Roberts points out, "I like our hand best of all. We're still in the best position to offer the full complement of broadband services."[39]

Set-Top Boxes and CableCARDs

Beginning in 2005, the FCC adopted a set of rules designed to help smooth the transition to digital television. The FCC's new "plug-and-play" rules will ensure that future cable systems are compatible with DTV receivers and related consumer electronics equipment. The FCC's plug-and-play rules will facilitate the direct connection of customer premises equipment, such as television receivers, set-top boxes and DVRs, to cable television systems without the need for a set-top box. In sum, the plug-and-play rules are crucial toward building products and advancing services to help spur the development of digital television.

CableCARDs

A CableCARD is the size of a credit card and plugs directly into the back of a digital television set, personal computer or digital video recorder; it eliminates the need for a set-top box. Previously, the set-top box was rented to the consumer by the cable operator for a nominal monthly fee. The Cable-CARD concept was developed by the cable industry in response to the 1996 Telecommunications Act, which required the industry to provide noncable companies the ability to access the network. Specifically, the goal was to create a more competitive market for third-party set-top box and consumer electronics manufacturers (i.e., HDTV, DVR and DVD, etc.). Section 304 of the Telecommunications Act directs the FCC to "assure the commercial availability to consumers of multichannel video programming and other services . . . from manufacturers, retailers, and other vendors not affiliated with any multichannel video programming distributor."[40]

Beginning July 1, 2007, cable companies are no longer allowed to use integrated security features that tie their cable boxes directly to their own service.[41] Instead, customers are able to simply get a CableCARD from their cable company and insert it into the set-top box of their choice.

Cable Television and Retransmission Consent Agreements

Retransmission is an option granted to U.S. television stations as part of the Cable Act of 1992, which grants local or area television stations "must-carry" rights (i.e., the cable operator must carry the station on the system) or allows them to elect cash payment (or the equivalent). Typically, small stations like a religious channel will elect must-carry status, knowing that the station will be given a guaranteed slot on the cable system. In contrast, a television affiliate station may elect cash payment (or the equivalent), knowing that the station is too high-profile not to be carried on the cable system. The cable operator, however, can refuse to pay the said broadcast station. In lieu of cash compensation, the broadcast station (or parent company, e.g., Viacom, Walt Disney, etc.) may work out an agreement whereby the cable operator agrees to carry additional forms of broadcast or cable television programming on the system.

Dual Carriage Ruling

In September 2007, the FCC voted unanimously to require cable systems nationwide to deliver hundreds of local TV stations in analog and digital formats to their customers for three years after the nation's full-powered stations suspend their analog broadcast. The requirement to carry TV stations' primary programming service in both formats would start in early 2009 and last until 2012. According to the FCC's dual carriage ruling, a cable operator would be required to carry:

- a local broadcaster's digital signal in analog and digital formats;
- the signal only in digital format, provided that all subscribers have the necessary equipment (digital set-top boxes) to view the broadcast content;
- the high-definition signal of broadcasters in HDTV format.

Commissioner Kevin Martin's stated goal is to protect the millions of viewers who use only analog TV sets to watch programs provided by their cable operators. The dual carriage rule provides such viewers with additional time to acquire digital set-top boxes or TVs in order to view local TV stations.[42]

Concluding Remarks

The term "smart cities" speaks to the importance of economic development and revitalization of a community's downtown and major public resources (i.e., schools, housing, parks, library, museums, etc.). What makes for a smart city depends on context, perspective and time frame. The common thread that ties all cities together is a recognition of the importance of economic development. Historically, schools, business and transportation infrastructure have been at the center in promoting the cause of community development. Starting in the decade of the 1990s, telecommunications and information technology have also come to be seen as a critical element in helping to advance economic growth. In particular has been the rapid deployment of high-speed Internet access throughout the world's major cities.

The cable industry is currently undergoing a major redefinition as to its core business. While television entertainment will continue to be the main engine that drives cable television forward, the very nature of programming will undergo a profound change. Today's cable operator is much more than a purveyor of television entertainment. Rather, cable delivery of broadband communication services makes possible a whole host of utility and value-added features, including local government, public safety, health care, education and business.[43] Table 4.6 provides a few examples.

In particular, communities that utilize geographic information systems (GIS) depend heavily on high-speed Internet access for purposes of database management, electronic mapping, public safety, tax assessment, etc. As we think about the future of cable television, the conversation is no longer just about television entertainment. Instead, the conversation is about enhanced information services and what it means for a community and its citizens. In a multichannel universe, the origins of entertainment-, information- and utility-based services become less distinguishable. The future of electronic media will come to include a variety of entertainment and information-based services and give new meaning to the term "programming."

Table 4.6 The Future of Entertainment and Information-Based Cable Service

1. Multichannel television entertainment:
   —basic and premium services;
   —digital and HDTV;
   —video on demand;
   —parental control;
   —à la carte program selection.
2. High speed Internet access:
   —e-mail;
   —electronic commerce;
   —music downloads;
   —streaming video;
   —electronic banking;
   —on-line information gathering.
3. Cable telephony:
   —wireline telephony;
   —Voice Over Internet Protocol (VOIP).
4. On-line video gaming.
5. Home shopping.
6. Public safety and health.
7. Geographic information systems (GIS).
8. Education and specialized training.

5

TELECOMMUNICATIONS ECONOMICS II

Principles of Public Utilities, Common Carriers and Information Carriage

Public Utilities

The term *public utilities* refers to those business enterprises engaged in the delivery of essential- (or utilitarian-) type services to the public. The provision of such services is considered essential to basic quality of life. In principle, public utilities like water, energy (gas and electricity) and local telephone communication tend to be one-of-a-kind service providers in the communities or regions in which they operate. As such, they are subject to extensive local, state or federal regulation in terms of the rates they charge and the kinds of services they provide.[1]

Public utilities tend to exhibit three common features:

1   Public utilities are natural monopolies.
2   Public utilities provide essential types of service.
3   Public utilities exhibit cyclical patterns of service.

Natural Monopolies

Owing to economic and/or geographic factors, a business is considered a natural monopoly when it is the primary supplier of a service to a given area. Natural monopolies tend to be one-of-a-kind businesses (or service providers), because the cost of duplicating facilities would be considered both inefficient and prohibitive in cost. Historically, natural monopolies tend to include service industries such as water, gas and electricity, local telephone, community hospitals, airports and postal delivery. The construction of natural monopoly facilities requires extensive capital. They are considered fundamental to local and regional economic planning.

Essential Types of Services

Public utilities provide essential-type services to the consumer. Economists use the term *elasticity of demand* to describe the level of demand (or need) for a product or service. Elasticity of demand measures the level of demand response to a change in price. The more responsive the demand is to a change in price, the more elastic is that product or service. The real test is whether the demand for a proposed service is considered essential, desirable or optional.

Telephone Service Is Inelastic

Historically, the demand for telephone service would be considered inelastic owing to the essential nature of telephone service and the need to communicate. Similarly, the demand for gasoline (despite rising gas prices) would be considered inelastic owing to the essential nature of car transportation. A sudden increase in price, while objectionable to the consumer, would not dissuade most consumers from having a telephone set or owning a car. By contrast, the demand for a second-tier pay television service would be considered highly elastic, since a change in price would have a corresponding effect on the consumer's willingness to pay for that service.

The Availability of Good Substitutes

One important consideration in determining the elasticity of demand is the availability of good substitutes. To what extent can consumers find alternative substitutes to the existing service provider? Direct broadcast satellite, for example, offers a reasonable substitute to cable television. Similarly, cellular telephony and Voice Over Internet Protocol telephony (VOIP) offer a reasonable substitute to traditional wireline service. By contrast, there are limited substitutes for gasoline-powered automobiles. In sum, the availability of good substitutes can directly affect the price consumers pay for essential types of service.

Cyclical Patterns of Service

The demand for public utilities exhibits cyclical patterns of use that can be tracked daily, weekly or by times of the year. As an example, peak demand for electricity is during the summer, whereas peak demand for heat is during the winter. Similarly, telephone traffic exhibits cyclical patterns of use on a daily basis, with telephone traffic being the highest during the course of the business day. Accordingly, cellular telephone rates factor in cyclical patterns of use with special discounts (and incentives) being given on nights and weekends.

The Regulation of Public Utilities

The public utility concept originated in the U.S. and is a decidedly American institution. The regulation of public utilities was originally conceived to provide some method of control over those companies that were engaged in the provision of essential-type services to the public. Historically, the regulation of public utilities emerged out of a confluence of three factors:

1   the negative experience with the behavior and performance of the railroad industries and electric utilities during the latter part of the nineteenth century;
2   the legal outcome of Munn v. Illinois (1877), which authorized government to regulate business when there was a substantial "public interest" concern;[2]
3   an economic belief in the concept of natural monopolies.

The regulation of utilities can occur at the local, state or federal level. In the case of local telephony, most telephone issues are handled by state public utility commissions (PUCOs). They are typically charged with examining issues pertaining to telephony, gas and electricity, water, etc. The establishment of the state PUCO concept was designed to protect the state and local citizenry from the possible excesses of public utilities, since consumers could not go elsewhere for essential-type services. Such protections find Constitutional support in the 10th Amendment, which provides that powers not delegated to the federal government (and not specifically prohibited to them) may be exercised by the states. Under this broad authority, states have the right to legislate for the protection of health, safety and the general welfare of their citizens.

Despite widespread deregulatory trends, not all markets are considered competitive. In areas like water and gas, market barriers still preclude effective competition. As such, public utilities have certain rights and responsibilities. This can be seen in Table 5.1.

Table 5.1 Public Utilities: Rights and Responsibilities

Rights	*Responsibilities*
1 The public utility has a right to a reasonable return on investment.	1 The utility is responsible for providing safe service at a reasonable rate.
2 Public utilities enjoy a limited exemption from competition resulting from certification or franchise agreements.	2 The utility is responsible for providing safe and adequate levels of service.
3 Public utilities are often granted the right of eminent domain, that is, the right to access private property for the proper conduct of their business, e.g., stringing telephone wire across an adjacent property to a business or home.	3 The utility is responsible for providing service on a nondiscriminatory basis to all who are willing to pay for it.

The Justification for Public Utilities

Public utilities are engaged in the delivery of essential- (or utilitarian-) type services to the public. Moreover, they tend to be one-of-a-kind services in the communities (or regions) in which they operate. The principle of natural monopoly suggests that, owing to economic and geographic factors, there are times when a single company or organization can produce the desired service more efficiently (and at lower cost) than any combination of two or more firms. Economists refer to this as subadditive conditions. Subadditive conditions are said to exist when the introduction of competition creates inefficiencies in the marketplace. Proponents of natural monopoly theory would argue that the duplication of facilities contributes both to increased costs and to a possible decline in the quality of service.

Increased Costs

Consider, for a moment, what happens when two hospitals provide health care in a small to medium-size community. Both hospitals must provide a full array of services despite the fact that each hospital is underutilized. In short, there are not enough patients to fill the beds and to fully utilize the available services. The same analogy can be applied to cable television, where the cost of deploying two sets of wired networks in a small to medium-size community would increase the cost for both sets of providers. Since both systems are presumably being underutilized, the fragmentation of the market results in less income for everyone, which in turn means raising the price of service to offset the cost of operation. In the end, the cable operator has to raise prices.

Quality of Service May Suffer

A second problem is that the quality of service may suffer, since the business (or organization) is looking for ways to economize and cut expenses. This, in turn, can result in a serious deterioration of service for everyone. The counter-argument is that competition or the threat of competition tends to promote greater efficiency and innovation in the marketplace. The challenge, therefore, is to know when subadditive conditions apply.

Cable television, for example, is not considered a public utility in the traditional sense of the term. It does, however, exhibit some natural monopoly-like features. Most small to medium-size communities will typically have only one cable operator. While U.S. law does allow for competitive cable franchises, most cable operators elect not to offer cable service in small to medium-size communities in which there is already an established cable operator.[3] The problem, in short, can be attributed to subadditive conditions. There are not enough existing (or potential) subscribers to fully utilize two cable television systems. The risks of finding out (including franchise requirements, the cost of wiring the community, program negotiations and marketing expenses) pose significant barriers to entry for most would-be cable operators. As a result, the established cable operator in such communities tends to exercise a de facto monopoly status in the area of wired communication to the home. This is beginning to change in light of DBS and developments in Internet Protocol Television.

The Problem with Public Utilities

Critics argue that public utilities tend to be less efficient than competitive industries. As the sole provider of service, they have less incentive to be innovative and to keep costs down. Moreover, they are highly protective of their market lead. This can sometimes prompt such companies to engage in anticompetitive behavior. This was a critical issue involving the U.S. Justice Department's decision to bring a massive civil lawsuit against AT&T in November 1974.[4]

When Is Regulatory Oversight Unnecessary?

There are times, however, when regulatory oversight is unnecessary. Regulatory intervention is typically unnecessary:

1   when the market is contestable, that is, when potential competitors can enter the market and act as a disciplinary force on the incumbent;
2   when the cost of market entry is considered reasonable and accessible;
3   when the potential entrant poses a credible threat to the incumbent leader. The new entrant must be able to take over a large portion of the market (15–25 percent) in a reasonable period of time.

The new entrant must be able to enter the market quickly and establish itself as a credible force before the incumbent attempts to erect regulatory or economic barriers to entry. These conditions are more likely to exist if the market is characterized by rapid technological change. Advancements in new technology can radically transform the marketplace by enabling a new entrant to enter the marketplace and establish an altogether different approach to the delivery of a new technology or service. Perhaps the most telling example of this can be seen in the area of cellular telephony. A cellular telephone system relies on highly efficient frequency usage to provide over-the-air telephone service to cars and to hand-held portable phones. What is most important, however, is that cellular telephony does not require the same level of physical infrastructure as is true with terrestrial wire-based systems. It is the primary reason why developing (and developed) nations in eastern Europe, Africa and South America have opted for wireless services as compared to wire-based systems.

Common Carrier Services

A common carrier is any company engaged in the business of message delivery on a point-to-point or point-to-multipoint basis. It provides the network facilities capable of delivering a telephone conversation, electronic mail, Internet data transmission, facsimile, videoconferencing and satellite communication delivery. The service must be provided on a nondiscriminatory basis to anyone who is willing to pay for it.

Common carriers are typically regulated by appropriate state and federal agencies. Common carriers can include local exchange carriers (LECs), such as Verizon, AT&T and Qwest Communications, as well as cellular telephone providers like Verizon Wireless, AT&T, Sprint, T-Mobile and Alltel. Common carriers can also include satellite service providers like Intelsat (International), Loral Space and Communications, SES Americom (U.S.A.), TeleSat (Canada), ArabSat (Middle East), Palapa (Indonesia) NordSat (Scandinavia), etc.

The Principle of Universal Service

In the U.S., the telephone and mail industries operate under very different legal principles from those governing broadcasting, cable and publishing. In past years, common carriers have often evolved as natural monopolies, especially in the provision of local telephone and mail service. Common carriers are required by law to serve their customers impartially and on a nondiscriminatory basis. The common carrier must provide the communication link impartially and without discrimination as to the user. In most countries of the world, telephony has traditionally operated under the auspices of the national government, which has in past years combined telephone and mail services under an arrangement called Post, Telegraph and Telephone (PT&T). The telephony portion has changed significantly in recent years owing to worldwide privatization trends. In the U.S., telegraphy and telephony were allowed to develop in the private sector and were modeled after the railroad industry.[5]

Cross-Subsidization (Price Averaging)

Telephone and postal service needs to be universal; that is, it should be available in large cities and rural communities alike. But the volume of business and the physical cost of delivery are not the same in all locales. The historical solution for meeting the goals of universal service was best accomplished through a process called *cross-subsidization*, which involves the price averaging of telephone service. In short, some people pay more for the cost of service while others pay less, thus creating a so-called average price for everyone. The principle of price averaging is at the heart of the U.S. mail delivery system. The cost for delivering a first-class letter is the same whether it's going between Kalamazoo and Battle Creek, Michigan (20 or so miles apart), or New York to California (over 3,000 miles apart). The same principle applies to telephone delivery. In past years, business has traditionally cross-subsidized residential telephone service at the local level, and urban communities have traditionally subsidized the cost of telephone service for the surrounding rural communities.

Direct Cost

The principle of direct cost means that the user pays the actual cost for providing service to one's home or business. For business this can mean a tremendous cost saving, especially if that company or organization is heavily dependent on telecommunications technology. It no longer has to concern itself with subsidizing more costly residential service. As a consequence, direct cost also means that some rural telephone users are now paying higher telephone bills for local service than ever before. In such cases, the cost for local telephone service is based on the actual distance from the local exchange office.

Tariffs and Rates

A common carrier must provide business customers and private residential subscribers with a standard schedule of rate charges. All requests for rate increases (or changes in the local/state telephone rate structure) must be approved at the state level under the auspices of the state public utility commission. Long-distance telephony, however, is considered a form of interstate commerce. As such, all requests for rate increases (or changes in long-distance telephone rate structures) must be approved by the Federal Communications Commission.

Rate-of-Return (ROR) Regulation

Regulation has predominantly focused on the pricing of utility services. The traditional method for regulating the prices and profitability of utilities is rate of return (ROR) regulation. ROR allows the utility to earn a fair rate of return at prices determined by the state PUCO. This is accomplished by setting rates that will reasonably compensate the utility for its operating expenses plus a fair return (i.e., 8 percent) on the capital invested in the rate base.

These rates are based on a test year and do not guarantee the utility such a return. For instance, if the utility, compared to the test year, operates less efficiently, its earnings will fall below the granted potential. If it operates more efficiently, its earnings may be temporarily above the granted level.

ROR regulation allows a utility to pass on all of its operating expenses to the consumer. In principle, ROR regulation should also pass on any cost savings to the consumer in the form of a rate reduction. The problem, however, is that the said utility has no incentive to produce efficiently and/or save its customers money.

Price Cap Regulation

Price cap regulation is more in keeping with performance-based regulation, that is, to create rewards and incentives for effective utility management. The objective is to create a series of rewards and incentives for having achieved a certain efficiency of operations or conservation of resources. Price cap regulation has built into the regulatory framework a system of rewards and penalties. There are a number of ways to build in incentives, including targeted incentive plans, external performance indexing, and price and revenue indexing.

Critics charge that price cap regulation (and other types of incentive regulation) uses a poor selection of performance yardsticks, including best practice, industry average, etc. In addition, other regulatory and social goals such as low-income support programs may be left out of the plan.[6]

Information Carriage

Telecommunications and Deregulation

A basic tenet of free market competition is that the private sector is the primary engine of growth. Free market competition means opening one's banking and telecommunication systems to private ownership and competition and providing a nation and its citizens with access to a wide variety of choices.[7] In principle, the best way to accomplish the goals of a highly competitive marketplace is by minimizing (or limiting) government involvement in the marketplace mechanism. Deregulation presupposes the elimination of nonessential rules and regulations.

Until the late 1970s, the communications industry was clearly separated in terms of areas of responsibility. Broadcasters and cable operators were in the business of television. And telephone carriers were clearly in the business of message delivery. All this has changed. Beginning in the early 1980s, the United States under the Reagan administration actively began promoting a policy of economic deregulation. The policy was designed to foster greater economic competition by allowing the marketplace to establish priorities and professional standards of business conduct rather than intrusive government intervention. Nowhere was this more pronounced than in the fields of cable and telephone communication, evidenced by the passage of the Cable Communications Policy Act of 1984 and the divestiture (or breakup) of AT&T in 1984.

America's commitment toward economic deregulation, in combination with the development of several important communication technologies, including cable television, the communication satellite, the personal computer, the Internet and high-definition television, has transformed the telecommunications marketplace. In today's telecommunications business environment, telephone service providers like AT&T and Verizon now offer video and other broadband residential services. Conversely, cable operators like Comcast and Cox now offer cable telephony as well as high-speed Internet access. The once-clear lines of business separation are no more.

Telecommunications and Privatization

Today, the level of economic restructuring and consolidation is unprecedented in the history of international business and commerce. The globalization of economic activity has forced many nations of the world to carefully consider their national economic policies. The once-sacrosanct government monopolies (i.e., airlines, steel and telecommunications) are facing the pressures of international competition. There is a clear recognition that, if such government-protected monopolies do not move fast enough in providing advanced services at the right cost, they will soon find themselves being outperformed by their international rivals. The result is a continuing movement to privatize (or sell off) state-owned companies.

The common motivation behind by such regulatory and economic reforms is the perceived inefficiency of central planning and government-protected monopolies. Government-owned enterprises tend to be inefficient operations and can be characterized by poor financial performance, overstaffing, dependence on government subsidies, highly centralized and politicized organizations, a strong adherence to rules and regulations, and technical noncompetitiveness.

Privatization is a highly political process that involves the conversion (and/or selling off) of state-owned enterprises (SOEs) into the private sector. The primary objective is to allow a market economy to flourish and thereby create opportunities and incentives for economic development. The successful privatization of SOEs is intended to improve the quality of goods and services while simultaneously reducing the role of the state in the economy. The selling off of SOEs, in particular, represents a way for government to raise cash that can be applied toward other government supported services. Another related objective of privatization is to promote the development of new technologies and services through foreign direct investment. The resulting competition is presumed to increase productivity and operating efficiency.[8] Privatization has been especially important in the fields of international broadcasting and telephony, where government-owned facilities are fast giving way to the private sector. The challenge of regulatory reform and privatization has proven especially difficult for those countries whose planning structures were once highly centralized.

Privatization and the Provision of Universal Service

As mentioned earlier, public utilities have no incentive to be efficient and innovative. In a world that has become increasingly deregulated and privatized, such companies find themselves being faced with outside competition in what were once "secure" markets. This was certainly the case for the U.S. postal service when a new upstart company called Federal Express began offering business customers overnight mail delivery service in direct competition. It was a novel concept whose success was immediate. Since then, overnight mail delivery has blossomed into a multibillion-dollar industry.

AT&T: The Breakup of the Bell System: A Case Study Analysis

Prior to 1984, AT&T (then called the Bell System) was the largest corporation in the world. In 1983, its assets were estimated to be worth $150 billion, making it bigger than General Motors, IBM and General Electric combined. AT&T's annual revenues were nearly $70 billion, representing approximately 2 percent of the U.S. gross national product. The company employed slightly less than one million people, thus making it the largest private employer in the United States. The Bell System provided residential and business customers with end-to-end telephone service for approximately 80 percent of the U.S. market. The company's organizational structure can be seen in Table 5.2.

The divestiture of AT&T was the culmination of a long history of legislative, judicial and regulatory decisions intended to foster competition in the field of telecommunications.[9] The U.S. Justice Department's case against AT&T took more than seven years to litigate and cost AT&T an estimated $375 million. The cost to the Justice Department (and the American people) was an estimated $18 million. The breakup of AT&T, effective January 1, 1984, was the largest corporate divestiture ever undertaken. AT&T's total assets were suddenly reduced to just under $40 billion dollars. The breakup of AT&T, more than any other regulatory action, forever changed telecommunications in the United States. Moreover, it created a ripple effect that was felt around

Table 5.2 AT&T: Organizational Structure (Prior to Divestiture Agreement, 1984)

Western Electric	Equipment manufacturing
Long Lines	Long-distance telephone communication
22 Bell Operating Companies	Local and regional telephony
Bell Research Labs	Research and development

the world. Let us consider, for a moment, the causes and consequences of the AT&T divestiture agreement.

The U.S. Justice Department Challenges AT&T: The Changing Regulatory Climate

In 1949 the U.S. Justice Department filed a major antitrust suit against AT&T and its Western Electric manufacturing subsidiary, claiming that both companies were in violation of the Sherman Antitrust Act. Both organizations were accused of restricting trade in the manufacture, distribution and sale of telephone equipment. The U.S. Justice Department wanted AT&T to divest itself of Western Electric and for the latter company to give up its 50 percent ownership of stock in Bell Research Labs (AT&T's research and development facility).

The 1956 Consent Decree

The suit dragged on for seven years and was settled out of court in 1956. The 1956 consent decree (or final judgment) permitted AT&T to remain intact, but required the company to restrict its business to traditional voice communication services. The Bell System would be subject to significant regulation. According to the terms of the 1956 consent decree, AT&T was precluded from using its own technology and research for the purpose of entering into other lines of business, and was required to license its patents to all foreign and domestic applicants on payment of reasonable royalty fees.[10] Interestingly, one of the first foreign applicants to take advantage of AT&T's work in the area of transistor communication was a small Japanese start-up firm called Sony.[11] The implication was clear. By licensing its patents to all would-be applicants, the Bell System was indirectly fostering competition against itself. More importantly, AT&T's senior management had failed to anticipate the future developments in new technology; even within their own Bell Research Labs.[12]

The Above 890 Decision

The 1956 consent decree may have denied AT&T entry into new lines of communication service, but it did not prevent other companies from entering into AT&T's own market of local and long-distance telephony. In 1959 and 1960, the FCC undertook a review of its microwave policy towards the private use of microwave facilities in what became known as the Above 890 decision.[13] The FCC considered whether there were sufficient frequencies to meet the needs of both public and private carriers in the delivery of microwave communication service. The FCC ruled in favor of allowing the private use of microwave communication facilities.[14]

MCI and Competitive Challengers

One of the beneficiaries of that decision was a small start-up company called Microwave Communications Inc. (MCI). In 1972, MCI established the first in a series of private microwave links that began with the cities of St. Louis and Chicago. In its 1968 filing, MCI claimed that its intended users represented a market that was not being adequately served by AT&T. The proposed MCI St. Louis to Chicago microwave link was designed for low-volume users who needed communication services for short periods of time. The MCI service was cheaper than AT&T's tariffed rates, since users would have to supply their own distribution links at both ends. In effect, MCI was proposing to offer its customers a bypass solution, that is, an alternative (albeit private) approach to information delivery.[15] By the end of 1973, MCI had established an $80 million coast-to-coast network servicing 40 U.S. cities.[16] Southern Pacific Communications (later to be named Sprint) would soon follow with a second coast-to-coast network.

The senior management of AT&T was clearly disturbed by the incursion into their market. In their view, competitors like MCI and Sprint would undermine the company's ability to offer universal service at an affordable rate. It was also in violation of the Kingsbury Agreement dating back to 1913 that effectively gave AT&T a government-sanctioned monopoly in the provision of voice communication service.[17] AT&T took the position that such private carriers as MCI have the ability to creamskim, that is, to go after the "desirable" high-traffic routes without assuming any obligation to serve the less desirable low-traffic routes. This, according to AT&T, would destabilize the company's commitment to universal service and result in higher prices for everyone.[18] AT&T's senior management further argued that the attachment of non-Bell equipment to the network would eventually degrade the quality of the network. As AT&T president William Ellinghouse later commented, "we've got the worst of all worlds. We're regulated, but we have to compete too."[19]

Not everyone saw it that way. MCI took the position that it was offering business customers alternative choice and cost-effective solutions that were previously unavailable to them resulting from the grand monopoly system imposed on them by AT&T and the U.S. government. Companies like MCI and Sprint soon felt the effects of the AT&T colossus, including predatory pricing, restrictive tariffs, enormous legal filings before the courts, and placing restrictions on common carrier access to the local network. In 1974, MCI filed a suit against AT&T

claiming that the Bell System had engaged in a variety of anticompetitive practices. Between 1968 and 1974, no fewer than 35 private antitrust suits were filed against AT&T.

The Promise of Enhanced Information Services

In the early 1970s, there was beginning to be much public talk about the dawning of a new information age, one in which the nation's telephone network could offer users a variety of enhanced information services. From AT&T's perspective, the Bell System was in a perfect position to offer many of these kinds of services. The restrictions from the 1956 consent decree, however, precluded AT&T from offering anything but traditional telephone service. Clearly, the management at AT&T began to chafe under the now-onerous restrictions of the 1956 consent decree. AT&T sought legislation that would relax restrictions that had prevented the company from entering into new lines of communication service. These developments raised significant issues of public policy regarding the appropriate boundary lines between regulated "voice telephony" and unregulated competitive enhanced information services.[20]

United States v. American Telephone and Telegraph Company

In 1974, officials at the U.S. Justice Department began to take a look at a private antitrust suit that was filed against AT&T by MCI and several other companies. In November 1974, the Justice Department superseded all private litigation by initiating its own legal suit against AT&T in what would become the largest civil lawsuit in U.S. history. The plaintiff was the U.S., and the defendant was the largest corporation in the world. At issue was the future of competitive telecommunications services in the U.S. Unlike many lawsuits, this one would have no clearly defined heroes and villains. As writer Trudy Bell points out, "The suit was as much a clash between the fundamentally opposing social philosophies of laissez-faire economics and corporate stewardship of the public interest as it was about violation of antitrust laws."[21]

Between 1974 and 1980, the U.S. Justice Department and AT&T went through a discovery phase in which both sides gathered documents. There had been a few unsuccessful attempts to settle the case out of court. The premise behind the lawsuit was simple. The Justice Department alleged that AT&T monopolized the business of long-distance telephony by exploiting its control over the local exchange market. In short, AT&T made it difficult for other long-distance carriers to interconnect with the company-owned local exchange carriers. The Justice Department further alleged that, since Western Electric was the primary supplier of telecommunications equipment for the Bell

System, it too was engaged in restricting competition from other manu-facturers and suppliers of customer premises equipment. In short, AT&T allegedly denied the benefits of a free and competitive marketplace to the purchasers of telecommunications equipment.[22]

The trial itself was an intense human drama. Many observers agree that the outcome may have been determined as much by individual personalities as by evidence and legal precedent. As in most govern-ment civil suit cases, the relief being sought was not punishment for past deeds but rather a preventative cure from all future violations. Federal District Judge Harold H. Green was assigned as chief judge. In July 1981, AT&T submitted a 500-page brief moving for dismissal of the case on the ground that the plaintiff had not made its case. Judge Green, however, had no intention of dropping the case and denied the motion to dismiss the case. According to George Saunders, chief trial lawyer for AT&T, "Before AT&T even put in any evidence, we knew we were confronted with a judge who wasn't hearing our side of our case. That was the concern."

United States v. AT&T required the company to devote some 3,000 people to the case, not to mention the time required of major corporate officials who had to prepare testimony. By the time the case was com-plete, it was estimated that some 7 million documents were entered into evidence by both the government and AT&T. In the meantime, AT&T was facing a barrage of other lawsuits at the rate of one every four months by such plaintiffs as ITT and Litton Industries. The ongoing litigation was draining company resources. It was at this point that AT&T CEO Charles Brown was faced with three options: 1) submit to an onerous injunctive decree and keep the company intact (similar to the 1956 consent decree); 2) appeal the probable verdict and fight the litigation, which might take years; or 3) accept the proposed divestiture in exchange for being released from the 1956 consent decree.[23] According to Howard Trienens, general counsel to AT&T, "even if we won the case, we would be tied up with information flow restrictions and not freed from the 1956 consent decree."[24] There was also the question of techno-logical inevitability. Going forward, the decades of the 1980s and 1990s looked to be a period of rapid business growth and technological change. It is questionable whether the existent AT&T monopoly structure could have withstood the communication demands of large corporate users.

The trial was recessed for the holidays with the plan that it would be resumed after the New Year. It was at this point that several initiatives were put forth by the Justice Department to settle out of court. Much to everyone's surprise, the management at AT&T showed a willingness to accept in principle (with some modifications) the terms put forth by the Justice Department. By December 31, Assistant Attorney

General William Baxter felt that an agreement on both sides was close enough for him to make a general announcement that negotiations were underway.

The Modification of Final Judgment (MFJ)

Judge Green was alerted to the proposed settlement in early January, and it took the next eight months with continued modifications before an agreement was finally signed on August 11, 1982. The settlement, less than nine pages long, became the Modification of Final Judgment (MFJ), the title referring to the fact that it modified the consent decree of 1956. Divestiture would effectively take place as of January 1, 1984.

Under the terms of the agreement, AT&T would spin off its 22 Bell Operating Companies in exchange for being released from the 1956 consent decree.[25] AT&T would retain AT&T Communications (long-distance communication), Bell Laboratories (research and development) and the right to enter into new information technologies and services. The latter would be called AT&T Information Systems. The 22 Bell Operating Companies (BOCs) would become the nation's primary suppliers of local telephone service. The 22 BOCs would be reorganized into seven regional holding companies, as noted in Table 5.3.

The Consequences

Did AT&T have to accept the Justice Department's proposal for full divestiture? According to Gerald A. Connell, chief trial lawyer for the Justice Department, "My guess is that Green would have entered a decree that would have had a lot of injunctions for giving competitors equal access to the network."[26] According to Sterling, Bernt and Weiss, the decision to divest was prompted by a realization that, given the regulatory and legislative restrictions that the company would have been placed under even if AT&T had won the case, the future of the company would have been much more bleak than in accepting divestiture.[27]

In the final analysis, this case was as much about differences in

Table 5.3 The Seven Regional Holding Companies post Divestiture (1984)

1 NYNEX
2 Bell Atlantic
3 Bell South
4 Ameritech
5 Southwestern Bell
6 US West
7 Pacific Telesis

economic philosophy (and the future of telecommunications) as it was about the alleged activities of the Bell System. The breakup of AT&T (and the subsequent competition that followed) ushered in a whole new era in telecommunication products and services for business and residential consumers, including: 1) customer-owned telephone sets, 2) facsimile, 3) caller ID and voicemail, 4) cellular and PCS telephony, 5) the Internet, 6) electronic mail and 7) videoconferencing.

The AT&T divestiture may well be considered the latter-day shot heard round the world. The events surrounding the AT&T breakup sent a loud and clear message to the world's PT&T entities that government-protected monopolies were a thing of the past and that global competition in the field of telecommunications had arrived. It would prove to be an altogether new and unfamiliar world for companies like British Telecom, NTT and Deutsche Telekom, to name only a few, that were used to government subsidies and whose financial and technical performance was never fully tested by the marketplace. In the new deregulated and privatized world of telecommunications, such companies would be expected to become technically competitive and self-sufficient. Nearly a quarter-century has transpired since the breakup of the old AT&T, but the effects of divestiture are still being felt today.

6

TELEPHONY

The Telephone Industry Structure

The telephone industry reaches nearly 95.1 percent of all U.S. homes and touches virtually all phases of U.S. consumer and business activity. The term *common carrier* is used to describe those companies engaged in the business of message delivery on a point-to-point or point-to-multipoint basis. Common carriers offer their service on a nondiscriminatory basis to anyone who is willing to pay for it. In principle, they do not interfere with the content of the message. Common carriers are regulated by appropriate state or federal agencies.

Prior to 1984, approximately 80 percent of the public switched telephone network in the U.S. was part of AT&T (or the Bell System of communication). As a monopoly, AT&T was a full-service provider and handled all aspects of the telephone call. As a result of the divestiture agreement (see Chapter 5) there were essentially two types of wireline carriers in the U.S., local exchange carriers (LECs) and interexchange carriers (IXCs) or long-distance carriers. Today, there is no longer the formal distinction between local and long-distance telephone service providers. The combination of changing market conditions (i.e., mergers and acquisitions and cross-media ownership) and advancement in telephone communication technology (cellular telephony, the Internet, Voice Over Internet Protocol, etc.) has eroded the once formal distinction.

Local Exchange Carrier (LEC)

The local exchange carrier (LEC) is the telephone company that provides local and long-distance telephone communication. The LEC is responsible for telephone service provision, network management, customer service and billing. In addition, the LEC provides the basic gateway to the national and international systems of telephone communication. The LEC also provides enhanced information services such as caller identification (caller ID), high-speed Internet access (DSL) and high-speed data lines (T1–T4) as well as

SONET fiber optic carriage. Several of the more notable U.S. LECs include Verizon, AT&T and Qwest Communications. The term *ILEC* (incumbent LEC) is sometimes used to describe the traditional Regional Bell Operating Companies.

The local exchange market also consists of competitive local exchange carriers (CLECs, pronounced *see-leks*). CLECs are telephone companies that directly compete with the traditional Regional Bell Operating Companies. CLECs will sometimes operate their own network, but are often resellers of a telephone service; that is, they purchase traditional telephone service at wholesale levels and then turn around and resell it to the public at discounted rates. Examples of CLECs include companies like Frontier and Covad Communications. Being a reseller saves the CLEC from having to invest in telephone networking equipment, including switches, fiber optic cable, pole attachments, etc.

Regional Bell Operating Companies

As a consequence of the AT&T divestiture in 1984, the original 22 Bell Operating Companies responsible for local telephone service were spun off and reorganized under seven Regional Bell Operating Companies (RBOCs). The original seven RBOCs were identified in Chapter 5 as 1) NYNEX, 2) Bell Atlantic, 3) Bell South, 4) Ameritech, 5) Southwestern Bell, 6) US West, and 7) Pacific Telesis.

LEC Merger and Consolidation

Today, there are three RBOCs compared to the original seven in 1984. This can be seen in Table 6.1. In the years following the breakup of AT&T, Southwestern Bell Corporation (SBC) acquired both Pacific Telesis (1997)

Table 6.1 Telephone Communication in the United States

1984	200X
1 NYNEX	1 AT&T (formerly SBC):
2 Bell Atlantic	—Pacific Telesis
3 Bell South	—Ameritech
4 Ameritech	—AT&T (IXC)
5 Southwestern Bell	—Southern Bell
6 U.S. West	2 Verizon (formerly Bell Atlantic):
7 Pacific Telesis	—NYNEX
	—GTE
	—MCI (IXC)
	3 Qwest Communications:
	—acquired US West

139

and Ameritech (1999). The company acquired long-distance carrier AT&T for $16.9 billion in 2005, and the combined entity was renamed AT&T in 2006. In late 2006, AT&T acquired Bell South Communication for $67 billion. The combined set of services now operate under the AT&T brand. Similarly, Bell Atlantic acquired NYNEX Corporation (1996) and independent telephone company GTE (1998). The combined company was formally incorporated and renamed Verizon in June 2000. In 2005, Verizon acquired long-distance carrier MCI for $8.5 billion.

Telephony: System Overview

Telephony (or telephone communication) is the science of converting voice, data or video information into electrical signals which can be transmitted over physical wire or through the air on a point-to-point or point-to-multipoint basis. Telephony is a system of communication that consists of two basic parts, including the telephone handset and box (or terminal equipment) and the physical network.

Telephone Handset and Box

The telephone handset functions as a transmitter and receiver. The telephone handset is the instrument that is held up to the mouth and ear. The transmitter is the end spoken into. It changes the human voice (or acoustic sound waves) into electrical signals that are transmitted via wire to the called party.[1] The receiver performs the inverse operation of the transmitter; that is, it changes the electrical signal back into human voice (or acoustic sound waves).[2]

The telephone box houses the electrical circuitry that performs several important functions, including equalization. This is the method by which signal strength coming into the telephone set is kept constant regardless of the distance traveled. The telephone box also contains the *hook switch*, which serves as the on/off switch of the telephone. When the phone is turned on (or the handset is lifted off the cradle), the telephone box activates a set of relays to the LEC's central office switch indicating that the user wishes to place a call. The central office switch, in turn, activates the dial tone, letting the user know that the call can be placed. A third important function of the telephone box is the ringer, which notifies the user of an incoming call.[3]

The Importance of Touchtone

Traditional telephone service to the home is considered a narrowband medium, that is, one channel with a limited bandwidth allocation. U.S. telephone companies allocate 4 KHz of bandwidth for a standard voice channel. Starting in the mid-1970s, one important innovation was the development of dual-tone multifrequency capability (or touchtone). Instead of a rotary dial, touchtone generates bursts of audible tones. Each numeric (or function) key consists of two frequencies (Figure 6.1).[4] What is most important, however, is that touchtone provides the basis for interactive capability with a host telephone system or computer. Such two-way capability means that users can access information by encoding information via their telephone handset.

High Group Frequencies (Hertz)

	1209	1336	1477
697	1	ABC 2	DEF 3
770	GHI 4	JKL 5	MNO 6
852	PRS 7	TUV 8	WXY 9
941	*	OPER 0	#

Low Group Frequencies (Hertz)

Figure 6.1 Dual-Tone Multifrequency (Touchtone) Display.

Telephone Switching and Routing

Telephone switching and routing are the combined activities of connecting and routing phone calls. The traditional telephone system of communication is designed as a circuit switched (or line switched) network. The phone call goes from the subscriber's telephone over telephone lines to a central office (CO) switch maintained by the LEC. When a telephone call is placed, the CO master switch automatically locates a circuit before putting the call through. The speaking parties stay connected on that line until the phone call is complete.

Local Loop

The term *local loop* is used to describe the connection between a residence or business and the LEC's central office (Figure 6.2).

Telephone Lines to the Home

The phone lines coming into a house typically consist of a twisted pair of copper wires, one for incoming, the other for outgoing communication (Figure 6.3). It is twisted to reduce crosstalk (or induction) between adjacent lines. The more twists per foot, the better the reduction in crosstalk. As a

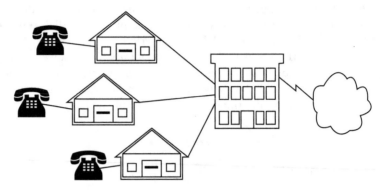

Figure 6.2 The LEC and Local Loop.

Figure 6.3 Twisted Copper Pair to the Home.

narrowband medium, twisted copper pair is the most technically limited in terms of information-carrying capacity. It is sufficient to carry acceptable voice conversations and computer data over a short distance of a few miles. Beyond this distance, the bandwidth capability is severely diminished. The traditional copper pair of lines, however, is steadily giving way to fiber optic cable to the home in order to accommodate high-speed Internet access and other enhanced information services, such as television.

Star Network Design

When engineers discuss the topology of a network, they are describing how the physical parts of the network are configured. Telephony utilizes what is called a star network configuration. Every terminal in the star can be connected to every other terminal through a central switch. Each terminal can transmit and receive information (Figure 6.4).[5]

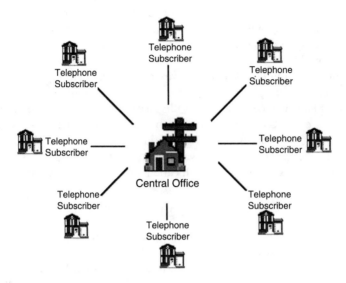

Figure 6.4 The LEC and Local Loop.

Illustration: Chan, Chin Bong.

Class 5 Telephone Switch

Today's telephone network utilizes a Class 5 telephone switch. The Class 5 telephone switch is located at the LEC's end office and performs several functions. They include:

1 detecting when a user wants to make a phone call;
2 establishing the connection and route between the two parties (i.e., defining the nature of the circuit to be used, including SS7 interface);
3 ringing the called party;
4 detecting when the call is complete;
5 billing information and record keeping;
6 network diagnostic functions.

If the call is outside the local exchange area, the Class 5 switch will send the call over a series of trunk lines that is routed to the intended LEC and its switching center.

Public Switched Telephone Network

The public switched telephone network (PSTN) represents the complex web of national and international common carriers, switching facilities and electronic pathways that makes voice and data communication possible for business and residential users. The original telephone system of communication was designed as a circuit switched network. In practice, the phone call goes from the subscriber's telephone over telephone lines to the Class 5 telephone switch located at the LEC's end office. When a telephone call is placed, the master switch automatically coordinates a temporary circuit before putting the call through. The speaking parties stay connected on that line until the phone call is complete. Prior to the AT&T divestiture (1984), the U.S. telephone network was organized into classes numbered 1–5, with Class 5 assigned to the LEC end office. Classes 1–4 were designated as toll centers (Figure 6.5).[6] The nation's telephone network was connected to the international set of telephone networks through a switch called an international gateway.

LATA

After divestiture, the geographical service areas were redrawn according to a U.S. Justice Department designation called local access transport areas (LATAs). The 146 LATAs were smaller than the original Bell telephone service areas. The LECs further divided each LATA into local and toll market calls. The toll market was considered a long-distance call and was hence more expensive. Calls placed between LATAs were considered interLATA and had to be carried by a long-distance carrier.[7] The principle of Dial 1 was established as a way to ensure equal access for all would-be long-distance carriers. Dial 1 is a software protocol that tells the LEC switch which carrier is responsible for executing the long-distance call.[8]

Digital Switching Technology

Since 1984, the combination of competitive telephone services and advancements in digital switching technology has allowed many of the switching levels previously described to be combined. Today's PSTN consists of fewer levels, consolidating many of the functions of the old Bell telephone switching hierarchy into two layers: Class 5 and Class 4 (toll offices). Long distance is accomplished through a point-of-presence (POP) connection to each LEC end office (EO). It serves as an interface point between the long-distance carrier and the LEC in the provision of long-distance service (Figure 6.6). Point of presence is also a location and access point to the Internet. It houses servers, routers and ATM switches, as well as digital/analog call aggregators.

In the years following the AT&T divestiture, several major developments have altered the basic design and operation of the modern telephone network, including advancements in digital switching, improvements in modern signaling systems and the introduction of fiber optic technology.[9] While the basic architecture of the PSTN remains largely circuit switched, the network is controlled digitally, thus permitting voice and data signals to be transferred digitally within the network.[10] Over time, the digitization of the network

144

- The international gateway provided access to the international telephone network(s) for purposes of voice and data communication.

- The *Class 1* (regional) center provided access to regional toll areas as well as the international gateway.

- The *Class 2* (sectional) office provided access to the regional center. Only two routes were available at this level; one to its peer in the destination calling area and one to the Class 1 regional office.

- The *Class 3* (primary) office supported calls placed within the same state or adjacent geographic area. It also served as an overflow switching center.

- The *Class 4* (toll) office allowed the Bell System to aggregate its facilities and use high-capacity trunk lines in order to interconnect with other Class 4 offices. A call sent between two end offices (that were not connected together) would be routed through a Class 4 toll office.

- The *Class 5* (end office) switch is maintained by the LEC and provides local telephone service to the end user.

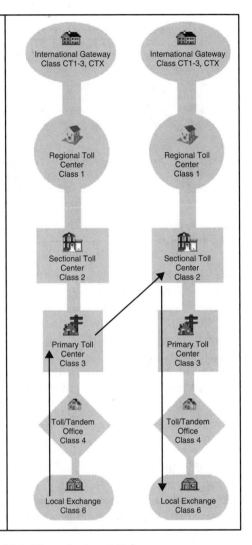

Figure 6.5 The U.S. Telephone Switching Hierarchy (pre-1984).

has evolved to a more general-purpose computing platform (including out-of-band signaling) which provides the basis for packet switching and Internet data transport.

Out-of-Band Signaling

Out-of-band signaling is a technique whereby the call set-up and management do not take place over the same path as the conversation. A circuit switched

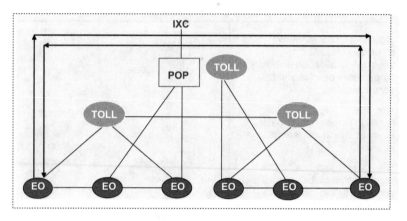

Figure 6.6 Consolidating Switching Centers: Three-Layer Network Hierarchy.

Source: R. Gershon.

call, for example, is considered in-band; that is, we hear the dial tone, dial digits and ringing over the same channel on the same pair of wires. When the call is established, we talk over the same path that was used for the signaling. In contrast, out-of-band signaling establishes a separate digital channel for the exchange of signaling information. This channel is called a signaling link. Signaling links are used to carry all the necessary signaling information between nodes, including the dialed digits, trunk selected, and other pertinent information, rather than the trunk lines which will ultimately carry the phone call.[11]

Signaling System 7 Network

Starting in the late 1970s, AT&T began to implement a new signaling and control system, referred to as Common Channel Signaling 7 (CCS7).[12] The CCS7 made use of a separate out-of-band signaling approach in which the signaling and supervisory information associated with the call set-up was different than the actual conversation path. This, in turn, led to the establishment of the Signaling System 7 (SS7) call processing standards later adopted by the International Telecommunications Union (ITU). Today, the SS7 telephone protocols define the basic procedures for the set-up, management and completion of a call between telephone users.[13] The SS7 telephone protocols are used to complete the vast majority of the world's PSTN calls. All public telephone networks are required to have an SS7 connection.

Specifically, SS7 is a set of global standards prescribed by the ITU that defines the procedures and protocols by which network elements in the public switched telephone network organize and coordinate digital signaling

- *Signal switching points (SSPs):* SSPs are telephone switches (end offices or tandems) equipped with SS7-capable software and terminating signaling links. The SSPs perform call processing; that is, basic call set-up, management and teardown of calls.

- *Signal transfer points (STPs):* STPs are the packet switches of the SS7 network. They essentially act as message routers. They receive and route incoming signaling messages towards the proper destination.

- *Signal control points (SCPs):* SCPs are databases that provide information necessary for advanced call processing capabilities (i.e., 911 emergency, toll-free 800 telephone calls, etc.).

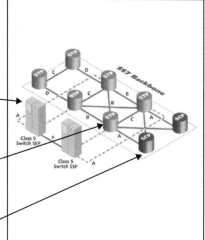

Figure 6.7 Signaling System No. 7 (SS7) Network Design.

Source: Adapted from Steven Shepard, *Telecom Crash Course* (New York: McGraw-Hill, 2002), 147.

information involving call set-up, control, network management and network maintenance. The SS7 call processing standards address several important network elements, including:

1   the basic call set-up, management and teardown;
2   the basic interface to wireless services such as personal communications services, wireless roaming, and mobile subscriber authentication;
3   network add-on features such as toll-free numbers (800/888), prepaid telephone calls and emergency communication (911, etc.);
4   enhanced call features such as call forwarding, calling party name/ number display, and three-way calling;
5   local number portability (LNP);
6   international network security;
7   network diagnostics and maintenance.

The SS7 network consists of a number of switches and application processors interconnected by transmission circuits. An SS7 network has three distinct components, as shown in Figure 6.7.

Packet Switching

Packet switching represents the ability to take a digital communication message and divide it into equal-sized packets of information. The said packets are then sent individually through the network to their destination, where the entire message is reassembled after all the packets arrive. The principle of packet switching was first developed by electrical engineer Paul Baran in the early 1960s while working for the RAND Corporation. He was asked to perform an investigation into survivable communications networks for the U.S. Air Force. Further development of packet switching technology was continued through the work of Donald Davies and Leonard Kleinrock, who did early research in the area of digital message switching as part of their work on the ARPANet (see Chapter 8), the world's first packet switching network and forerunner of the Internet.

Today, packet switching dominates data networks like the Internet. An e-mail message or VOIP telephone call from San Francisco to New York is handled much differently than with circuit switching. In a circuit switched network, digital data go directly to the receiver in an orderly fashion, one after another on a single track. The main disadvantage of a circuit switched call is that only one set of users can communicate over the circuit at one time. With packet switching, system routers determine a path for each packet on the fly, dynamically, ordering them about to use any route available to get to the destination (Figure 6.8). Other packets from other calls race upon these circuits as well, making the most use of each track or path, quite unlike the circuit switched telephone call that occupies a single path to the exclusion of all others.

A typical packet length on the Internet is about one kilobyte (or a thousand characters). A large message may be divided into thousands of individual packets. The beginning of a packet is called the "header" and records the following information:

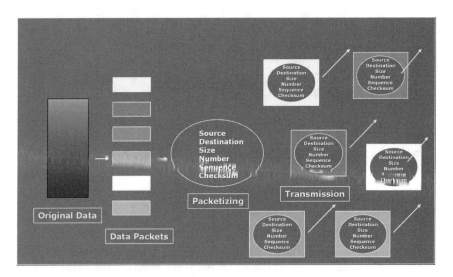

Figure 6.8 Packet Switching Overview.

- *source*—the Internet Protocol (IP) address of the computer sending the packet;
- *destination*—the IP address of the destination computer;
- *size*—the combined length of the header and data packet in bytes;
- *number*—the total number of packets in the complete message;
- *sequence*—the number of this packet in the whole list of packets making up the said communication;
- *checksum*—redundancy check, a measure for assessing the integrity of the received packets being sent.

After getting to their destination point, the individual packets are reassembled in order by a packet assembler. The difference in routing paths practically ensures that packets will arrive at different times. This approach is acceptable when calling up a website or downloading a file, since a short delay is hardly noticed. Delays in packet switching for voice, however, can cause voice quality to suffer and are highly noticeable, as anyone who has talked over the Internet can tell you. A circuit switched call remains the best-sounding call, because information goes in sequence with very little delay. The challenge going forward will be to improve the quality of voice over "packet switched" Internet Protocol telephone communication. For this reason, telephone carriers do not use the general Internet to route VOIP calls. Instead, they build specialized packet switched networks dedicated for this purpose. VOIP calls over such networks are fast becoming the near equal of circuit switched calls.

Transmission

Transmission is concerned with the ability to move information from one location to another. Transmission includes both the method of signal carriage (modulation and multiplexing schemes) and the physical pathways used to complete an end-to-end communication link.

The Telephone Number

In order for telephone calls to reach their proper destination, subscribers must have telephone numbers that are both unique and recognizable by all switches in the public network. The assigning of a worldwide telephone numbering plan is accomplished under the auspices of the International Telecommunications Union (ITU) and the International Telegraph and Telephone Consultative Committee (CCITT), which handles telephony matters. In the U.S. and Canada, the North American Numbering Plan (NANP) is implemented by the North American Numbering Plan Administration, a private group overseen by the FCC. The actual assignment of telephone numbers falls to the major LEC within a geographic service area.

The telephone number provides a numerical address for all telephone users. The NANP is a nationally and internationally accepted standard for the switching and routing of telephone calls. The standard telephone number consists of four parts, including:

010	Country code
269	Numbering plan area (or area code)
387	Local exchange prefix (or central office code)
6160	Individual subscriber line (or telephone address)

Fiber Optics

Optical fiber is thin strands of extremely pure glass capable of transmitting large quantities of information over long distances with little signal loss.[14] Starting in the early 1980s, America's IXCs began installing fiber optic communication lines on high-traffic, long-haul routes, thus replacing microwave radio transmission systems. Today, fiber optic transmission is responsible for the vast majority of interexchange telephone traffic. In a matter of two decades, fiber optics has come to the forefront of communication technology. Fiber optic communication is primarily used in three distinct communication environments: 1) long-haul "interexchange" telephone communication, 2) local area networks for data distribution and 3) in combination with coaxial cable to serve as the backbone for modern cable television systems in a configuration referred to as hybrid fiber–coax. The fiber optic portion of the network extends the cable signal from the system head-end point along the main trunk lines to a junction box where it connects to coaxial cable for distribution into people's homes and businesses.

Fiber optics uses light as a method for encoding a transmitted signal. A standard fiber optic link consists of three parts, including: a light source, optical fiber as the primary transmission medium, and a transducer (receiver/detector). The light source is a light-emitting diode (LED) or an injection-laser diode (ILD) laser. The LED modulates an incoming electrical signal into an optical one, which is then transmitted down the line.[15] The optical fiber consists of two layers of different types of glass, surrounded by a protective acrylate coating. The two layers are the core and the cladding. The light is guided through the core region, where it is detected at the receiving point.[16] At the receiving end, the transducer converts the optical signal back into an electrical signal (Figure 6.9). The electronic information is then ready for input into electronic-based communication devices, such as a computer, telephone or television set.

There are two basic types of optical fiber. They are single-mode and multi-mode fiber. The main challenge in deploying optical fiber is the ability to maintain an accurate signal over distance without signal loss (i.e., attenuation). Part of the problem has to do with the fact that optical fiber does not

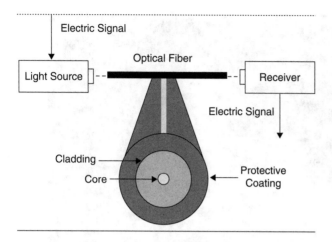

Figure 6.9 Fiber Optics Transmission Path.

transmit all wavelengths of light with the same level of efficiency. The attenuation of light signals is much higher for visible light than for light in the near infrared region. There are two key factors in determining which fiber type to use for a given application: 1) distance and 2) bandwidth.

Single-Mode Fiber

Because of the small physical core diameter of a single-mode fiber, only one ray of light propagates at the desired operating wavelength. With only one mode, it is easier to maintain the precision and integrity of each light pulse than with multiple modes. Single-mode fiber is best suited for long-distance telephone trunk lines as well as applications that require extremely high bandwidth such as cable television. Single-mode fiber has a narrower core diameter, generally 8–10 microns, with a 125-micron cladding (Figure 6.10).[17]

Multimode Fiber

A multimode fiber allows more than one ray (mode) of light, usually hundreds, to propagate at the operating wavelength. The larger the multimode fiber core diameter, the higher the number of modes propagating through the fiber. Multimode fiber is best suited for short-distance applications such as local area networks (LANS) or campus environments where transmission distances are between three and five miles and can accommodate multiple splices or connectors.[18] Multimode fiber has a larger core diameter, generally 62.5 microns, with a 125-micron cladding.

Let us consider for a moment what are some of the distinct advantages that fiber optics offers when compared to other transmission media (Figure 6.10):

Single-Mode

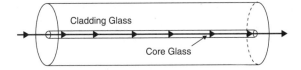

Multimode

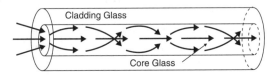

Figure 6.10 Comparison of Single-Mode and Multimode Fiber.

- *Broad bandwidth capability:* Fiber optic systems offer users more potential bandwidth than any other type of transmission medium. An actual fiber strand is a few microns wide in diameter, or the equivalent of 6/1000s of an inch thick. When bundled together in a duct or passageway, the combined bandwidth provides more than sufficient capacity for most voice, data and video applications. Moreover, it allows for expanded growth as information needs change. Consider that a conventional 3-inch-thick telephone trunk cable contains approximately 1,200 pairs of copper wires, which is the equivalent of 14,400 telephone conversations. By comparison, a 1/2-inch-thick fiber trunk cable contains approximately 72 pairs of fiber, which is the equivalent of 3.5 million telephone conversations.

- *Immunity from electromagnetic noise and interference:* Fiber is not susceptible to electromagnetic interference and radio frequency interference (RFI) as compared to twisted wire pairs, coaxial cable and satellite. It is durable, nonflammable and resistant to extremes in temperature. Fiber's durability becomes particularly important when it comes to cable routing, since it is likely to be placed in some rather harsh and noisy environments. Its light weight and flexibility make it ideally suited for placement in such conduits as subway routes or elevator shafts, or to be aerially placed above a railroad track or positioned beneath a street. Moreover, it can be used in select environments where corrosive chemicals are used.

- *Speed and reliability:* Today's single-mode fiber using SONET standards can achieve transmission speeds for voice and data traffic ranging between 5 and 10 Gbps.[19] Alternatively, today's multimode fiber can achieve speeds ranging between 600 Mbit/s and 2.4 Gbit/s depending on the size and thickness of the multimode fiber.[20] In addition to high-speed transmission, fiber optics is capable of achieving high levels of accuracy. Refinements in the manufacturing process have enhanced fiber's ability to transmit light considerable distances with minimal signal loss. Lower attenuation rates allow for greater spacing between repeaters across the communications link. Fiber optics is the transmission method of choice for long-distance communication.

- *Security:* Since fiber optic cable emits no radiation, it is virtually impossible to intercept the signal transmission without immediate detection. Moreover, a break in a fiber optic cable can be easily located to within a few inches, thus assuring security and maintenance of the system.

- *Cost:* Fiber compares favorably with other transmission media in terms of cost. Unlike copper, which is a costly depleting resource, fiber's primary composition is sand, one of the most abundant resources on earth. This, coupled with improved manufacturing techniques, has led to a significant decrease in production costs. In addition, fiber optic cable is more flexible and lightweight when compared with traditional coaxial cable. The latter is heavier and occupies more space, which in turn requires more duct work and takes longer to install. As an example, 15 pounds of fiber optic cable is the equivalent of 100 pounds of coaxial cable.

T1 (DS1) Transmission Lines

The volume of information can pose a problem for some communication systems since they may not have sufficient channel capacity to transmit the information. Thus, special telephone lines need to be installed to handle the large data flow. The T1 line developed by AT&T in the 1960s is one of several industry standards for high-speed digital communication. A more concise term is DS1. In a T1 line, digitized voice channels are multiplexed in groups of 24, requiring an aggregate of 1.544 Mbps of transmission bandwidth. It is also flexible enough to integrate voice, data and video communication. Since 1980, the leasing of T1 service has become a standard telephone service offering to prospective clients. T1 often provides more capacity than most users need. Therefore, effective management presupposes the use of a T1 TDM multiplexer that will divide the T1 bandwidth into slower speeds that are compatible with regular communication and data processing applications. A standard digital voice channel operates at 64 Kbps. T3 (or DS3) operates at 44.736 Mbps and operates with a channel capacity of 672 voice channels (Table 6.2). T-carrier is now being replaced by SONET, a digital fiber optic transport standard used worldwide.

Table 6.2 North American Digital Transmission Hierarchy

Digital Signal	Bandwidth	Channels	Carrier Designation
DS	64 Kbps	1 channel	None
DS1	1.54 Mbps	24 channels	T1
DS2	6.312 Mbps	96 channels	T2
DS3	44.736 Mbps	672 channels	T3
DS4	274.176 Mbps	4,032 channels	T4

Optical carrier (OC) levels describe a range of digital signals that can be carried on a SONET-based fiber optic network. The number in optical carrier level is directly proportional to the data rate of the bit stream carried by the digital signal. The main SONET optical carrier levels can be seen in Table 6.3.

Table 6.3 SONET Optical Carrier Level and Transmission Speeds

Digital Signal Optical Carrier Level	Transmission Speed
OC-1	51.84 Mbps
OC-3	155.52 Mbps
OC-12	622.08 Mbps
OC-192*	953.28 Mbps

* OC-192 connections are the most common for use on the backbones of large ISPs.

Telephone Management and Service Provision

The telephone has become so ubiquitous in our everyday lives that we take it for granted. We don't pay much attention until it doesn't work. Owning a telephone has become a right. People expect good telephone service and it's the LEC's job to give it to them. Rarely do people think about their telephone service when it works correctly, but they feel very inconvenienced when it does not work. LEC telephone service requests fall into five general categories, as shown in Table 6.4.

Basic Telephone Service

Today, basic telephone service includes both local and long-distance telephone communications. All of the major local exchange carriers (LECs) offer combined local and long-distance telephone service packages for a flat rate. Basic telephone service is also offered by competitive local exchange carriers (CLECs), which effectively are sellers of basic telephone service at a discounted rate from an incumbent local exchange carrier (ILEC). The one difference, of course, is that CLECs are not necessarily able to offer enhanced information services such as high-speed Internet access, since that is considered an information rather than a telephone service. Cellular telephone carriers are also in the business of providing basic telephone service, and this is the subject of Chapter 8. For many consumers, especially young working professionals and students, the cell phone (i.e., wireless) approach represents their one and only telephone. Depending on the service plan, basic telephone service can include a number of value-added features that were once considered extra, including caller ID, voicemail, differences in handset design, etc.

Enhanced Information Services

As telecommunications requirements become more complex, both residential and business customers are willing and able to spend more of their discretionary income on enhanced information services. Enhanced information services represent the high-growth portion of the LEC's business. The advent of digital subscriber line (DSL, i.e., high-speed Internet access), Voice Over Internet Protocol (VOIP) and emerging Internet Protocol Television (IPTV) has redefined, and will continue to redefine, the business of telephone

Table 6.4 General Categories of Telephone Service Requests

1   Basic telephone service:
     —local and distance.
2   Enhanced information services:
     —facsimile;
     —high-speed Internet access;
     —Voice Over Internet Protocol (VOIP);
     —Internet Protocol Television (IPTV);
     —desktop video.
3   Information about billing.
4   Telephone maintenance and repair.
5   Request for small business consulting.

Table 6.5 LEC Enhanced Information Services

Custom Calling Features	Equipment and Services
Caller identification (caller ID).	Digital subscriber line (DSL):
Voicemail.	—high-speed Internet access.
Call forwarding.	Voice Over Internet Protocol (VOIP).
Caller ID blocking options.	Internet Protocol Television (IPTV).
Call return.	Facsimile (fax).
Three-way calling.	Paging services.
Repeat dialing.	Videoconferencing (desktop video).

communications. Table 6.5 divides enhanced telephone services into two basic categories: 1) custom calling features and 2) equipment and services.

Digital Subscriber Line (DSL)

DSL is a high-speed Internet service provided by the local exchange carrier to both residential and business subscribers. Although DSL is technically referred to as asymmetric digital subscriber line, it is actually a subset of a broader group of standards that are referred to as xDSL. DSL is considered asymmetric because a greater amount of bandwidth is allocated for the downloading of information as compared to the uploading portion. The service requires the upgrading of equipment and is carried over unshielded twisted-pair copper lines to the end user. Greater speed and throughput are accomplished by utilizing available bandwidth that operates beyond the regular voice range (i.e., 300 Hz to 3,300 Hz). The user is assigned his/her own dedicated line. DSL operates in a continuous "on state." It should be noted that distance limits between the telephone company switch and the subscriber location can sometimes affect the availability and performance of DSL service offerings.

Today, broadband communication to the home is offered primarily through cable television or DSL in that order. While there are alternative approaches (i.e., Ethernet connections, power utility lines and one-way satellite distribution), none compare with the widespread diffusion of cable television and DSL. According to the DSL Forum, the number of DSL customers has reached over 200 million worldwide, with more than 20 percent living in China.[1]

Voice Over Internet Protocol (VOIP)

Internet telephony (or VOIP) represents the ability to conduct a telephone call via the Internet. The Internet was not originally designed for real-time traffic such as voice and video. In past years, the quality of voice traffic was not good. This has changed dramatically since 2004. Today, the benefits of using IP as a generic platform to support both data and voice communication have started to have far-reaching effects in both the business and the residential sectors. The major reason has to do with cost. The ability to switch and route telephone calls via the Internet using packet switching technology is much less expensive when compared to traditional telephone communication. VOIP telephone calls require a special adaptor which plugs into a high-speed Internet connection. When the user places a call, the adaptor converts the analog signal of the phone call into digital packets which are then sent over the Internet. The call travels via the Internet to a hub location near the call's destination. The hub converts the call back into an analog signal and funnels it into the local phone network. The LEC transmits the call to the phone dialed by the user. Some of the better-known U.S. VOIP companies include Vonage and AT&T CallVantage.

Research consulting group Frost & Sullivan estimate that the consumer VOIP market revenues will reach $4.07 billion by 2010, representing an increase of more than 1,300 percent over the $295.1 million spent in 2005.[22] Further, Frost & Sullivan expect the entry of non-traditional telecommunications companies, including cable operators, Internet service providers (ISPs) and non-telecom companies, into the voice market to drive the number of North American VOIP lines up to 18 million from 1.5 million in the same period. Not surprisingly, ILECs tend to view VOIP as a threat to their market share and revenue. ILECs have lost an estimated 15 million access lines to their non-traditional competitors, though many of these were data lines and second residential lines.[23]

Internet Protocol Television (IPTV)

IPTV is a method for transporting multichannel television over the Internet, hence the term Internet Protocol Television. IPTV relies on the Internet and packet switching technology as the basic platform for video picture and audio delivery. Because electronic information travels at the speed of light, the breaking up and reconstitution of video and audio data are generally not detectable to users. Companies like Verizon and AT&T are heavily investing in IPTV as the basis for entering the broadband video market of the future.

Television programming is received from satellite and local broadcast sources. It is then stored in local nodes, such as the central office of the LEC and called up by users at home. While traditional cable systems devote a slice of bandwidth for each channel and then transmit them all at once, IPTV uses a "switched video" architecture in which only the channel being watched at that moment is sent over the network, freeing up capacity for other features and more interactivity. The principal advantage of IPTV is that it employs a more dynamic bandwidth allocation scheme, thus making it more bandwidth efficient. At the LEC site, the selected channel (i.e., programming content) is

IP encapsulated, that is, converted into a packet format and transmitted. The data then travels across the LEC's fiber optic network to households that have a DSL connection (or fiber to the home) and that subscribe to IPTV. The television programs are distributed to the user's television set over the DSL line, where a set-top box (STB) descrambles the packetized information into a viewable program.

IPTV represents a fundamental shift in terms of how people watch television. Instead of television being one-directional from programmer to consumer (with all its implied programming assumptions), tomorrow's viewers will approach television the way they do the Internet. Television viewing will be a far more interactive experience where traditional television program formats give way to people calling up programs they want to see. Today's DVR technology has already provided the catalyst in terms of giving consumers far more control of program selection and scheduling. IPTV represents a natural progression of that same idea.

Information about Billing

The LEC is responsible for providing its customers with a billing statement once a month breaking down the cost of service. Telephone billing operates as a real-time transaction-based service whereby flat-rate charges, toll charges and enhanced information services must be tabulated and recorded into the customer's telephone bill. The information is automatically processed by the LEC's digital switch and recorded electronically onto a central server. The raw data is later transported over a dedicated link to a regional billing center. The billing center then computes and creates the actual bill for the customer. The information generated in the course of billing can be used for purposes of consumer analysis as well as direct marketing to the customer.

Telephone Maintenance and Repair

It is the LEC's responsibility to ensure that all telephone equipment and communication facilities are operating properly. When there is a power outage (or break in the telephone line) it is the LEC's responsibility to ensure that the problem is corrected within a reasonable amount of time. The correction should be accomplished with the least possible disruption to the existing subscriber base. The importance of maintenance and service cannot be overestimated. It is here that the LEC's credibility and effectiveness are usually judged. To that end, the customer service representative (CSR) is critical in ensuring good customer relations. Most telephone users will never have occasion to go beyond the customer service representative in terms of communicating with the LEC. The issue becomes all the more important as the LEC looks to compete in the area of enhanced information services.

Request for Small Business Consulting

International business has been transformed by the power of instantaneous communication. The combination of computer and telecommunications has collapsed the time and distance factors that once separated nations, people and business organizations. Today's business environment has been transformed by the ability to engage in intelligent networking. The once highly centralized organization has become increasingly decentralized. Levels of organizational hierarchy are giving way to flatter (and more decentralized) organizations. One major consequence of decentralization is that many of today's large corporations are operating with smaller staffs in decentralized locations and/or outsourcing some of their work altogether. The aforementioned business start-ups, in turn, require telecommunications and information technology to support their business operations. The LECs, as well as private companies, now offer small business consulting for the small business start-up.

Telecommunications Consulting for Small Business Operations

Understanding Your Client's Business

As a telecommunications consultant, your first task is to understand what are the unique communication requirements of your client's business. There is no way to properly design a system of communication without knowing the information requirements of that organization.

Questions to consider are:

1   What is the purpose of your client's organization?
2   What determines the success of your client's organization? Is it marketing, finance, education, manufacturing, customer service, etc.?
3   What role does telecommunications play within your client's organization? How can telecommunications be used to promote greater efficiencies?

Evaluating Your Client's Present System of Communication

A second important task is to become familiar with your client's existing system of communication. This includes developing an accurate inventory of telecommunications equipment and services. Consider that many organizations spend thousands of dollars annually on telecommunications equipment and services and seldom conduct an inventory of their system. In short, they have no idea what they are paying for or why.

Identify Costs

As a telecommunications consultant, you have to know how much your client is spending on telecommunications. Monthly and annual expenses can be broken down into three categories: 1) recurring monthly charges, 2) usage charges and measured service and 3) installation, maintenance and other service charges.

Recurring Monthly Charges

Recurring monthly charges are monthly rental charges for equipment and other facilities provided by the phone company and other vendors. This is sometimes referred to as equipment and line charges. Recurring monthly charges can be broken down according to equipment rentals such as Internet broadband access fees, monthly wireless cell phone charges, pager fees, etc. In addition, depending on the nature of the business or organization there may be monthly charges for high-speed telephone and data lines such as T1 and ISDN lines.

Usage Charges and Measured Service

Usage charges and measured service refer to all message unit charges (i.e., text messaging, etc.), toll charges (i.e., international long-distance) and various other specialized vendor services such as three-way calling or group conference calls. Cell phones typically have a number of usage charges attached to a service plan, including text messaging, cell phone picture delivery, etc. It's important to know how much your client spends (or expects to spend) on these various types of service.

Installation and Maintenance Charges

Depending on the complexity of the organization, installation and maintenance charges are the client's total monthly and yearly expenditures for installation equipment, maintenance and servicing of equipment. Most of this information can be analyzed according to your client's phone bills and vendor invoices.

Designing a Future Communication System

In designing a future telecommunications system, the consultant needs to consider what are the communication features and applications that are most critical to the client's business and professional needs. Specifically, what does the client expect to be the real benefits to its operation in terms of productivity, efficiency and cost savings? The new system needs to be scalable whereby it should be designed to accommodate future growth and development.

Consultant or Vendor

Before designing a future communication system, a basic decision will have to be made as to whether the client will work with a consultant, vendor or both. A consultant is a third party with expertise in a particular field that a client hires to assist in designing a telecommunications or information technology system. A vendor is an organization licensed to sell and distribute a specific product or product line (e.g., Nortel, AT&T, 3Com, Avaya, etc.). Some companies offer both services.

The Business Communication Planning Model

The selection of communication technology should offer a wide selection of possibilities based on how much information capability the client wishes the organization (or project team) to have. To that end, it is important to develop a framework for planning and selecting the proper computer and information technology. There are six criteria that should be observed when selecting different information technologies. We will refer to this as the business communication planning model (Table 6.6).

Table 6.6 The Business Communication Planning Model

1 Communication features and applications.
2 Equipment and service costs.
3 Reputation of vendor or service provider.
4 Service and maintenance support.
5 Installation of new equipment and service.
6 Training and development.

Planning model design: R. Gershon.

Communication Features and Applications

In this first category, we ask the question: what are the communication features and applications that are most important to the client's business operations in terms of productivity, efficiency and cost savings? Some clients need an entire system of communication and information technology, whereas others need a specific application. Features and applications break down into a number of subcategories (Table 6.7).

Table 6.7 Communication Features and Applications

Traditional wireline service	Telephone handsets. Telephone switching equipment (PBX, Centrex, etc.). Facsimile (or fax) capability. Voicemail capability. Six- to 12-party audioconferencing capability. Telephone lines coming into the building or residential facility (T1–T2, digital ISDN lines).
Wireless service capability	Cellular telephone equipment (number of units). Cellular text messaging capability. Pagers. Wi-Fi or WiMAX access capability.
Broadband access	High-speed Internet access (DSL, cable, Ethernet, etc.). Electronic mail (e-mail). Specialized information databases (stock quotations, news feeds, etc.). Voice Over Internet Protocol (VOIP) solutions.
Videoconferencing capability	Full-time videoconferencing equipment and room. Occasional videoconferencing capability (lease facilities options). Desktop video capability.
Computer support services	Network installations, security and maintenance: LAN and WAN design and implementation including wireless. NIC card installations, Ethernet cabling installation, hubs, routers, bridges, firewalls, VPN, server set-up and configurations. Associated software set-up and configurations. Hardware support/upgrades: RAM, hard drives, CD/DVD drives, motherboards, modems, sound cards, video cards, USB, firewall, printers, digital cameras, scanners, personal computer systems. Software support/upgrades: Operating systems: Windows XP (Home and Professional), Windows 2003 Small Business Server, Windows 2003 Server, Macintosh OSX. Hardware troubleshooting and repairs: Drives (hard drive, CDR, CDRW, DVD, USB, zip), boot failures, power failures, etc. Software troubleshooting and repairs: System failure troubleshooting, virus and spyware removal, boot problems/failure analysis, unexpected locking problems analysis, hardware failure analysis, general troubleshooting and analysis.

Equipment and Service Costs

The selection of equipment and service provision will depend largely on how the client views the role of computer and information technology. Does the client see telecommunications as a business tool or a controllable expense? In short, what are the client's budgetary constraints? Consider that an investment/brokerage firm, for example, may spend as much as 45 percent of its operating costs on telecommunications. The amount of money devoted to communication and information technology will say a lot about its relative importance to the client's business operations.

Reputation of Vendor or Service Provider

Buying the right equipment from the right vendor is critical from the standpoint of planning. A company that has an established track record in the fields of communication and information technology is important when it comes to quality equipment and software reliability. The client presumably wants to buy this equipment only once. But, equally important, a company with a strong track record will be there to support your client when and if there is a problem or a need to upgrade the existing system of communication.

Customer Service Support

Depending on the equipment and software product, customer service support may be of paramount importance to your client. This is especially true for the person or business operation that has neither the time nor the money to spend on complex service agreements.

Installation of New Equipment and Service

What are the time frame and method for installing and testing out new equipment? This becomes especially important to the client since he/she has the right to expect the project installation to be as unobtrusive as possible. When introducing a new system of equipment, the consultant must allow sufficient time to cut over the new system without disabling the present system. In other words, it must have minimal impact on your client's business as a whole. Depending on the size and complexity of the operation, it may be necessary to design a parallel system that allows for back-up and contingency.

Training and Development

A final consideration is training and development. How easy or difficult will it be for your client and staff to learn the new system? How much training will be needed in order to transition to the new system? Depending upon the complexity of the system, the consultant should be prepared to arrange for the appropriate level of training and development, which can include providing support materials, in-house presentations and/or access to a telephone or Internet support capability to answer all questions during the start-up phase.

Evaluating Different Vendor Proposals

In the design process, the telecommunications consultant is responsible for determining the system requirements. Once the requirements are outlined, they are sent to prospective vendors as a request for proposal (RFP). The vendor identifies (or specs out) the necessary hardware, software, installation, and training costs associated with the project and submits a completed proposal (and cost summary) to the consultant. The consultant, for his/her part, must evaluate the different vendor proposals and balance the competing requirements in selecting the best vendor and proposed set of services. Table 6.8 provides a consulting checklist for evaluating vendor proposals based on the criteria first identified in the business communication planning model. The criteria are typically weighted depending on the project and client requirements. The telecommunications consultant, however, may choose to weigh the criteria differently. The planning model checklist allows the consultant to attach an assigned numeric value for each vendor proposal across six categories that can be totaled and scored and used as a basis for comparison.

Table 6.8 Business Communication Planning Model: A Checklist for Small Business and the Professional User

Selection Criteria	Weight	Vendor A	Vendor B	Vendor C	Vendor D
Communication features and applications	40%				
Equipment and service costs	20%				
Reputation of vendor or service provider	5%				
Customer service support	20%				
Installation of new equipment and service	10%				
Training and development	5%				
Total	100%				

Planning model design: R. Gershon.

Making the Recommendation

As a telecommunications consultant, be prepared to develop a justification to your client explaining the need and intended benefits that will result from implementing the new system of communication. In your analysis and recommendation, your goal is to provide optimum solutions that are cost effective in order to meet your client's present and future needs. As a general rule, organize your client presentation according to the seven criteria listed in Table 6.9.

Though a vendor has been selected to implement the new system, it is still your project! Whether you're a consultant, vendor or both, don't plan on an 8–5 work day. Most telecommunications system installations take place on nights and weekends, many times requiring 12- and 16-hour days. Plan to manage the project throughout and pay close attention to detail. Never assume. After the installation is complete, make sure the client has accepted the project as complete and is satisfied with the outcome. The training and development sequence should be in place. Be ready for several weeks of telephone calls and questions regarding new (or unfamiliar) features of the system. Be ready for follow-up meetings as needed to complete the project installation. In the final analysis, a smooth project installation establishes your credibility as a consultant and is a reflection of your organization.

Table 6.9 Telecommunications Consulting: Seven Criteria for Presentation Analysis

1 Features and applications.
2 Benefits to your client's business operation.
3 The cost of the system.
4 Ease of use.
5 Potential to grow and accommodate future changes (i.e., scalability).
6 Plan for implementation.
7 Customer support, including training and development, maintenance, technical support, etc.

Planning model design: R. Gershon.

Verizon Communications: A Case Study

Verizon Communications Inc. was formed on June 30, 2000, with the merger of Bell Atlantic Corporation and GTE Corporation. The Verizon logo was selected because it graphically illustrates two words: *veritas*, the Latin word connoting certainty and reliability, and *horizon*, signifying forward-looking and visionary. While Verizon is a twenty-first-century company, the mergers that formed Verizon were many years in the making, involving companies with roots that can be traced to the beginnings of the telephone business in the late nineteenth century.

Bell Atlantic and NYNEX

Bell Atlantic and NYNEX were two of the original seven Regional Bell Operating Companies (RBOCs) formed in the aftermath of the AT&T breakup in 1984. Ten years later, Bell Atlantic undertook a major initiative by forming a joint wireless partnership with NYNEX in June 1994. The combined wireless businesses was expected to cover 55 million potential customers along the east coast and in the southwest. The joint venture began operations in July 1995 under the name Bell Atlantic NYNEX Mobil. The Bell Atlantic–NYNEX wireless partnership marked the beginning of what would later become Verizon

Wireless. This partnership also developed into a relationship between the two RBOCs that resulted in an announcement on April 22, 1996, that Bell Atlantic and NYNEX had agreed to merge their entire set of operations in a transaction then valued at $23 billion.

The Bell Atlantic–GTE Merger

In 1984, there were more than 1,400 local phone companies that were not part of the Bell System. These so-called "independent" telephone companies are family-owned businesses or subscriber-owned cooperatives that serve one or more small communities. Many still exist today, primarily in rural areas. The independent telephone industry began in 1893, when Alexander Graham Bell's original patents expired. For those communities wanting telephone service, the creation of independent phone companies provided an alternative solution rather than waiting for the Bell System to deploy its services, which depending on time and location could take years.

GTE represents one of the best known of the original independent telephone companies. Its success was due in large measure to a long history of acquisitions and mergers, beginning with the acquisition of hundreds of small telephone companies. Prior to its merger agreement with Bell Atlantic, GTE was the largest independent telephone company in the U.S., with 1999 revenues of more than $25 billion. GTE owned numerous local telephone properties in such diverse locations as California, Hawaii and Virginia.

GTE had more than 7.1 million wireless customers in the U.S.

Bell Atlantic was even larger than GTE, with 1999 revenues of more than $33 billion. Its domestic telecom unit served 43 million access lines, including 22 million households and more than 2 million business customers. Its global wireless unit managed one of the world's largest and most successful wireless companies, with 7.7 million subscribers. The Bell Atlantic–GTE transaction, valued at more than $52 billion at the time of the announcement, was designed to join Bell Atlantic's sophisticated voice and data network with GTE's national footprint and long-distance expertise. The purpose was to create a combined company with the scale and scope to compete as one of the telecommunications industry's top-tier companies. This combined company would be able to provide local, long-distance and Internet communication nationwide as part of a full package of services.

When Verizon Communications began operations in mid-2000, the leaders of Bell Atlantic and GTE shared management responsibility for the newly combined company. Former GTE chairman and CEO Charles R. "Chuck" Lee became Verizon's founding chairman of the board and co-CEO, while former Bell Atlantic CEO Ivan Seidenberg became

Verizon's founding president and co-CEO. In accordance with a leadership transition plan announced at the time of the merger, Lee retired from Verizon in 2002. Seidenberg is currently chairman and CEO.

During its first five years (2000–2005), Verizon invested a total of more than $72 billion to maintain, upgrade and expand its technology infrastructure. Verizon's strong cash flow ($22 billion in 2005) enabled the company to maintain a healthy level of investment in growth areas, particularly broadband and wireless communication, even as the company has reduced total debt by more than $20 billion since 2002.

MCI Acquisition

William G. McGowan organized MCI Communications Corporation (first known as Microwave Communications Inc.) in 1968, when the FCC's Carterfone decision allowed competition with the Bell System for telephone equipment. By 1972, MCI had begun offering point-to-point private line service between Chicago and St. Louis, and by 1973 the company had annual revenues of $15 million in a relatively small segment of the telecommunications market in competition with AT&T.

The 1982 MFJ, which opened the long-distance market to competition, was a turning point for MCI. It steadily built a nationwide network as well as expanding internationally. MCI grew to become the second largest long-distance telephone company, with a well-established brand. Part of the company's success included building a fiber optic network spanning more than 46,000 miles and offering dozens of new services in more than 150 countries. Its success, however, would be short-lived with the arrival of WorldCom Inc.

Starting in the mid-1990s, Mississippi-based WorldCom Communication quickly rose to become the number two long-distance telephone carrier in the U.S. Along the way, the company used its soaring stock to make 70 acquisitions, including a hostile takeover of MCI in 1998. WorldCom, like other telephone companies, got caught in the crosshairs of a changing telephone marketplace as well as changes in technology. Beginning in early 2002, WorldCom suffered a stunning reversal of fortune. WorldCom became the focus of intense scrutiny by regulators and law enforcement officials after the disclosure that the company improperly overstated earnings by $3.8 billion in 2001 (later estimated to be $11 billion) and the first quarter of 2002. WorldCom CEO Bernie Ebbers would later be indicted and sent to prison, but not before leaving the company $30 billion in debt, not to mention a tarnished reputation. WorldCom subsequently discharged 17,000 of its employees (or 28 percent of the company's workforce). The company saw its stock plummet from a one-time high of $64.50 per share to stock that in 2003 was trading at 83 cents per share.

On February 14, 2005, Verizon announced that it would acquire MCI in a move designed to enhance Verizon's long-distance telephone capability as well as MCI's Internet and data communications network. The merger closed on January 6, 2006, in a transaction valued at approximately $8.5 billion.

Entry into Broadband Delivery

Starting in 2004, Verizon began a major initiative to deliver broadband communication to the home using fiber optic delivery. The project, called "FIOS," combines the best elements of IPTV with fiber optic delivery. FIOS is Verizon's answer to those cable companies that now offer telephone communication as part of their full set of service offerings. Verizon will spend $20 billion over the next ten years to upgrade its network.[24]

Verizon plans to spend as much as $23 billion by 2010 to make fiber optic connections available to 18 million households in the U.S.[25] Once the massive upgrade is completed, Verizon will operate one of the most sophisticated broadband residential networks in the U.S., reaching 28 states and the District of Columbia. The FIOS network will be capable of delivering a broad array of information and entertainment services to the home, including telephone, high-speed Internet and multichannel television. In sum, Verizon has positioned itself as a full-service telecommunications provider and has adopted a bundling strategy going forward by offering consumers various service level options. This can be seen in Figure 6.11.

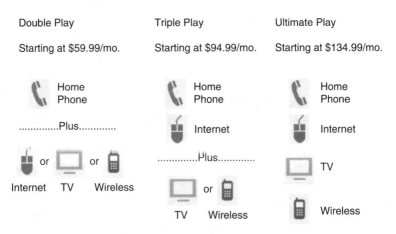

Figure 6.11 Verizon: Broadband Bundling Strategy.

Source: Verizon, Inc.

Strategic Challenges Going Forward

National Cable Franchise Policy

The current system of local cable franchising is about to undergo a major change. House Energy and Commerce Committee chairman Representative Joe Barton supports replacing the nation's existing system of local cable TV franchising with a national scheme, an approach supported by the U.S. telephone companies AT&T and Verizon.[26] Phone companies would be granted ten-year national video franchises with automatic renewal.[27] The NCTA, for its part, is lobbying hard to ensure that a national franchising policy would include cable service providers as well.

IPTV Telephone Franchising

As the nation's major telephone companies move ahead to wire local communicates for IPTV capability, they are being challenged by local community governments to obtain video franchises similar to cable television operators. Those franchises typically require cable TV providers to wire an entire community, not just the wealthiest areas, and pay a 3–5 percent franchise fee. Federal law generally requires phone companies to obtain franchises for video services that use the public right of way. Major LECs like AT&T and Verizon insist that they shouldn't have to negotiate franchise agreements to offer premium television and information services to consumers. The battle is pivotal. Franchise requirements could delay or add huge costs to the phone companies' plans. Equally important, franchise agreements can take months to negotiate. This, in turn, could slow the rollout process for the telephone companies in their race to offer broadband residential services.

America's major cities and towns see it differently. At issue is the fact that the nation's cities stand to lose a major source of revenue in the form of franchise fees that underwrite the cost of community access television as well as supporting various other community activities. For organizations like the National League of Cities, the cable television franchise is a rights-of-way issue. Broadband (and IPTV) delivered services simply represent a different video delivery platform that uses city streets and byways.

The stakes are high for the major LECs as well. The cost of implementing broadband video services is very expensive, especially fiber to the home. The phone companies, for their part, do not want to negotiate separate franchises with each and every community as well as commit to a franchise fee obligation. Both AT&T and Verizon have lobbied at both the state and the federal level to change the current laws involving community franchises. On June 8, 2006, the U.S. House of Representatives passed H.R. 5252, the Communications Opportunity, Promotion, and Enhancement Act of 2006, that would make it easier for telephone companies to enter local communities and offer broadband video services.

On June 28, 2006, the U.S. Senate Commerce Committee approved a major communications video franchising reform bill after a long and heated debate on the issue of network neutrality. The bill passed by a vote of 15–7. The bill streamlines the video franchising process and is similar to the bill already passed in the House but with more local oversight than the House's more national version. Both bills create a de facto national franchise that will help telephone companies more easily roll out video and broadband service and that provide similar opportunities for cable operators once a competitor enters the market. The enactment of a national video franchising bill is in keeping with the government's efforts to revise the 1996 Telecommunications Act and recognition of the Internet to near-utility status.

Similar efforts have occurred at the state level as well. In September 2005, the telephone companies won a major victory in their efforts to launch video services in Texas when Governor Rick Perry signed legislation replacing city-by-city franchising with a single, statewide franchise. The wide-ranging telecommunications bill also deregulates some of the wireline services of the incumbent local providers, including AT&T and Verizon Communications Inc. Other states have passed or are considering legislation that would eliminate the need for both telephone and cable companies to have to negotiate individual franchise deals with hundreds of communities.[28]

In March 2008, the FCC passed a set of rulings designed to streamline the cable franchising process and prohibit local authorities from "unreasonably refusing to award competitive cable franchises." The ruling imposes a 90-day time limit on local regulators for approving applications by new entrants in cable and other pay television services. Municipalities need to approve or reject franchise applications within 90 days or they are considered approved. In June 2008, the U.S. Court of Appeals for the Sixth Circuit dismissed a petition by cable operators and local governments to overturn the FCC ruling.

Concluding Remarks: Net Neutrality

As the delivery of broadband services continues to unfold, an emerging issue that has taken center stage is the question of net neutrality. Internet service provider (ISP) companies like AT&T and Comcast (cable television) would like the ability to charge major users of the Internet a higher fee to deliver information content to consumers. Currently, most websites take approximately the same amount of time to download information on to a user's desktop or laptop computer (assuming a high-speed connection). A sticking point for many ISPs is that different content providers use varying amounts of bandwidth (i.e., information-carrying capacity) in order to deliver audio, video, mass e-mailings, etc. to the end user. The presumption going forward is that major application services like e-commerce mailings and IPTV will require major amounts of bandwidth.

The question before the U.S. Congress is whether companies like AT&T and Comcast—that provide the on-ramps to the nation's intelligent networks—should have the right to impose a toll system on those companies that want faster delivery times and that use enormous amounts of bandwidth. For companies like AT&T and Comcast the issue boils down to cost. The ISPs make the argument that certain purveyors of information and entertainment on the Internet use a disproportionate amount of carriage capacity and thereby place greater demands on the network while decreasing the speed for everyone else. Such companies would like the ability to impose a fee structure on those companies that are heavy users of the Internet.

Critics of the toll system approach argue that it is wrongheaded in principle and a throwback to the past where common carriers are attempting to impose a metered system on information traffic flow. As Penn State's Robert Frieden writes, "Faced with ever increasing bandwidth requirements, incumbent carriers have resurrected a decidedly Bellhead notion that they should implement technological innovations that can 'sniff' and meter Internet traffic and thereby identify cost causers with greater specificity."[29]

Nor is the problem simply confined to the matter of technical downloading speeds. The imposition of a metered system raises the specter that powerful companies such as AT&T, Verizon, Comcast and Time Warner would exercise an enormous gatekeeping ability and control too much of how the Internet is used. Specifically, the major ISPs would have an incentive to build and manage a broadband network in a manner that favors their own applications (or favored clients) over competitors' applications. Imagine a scenario in which the ISP launches its own music or movie download service and positions it on "the fast-download lane" in front of competing services such as iTunes, Yahoo Music and others.[30] It would be analogous to a supermarket that favors and allocates the best shelf space for its own products. Alternatively, let's assume for a moment that preferred major clients like Google and Microsoft would be willing and able to pay higher fees in order to have their sites come up more quickly. What does this mean for start-up Internet companies and non-profit organizations that have less money to spend but require a lot of bandwidth?

Critics of the metered system approach favor so-called "net neutrality," whereby the ISP is strictly a carrier and does not get involved with information content. They take the position that, given the limited broadband options, the telephone and cable duopoly would have both the incentive and the ability to exploit access and control over the Internet and thereby restrict competition and innovation.

Supporters of net neutrality argue that inexpensive free-speech vehicles such as blogs and social networking sites could be stifled. As Massachusetts senator John Kerry writes:

Free and open access to the internet is something all Americans should enjoy, regardless of what financial means they're born into or where they live. It is profoundly disappointing that the Senate is going to let a handful of companies hold internet access hostage by legalizing the cherry-picking of cable service providers and new entrants. That is a dynamic that would leave some communities with inferior service, higher cable rates, and even the loss of service. Not to mention inadequate internet service—in the age of information.[31]

Not so, say the major ISPs. Industry officials point out that these scenarios aren't happening now and that net neutrality attempts to solve a problem that doesn't exist. They make the argument that ISPs fully understand that customers won't tolerate a differential treatment of the Internet. More to the point, it's in everyone's best interest to keep all Internet traffic flowing at an equal speed. The problem, however, is that traffic flow bottlenecks will in time become everybody's problem, and the imposition of a fee structure provides an incentive to upgrade networks and launch next-generation network services.

7

SATELLITE COMMUNICATION

Satellite Communication

A communication satellite is essentially a microwave relay in the sky, operating at 22,300 miles above the earth's equator. It receives microwave signals in a given frequency and retransmits them at a different frequency. Satellites provide an efficient means of reaching isolated places on the earth and are considerably less expensive than terrestrial communication links for select applications. Communication satellites are a versatile form of wireless communication. What distinguishes communication satellites from other forms of wireless communication (cellular, paging, etc.) is their high orbital position and movement.

Geosynchronous Orbit

The term *geosynchronous orbit* (GSO) refers to a satellite that operates at 22,300 miles above the earth's equator. The satellite rotates at the speed of the earth. Hence, the satellite appears to be stationary in its orbital position.

Fixed Satellite Services

The term *fixed satellite services* (FSS) is used to describe satellites that operate in the GSO. Satellites that operate in the GSO can provide 24-hour service, which is essential for broadcasting, cable television, telephony and Internet communications.

Satellite Links

In principle, a complete satellite link requires a line-of-sight path extending between the earth station and the satellite. The term *uplink* refers to that portion of the satellite link where a signal is being transmitted from the earth station to the satellite. The term *downlink* refers to that portion of

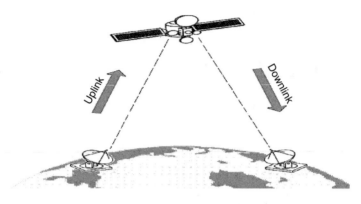

Figure 7.1 Satellite Transmission Link.

Illustration: Chan, Chin Bong.

the satellite link where a signal is being transmitted from the satellite to the earth station below (Figure 7.1).

Transponder

A transponder is a contraction of two words: transmitter and responder. A transponder is analogous to a channel. A transponder provides the connection between the satellite's receiver and transmitter antennas. It receives the signal in one frequency and then converts it to another for the downlink portion. Satellites operate in the super high frequency (SHF) range, which is measured in GHz or billion cycles per second. Satellite engineers recognize that the higher the frequency, the greater the susceptibility to weather conditions, which can degrade performance. Therefore the higher frequency is always assigned to the uplink portion, whereas the lower frequency is assigned to the downlink. Table 7.1 provides a listing of the six major satellite bands and their corresponding application.

A communication satellite contains 24–96 transponders plus spares

Table 7.1 Satellite Frequency Bands

L-band	1.0–2.0 GHz	Mobile satellite services.
S-band	1.55–3.9 GHz	Satellite radio.
C-band	3.7–6.2 GHz	Broadcast and cable television.
X-band	8.0–12.0 GHz	Military satellites and satellite image.
Ku-band	11.7–14.5 GHz	Cable television, DBS and VSATs.
Ka-band	17.7–21.2 GHz	Broadband and inter-satellite links.
	27.5–31.0 GHz	

Source: Satellite Industry Association, "Satellite Industry Overview," Available at: http://www.sia.org/ (retrieved July 5, 2006).

depending on the size of the satellite. The transponder bandwidth can vary in size, and can be 36 MHz, 54 MHz or 72 MHz. A single transponder can deliver a digital combination of voice, data and television channels. Many of today's satellites use a hybrid approach, that is, a combination of C- and Ku-band set of transponders. Subsequent improvements in digital video compression using an MPEG 2 standard format allows satellite common carriers to maximize their transponder delivery capability. This becomes especially important when it come to the delivery of cable and DBS video signals.

Footprint

A satellite footprint refers to the signal's area of coverage. The HBO signal, for example, utilizes an east coast and west coast feed in order to blanket the entire U.S. Similarly, DirecTV uses a total of six satellites, including spot beams, to deliver DBS service to the U.S. Therefore, any earth station that falls within the footprint of a satellite-fed signal and that is locked on to the appropriate transponder is capable of receiving the same signal. Figure 7.2 illustrates a satellite footprint with specific reference to an Intelsat C-band satellite footprint and its coverage in North America. Figure 7.3 provides additional examples of Intelsat satellite footprints.

Earth Station

The earth station (or satellite dish) is the antenna that receives satellite-fed voice, data and video signals. While some earth stations are capable of transmitting and receiving signals, most satellite dishes such as a cable head-end or DBS receiver are television receive only (TVRO) devices. The satellite dish contains a parabolic reflector as well as the internal electronics for down-linking and converting the signal. By forming an arc, the parabolic dish concentrates incoming signals to a small point at the center above the dish (Figure. 7.4). The larger the diameter of the reflecting surface, the greater the sensitivity to weak incoming signals.[1] Once the signal has been concentrated and delivered to the focal point, it must be collected and passed on with a minimum of signal loss. This is the function of the feedhorn, which is bolted to the mouth of the low noise block converter.

Signal Quality and Strength

In designing the proper satellite communication link, there comes a tradeoff in design. Either one builds small satellites with large earth stations or large satellites with small earth stations. In short, amplification of the signal has to happen at one end or the other. During the decades of the 1960s and 1970s, companies like AT&T, RCA and Ford Aerospace built small satellites and

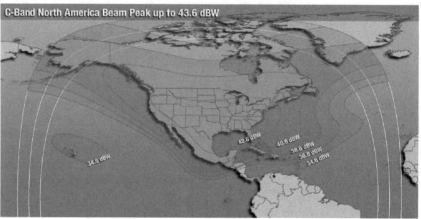

Figure 7.2 Satellite Communication Footprint.

Illustration: Chan, Chin Bong; C-Band North America footprint illustration: Intelsat.

large earth stations because there was no practical way to launch large satellites with heavy payloads. Subsequent improvements in satellite design and launch capability have allowed designers to put more amplifying power in the satellite (or space segment end). This, in turn, has led to a corresponding decrease in the size of earth stations. The direct beneficiaries of such design changes have been the DBS, VSAT, global satellite telephone and high-speed Internet delivery businesses.

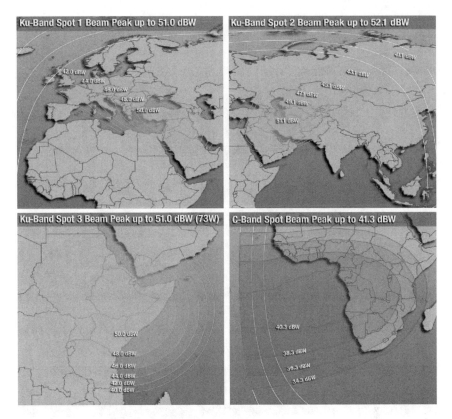

Figure 7.3 Intelsat Communication Satellite Footprint.
Source: Intelsat.

Satellite Design Characteristics

The design of a satellite must operate in a high vacuum environment. Once the satellite achieves GSO, there are no wind or weather shifts. Satellites are solar powered. The radiation from the sun enables the satellite to generate electricity through the use of solar cells. The basic design to a communication satellite generally comes in two forms: 1) spin stabilized and 2) body stabilized (Figure 7.5). A spin stabilized satellite is balanced by spinning the main body (at 100-plus revolutions per minute). To keep the antenna pointing to earth, the antenna subsystem must be despun; that is, the antenna subsystem remains stationary while the body of the satellite spins. A body stabilized satellite (also called a "3 axis" stabilized satellite) looks like a large box, with extended wings needed to power the satellite. A body stabilized satellite uses flat panel solar arrays which are oriented toward the sun.[2] The vast majority of communication satellites being designed today are body stabilized "3 axis" satellites.

Figure 7.4 Parabolic Dish and Signal Concentration.

Figure 7.5 Satellite Primary Design Formats (left: spin stabilized satellite—Astra 3A satellite; right: body "3 axis" stabilized satellite—DirecTV satellite).

Source: Boeing Corporation, Satellite Division.

Telemetry, Tracking and Command

The satellite is designed to send continuous information about its own flight-path performance and on-board instrumentation data to earth. A telemetry, tracking and command (TT&C) center monitors the spacecraft's condition and is able to control it from the ground. A separate radio link is used to provide ground station command with information. One of the important responsibilities of the TT&C is space-station keeping. A satellite tends to drift out of its assigned orbital slot owing to the effects of the sun, moon and gravitational pull. In order for the satellite to perform optimally, it must be kept within a specified longitudinal and latitudinal tolerance range of its assigned orbital position. Before the satellite reaches the outer limits of its north–south east–west tolerance range, the TTC will reposition the satellite.[3] A set of signals are sent from TT&C ground control to the satellite, which in turn fires up a series of control thrusters. The control thrusters rely on the use of jet propulsion rockets. The satellite is then repositioned into its proper orbital position and tolerance range.

Satellite Advantages

Economies of Scale

Cost bears no relationship to the distance involved and/or to the number of users. When considering any distance greater then a few hundred miles, the cost of broadcasting via satellite is significantly less expensive than landline transmission. This is because only one relay station is involved, namely, the satellite. The satellite's footprint (or area of coverage) permits many earth stations to simultaneously receive the same signal. Therefore an economy of scale is realized, because it costs no more to transmit television to one earth station than it does to 5,000 so long as they fall within the same footprint. This is the underlying economic assumption that makes direct broadcast satellite possible.

Wide Area of Coverage

Satellites provide wide area coverage where distance and terrain are not critical factors. This becomes especially important for mobile communication for ships at sea or fleet management. Satellite communication is also good in rural areas that may not have established terrestrial communication links. This is one of the special appeals of direct broadcast satellites for people living in the rural countryside.

Rapid Installation of the Ground Network

The installation of an earth station is relatively inexpensive and can be accomplished quickly. In addition, there is a lower cost per added site. This has been especially important for mobile news operations in the field as well as military communication.

Satellite Disadvantages

Delay Factor

A satellite transmission takes a quarter-second to complete. While this is not a problem for broadcasters, it is problematic when one is conducting an international telephone call via satellite.

Piracy

A satellite transmission intended for a specialized audience can be easily intercepted by someone equipped with an earth station and locked on to the appropriate satellite and transponder. The problem of signal piracy can be especially problematic to a corporation, pay cable television service or news operation that wants to keep its information proprietary. Thus most cable television networks and news organizations encrypt their primary transmission feeds.

Satellite Applications

Satellite communications are principally used in situations that require a form of distribution on a point-to-multipoint basis, that is, a major uplink site with several downlink locations.

Broadcast Television

The television networks use satellite communications as the primary method for transmitting all of their long-haul feeds, including affiliate feeds, news and syndicated programs. Moreover, satellite's flexibility to uplink and transmit from remote sites gives national and local news services untold capability for newsgathering purposes. Satellite newswire and remote publishing saves on publishing and distribution costs for all the major electronic and print news media organizations.

Cable Television

As mentioned in Chapter 4., HBO's 1975 decision to use satellite communication not only reshaped HBO's own method for distributing programs but also transformed broadcast and cable television forever. The subsequent merging of satellite and cable communications would unlock a floodgate of new cable programmers who were equally capable of leasing satellite time, including Ted Turner's UHF station WTBS (1978) and CNN (1980). Both HBO and Turner's commitment to use satellite communication led to a new concept in cable television called *cable networking*, where future cable programmers like USA, ESPN and MTV would use the satellite–cable interface as a way to create and distribute programming exclusively to cable operating systems.[4]

Direct Broadcast Satellites

Direct broadcast satellites (DBS) represent a new generation of highly powered satellites capable of delivering television programs to users equipped with small earth stations (parabolic dishes) approximately 18 inches in diameter. Today's generation of DBS satellites are much larger in size and utilize digital compression techniques that allow them to offer 250-plus channels of service. A direct broadcast satellite provides 15–20 times greater signal strength than a traditional fixed satellite service. In the U.S. today, there are two DBS system offerings, DirecTV and EchoStar, which began in June 1994 and December 1996 respectively (Table 7.2).

Table 7.2 U.S. Direct Broadcast Satellite Services

DBS Program Service	Location	Owner	Launch Date	Number of Subscribers
DirecTV	El Segundo, CA	News Corporation Ltd.	June 1994	16 million
EchoStar	Englewood, CO	EchoStar Communications	December 1996	12 million

DirecTV

The DirecTV Group is headquartered in El Segundo, California, and is composed of two operating units—DirecTV U.S. and Latin America. DirecTV began as a subsidiary of Hughes Communication under the leadership of Eddie Hartenstein. The company was acquired by Rupert Murdoch's News Corporation Ltd. in 2003 and is the largest provider of DBS television service in the U.S. DirecTV has an estimated 16 million subscribers. DirecTV programming is distributed by six high-powered satellites. Each satellite has multiple transponders that relay the DirecTV signal from the company's two broadcast centers to home satellite receivers. The D4-S satellite is a "spot beam" satellite which allows signals to target specific areas within the U.S., and is used by DirecTV to deliver local programming. DirecTV transmits more than 130 basic entertainment channels, 31 premium movie channels and over 33 regional and specialty sports networks, as well as local channels in select markets.[5]

The Dish Network EchoStar

EchoStar Communications Corporation is headquartered in Englewood, Colorado, and is home to the Dish Network. EchoStar began in 1980 when chairman and CEO Charlie Ergen entered the satellite television industry as a distributor of C-band TV systems. In 1987, EchoStar filed for a DBS license with the FCC and was granted access to orbital slot 119 degrees West longitude in 1992. The company continued to upgrade its facilities and formally established its own DBS service on December 28, 1995, with the successful launch of EchoStar I. That same year, EchoStar established the Dish Network brand name.[6] Today, EchoStar provides DBS service through its Dish Network to over 12 million customers located throughout the U.S. There are two satellites that make up the EchoStar satellite network, providing 250-plus channels of digital video as well as audio and data services.

Satellite Radio

Satellite radio has become an important alternative to traditional radio in the U.S. Satellite radio is a national service that provides point-to-multipoint digital delivery to users equipped with specialized antennas. There are two major satellite radio companies in the U.S. and one international. The U.S based services include XM Radio, which uses two satellites, and Sirius Radio, which uses three. Satellite radio has seen a dramatic increase in popularity among users throughout the U.S. The main appeal of satellite radio is the diversity of its music offerings. Both XM and Sirius offer a wide variety of music and talk-show formats to its listeners. Satellite radio is also a service that is highly mobile; the user can access the service from a car, anytime, anywhere.

Voice and Data Communication

Before the advent of suboceanic fiber optic cable, satellite communication was the principal transmission method for international voice communication. FSS is still used for some voice communication links as well as back-up. However, the vast majority of international voice traffic goes by suboceanic fiber optic cable. The principal reason has to do with the quarter-of-a-second delay factor cited earlier. Conversely, satellite communications offer up important opportunities in the area of high-speed Internet and data transport where the delay factor is not a significant issue.

Very Small Aperture Terminals (VSATs)

VSATs are micro-earth stations that are used for the receipt of data communications on a point-to-multipoint basis. Starting with host computer, the data is formatted into addressed packets and sent via satellite to the receiver's micro-earth station. VSATs can often be seen atop a gas station that uses the small earth station for verifying credit card information, as well as newspapers and radio stations that use them to downlink newswire feeds.

Mobile Satellite Communication

Mobile satellite communication involves using satellites for direct, albeit flexible, transmission to moving vehicles or remote platforms. They are used in such industries as 1) trucking, 2) maritime communication and 3) offshore oil and gas drilling. Mobile satellite communication depends on the use of global positioning satellites (GPS) for the purpose of detecting the location of a moving vehicle or ship at sea. In the GPS system, a constellation of 24 satellites circle the earth in near-circular inclined orbits. They operate in low earth orbit (Figure 7.6). A GPS receiver on the ground computes its present position by comparing the time taken by signals from three or four different GPS satellites to reach the receiver. By receiving signals from at least three satellites, the receiver's position (latitude, longitude and altitude) can be accurately determined.

The Business of Satellite Communication

The satellite industry can be divided into four areas: 1) satellite carriers, 2) satellite manufacturing, 3) satellite launch services and 4) ground equipment.

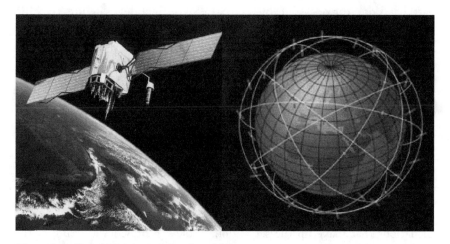

Figure 7.6 Global Positioning Satellite System.

Satellite Carriers

Satellite carriers are in the business of selling satellite time and capability. This can include everything from the outright sale of a transponder to selling satellite time on a per-use basis. Most satellite carriers also provide customers with full networking capability, that is, the ground segments necessary for establishing end-to-end connectivity.

Satellite Manufacturing

Satellite manufacturers are those companies engaged in the design and construction of a communication satellite. The two critical issues for the manufacturer of a communication satellite are reliability and production schedule. The average production time for a communication satellite ranges between 25 and 40 months.[7] Several of the more notable satellite manufacturers include: 1) Boeing, 2) SS Loral, 3) Lockheed Martin, 4) Alcatel 5) EADS Astrium and 6) Orbital Science.

Satellite Launch Services

The physical launch of a satellite represents the second most expensive part of deploying a satellite. It requires that the satellite carrier (or government agency) contract with a satellite launch company, which is responsible for scheduling and building the launch vehicle that will be used to place the satellite into orbit.

Ground Equipment

Ground equipment is the satellite equipment and components, including earth stations (broadcast, cable, DBS, VSATs, mobile), satellite tracking and telemetry equipment, television monitors, cabling, mobile trucks, etc.

World satellite industry revenues have averaged annual growth of 10.5 percent for the period 2001–2006. In 2006, the combined satellite industry achieved worldwide revenues of $106.1 billion. Figure 7.7 provides a comparison of the satellite industry by segment areas for the years 2001–2006.

Satellite carrier services were responsible for 59 percent of worldwide revenues, followed by ground equipment (27 percent), satellite manufacturing (11 percent) and launch services (3 percent).[8]

The Business of Satellite Common Carriage

Satellite carriers operate at the international, regional and domestic levels. Regional carriers are often partially government subsidized by a consortium of nations that make up the set region. Table 7.3 provides a listing of the major international and regional satellite carriers.

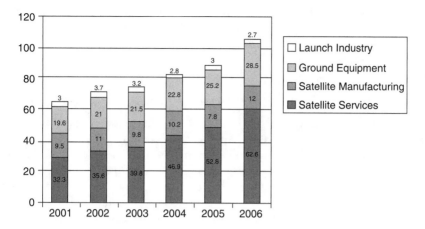

Figure 7.7 International Satellite Revenue (in billion dollars): Four Area Segments, 2001–2006.

Source: Satellite Industry Association, "State of the Satellite Industry Report," Available at: http://www.sia.org/PDF/2007StateofSatelliteIndustryReport.pdf (retrieved October 22, 2007).

Table 7.3 International and Regional Satellite Carriers

International Carriers	Regional Carriers
Intelsat:	EutelSat (Europe)
—Loral Space and Communications	TeleSat (Canada and North America)
—PanAmSat	Palapa (Malaysia and Southeast Asia)
SES Global:	NordSat (Scandinavia)
—SES Americom	ArabSat (Middle East)
—SES Astra Europe	SatMex (Mexico and Latin America)
—SES New Skies	
Inmarsat	
Stratos	
Globalstar	

Satellite communication is a capital-intensive industry. It is a business characterized by high start-up costs in terms of satellite manufacturing and deployment. Once the satellite has been successfully launched and placed into orbit, the cost of delivering service is relatively low. The challenge for the satellite operator is to build a strong customer base in order to offset the high cost of investment. An analogy can be drawn between deploying a satellite and constructing a large commercial building. Both need to be filled with high-quality tenants. The best tenants are broadcast and cable programmers which require guaranteed satellite time 24/7 and will typically purchase transponders outright or commit to long-term leases. Continuing with the commercial building analogy, lost satellite time cannot be recouped or regained. The satellite carrier, however, does have the ability to subdivide the service offerings into various increments (i.e., short-term lease and occasional use).

Satellite Transponder Sale and Lease

In a satellite transponder sale or lease arrangement, users will typically have their own transmit and receive earth stations. Selling/leasing is the most attractive arrangement because the customer is making a long-term commitment for satellite use. Broadcast and cable programmers, for their part, look to be associated with dedicated satellites (i.e., so-called satellite neighborhoods) where the primary clientele are other programmers. This also makes it easier for the cable operator, which doesn't have to maintain multiple earth stations. The contract length can range between two years and the life of the satellite. The satellite carrier, in turn, must provide the user with transponder access and guarantee. In other words, when and if a transponder does not perform as required, the satellite carrier must take action to restore service as soon as possible. Often, the satellite carrier maintains a spare satellite or unused transponders to meet such occasions.

Short-Term or Recurring Satellite Use

A short-term lease is attractive, but not as lucrative as full-time use. Under this arrangement, there will be significant gaps in satellite use. The contract terms can range from monthly to two years. An example of a short-term or recurring satellite user might be a company that hosts periodic videoconferences to its national and international affiliate sites or a university engaged in satellite education extension courses.

Occasional Satellite Use

Occasional satellite users make no commitment for recurring service, thus reserving satellite time on an as-needed basis. This represents the least attractive approach, unless the satellite carrier has an extensive coordination plan of part-time users. Transponder resources are booked through a reservation desk. This approach is typically used by business or nonprofit organizations requiring satellite capability for conducting specialized activities such as a worldwide business videoconference or transmitting a major sporting event.

Tied to short-term and occasional-use satellite contracts is the principle of preemptible satellite time. Depending on the contract arrangement, the user may be given a discount in terms of satellite cost, knowing that the service can be interrupted or canceled if the satellite carrier has a need to reclaim the satellite or time allocation.

The Business of Satellite Launch and Deployment

Frequency Coordination and Registration

Before a satellite carrier can build and locate a satellite, the carrier must obtain the proper international frequency assignment. The process of international frequency coordination is complex process given the fact that the electromagnetic spectrum used for satellite communications is a limited (or fixed) resource that must be shared by all nations and users. The high cost of satellite deployment, therefore, requires good cooperation between and among users. Such cooperation, however, can break down when and if satellite operators behave independently as if they own the spectrum and orbital positions. The International Telecommunications Union (ITU) is charged with overseeing frequency coordination and registration so that everyone's best interests are served.

The registration process typically begins three to five years in advance of the satellite's actual launch and deployment. Frequency coordination and registration happen in three steps. The satellite carrier begins by applying to the nation's representative to the ITU. In the U.S., the FCC serves as the U.S. liaison organization to the ITU. There are basically two types of frequency coordination: 1) terrestrial—for radio and land-based microwave transmitters and 2) space coordination—for satellite deployment and frequency assignment.

ADVANCE PUBLICATION OF INFORMATION (API)

The API is submitted to the ITU and provides a general description of the proposed satellite network. The API step is a prerequisite for coordination, allowing any host government administration to assess the potential impact of a proposed satellite deployment on existing or planned satellite networks. The API allows for comments and reactions. Comments are expected within four months of the publication. A complete effort is made to resolve all disputes between neighboring countries, including the possible change in a frequency assignment.

PROCEEDING WITH THE COORDINATION PROCESS

After comments have been forwarded, coordination must occur with planned or existing satellite networks. The coordination of satellite networks is a bilateral activity where the newcomer must approach the incumbent and obtain its agreement regarding the potential for interference. An affected administration will evaluate the technical characteristics of the proposed satellite network and inform the filing administration if it agrees with the proposed operation. The basic criteria for acceptable interference levels are set by the ITU at relevant World Radio Conference (WRC) and Radio Regulations Board (RRB) meetings.

The question may be asked: what motivates agreement and coordination between international telecommunication entities? In the final analysis, all nations and users have a collective stake in the successful outcome of such discussions. One of the primary goals of the RRB is to ensure that all administrations make every effort to overcome difficulties, in a manner acceptable to the parties concerned. There is a clear recognition that all nations (and their respective carriers) have a legitimate right to put up a satellite. At the same time, the RRB recognizes that those satellite networks that have already entered into the coordination process have priority over newcomers.

NOTIFICATION OF FREQUENCY ASSIGNMENTS

This is the last step in the regulatory process. It occurs after the coordination of frequencies has been fully resolved. The RRB will verify that the entire coordination process is complete. Afterwards, the RRB will record the assignments in a master register, and the new operator is free to begin the planning process for satellite manufacturing and launch.[9]

Satellite Launch Services

Once the carrier has been given a notice of frequency assignment, the carrier must contract with a satellite launch company, which is responsible for scheduling and building the launch vehicle that will be used to place the satellite into orbit. The physical launch of a satellite is technically challenging, as well as the second most expensive part of deploying a satellite.

THE U.S. SPACE SHUTTLE PROGRAM

The U.S. Space Shuttle was the world's first reusable piloted spacecraft. It was designed as a multipurpose vehicle capable of conducting scientific experiments as well as deploying satellites into low earth orbit. While the Space Shuttle proved successful in the deployment of satellites, its complex design and refurbishing delays led to a number of setbacks.[10] In the aftermath of the January 1986 Space Shuttle *Challenger* disaster and a report released by an investigatory commission, President Ronald Reagan announced that NASA would withdraw from the business of launching commercial satellites.[11] This, coupled with the destruction of Space Shuttle *Columbia* in February 2003, all but eliminated NASA from the commercial satellite launch business.[12] Since then, the satellite launch void has been filled by a number of international players, including Arianespace, France,[13] and Lockheed Martin, U.S.A. Table 7.4 provides a listing of both U.S. and international satellite launch service companies.

Table 7.4 Satellite Launch Services: U.S. and International

U.S. Launch Service Providers	International Launch Service Providers
Lockheed Martin (Atlas).	Arianespace (Ariane).
Boeing (Delta).	International Launch Services: Joint venture between
Orbital (Pegasus).	Lockheed Martin (U.S.A.) and Khrunichev State Research and
SpaceX (Falcon).	Production Space Center (Russia) (Atlas/Proton).
	Sea Launch: Joint venture between Boeing (U.S.A.), Russia, Ukraine and Norway.
	PSLV (India).
	Great Wall (Long March) (China).
	Mitsubishi (H2A) (Japan).

Satellite Deployment Phase

A critical moment in the life of every satellite occurs when it first leaves the earth. Dwarfed by the enormous launch rocket(s) needed to overcome gravity and atmospheric resistance and to attain escape velocity, the fragile satellite starts its journey as a mere passenger.[14] The term *perigee stage* refers to the low earth orbit position of the satellite once it has been separated from the rocket (approximately 184–200 miles). Only after it reaches an elevation of about 200 miles does the satellite ignite its own rocket motors to carry it into GSO or other orbital locations. Failure of a satellite's onboard motors to ignite and other such difficulties can leave hardware worth $500 million stranded uselessly in low earth orbit. The *apogee stage* refers to the attainment of GSO. Another potential failure point is when the satellite has reached its proper orbital location but is unable to deliver the full range of signaling capability.

Satellite Launch Insurance

Satellites are expensive to build and launch. Satellite carriers will usually buy insurance, but the premiums are enormous—oftentimes 20–23 percent of the value of the satellite.[15] There are different types of coverage that are available. 1) Pre-launch insurance covers damage to a satellite during the construction, transportation and processing phases prior to launch. 2) Launch insurance covers losses of a satellite occurring during the actual launch phase of a project. It insures against complete launch failures as well as the failure of a launch vehicle to place a satellite into the proper orbit. 3) In-orbit policies insure satellites for technical problems and damages once a satellite has been placed into its proper orbit. When and if a satellite fails to execute properly the financial fallout can be significant for all parties concerned. The satellite manufacturer and/or launch company, for example, when doing business with future clients, is likely to face increased premiums and other difficulties associated with the past failure. The satellite carrier, for its part, must honor existing contracts with prospective buyers by either finding an alternative satellite or voiding the user contract altogether.[16]

Intelsat: A Case Study

The early 1960s saw the beginning of satellite development in the U.S. In 1962, the U.S. Congress passed the Satellite Communications Act, which created an organization called the Communications Satellite Corporation (Comsat). Comsat was responsible for overseeing the development of satellite communication in the U.S. In 1964, the U.S. and 13 other nations founded the International Telecommunications Satellite organization (Intelsat) for the express purposes of advancing satellite communications on a worldwide basis. Intelsat was established as a nonprofit global consortium whose mission was to provide high-quality international satellite distribution of voice, data and video on a non-discriminatory basis to those nations of the earth and organizations requiring such services.

The launch of Intelsat I (Early Bird) in 1965 put the first commercial communications satellite into orbit, providing television and voice services between North America and Europe.[17] The next several years would produce an entire generation of satellites and the growth of the Intelsat network. However, it was not until July of 1969 that Intelsat achieved global communications. The Intelsat III satellite completed the first global satellite communications system when it was launched above the Indian Ocean, allowing it to relay signals with two other satellites positioned above the Atlantic and Pacific Oceans and thus provide coverage on a global scale.

In 1974, Intelsat was drawn back to the events that were partly responsible for its creation: the Cold War. Intelsat helped establish the technical foundation for a direct communications link between the White House and the Kremlin. The Cold War had escalated to the extent that leaders on both sides needed a reliable communication method in case of emergencies. Intelsat was able to provide the backbone of the communication's link through its satellites. Beyond that, Intelsat has utilized its global communications ability to provide worldwide coverage of Olympic Games for more than three decades. By 1990, Intelsat had 15 satellites and provided international telecommunications service to 174 countries, territories and dependencies, as well as furnishing domestic telecommunications service to more than 30 nations. The Intelsat network carried over 70 percent of the world's international voice traffic and virtually all international television transmission.[18]

Intelsat's Business Operations

Intelsat was established as a nonprofit global consortium, not only to share the economic investment associated with satellite communications, but to develop an international communications network that would link geographically isolated and underdeveloped nations.[19] The Intelsat global satellite system comprises two elements—the space and ground segments. The space segment consists of the satellites and commercial network owned by Intelsat, including tracking, telemetry and control. The ground segment consists of earth stations owned and operated by the telecommunication entities in the countries in which they are located.[20]

Revenues for the Intelsat system were derived from utilization charges and after deduction of operating costs (and reinvestment) they were distributed to member nations in proportion to their investment share. At one time, the U.S.A. held an investment share of approximately 26.4 percent. Part of Intelsat's mission was to provide satellite communications capability for developing nations while ensuring its commitment to offer such services at an affordable rate.[21] One way to accomplish that goal was through the principle of global price averaging (or cross-subsidization). Intelsat would subsidize low-traffic routes with the surplus money derived from high-traffic routes (e.g., New York to London).

The Privatization of Intelsat

The decade of the 1980s was a time of rapid business and technological change. Private companies, such as PanAmSat and Orion in the U.S., were petitioning the FCC for licenses to launch private commercial satellites in direct competition with Intelsat's high-traffic routes. In the meantime, AT&T was working on TAT-8, which was a suboceanic fiber optic cable that would be capable of supplying high-speed international communications at a fraction of the cost of satellite communications.[22] All this came at a time when the U.S. government was promoting the cause of international business development through its stated policies of deregulation and privatization. The privatization of the satellite industry was more fully expressed when U.S. president Ronald Reagan articulated his 1984 Open Skies Policy, which fully recognized the value of allowing private companies to compete in the field of satellite communications. The combination of competitive, technological and policy factors was the beginning and the end for Intelsat as a protected intergovernmental organization (IGO).

Though Intelsat was offered some guarantees given its IGO status, it was clear that such special protections would not be sufficient to allow it to compete in a highly competitive market. According to Sean Murphy:

> It became apparent that for INTELSAT to survive in the global market, it would need to operate with much greater flexibility than was possible for an international organization. For instance, INTELSAT faced difficulties in obtaining expeditious decisions from its forty-eight-member board, whose meetings had to be translated into INTELSAT's three official languages.[23]

In 1999, in response to the aforementioned changes, the Intelsat board of governors recommended the full privatization of Intelsat. In supporting Intelsat's decision, the U.S. Congress passed the Open-Market Reorganization for the Betterment of International Telecommunications (ORBIT) Act. Intelsat became a privately held company on July 18, 2001, and was renamed Intelsat Ltd.[24] One of the provisions of the ORBIT Act was that Intelsat Ltd. would continue to offer satellite communications for underdeveloped nations. To that end, a small piece of Intelsat was spun off into an IGO now called the International Telecommunications Satellite Organization (ITSO). As an organization, ITSO possesses no satellite infrastructure and has only the law to ensure that Intelsat Ltd. will continue to offer required services to those nations that request such assistance.

In 2004, Intelsat Ltd. acquired Loral Communications, making it the second largest satellite communications provider in the world.[25] On January 28, 2005, Zeus Holdings Ltd., a consortium of private partners including Apax Partners, Apollo, Madison Dearborn Partners and Permira, acquired Intelsat Ltd.[26] The acquisition was made to fulfill the requirements of the ORBIT Act, which required that the primary shareholder(s) of Intelsat must be a party other than its original member nations. The acquisition created Intelsat Holdings Ltd., the current version of Intelsat.

On July 3, 2006, Intelsat announced the completion of its merger with PanAmSat Holding Corporation. With the addition of PanAmSat's satellite fleet and video market expertise, the combined Intelsat and PanAmSat organization is now the largest provider of fixed satellite services. The total value of the transaction, including PanAmSat debt, was approximately $6.4 billion. The new Intelsat has a combined fleet of 51 satellites and a complementary terrestrial infrastructure including eight owned teleports.[27]

8

CELLULAR AND WIRELESS COMMUNICATION

Historical Overview

A cellular telephone (or cell phone) is a long-range, portable communication device that enables mobile communication to occur. Cell phone technology relies on a highly sophisticated network of radio communication frequencies that provide over-the-air telephone service to users with hand-held portable phones. Cellular systems are designed to interface with the public switched telephone network, which enables users to make both local and long-distance telephone calls.

Cellular "radio" telephone technology was pioneered in the 1970s at Bell Laboratories in the U.S. World War II proved to be an important testing ground for early mobile radio communication. While radar was perhaps the most publicized achievement, other telecommunication discoveries were being realized as well, including the first portable FM two-way radio, known commonly as the "walkie-talkie backpack radio," designed by Dan Noble at Motorola Corporation. Shortly after the war, the July 28, 1945 issue of the *Saturday Evening Post* featured the comments of then FCC commissioner, E.K. Hunt, who in an article entitled "Phone Me by Air" discussed the future of wireless communication. He called it "citizen radio." In 1947, the technical principles of cellular telephony were first articulated by D.H. Ring in a technical briefing paper at Bell Labs. Ring's paper, with contributions from W.R. Young, identified several critical elements necessary in order to make wireless communication a possibility. Ring's briefing paper called for the development of geographical coverage areas called "cells," a low-powered transmitter in each cell, traffic to be controlled by a central switch and the importance of frequency reuse in different cell sites.[1]

Mobile Telephone Service

On June 17, 1946, in Saint Louis, Missouri, AT&T and Southwestern Bell demonstrated the first American commercial mobile radio telephone service. It was simply called Mobile Telephone Service (MTS). MTS technology used one high-power transmitter to cover an entire service area. In 1947, the Bell System submitted a request to the FCC for additional spectrum space. The FCC allocated a few more channel assignments in 1949, but gave half to other radio common carriers (RCCs) wishing to offer mobile service. Starting in 1964, the Bell System introduced Improved Mobile Telephone Service (IMTS), which served as a replacement for the badly aging MTS system. IMTS utilized a full-duplex approach, whereby people didn't need to push a button in order to talk. Basic voice conversations went back and forth just as in a regular telephone call. As IMTS became available in other major U.S. cities, the demand for service far exceeded the supply, thereby creating long waiting lists.[2] In 1976, for example, only 545 customers in New York City had access to IMTS service, with 3,700 customers on a waiting list.

The Chicago AMPS Test

Despite the early work in MTS, the real move toward modern cellular telephony did not begin in earnest until 1978. A year earlier, the FCC approved AT&T's request to begin testing a cellular telephone system. The main test site was Chicago, Illinois. In July 1978, AT&T and its Illinois Bell subsidiary initiated test operations of its analog-based Advanced Mobile Phone Service (AMPS).[3] The trial test called for ten cells covering 21,000 square miles. Starting in December, interested subscribers could lease car-mounted telephones. Despite a slow start, the Chicago AMPS test successfully demonstrated the feasibility of cellular telephone switching technology.

U.S. Cellular Service Begins

The success of the Chicago AMPS test set the stage for the start-up of America's first commercial cellular service, which began operations in Chicago on October 12, 1983. The service was offered by Ameritech (and Illinois Bell) following the announced breakup of AT&T in August 1982. By the time the FCC granted its first commercial license to the Chicago system, the Commission was besieged with applications for other commercial licenses. At the time, it was taking 10 to 18 months of deliberation and more than $1 million in costs to award a single license. The FCC realized that "comparative hearings" were too slow and a new licensing procedure had to be found. On October 18, 1983, the FCC announced that lotteries would be used to award licenses in all markets below the top 30 systems. The FCC then spent the next six years refining the lottery process, as thousands of applications were filed for the remaining licenses. Between 1984 and 1988, U.S. cellular telephony experienced a compound annual growth rate of more than 100 percent. By 1990, construction permits had been issued for at least one system in every U.S. market.

International Developments

Research and development in the area of cellular telephony was not unique to the U.S. Work in the area of mobile telephone communication was taking place throughout the world, including in Japan, Sweden, Finland, Denmark, the U.K. and Germany. In Sweden alone, early experiments in over-the-air police radio began in Gothenburg, Sweden, as early as 1933. Technical developments in mobile radio were greatly enhanced by research that took place during World War II. At the end of the 1940s, the demand for mobile radio increased, as did the demand for its further connection to the nation's telephone network. In response, the Swedish Telecommunications Administration considered the time right to begin research and experimentation in mobile radio telephony. S. Lauhrén from the Swedish Telecommunications Administration was the chief architect of what many consider to be the world's first fully automatic mobile telephone system, with a Stockholm trial beginning in 1951. The Stockholm trial was later expanded to include the city of Gothenburg and went public in 1956.

For some time, there was ongoing discussion about the need for a nationwide mobile telephone system. To that end, the Swedish Telecommunications Administration established a working group under the direction of C.G. Åsdal, who later became chief for Televerket Radio. At the 1969 Nordic telecommunications conference at Kabelvåg, Lofoten, a new initiative was put forth by C.G. Åsdal, who together with other interested delegates proposed that the various Nordic telecommunications authorities should consider the question of implementing a common mobile telephone system in the future. The result was Nordic Mobile Telephony (NMT). The first cellular telephone system was officially inaugurated in Sweden on October 1, 1981. NMT was the world's first multinational cellular network. During the next decade, the NMT system would be introduced to other countries as well, both inside and outside of Europe.[4]

The success of mobile telephony in Sweden would spread to other Scandinavian countries as well, including Finland, where a young upstart company named Nokia (formerly the Finnish Cable Works) started a major electronics department in the 1960s that was conducting ongoing research in semiconductor technology. By 1988, Nokia was Europe's third largest television manufacturer and one of the largest telecommunications companies in Scandinavia. At the start of the 1990s, the country of Finland was in deep recession. Nokia's future success would depend heavily on the development and improvements in cell phone technology. Today, Nokia is among the world's leading manufacturers of cellular telephone sets.

Cellular Telephony: Design Characteristics

A cellular telephone system is designed to service customers within a specified geographical area, known as a cellular geographic service area (CGSA). The CGSA generally corresponds to a metropolitan area, including a central city, its suburbs and some portion of its rural fringe. The CGSA can also encompass two or more cities located relatively close together. Cellular systems are designed to interface with the public switched telephone network, thereby enabling the user to make both local and long-distance telephone calls.

A cellular telephone system consists of four major parts. They include:

1 cell site;
2 base station (BS);
3 mobile telephone switching office (MTSO);
4 cellular telephone.

Cell Site

The cellular geographic service area is designed as an interlocking grid of cell sites (or coverage areas). The CGSA is often visually depicted as a series of hexagonal zones or circles. Each cell has its own base station and a dedicated set of over-the-air frequencies. Areas of coverage overlap at the outer boundaries (Figure 8.1).

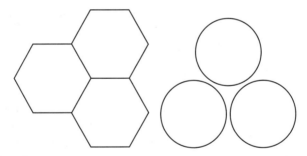

Figure 8.1 Cell Site Coverage Areas.

The use of the hexagonal zones dates back to the original AT&T telephone system engineers, who liked the regular balance and proportion of the hexagon as a way to experiment with and calculate vehicle traffic flow patterns. As Mark van der Hoek points out, the original Bell engineers drew their inspiration from the perfect symmetry of bees' honeycombs, otherwise referred to as honeycomb cell structure—hence the name *cellular* (Figure 8.2).[5]

In reality, cell sites are seldom perfect hexagons or circles. There are obvious gaps between and among cell sites. The cell size depends on population

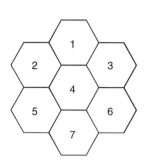

Figure 8.2 Honeycomb Cell Structure.

density (including the expected number of users), physical terrain and traffic. Cell sites will vary in size ranging from half a mile (urban centers) to five to eight miles (suburbs and rural fringe areas). In contrast, highly rural areas can have cell sizes closer to 25 miles owing to the lack of population density. There are an estimated 210,360 cell sites located throughout the U.S.[6]

The Principle of Frequency Reuse

Cellular telephone systems are organized into cell clusters. A cluster is a group of cells. The clusters are then repeated over and over again to form the entire CGSA. The number of cell clusters will vary according to the system design. Cell site cluster configurations are typically designed in one of four variations, including four, seven, ten and 21. Figure 8.3 provides an illustration of a seven-cell cluster configuration.

Cellular telephony operates on the principle of frequency reuse in nonadjacent cells; that is, users can operate on the same set of frequencies in nonadjacent cells without causing interference. Each of the seven numeric cells is assigned a block of frequencies that can only be used within that designated cell. The beauty of cellular telephony is the ability to reuse the same set of frequencies over and over again (in nonadjacent cells), thus optimizing spectrum efficiency and avoiding co-channel interference.[7] Cellular telephone capacity is measured in the number of calls per cell site.

Cell Splitting

Designing a cellular telephone system requires an appreciation for the fact that, as subscriber demand for cell phones increases, this in turn will have a direct effect on the availability of frequencies per cell site. This is especially true in major urban areas of the country. The solution for the telecom

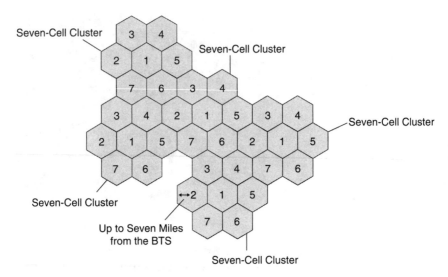

Figure 8.3 Seven-Cell Cluster Configuration.

Illustration: Chan, Chin Bong.

engineer is to engage in cell splitting, whereby a single cell is subdivided into a smaller cell cluster (Figure 8.4). Each cell is designed with its own dedicated set of frequencies and lower signal output. In this way, major urban centers can be split into as many micro-cells as necessary in order to provide acceptable levels of service in heavy-traffic regions.

Base Station (BS)

Each cell has its own low-power transmitter. The low-power transmitter is part of a base station (BS), which is located towards the corner (or contiguous points) of each cell. The transmitters in a cellular system are tailored to the size and shape of the cell.[8] The height of the transmitting antenna depends on the topology of the area it covers. The transmitters are low in power so that their signal does not spill over to an adjacent cell. This, in turn, allows for greater efficiency by dynamically allocating the same set of frequencies for reuse in nonadjacent cell sites (Figure 8.3).[9]

The Mobile Telephone Switching Office

The mobile telephone switching office (MTSO) oversees the primary switching and control functions for the cellular system. It is the radio equivalent of a Class 5 telephone switch. The MTSO interfaces with the public switched telephone network. The MTSO performs seven functions:

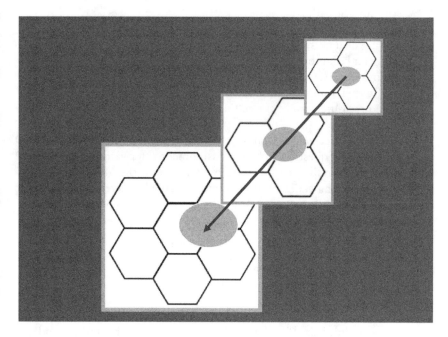

Figure 8.4 Cell Splitting.

Source: Richard A. Gershon, Western Michigan University.

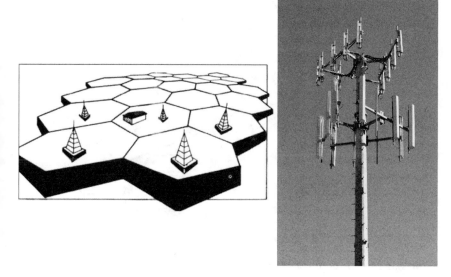

Figure 8.5 Cellular Telephone Base Tower and Transmitter.

1   setting up the call;
2   assigning channels;
3   changing channels;
4   ringing and dial tone;
5   disconnecting the call;
6   recording relevant telephone data for billing purposes;
7   test and measurement of the cellular telephone network.

Each base transceiver station is connected via landline to the MTSO (Figure 8.6). The request for a channel assignment is forwarded to the MTSO over a dedicated landline link. As the master switch, the MTSO automatically assigns incoming callers to unused radio channels, thereby ensuring that callers in adjacent cells are occupying different assigned frequencies.

Locating and Handing Off

As a car (or moving vehicle) passes from one cell to another, the system must be able to determine the location of the moving vehicle and automatically switch to an available frequency as it enters the new cell. The changeover must be smooth and without disruption to the telephone call. In order to accomplish this, the BS monitors the calls in progress and can

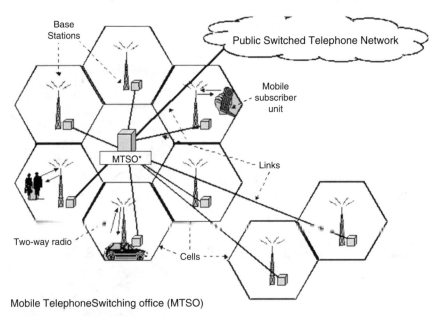

Figure 8.6 MTSO and BS Dedicated Landline Links.

Source: International Telecommunications Union, "Illustration of MTSO," Available at: http://www.itu.int/osg/spu/ni/images/mtso.gif (retrieved August 15, 2006).

sense the signal strength of the mobile units in its own area (and in the overlap areas of adjoining cells). The results are sent on to the MTSO, which determines when the telephone call should be handed off upon entering a new cell site. When the MTSO decides that a call should be handed off, it tells the cell site base transceiver station (BTS) to send a very short data-burst on the same voice channel to the cellular telephone mobile unit. The control data communicates to the mobile unit the new frequency assignment. The mobile unit automatically switches frequencies and the call continues. The handoff should be fast, with no detectable interruption (Figure 8.7).[10]

Dead Spots and Dropped Calls

Cell site coverage areas vary in size and shape. Sometimes, gaps (or empty spaces) are created between the coverage area of two or more adjacent cells. These dead spots can be caused by trees, tall buildings or other obstructions that block the user's cell phone from obtaining a clear signal. The result can be a dropped call when the user enters into that cell site location. Sometimes, cell sites exhibit a different problem when there are too many users within a specific cell site location, thereby maximizing the number of available frequencies. As the user passes into the new cell site location, his/her call might be dropped owing to the lack of available frequencies. In sum, the cell site is operating at maximum capacity and cannot accommodate another user.

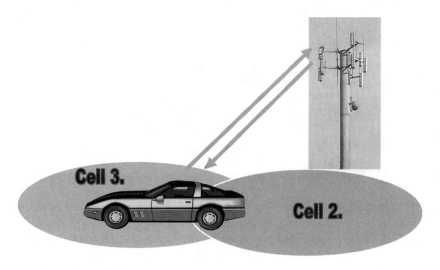

Figure 8.7 Frequency Channel Handoff.

Cellular Telephone (Cellular Mobile Unit)

A good way to appreciate the sophistication of a cell phone is to compare it to a CB radio or a walkie-talkie. Both CB radios and walkie-talkies are simplex devices; that is, the two people communicating share the same frequency. This, in turn, means that only one person can talk at a time. In contrast, a cellular telephone is considered a duplex device because two frequencies are required in order to communicate (i.e., one to transmit and one to receive). This, in turn, means that two people can talk simultaneously. In sum, a pair of frequencies is required to create one voice channel.

The cellular telephone is capable of tuning to all designated channels within a CGSA. The cell phone itself contains the actual mobile transmitting and receiving unit. The cell phone also contains a subscriber identity module (SIM), which is a detachable smart card containing the user's subscription information and phonebook. The SIM card performs three important functions, including access control to the network (i.e., authentication and ciphering), personalized services (i.e., text messaging, Internet access, etc.) and network branding and advertising (i.e., graphics display printed on the SIM card). Assuming the same service provider, the SIM card can be detached and inserted into a new phone when and if the user decides to change handsets.

To make a call, the user enters the telephone number through the keypad into the set's memory and then presses the "send" button. When the user places a call, the control unit in the cell phone transmits a digital message to the closest base station over a radio data link called a "control channel." The control channel message identifies the cellular customer (SIM authentication), gives the called number (address) and requests that the call be assigned a voice channel. Most cell phones utilize low-power transmitters and operate at signal strengths ranging from 0.6 watts to 1.6 watts.[11] The value of a low-power transmitter is twofold. First, the user's signal does not travel beyond the cell in which the phone is operating. Second, the power consumption of a cell phone, which is normally battery operated, is relatively low. Low power translates into smaller batteries and fewer of them.

Digital Cell Phones

Digital cell phones use the same radio technology as analog phones, but they use it in a different way. Digital communication offers several important advantages when compared to analog communication, including: 1) better quality, less noise, 2) more efficient use of bandwidth, 3) better throughput and speed, 4) increased capacity and security, and 5) convergence and multimedia displays. The latter point becomes especially important when it comes to providing enhanced services features, such as caller ID, text messaging, video streaming, high-speed Internet access and MP3 music downloading and playback. A second consideration has to do with available bandwidth. As more and more consumers subscribe to cellular telephone service and want to incorporate advanced features, the issue of bandwidth becomes a major consideration. Digital cellular can accommodate more users per cell site than was true with the traditional analog systems. Digital cellular converts the user's voice (and specialized applications) into binary format and then compresses it. This compression allows between three and ten digital cell phone calls to occupy the space of a single analog call.[12]

Multiple Access and Demand Assignment

As the demand for cellular telephone service started to increase in the early 1990s, telephone service providers found that basic engineering assumptions borrowed from traditional landline networks did not hold true in mobile systems. While the average landline phone call lasts at least ten minutes, mobile calls usually run 90 seconds or less. Telecom engineers, who expected to assign 50 or more mobile phones to the same radio channel, soon discovered that by doing so they increased the probability that a user would be unable to obtain a dial tone—this is known as call-blocking probability. As a consequence, the early cell phone systems became quickly saturated, and the quality of service decreased rapidly. The critical problem was insufficient capacity.[13]

Cellular radio spectrum, like premium office space, is a valuable but limited resource. When a large number of cellular users need to be interconnected to a central switching facility, there is a need to manage and provide over-the-air access to a multiple set of users. We refer to this as the problem of multiple access. The challenge for the telecom engineer is to make radio spectrum available to users in the most efficient way possible. In principle, there are two ways that spectrum can be assigned to users. The first approach is called a fixed assignment. Examples include broadcast radio and television stations, where the licensee is granted a dedicated radio or television channel for a specified period of time subject to renewal. The second approach is called demand assignment, where a radio channel is granted on an as-needed basis. Cellular telephony operates on the principle of demand assignment. When a user wants a radio channel, the request is made and the user is granted a temporary channel assignment. Cellular telephone systems achieve spectral efficiency by allowing more than one person to carry on a conversation by sharing the same frequency without causing interference (i.e., multiplexing).[14]

There are three common approaches to cellular telephone access (Figure 8.8). They include:

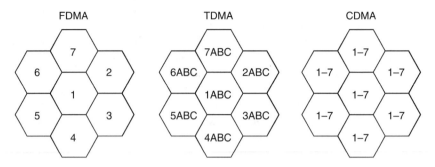

Figure 8.8 Comparison of Multiple Access Design Approaches.

- frequency division multiple access (FDMA);
- time division multiple access (TDMA);
- code division multiple access (CDMA).

Frequency Division Multiple Access

FDMA is a multiple access method in which users are assigned a specific frequency. FDMA implies that separate channels are allocated to users according to frequency separation, as illustrated in Figure 8.8. The user has sole claim to the assigned frequency for the length of the call or when entering into a new cell site. FDMA was traditionally used for analog transmission and is the oldest of the multiple access and demand assignment approaches. FDMA is less efficient in terms of spectrum use and allocation than either TDMA or CDMA.

Time Division Multiple Access

TDMA is a multiple access method that enhances the FDMA approach by splitting the designated cell site frequencies into time slots. TDMA is used in digital cellular and personal communication services (PCS)-based systems and is able to accommodate more users. Each user of a designated frequency is allowed to transmit sequentially in predetermined time slots. In short, only one person is actually using the channel at any given moment, albeit for a fraction of a second.[15] The user then gives up the frequency (or channel) to allow other users to have their turn. Channel capacity in a TDMA system is fixed and indisputable. Each frequency (or channel) carries a finite number of time slots, and the system cannot accommodate a new caller once each of the said time slots is filled (Figure 8.8).[16] TDMA is used as part of the Global System for Mobile Communications (GSM) standard for cellular telephone use.

Code Division Multiple Access

CDMA is a multiple access method which allows more than one person to carry on a conversation on a combined set of frequencies without causing interference. CDMA uses spread spectrum technology, which involves spreading (or scattering) the transmission over a range of frequencies rather than the user occupying a single channel (or designated frequency). In a CDMA system, every cell site shares the same set of frequencies. What distinguishes CDMA from the other two approaches is the fact that each telephone call is assigned a unique digital code that separates it from the multitude of calls that are being simultaneously transmitted. In sum, multiple calls are overlaid on each other on the same set of frequencies, with each call assigned a unique code (Figure 8.8).[17]

W-CDMA

Wideband code division multiple access (W-CDMA) is a wideband spread spectrum 3G mobile telecommunications air interface that utilizes the CDMA multiplexing scheme. It provides simultaneous support for a wide range of services with different characteristics on a common 5 MHz carrier. The W-CDMA method was developed by NTT DoCoMo and is designed to support high-speed Internet access, high-quality image transmission and videostreaming. W-CDMA can support mobile voice, data and video communication at speeds of up to 2 Mbps (local area) or 384 Kbps (wide area). W-CDMA is well suited to supporting the highly dense population centers of Europe and Asia.

Global System for Mobile Communication

Global System for Mobile Communication (GSM) is the most ubiquitous wireless standard for mobile communications in the world. The GSM Association (a major advocate group for the standard) estimates that 82 percent of the world's global cellular market uses the GSM standard. Its primary markets and territories include Europe, Scandinavia, Asia, Africa and parts of North and South America. Most GSM networks operate in the 900 MHz or 1800 MHz bands. Some countries in the Americas (including Canada and the U.S.) use the 850 MHz and 1900 MHz bands because the 900 and 1800 MHz frequency bands had been previously allocated. Newer versions of the GSM standard are designed to be backwards compatible with the original GSM standards. GSM uses a variation of TDMA for purposes of multiple access.

Development of the GSM standard began as early as 1982 by a working group operating within the European Telecommunications Standards Institute. The original working group was called Group Spécial Mobile, hence the acronym GSM. GSM uses a combination of TDMA and FDMA strategies. In addition to voice communication, the GSM (DCS 1800) is designed to include a variety of other services, including text messaging, caller ID and data transmission. What this means for consumers is that cell phone users are able to buy one phone that will work anywhere the GSM standard is supported. The GSM standard makes international roaming very common between mobile phone users traveling throughout the world.

The Business of Wireless Communication

U.S. Cellular Telephone Development

In the U.S., the wireless telephone industry has experienced dramatic growth, having achieved revenues of $138.8 billion in 2007, with service available to some 255,395,000 subscribers. This represents an estimated 81 percent of the total U.S. population.[18] The top four cellular telephone service providers are: 1) Verizon Wireless, 2) AT&T (formerly Cingular), 3) Sprint Nextel and 4) T-Mobile. Verizon and AT&T are the two most dominant carriers, claiming 31 percent and 30 percent respectively of U.S. cell phone market share.

Table 8.1 provides a brief comparison of U.S. subscriber growth patterns and annual cell phone revenues for the years 1987–2007.

International Cellular Development

The international growth rate of cellular phones has been even more dramatic. Cellular phones have proliferated throughout Southeast Asia, Latin America and Eastern Europe, where building cellular systems is proving to be faster and more cost-effective than building (or reconstructing) traditional

Table 8.1 Cellular Telephony Industry Estimates, 1987–2007: U.S. Subscriber Patterns and Annual Wireless Revenues (in thousand dollars)

Year	Estimated Total Subscribers	Estimated Annual Revenues
1987	1,230,855	1,151,519
1990	5,283,055	4,548,820
1993	16,009,461	10,892,175
1996	44,042,992	23,634,971
1999	86,047,003	40,018,489
2002	140,766,842	76,508,187
2005	207,896,198	113,538,221
2007	255,395,599	138,869,000

Source: CTIA—The Wireless Association, "Annual Wireless Industry Survey," Available at: http://www.ctia.org/content/index.cfm/AID/10316 (retrieved December 18, 2007).

telephone systems. This is particularly true in rural regions of the world with poor wireline infrastructures. The deployment of a cell phone system can be linked to the public switched telephone network and effectively bypass outmoded or unreliable local systems. In urban areas, cell phone deployment eliminates the challenges of implementing physical wireline systems that require negotiating rights-of-way clearance between carriers and cities (and home owners) as well as the arduous task of cutting up city streets and stringing wire on buildings and houses. Not surprisingly, developing countries account for a major portion of all wireless local loop subscribers. The number of cellular subscribers surpassed the 3 billion mark in August 2007. At current growth rates, global mobile penetration is expected to reach 50 percent by early 2008.[19]

Figure 8.9 provides a comparison of the top ten country leaders in cellular communication for 2006.

3G in Europe

After capitalizing on its success with GSM, Europe's telephone industry was well positioned to lead the way in twenty-first-century mobile technology. It should be noted that Europe has proportionately the highest number of cell phone users in the world. However, implementing 3G technology in Europe has proven to be an enormous challenge. Part of the difficulty can be attributed to the high cost for obtaining spectrum.[20] Starting in 2000, Europe's wireless carriers found themselves spending in excess of 100 billion euros to purchase spectrum space for a technology that was several years away

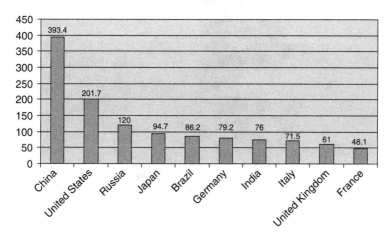

Figure 8.9 Top Ten Leaders in Cellular Communication (2006).

Source: International Telecommunications Union, "The 15 Leaders in Mobile Communication, 2006," Available at: http://www.itu.int/osg/spu/newslog/content/binary/MobileTop15_Jan20061.jpg (retrieved December 10, 2007).

in development.[21] The implementation of 3G has posed some significant technical challenges as well. 3G mobile phones cannot rival traditional broadband systems in terms of delivery speed and throughput. In short, consumers are unable to obtain the full range of Internet benefits in terms of speed, color and graphics.[22]

Another problem has to do with standards. In the late 1990s, when standards for 3G were being developed, the European authorities were determined to repeat the success of GSM. Rather than consider a U.S.-developed CDMA approach (which was both efficient and faster to implement), the European standards committee opted for W-CDMA, a European proprietary version. Most observers believe that the European standard selection was politically motivated. In the end, the implantation of 3G wireless technology has proven challenging, but the benefits are now beginning to be seen in terms of new communication service offerings.

Cell Phone Manufacturing

Today, there are five major cell phone manufacturers responsible for an estimated 80 percent of all international cellular telephone production. They are Nokia, Motorola, Sony Ericsson, Samsung and LG. Their respective level of global market share can be seen in Figure 8.10. It should be noted that, for 2007, Motorola saw a drop in market share of nearly 6 percent from the year before. In addition, there are a number of second-tier cell phone

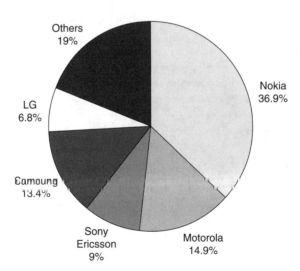

Figure 8.10 International Market Share: Cellular Telephone Manufacturers, 2007.

Source: Gartner Group and Information Week, "Nokia, Samsung Gain Cell Phone Market Share," Available at: http://www.videsignline.com/news/201802509 (retrieved December 5, 2007).

manufacturers as well, including Fujitsu, Panasonic (Japan), Ningbo Bird (China), Pantech Curitel (South Korea) and TCL–Alcatel (a joint venture— Hong Kong and France).

Cellular Telephone Plans

A typical cellular phone plan requires a one- to two-year contract that includes an initial activation fee as well as a penalty fee if the user ends the contract prior to the terms of the agreement. The monthly telephone charge can range from $40 to $200 depending on the number of voice minutes and specialized features. Additional minutes cost extra depending on the service plan as well as whether the time is peak or off-peak. Digital PCS service also offers à la carte charges for various types of enhanced services, including: text messaging, Internet access, music and video downloading, and roadside assistance.

Early Termination Fees

Many service providers either discount or give away what they call a cellular phone starter kit with a free (or discounted) phone as long as the user signs up for a service plan of one to two years. Most carriers utilize an early termination fee (ETF) as a way to establish the basic service plan. Even though most customers will never pay an ETF, they are part of wireless carriers' rate structures. ETFs are a means of ensuring customer consistency and reliability. ETFs secure a customer's commitment by offering a more attractive rate plan by committing to a specific term. ETFs are a common practice in many industries: airlines charge cancellation fees; car dealers assess fees for breaking leases; and many rental properties require non-refundable deposits. ETFs provide a measure of predictability to the revenue stream reasonably expected by wireless carriers in exchange for costs incurred to provide voice service.

Air Time Features

Air time charges are billed in full minute increments. Basic service features include:

- Unlimited incoming calls apply to calls received in the primary service area.
- Unlimited night and weekend minutes apply to calls made or received in the primary service area of 8 P.M. to 6 A.M. Monday–Thursday and 7 P.M. Friday to 6 A.M. Monday.
- Free long-distance applies to calls made from the primary service area to anywhere throughout the continental U.S.

- Expanded minutes apply to calls made or received to another user using the same cellular telephone carrier.
- Rollover minutes in the case of some carriers that allow the user to forward unused minutes into the next month. The sum total of minutes are swept at the end of the year.
- Directory assistance, taxes and network interconnect charges are additional.

Wireless Communication

Wireless communication is the transfer of information and entertainment services through the air without the need for physical wires. Historically, the term *wireless communication* referred to traditional radio technology. Today, however, wireless communication has come to mean the delivery of voice, data and Internet communication using a variety of devices that can include cell phones, personal digital assistants, laptop computers, etc.

Personal Communication Services or Smart Phones

Digital cell phones presuppose basic feature elements like voicemail, caller ID and long-distance telephone capability. Starting in 1995, the development of personal communication services (PCS) has steadily redefined the nature and purpose of cellular telephone communication. PCS emphasizes the *personal aspect* of wireless technology by advancing a number of enhanced feature elements, including:

1   e-mail;
2   personal planner;
3   text messaging;
4   cell phone cameras;
5   Internet access;
6   video imaging (sports clips on cell phones);
7   GPS locator;
8   combination cell phone/MP3 player.

Many industry watchers and device makers have coined the term *smart phones* as an alternative to *personal communication services*. Today's smart phones have built-in functionality that is programmable. The most current example of a smart phone can be seen with the 2006 introduction of the Apple iPhone. The iPhone is a multimedia Internet-enabled phone that uses a multi-touch screen with virtual keyboard and buttons. The iPhone's functions include voice communication, caller ID, an iPod (portable music player), Internet access, camera phone, text messaging and electronic mapping.

Central to this discussion is the importance of the electromagnetic spectrum, which provides the needed spectrum space in order to accommodate the various smart phone applications. In 1993, the U.S. Congress passed the Omnibus Budget Act, which authorized several auctions of the electromagnetic spectrum to be used for promoting greater competition in the PCS mobile phone market as well as the advancement of enhanced service features. The FCC subsequently conducted a series of auctions during the 1994–1996 time period, as well as in 2006. In January 2008, the FCC hosted a new round of auctions involving 62 MHz of spectrum in the 700 MHz range of frequencies.[23]

Cellular and PCS Network Standards

A wireless network standard is primarily a set of technical specifications involving the interface between cell phones, base stations and switching centers. The network standard details how voice or data is converted into electromagnetic signals.[24] Since the beginning of the original AMPS system, there have evolved several generations of mobile wireless standards. Each generation represents a progressive shift in terms of improving the kinds of information that can be sent over a wireless network, factoring in such important elements as connectivity, speed and throughput. Table 8.2 provides a brief summary of the four major generations of mobile wireless communication standards.

Bluetooth

Bluetooth represents an industry standard for personal wireless communication devices; referred to as personal area networks (PANs).[25] Bluetooth provides a way to connect and exchange information between Bluetooth-compatible devices such as PCs and laptop computers, digital cameras, cellular telephones, printers and videogame consoles using unlicensed short-range radio frequencies (i.e., typically 1–100 meters). Bluetooth simplifies the discovery and set-up of services between devices. For example, if a user has Bluetooth readiness built into his/her cell phone and laptop, the user can synchronize both laptop and cell phone for things like calendar events, e-mail and photo file sharing. Similarly, many of today's cars are equipped with Bluetooth readiness. This allows the user to receive a call on his/her cell phone, while enabling the call to be played through the vehicle's speakers. The radio is automatically muted. The Bluetooth specifications are developed and licensed by the Bluetooth Special Interest Group.

Wi-Fi

Wi-Fi s a wireless technology designed to improve the interoperability of wireless local area network devices based on the IEEE 802.11 standards.

Table 8.2 Mobile Wireless Communication Standards

First-generation wireless	*First-generation ("1G") wireless* was the original AMPS analog-based service created by AT&T and introduced into the Chicago market in 1983.
Second-generation wireless	*Second-generation ("2G") wireless* represents the slow, steady transition from analog to digital wireless throughout the early 1990s. 2G was capable of delivering voice and data speeds of 14.4 Kbs. The 2G standard became the starting point for additional enhanced wireless features, including caller ID and text messaging. By 2004, 97.4 percent of the U.S. cellular market was digitally based. 2G wireless has provided the basic platform for advancing cellular telephone diffusion throughout the U.S. TDMA, CDMA and GSM are designed to support existing 2G wireless communication systems.
Third-generation wireless	*Third-generation ("3G") wireless* represents a progressive shift in wireless communication. The goal is to provide Internet access that would allow users to obtain information and entertainment services via cellular and other hand-held portable devices. Some of the important features of 3G wireless systems include high-speed mobile Internet, e-mail and videostreaming. 3G is based on the ITU family of standards under the International Mobile Telecommunications program "IMT 2000." Japan was the first country to introduce 3G nationally, followed by Korea. By 2005, 3G was available in 40 countries and continues to become more fully diffused.
Fourth-generation wireless	*Fourth-generation ("4G") wireless* represents the future in wireless communication. It is still very much in the beginning stages of development. The long-term goal is to create a comprehensive Internet Protocol (IP) solution whereby voice, data and video can be streamed anytime, anywhere. The speed and throughput rate for 4G will be significantly higher than for 3G, approaching speeds of 100 Mbps both indoors and outdoors. 4G would provide additional technical benefits as well, including greater spectral efficiency, smoother handoffs across heterogeneous networks, and high network capacity (i.e., more simultaneous users per cell site).

As DSL and cable modem technology become more fully deployed, Wi-Fi provides a high-speed wireless Internet connection to computers within 50 meters of a small base station. Wi-Fi has become fairly commonplace in small dedicated professional and residential settings. Wi-Fi is widely used in offices, universities, libraries, cafes and other public places, as well as people's homes. In the case of residential dwellings, the Wi-Fi signal extends the broadband connection to other rooms, thus enabling more household users to access the Internet. Although many companies are working on ways to extend the range of Wi-Fi signals, it now takes hundreds of Wi-Fi base stations to cover the same area as a single WiMAX signal.

WiMAX

WiMAX represents the next generation in broadband wireless technology. WiMAX (Worldwide Interoperability for Microwave Access) is an IP-based high-capacity wireless network that can fully support high-speed Internet access at a range of up to 30 miles. WiMAX was created by a coalition of wireless industry professionals whose goal is to promote the compatibility and interoperability of devices based on the IEEE 802.16 standard. WiMAX allows a user, for example, to browse the Internet on a laptop computer without the need for a physical broadband connection such as cable modem, DSL or Ethernet cable. Subscribers value the flexibility, immediacy and power of wireless communication. WiMAX can be deployed as a new network installation or as an overlay to complement existing 2G and 3G wireless technologies. In addition, many broadband service providers are closely examining WiMAX for last-mile connectivity at high data rates. The resulting competition may bring lower pricing for both home and business customers, or bring broadband access to places where stringing cable is not cost-effective.

Mobile WiMAX is based on orthogonal frequency division multiple access (OFDMA) technology and has inherent advantages in throughput and spectral efficiency when compared to other multiple access approaches. Even though WiMAX can support VOIP, it is not expected to replace or compete with existing cellular telephone networks. WiMAX is still in the early stages of development, but it's poised for growth.[26]

There is growing international support for WiMAX deployment as well, since it can offer downtown urban centers the ability to offer users large-scale "hot spots" for Internet use. To be sure, WiMAX represents one of the important building blocks in making tomorrow's smart cities a reality. Taiwan and Australia are among the world's leaders in promoting the cause of WiMAX technology. In the U.S. today, there are two critical challenges restricting the future deployment of WiMAX technology. The first is the ability to obtain sufficient spectrum space to support WiMAX development in major urban centers around the U.S. The second challenge is the cost of WiMAX deployment and an uncertain return on investment. In August 2006, Sprint Nextel in partnership with Clearwire Communications announced plans to invest $5 billion over the following four years to build a so-called nationwide WiMAX 4G network. The first two cities would be Chicago and Washington, D.C. The proposed WiMAX network would let cell phones and laptop computers connect to the Internet throughout entire cities without the need for smaller, more localized Wi-Fi technology. The Sprint–Clearwire network would cover up to two miles from one base station to another and deliver speeds of up to 2 Mbps. In less than a year, Sprint and Clearwater have made the decision to scale back their original plans to build a nationwide high-speed wireless service. All this points to the difficulty of building a WiMAX network without fully understanding the expected demand for such services, given other existing methods for delivering high-speed Internet access.

Strategic Challenges: Discussion

Since the start of the twenty-first century, the phenomenal growth of cellular telephones has redefined the way business, government and individual users communicate on a day-to-day basis. A decade ago, the cell phone was used primarily for business and emergency communication. Today, cell phones have surpassed landline phones in terms of everyday use. The combination of increased network reliability, enhanced service features and more attractive rate plans has caused cell phone technology to become more widely diffused. At the heart of cell phone technology use is the principle of mobility, that is, the ability to communicate anytime, anywhere, without the need for physical wires. Location should never be a factor. For younger working professionals (as well as kids) cell phones are their only telephone device.

The digitalization of media and information technology has steadily transformed the cellular telephone into a multimedia "smart phone" device. Tomorrow's wireless phone is about sending and receiving high-quality, high-speed voice, data and video information across diverse network architectures. In the future, the wireless phone will become the quintessential, multitasking broadband device. For the user, this can include everything from checking on flight reservations, to being alerted to severe weather conditions, to using instant messaging to check on your children, to watching a sports video clip on your phone. Some observers have called it "broadband on the go." The Apple iPhone is just the beginning. . . . As mentioned earlier, the need to secure unused portions of the electromagnetic spectrum will become a high priority for those companies that wish to provide enhanced information and entertainment services in the future. Spectrum is a finite resource and is the principal reason why media, Internet and telecommunication companies bid an estimated $19 billion in the spring of 2008 for select portions of the electromagnetic spectrum. The FCC reported that the historic spectrum sale elicited twice as much revenue as the government had originally expected to raise. The major bidders included AT&T, Verizon, Google and Cox Communications. The stakes in terms of missing out on future information services were considered too critical to ignore.

Frequency licensing and efficient spectrum management are key network issues when considering today's wireless networks. New signaling techniques are being designed specifically to enhance present-day 2G and 3G networks. A major challenge in the future deployment of 4G technology is how to make the existing network architectures compatible with each other. A related issue is quality-of-service (QOS) standards. Quality of service refers to the measure of the performance for a system, reflecting its transmission quality and service availability (e.g., 4G is expected to have a reliability of at least 99.99 percent). Supporting QOS in 4G networks will be a major challenge. There are several QOS hurdles that will need to be addressed, including future bandwidth allocations, varying rate channel characteristics, fault tolerance levels, and handoff support among heterogeneous wireless networks.

9

THE INTERNET AND ELECTRONIC COMMERCE

The past two decades have witnessed the development of several new technologies that have expanded the world's geographical boundaries and hastened the pace of human communication. Foremost among them is the Internet. The Internet has been steadily woven into all aspects of business and leisure. The Internet has created a new business model that maximizes the potential for instantaneous communication to a worldwide customer base. It has fundamentally changed how retail trade is conducted in terms of information gathering, marketing, production and distribution. Secondly, the argument can be made that the Internet serves as the unofficial demarcation point that separates traditional media from so called new media. New media products and services like e-commerce (Amazon.com, eBay), MP3 file sharing (iTunes), social networking (MySpace, Facebook) and on-line reservation systems (airline, hotel and theater) are the direct consequence of the Internet and the power of intelligent networking.

Historical Overview

ARPANet

The beginnings of the Internet can be traced back to the early 1960s. At the peak of the Cold War, researchers in the Advanced Research Projects Agency (ARPA) of the Department of Defense built a computer network to share resources among defense strategists, researchers and contractors in different parts of the U.S.[1] The original ARPA network (known as ARPANet) provided a unique peer-to-peer communication network between and among defense personnel, educational institutions and federal agencies that were linked to it. The original ARPA network was designed to withstand a nuclear attack. The original concept behind ARPANet presupposed three important design elements, including a distributed architecture. No single network or person controlled the flow of information. This was done as a defense measure against possible attack and/or if someone tried to destabilize the network from a single gateway point (Figure 9.1). Second, the ARPANet provided

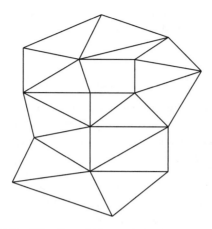

Figure 9.1 ARPANet Distributed Network Architecture.

open access (or permeability). A person connected to any node of the network could access the network and/or communicate with anyone else on the network via different gateway points. Third, the ARPANet provided free switching and routing of all data communication messages. The ARPANet carried the main bulk of data without charging for the service.

In 1983, ARPA took all military- and defense-related nodes off the ARPANet and created a separate network. The remaining civilian nodes, which came to be known as the Internet, consisted of smaller networks in educational institutions, research institutions, major corporations and federal agencies. In 1990, ARPA handed over the primary organization and transport responsibility to another federal agency, the National Science Foundation (NSF). NSFNET served as the primary carrier transport (or backbone) of the newly emerging Internet until 1995.

World Wide Web (WWW)

As the popularity of the Internet increased, newcomers often found the arcane navigational commands a difficult task. Such would-be users had to master a complex set of computer commands and procedures before they could access the Internet. What was needed was an easy-to-use communication procedure that could link various programs. In 1989, Tim Berners-Lee of CERN, a Swiss physics lab, developed a navigational protocol for the Internet and distributed the program for free. This protocol was based on the principle of hypertext (or non-linear text), which is the foundation of multimedia computing. Lee's hypertext markup language (HTML) protocol does not require any specialized computer skills other than the ability to point the mouse and click on text or graphics. The hypertext protocol allows the user to navigate the Internet by moving from one document to another (or from one computer

THE TELECOMMUNICATIONS INDUSTRY STRUCTURE

host to another). Lee's contribution to the development of the Internet cannot be overestimated. The HTML protocol forms the basis for the world wide web concept.

The Internet Today

The success of the Internet today is due to a combination of factors, including hypertext linking, improved website design and powerful search engines like Google and Yahoo. This, in combination with high-speed Internet access via cable modems and DSL technology, has greatly improved navigation, organization and speed. The Internet has transformed today's business and social environment. As noted communication scholar Everett Rogers points out, once a primary technology (or innovation) has been fully diffused into a system there is no going backward. Basic patterns of social and organizational behavior are forever changed.[2] Moreover, the systemic consequences are both direct and indirect. According to Rogers,

> One problem in measuring the consequences of innovations is untangling cause-and-effect relationships. Ideally, we should only measure the consequences that are exclusively the outcome of an innovation. . . . But many important consequences are unanticipated and indirect.[3]

The International Dimension

The Internet is becoming steadily diffused on a worldwide basis. According to Paul Saffo, Institute for the Future in Menlo Park, California, it takes 30-plus years for a major technology to reach the full bloom of social acceptance.[4] The growth of the Internet has exceeded Saffo's estimate by nearly half. Table 9.1 provides a comparison of the top 20 countries in terms of Internet usage, as well as penetration rate as a percentage of population. The United States has the highest level of Internet usage by country, followed by China. What is important to remember is that the figure depicting Internet usage is to some extent tied to the country's overall population figure. India, for example, ranks fourth on our list with an estimated 42 million Internet users. However, that figure represents only 3.7 percent of the country's overall population. In contrast, the country of Norway, not ranked on our list, has an estimated 4 million users, representing a penetration rate of 88 percent of the country's population. Similarly, Iceland has an estimated 258,000 Internet users, representing a penetration rate of 86.3 percent of the country's population. Thus countries like the Netherlands, Sweden, Israel and Switzerland, for example, have relatively high penetration rates given the size of their respective populations.

Another important consideration is the growth of the Internet according

Table 9.1 Top 20 Internet Usage by Country and Penetration Rate as a Percentage of Population Base

Country or Region	Internet Usage (millions)	Penetration (Percentage of Population)
1 United States	211	69.7
2 China	162	12.3
3 Japan	86.3	67.1
4 Germany	50.4	61.1
5 India	42.0	3.7
6 Brazil	39.1	21.0
7 United Kingdom	37.6	62.3
8 South Korea	34.1	66.5
9 France	32.9	53.7
10 Italy	31.4	52.9
11 Russia	28.0	19.5
12 Mexico	22.7	21.3
13 Canada	22.0	67.8
14 Spain	20.0	43.9
15 Indonesia	20.0	8.9
16 Vietnam	16.5	19.4
17 Turkey	16.0	21.1
18 Australia	15.0	71.9
19 Taiwan	14.5	63.0
20 Philippines	14.0	16.0

Sources: ITU, Nielsen Research, CI Almanac, "Internet World Stats," Available at: http://www.internetworldstats.com/top20.htm (retrieved May 10, 2008).

to continental region. Table 9.2 provides a comparison of Internet penetration by continental region as a percentage of overall population base. North America followed by Oceania/Australia and Europe have achieved the highest degree of Internet penetration as a percentage of population. However, the Middle East followed by Africa and Latin America/Caribbean have experienced the highest growth rate as a percentage of population between 2000 and 2008.

Electronic Commerce

Electronic commerce (EC) represents the ability to sell goods and services electronically via the Internet. The combination of intelligent networking and advancements in computer and communication technology has created a vast global playing field where buyers and sellers from many different countries are free to participate.[5] This chapter will examine current developments in the area of EC. A special emphasis is given to the importance of strategic marketing. A central theme throughout this chapter is that we are witnessing the demassification of media and entertainment products, made possible by the Internet and just-in-time manufacturing trends. For marketers, the

Table 9.2 Internet Penetration Rate as a Percentage of Continental/Regional Population Base

	Percentage of World Population	Internet Penetration as a Percentage of Population	Percentage of World Usage	Percentage Growth Rate 2000–2008
Africa	14.2	5.3	3.6	1,030.2
Asia	56.6	14.0	37.6	363.4
Europe	12.0	47.7	27.1	263.5
Middle East	3.0	21.3	3.0	1,176.8
North America	5.1	73.1	17.5	127.9
Latin America/Caribbean	8.6	23.8	9.8	659.9
Oceania/Australia	0.5	57.0	1.4	154.0
World total	100.0	21.1	100.0	290.0

Source: Internet World Statistics, "Internet World Stats," Available at: http://www.internetworldstats.com/stats.htm (retrieved May 10, 2008).

steady shift from mass to micromarketing is being driven by a combination of technological change and strategic opportunity. As marketers fully realize, the actual purchase of a product or service on-line represents only one aspect of an EC transaction. Whether it's obtaining background information about a vacation destination spot using Expedia or comparing prices about a potential car purchase using *Kelley Blue Book*, EC is also about information exchange. In short, consumers need information before they can make an informed buying decision.

At the start of the twenty-first century, EC has created a new business model that maximizes the potential for instantaneous communication to a worldwide customer base. EC has taken the principle of exchange efficiency to a whole new level in terms of retail trade. There are three kinds of e-commerce transactions. They include business-to-consumer (B2C), business-to-business (B2B) and consumer-to-consumer (C2C). B2C EC involves selling products and services directly to consumers via the Internet. B2C comes in two general formats, which are: traditional retailers (e.g., Sears, Target, Lands' End, etc.) and those companies whose primary business model depends on the Internet as the basis for retail trade (e.g., eBay, Amazon.com, Dell Computers, etc.). The EC merchant, in turn, is willing and able to provide prospective customers with 24/7 technical support capability (e.g., Dell Computers, Gateway Computers, etc.), as well as the ability to track the status of their package delivery via the Internet (e.g., Federal Express, UPS, etc.).

B2B EC involves on-line communication between businesses to sell products and services and to exchange information. B2B dramatically changes the structure of the traditional business supply chain, which normally consists of raw material suppliers, a manufacturer, a distributor and a retailer. Prior to the Internet, the said players communicated with each other through electronic data interchange (EDI). Any one of these parties can now transact with each other via an "intranet exchange," that is, private internal web communication. Information flows in all direction between various members of the supply chain. Moreover, any one of these parties can also transact with the customer directly. The so-called middlemen (i.e., distributors and retailers) become less important to the direct delivery of goods and services.

C2C EC involves the exchange of goods, services and information directly between consumers. EC websites like eBay and Craigslist.com provide opportunities for consumers to display and sell anything from consumer electronics to trading stamps. C2C also includes the exchange of information through Internet forums that appeal to special interest groups. Through these forums, buyers do more than consume product information. They help generate useful information, which in turn can influence and facilitate purchasing decisions. In sum, the Internet has created a virtual community of users throughout the world equally capable of buying and selling on-line as well as providing useful information.

In this chapter, we will consider three aspects to the business of Internet communication and electronic commerce. They include: 1) portals and search engines, 2) marketing and 3) supply chain management.

Portals and Search Engines

Portals can trace their origins to search engines, which are primarily software tools that help the user perform key word searches and locate specific information throughout numerous Internet host sites. Portals are responsible for organizing and classifying information resources on the Internet. Today's portals are to the organization of content what the HTML protocol is to Internet navigation. Examples of portals include Google, Yahoo, LexisNexis and WebMD, to name only a few. The portal, in combination with hypertext linking, has made using the Internet far more accessible than in years past.

Why Portals?

By the late 1990s, the Internet had become the wild, wild west of communication. As one writer put it, accessing the Internet for the first time was a "little like taking a farm boy from the Midwest, putting him in the middle of Manhattan, and telling him to go have the time of his life."[6] With so many newcomers and given the increasing complexity of host sites and information content, there was an obvious need for search directories that would help organize and give direction on the Internet.

The basic reason for creating a portal is simple. By becoming the principal gatekeeper of people's on-line experience and information search, the portal companies expect to lay claim to a market share of loyal users who will rely on them not only to help navigate the Internet but to buy goods and services as well. In exchange for trusted advice and guidance, such companies hope to influence the user's web browsing and viewing experience. Moreover, the major portals are well positioned to capitalize on various kinds of advertising opportunities. It should be pointed out that the importance given to portals is by no means a uniquely American phenomenon. Internationally, the most widely visited websites tend to be portals. Table 9.3 provides a listing of the 15 most widely visited websites in the U.S.

Planning and Design Considerations

The key to building a successful portal is to make it an integral and valuable part of the user's Internet experience. Two important features found in most portals are the aggregation of content and personalization.

Aggregation of Content

The primary responsibility of a portal is to collate data from a variety of information sources around the world. This is accomplished through international alliances and distribution relationships. The portal is responsible for the organization and classification of information, thus making it possible for key word and context-based search information. Today's portals blend the best features of the dictionary, encyclopedia and Yellow Pages into one integrated search engine. The aggregation of content provides the basis for comparison shopping, whereby the user can locate and compare prices (and features) among a wide variety of merchants and service providers both regionally and nationally.

Table 9.3 Top 15 Most Widely Visited Websites in the U.S.

1 Google
2 Yahoo
3 My Space
4 YouTube
5 Facebook
6 MSN Windows Live
7 Wikipedia
8 Microsoft Network
9 eBay
10 AOL
11 Blogger.com
12 Craigslist
13 Amazon.com
14 Go
15 Photobucket

Sources: Nielsen Net Ratings; Alexa.

Personalization

Portal software permits users to receive personalized information in the form of specialized content (e.g., daily news updates, stock reports, weather, newly released books and publications, medical information, etc.). Personalization reflects the principle of push-vs.-pull technology, whereby the portal downloads topical information to a person's PC that is unique (or relevant) to that user. In addition, the portal provides registered users personal communication tools such as professional news updates, e-mail accounts, special offers and address books.[7]

The Future of Portals

Many of today's better-known portals (e.g., Google, Yahoo and AOL) are positioning themselves to become multilevel Internet companies. They want to become a one-stop, full-service site with content and links to a whole host of information, entertainment and value-added services. Such companies want to create an integrated service brand to prospective users. In contrast, there is also a move toward more narrowcasted portals that are designed to serve more highly specialized audiences. They are looking to serve the more sophisticated user who has defined information needs. As an example, WebMD advertises itself as the number one portal for obtaining information about health issues. The website, available at http://www.webmd.com/, provides useful medical news and information about a variety of health issues as well as providing users with information pertaining to finding doctors, hospitals and specialized treatment centers. WebMD is an example of a specialized portal.

Internet Marketing

The Internet has become an integral part of any marketing and public relations strategy for companies looking to promote their products and services. Virtually all major businesses and government and nonprofit organizations maintain a website. A well-designed website has become an essential marketing and public relations tool. An effective organizational website provides the user with:

1   contact information;
2   a directory to personnel, professional staff and sales contacts;
3   a description of products and service offerings;
4   current news information and press releases;
5   investor relations, including a copy of the company's annual report;
6   information items, including reports, conference slide presentations, relevant URL links, etc.

Branding

Through the years, branding has emerged as a specialized field of marketing and advertising, and the burgeoning field of business literature reflects this pattern. David Aaker's seminal work *Managing Brand Equity* suggests that a highly successful brand is one that creates a strong resonance connection in the consumer's mind and leaves a lasting impression. According to Aaker, brands can be divided into five key elements: brand loyalty, brand awareness, perceived quality, brand associations and proprietary brand assets.[8] Global media brands, like Sony, Disney, HBO, Microsoft and MTV, represent hardware and software products used by consumers worldwide. Such products are localized to the extent that they are made to fit into the local requirements (i.e., language, manufacturing, marketing style) of the host nation and culture. To that end, a successful brand name creates a resonance or connection in the consumer's mind toward a company's product or service.

The Internet and Brand Extension

A successful television program is one that engenders a strong brand identity. As Alan Albarran points out, audiences tend to watch programs as opposed to television networks, stations or channels.[9] Programs that attract and hold audiences become recognizable brands for the program producers. The challenge for today's broadcast and cable programmers is to establish and preserve a loyal audience following given the number of competing television program services coupled with other media choices.

Television Websites

In response, broadcast and cable programmers are having to adapt new strategies to address a changing and ever more competitive television marketplace. Foremost among the important strategies going forward is to establish an attractive and engaging television website presence. A strong website presence promotes both network and program identity. Louisa Ha makes the argument that there are three distinguishing website strategies employed by today's broadcast and cable networks. They include: 1) the welcome-all model, 2) the fans-friendly (in-depth) model and 3) the hello model.[10]

The welcome-all model provides a general introduction; it is the one-site-fits-all approach characterized by the major television networks (i.e., CBS, NBC, ESPN, PBS, etc.). The fans-friendly model targets the loyal television viewer who has a greater understanding of specific programs, characters, story line, etc. The fans-friendly website is more sophisticated in its design and displays a higher level of interactivity (e.g., ABC's *Desperate Housewives* and *Lost*, Fox's *American Idol* and CBS's *CSI*. In the case of Fox's *American Idol*, fans are routinely polled to give their opinions regarding the program's ongoing performers. Last, the hello model is an investment into the future and represents up-and-coming broadcast and cable networks.

Researchers Louisa Ha and Sylvia Chan-Olmsted conducted two studies that looked at how broadcast and cable networks use the Internet as a method of brand extension. The authors posit that television programming supported with a visible website presence enhances the viewing experience of TV viewers. Brand extension in the television industry can and does translate into audience loyalty towards a particular network or program. One of the most important ways that the Internet adds value to conventional television viewing is by creating interactive experiences. Such interaction becomes an essential tool in leveraging the television program experience.[11] Ha and Chan-Olmsted devised a framework for understanding the strategies employed by television networks and stations in promoting brand extension. They include: 1) playfulness, 2) choice, 3) connectedness, 4) information collection and 5) reciprocal communication.[12] In a 2001 study, the authors conclude:

> While a good web site may not compensate for mediocre programs, it [certainly adds] value to the programs that have already been well received and thus nurture[s] the loyalty of its audience. Furthermore, as the subjects both with and without prior web site exposure agreed that they explored only their favorite program/TV stars on the web-sites, we see a clear "selective exposure behavior" exhibited by the users of the websites, demonstrating certain reinforcement and supplemental functions of the sites.[13]

Micromarketing and Personalization

As Ithiel de Sola Pool once wrote, the mass media revolution is undergoing a reversal: "instead of identical messages being disseminated to millions of people, intelligent networking permits the adaptation of electronic messaging to the specialized or unique needs of individuals."[14] This has proven especially true in the area of the Internet and marketing communication. More and more, we are witnessing the demassification of media and entertainment products made possible by Internet and just-in-time (i.e., made-to-order) manufacturing trends. For marketers, the steady shift from mass to micro-marketing is being driven by a combination of technological change and strategic opportunity. From iPods to digital video recording, consumers now have the ability to compile, edit and customize the media they use.[15]

Broadcast television and large-circulation newspapers are no longer seen as the primary or best means of advertising to smaller niche audiences. The lessons of cable television have underscored the importance of narrowcasting. But even cable television has its limits as a medium of communication. More and more companies are using the Internet to communicate and personalize the information exchange between the advertiser (or retailer) and the end consumer. As Sylvia Chan-Olmsted points out, the Internet's interactive capability changes the basic relationship between the individual and media, challenging marketers to shift their emphasis from persuasion to relationship building. "As communication channels continue to proliferate and fragment, successful media firms will have to focus on consumers, rather than on systems of distribution or types of media content."[16] One indication of this trend was a comment made by Coca-Cola president Steven Heyer when he declared that Coke was moving away from broadcast television as "the anchor medium" toward more direct experience-driven marketing.[17] Personalized marketing involves knowing more about the particular interests and buying habits of one's customers. As an example, Amazon.com routinely sends out information updates to its customers notifying them of newly published books based on information obtained and analyzed from past purchasing selections.

Internet Advertising

The field of advertising is undergoing a major change. More and more of today's advertising is shifting from traditional mass media to the Internet. After nearly a century of traditional advertising and its corresponding one-way messages, today's consumers have become a lot more sophisticated and demanding in terms of their expectations. The days of the passive television viewer are long gone. The combination of increased viewing options and simple technologies like the TV remote control and digital video recorders has enabled today's viewer to expect more from advertisers. To that end, the Internet allows marketers to achieve a level of interactivity with consumers that other traditional media cannot match.

One of the longstanding criticisms of advertising is that it is something of a blunt instrument. Traditional advertising tends to be mass oriented, that is, advertisements directed to the public at large (i.e., newspapers, broadcast television, billboards, etc.). The audience composition is often broad and difficult to define. More specifically, audience research groups are routinely challenged to devise better ways for evaluating who is actually seeing the advertisement. One of the unique benefits of Internet advertising is that it is directly tied to the user. Search (and search engines) is the most common web activity because people go on-line with a purpose. The user actively seeks out the content that is displayed on his/her screen. If the corresponding ad display is relevant, it is going to leave a more lasting impression.

A significant number of companies, from transnational corporations to small businesses, utilize Internet advertising as part of their basic marketing strategy. Internet advertising typically involves two distinct players. The first is the advertiser (or advertising agency) responsible for placing the advertisement. The second is the publisher (or search engine host) responsible for displaying the advertisement. An industry oversight group called the Interactive Advertising Bureau (IAB) has established technical guidelines for determining ad display size and graphic requirements as well as evaluation methods. There are five types of Internet ads: banner ads, interstitials, rich media, 3-D visualization and key word searches.

Banner Ads

Banner ads are small, usually rectangular graphics that appear on a number of business and organizational websites. They function similarly to roadside billboards. An example might be a picture of the Visa logo accompanying a directory to city dining. When viewers click on the banner, they are linked to that advertiser's website. This action is known as a *click-through*. In many cases, banners are delivered by a central ad server.[18] The ad display is known as an *impression* and is reported whenever an individual ad is displayed on a website. The rates for banner ads are based on the number of impressions (or times) the advertisement appears in pages viewed by users. A variation on the banner ad concept is *buttons*, which are located at the bottom of a web page. Clicking on the button takes the on-line viewer directly to the advertiser's website.

Interstitials

Interstitials are ads that appear between screen changes on a website, particularly when a new screen is loading. *Pop-ups* and *pop-unders* are a form of interstitials. These ads suddenly appear in a new window in front of or behind the window being viewed. Because these ad exposures are forced, interstitials are often considered to be intrusive. Such ads are often associated with lotteries, special offers, vacations and pornography.[19]

Rich Media

Rich media involve the use of highly interactive and visually attractive ad displays. They tend to hold consumer attention better than traditional banner ads. Rich media ads are of high quality and include animations, streaming audio and video. The ever increasing availability of broadband Internet has enabled this format to flourish.

3-D Visualization

3-D visualization is a form of advertising that allows users to interact on-line with simulated products. As an example, one Verizon ad allows consumers to inspect several of its phone products by rotating them from any angle as well as zooming in and out for details. This type of advertising is often used with consumer electronics.

Key Word Search

Key word search, also known as contextual advertising, involves text-based ads and links that appear next to a search engine result. An advertiser buys search terms from the search engine site and pays only if consumers click through to its site. The term *click-through* (or *hit*) refers to the number of times viewers respond to a specific website or advertisement. An advertisement that generates a large number of hits can be considered successful in terms of promoting consumer interest. Key word searches are typically associated with search engines like Google and Yahoo. As an example, Miller Brewing might contract with Google and Yahoo so that every time someone conducts a search using the terms "beer," "party" and/or "friends" a text-based ad for Miller Genuine Draft Beer accompanies the requested site.

In general, there are three kinds of key word matching options: broad matching (based on topical interest), exact matching (word for word) and phase matching (based on the context or situation). In principle, a key word search allows an advertiser to target a message to an audience that is already interested in it. Moreover, key word searches offer the benefit of measurable value; that is, one can measure (or tally) the number of people who click through to the advertisement. This enables the publisher (or search engine firm) to offer prospective advertisers different pricing options ranging from maximum cost per click, where the advertiser sets a prescribed limit on the number of hits it is willing to pay for, to a cost-per-click option, where the advertiser is charged based on the total number of hits.

Other On-Line Promotional Tools

In addition to advertising, marketers use a number of other on-line promotional tools including content sponsorships, viral marketing and on-line social networks.

Sponsorships

Companies sponsor special content on websites to create and maintain a positive association between the company's brand and the website experience. Sponsorships typically include placement of a sponsor's logo or brand name in carefully targeted sites where they can offer relevant information or service to the audience. For example, E-Trade sponsors the Markets section on msnbc.com, which provides up-to-the-minute financial market information; and Nationwide insurance sponsors the NASCAR Up-to-Speed Challenge contest on ESPN.com, which also includes the ability to obtain an insurance quote.

Viral Marketing

Viral marketing is the Internet version of word-of-mouth communication. It involves creating a website, video, interactive game, e-mail message or some other event that is so infectious that consumers will want to pass it along to their friends. Because the content comes from a friend, the receiver is more likely to pay attention to it, use it to make informed purchasing decisions, and pass it along to others voluntarily. For example, OfficeMax launched its "ElfYourself" website for the holiday season, which allowed consumers to personalize a dancing elf and e-mail it to others. The site drew 36 million visits in nearly five weeks and increased traffic to its website by 20 percent without any paid advertising.[20] Viral marketing often uses existing social networks, like Facebook and YouTube, as conduits.

On-Line Social Networks

On-line social networks, such as Facebook, MySpace, YouTube and Second Life, are web communities that provide consumers with on-line places to congregate, socialize and exchange information. Marketers recognize the targeting potential of these websites and continue to explore ways to reach consumers via these on-line communities. Users of these social networking sites often will list their favorite products or interests (e.g., television programs, brand of coffee, music), which advertisers can then use to create offers or experiences tailored to that user. For example, a Facebook user who rents a movie on Blockbuster.com can be asked if he would like to have his movie choice broadcast out to all his friends on Facebook. If he agrees, his friends will receive the message, along with an ad from Blockbuster.[21]

In addition, companies have established a brand-based presence in Second Life. For example, Pontiac created Motorati Island, a place dedicated to car enthusiasts and car culture. Visitors can race at Pontiac Raceway Park and play other kinds of on-line games that all contribute to the Pontiac brand experience.[22] Other companies have decided to build their own targeted web communities, or microsites. For example, Nike has established the Nike Plus website, where 200,000 runners can upload, track and compare their performances. Regardless of the approach, these on-line social networks provide opportunities for like-minded consumers to gather together, as well as opportunities for companies to provide those consumers with ad displays and brand experiences that will ultimately influence purchasing decisions.

The Internet and Supply Chain Management

Supply chain management (SCM) is a complex business model that takes into consideration the entire set of linking steps necessary to produce and deliver a product to the end consumer. A supply chain consists of the intermediary steps from the point of product inception (inclusive of the purchase order) to the delivery of the finished good(s) to the consumer. A supply chains consists of the following intermediary steps:

- research and design teams;
- intermediate and end product manufacturing;
- marketing and sales;
- product ordering and storage;
- wholesalers;
- retailers and/or direct sales;
- distribution and delivery to the end consumer.

SCM has two distinct and equally important parts: 1) the philosophy and 2) the methodology. SCM philosophy is grounded in the belief that everyone involved in the supply chain is both a supplier and a customer and requires access to timely, up-to-date information. The goal is to optimize organizational efficiency and to meet the needs of any and all suppliers and customers. SCM methodology has to do with the specifics of strategy implementation. The organization starts by identifying the existing supply chain processes and evaluating them against best practices. Through process reengineering, all non-essential elements are eliminated. SCM forces companies to move away from an organizational structure designed around functional silos toward one designed around the end-to-end flow of business processes. Information is key. To that end, an essential element of any SCM methodology is the ability to share timely information across the entire supply chain system. A well-designed SCM system gives automated intelligence to an extended network of suppliers, manufacturers, distributors, retailers and a host of other trading partners.[23]

Organizational Control

Since the late 1940s, there has been a slow, paradigmatic shift away from top-heavy, centralized decision making toward decentralization where greater responsibility has been given to the regional manager for routine decisions. The combination of computer and telecommunications technology has had a major effect on the spatial reorganization of activity for the transnational organization. Time and distance factors have become less important in determining where a company chooses to locate.[24] One important consequence is that organizational hierarchies tend to be flatter, thereby allowing direct communication between and among organizational players.[25]

The term *organizational control* is used to describe a system-wide method for managing, tracking and evaluating an organization's domestic and foreign operations. Organizational control enables the complex organization to strategically plan, allocate resources and take corrective action in order to meet changing conditions. At the heart of organizational control is the intelligent network, which can be likened to the vital nervous system of an organization. It is responsible for integrating information and communication both internal and external to the organization.[26]

The intelligent network performs the proper switching and routing of electronic communication between a global set of users that might include senior project managers, research and design teams, manufacturing and distribution, sales and marketing, etc. The intelligent network provides the capability for increased and faster communication in the field and the flattening of organizational hierarchies. In the design of an SCM system, every event or task that takes place is considered both a source and a delivery point. By allowing information to flow in all directions, the intelligent network provides the structural links and coordination of activities that make global communication possible between an organization's various operating divisions.

Supply Chain Management and ERP

A supply chain is connected by transportation and storage activities and coordinated through planning and networked information activities. When engineers discuss the architecture of a network, they are describing how the physical parts of the network are organized, including: information pathways (configurations), 2) terminals (gateways and access points) and 3) data enhancement equipment (software protocols and add-on devices). Central to any discussion of supply chain management and intelligent networking is the principle of enterprise resource planning (ERP), which attempts to integrate all departments and functions across an entire company onto a single computer system using a common database and a shared set of reporting tools.[27]

Dredden and Bergdolt define enterprise resource planning as "information systems that integrate processes in an organization using a common database and shared reporting tools."[28] While the reality is that many organizations maintain highly diverse and sometimes incompatible software, the goal of an ERP system is to replace stand-alone programs such as accounting, manufacturing, human resources, warehousing and transportation and replace them with a single unified software program. Consider, for example, the placement of a purchase order for a laptop computer. The customer service representative (CSR) takes the order and sets into motion a kind of software road map that will enable the said purchase order to be completed by the various players who make up the supply chain. The CSR has access to all of the pertinent information in order to complete the transaction, including the customer order information, credit rating (where appropriate), order history, production status, warehousing and distribution.

Just-in-Time Manufacturing

Telecommunications has collapsed the time and distance factors that once separated nations, people and business organizations. Communication is instantaneous. The combination of high-speed voice, data and video communication allows both large and small organizations the ability to coordinate the production, marketing and delivery of products on a worldwide basis. The full impact of instantaneous communication can be seen in the area of SCM, global inventory management systems and just-in-time manufacturing capability.

Most companies have access to excellent hardware and software capability that enables them to operate in an international business environment. The distinguishing factor often centers on speed and turnaround time. Faster product cycles and the ability to train and produce worldwide production teams have transnationalized the manufacturing and distribution process. It is the ability to apply time-based competitive strategies at the global level that enables the transnational corporation to manage inventories across borders. As researchers Goldhar and Lei observe:

> We are now in a global competitive environment in which flexibility, responsiveness and low cost/low volume manufacturing skills will determine the sustainability of competitive advantage. The strategic picture is clear. . . . [Today's manufacturers] must also manage that most precious of all resources—time.[29]

At the heart of time-based competitiveness is just-in-time manufacturing, which allows a company to meet an order in the least amount of time. Just-in-time manufacturing (and delivery) relies on the use of supply chain management and ERP systems for the purpose of tracking customer orders. ERP systems are designed to interface with universal product codes (i.e., bar codes) or radio frequency identification (RFID) tags, which enables a manufacturer or service provider to track the status of a product throughout the entire manufacturing and delivery cycle. An RFID tag can be applied to or incorporated into a product, animal or person for the purpose of identification using radio waves. RFID tags can be read from several meters away and some beyond the line of sight of the reader. RFID tags are expected to become an integral part of supply chain management operations in the future, thus improving the efficiency of inventory tracking and management.

In summary, SCM systems integrate and optimize both internal and external processes to the organization. This includes dealing with external business partners across the entire supply chain.[30] The real value of SCM (and intelligent networking) is that everyone who is part of the extended supply chain has access to all of the relevant information contained on the SCM system. In contrast, ERP systems tend to focus on internal business processes within the boundaries of a single organization. The ERP system coordinates and integrates all information planning activities within a single organization. This can include reacting to customer needs (e.g., answering customer inquiries about production status, delivery dates, etc.).

Product Ordering, Storage and Distribution

The principle of "exchange efficiency" is an important concept found in management theory. It has to do with creating the optimum conditions through which a consumer can obtain a product or service. Traditional examples of exchange efficiency can be seen with speed lanes in a supermarket, which allow customers to move quickly through the checkout line. Similarly, the principle of exchange efficiency can be seen with companies that specialize in catalogue shopping such as L.L. Bean and Lands' End, to name only two. In the latter examples, exchange efficiency is made possible because of an easy-to-use catalogue (or Internet website), supplemented with a 24-hour-a-day toll-free telephone number and three-day shipping. Today, electronic commerce has taken the principle of exchange efficiency to a whole new level in terms of retail trade and distribution.

EC is not exempt from good business planning. The same rules of product planning and distribution apply. The difference, however, lies in the value proposition to the consumer. In short, what does the e-merchant offer in the way of value-added benefits that would prompt the customer to consider engaging in an EC transaction? The value proposition for an eBay customer is the combination of availability and convenience of hard-to-find goods and services. The value proposition for an Amazon.com customer is the combination of convenience and cost savings in terms of shopping for books and other items on-line. What EC does best is simplify the process of ordering products and services and delivering them to the end consumer. We call this *exchange efficiency*. As an example, Apple iTunes has eliminated the need for traditional bricks-and-mortar music stores by making it easy for consumers to download music for a set fee. Likewise, ordering airline tickets on-line (or e-ticketing) has revolutionized the way people purchase airline tickets. The need for the traditional travel agent (or middleman) has become greatly reduced. Both Apple iTunes and e-ticketing are the quintessential forms of exchange efficiency.

Customer Oriented

Another important element is recognizing the importance of building good customer relations between the EC merchant and the consumer. The relationship begins with an attractive, secure and easy-to-use website. To that end, the EC merchant needs to be customer oriented. Many factors go into making this possible.

It starts by making the purchasing experience user friendly. The mechanics of the purchase selection should be easy to execute. The customer should feel confident that his/her purchase is both confidential and secure. Credit card transactions represent some 90 percent of all on-line purchases. Customer order information should be encrypted with e-shopping carts and electronic payment services, like credit cards and PayPal.

Second, the EC merchant should service its customers with personalized attention (i.e., personalized messages, purchase suggestions, membership programs, special offers and discounts). In short, the EC merchant should provide an incentive for the customer to return.

Third, the EC merchant should provide good customer support, including a willingness to answer any and all questions. While the relationship may be virtual, real questions demand real answers that are timely and supportive. Much of Dell Computers' success, for example, is built on its reputation for good customer support. Over time, Dell Computers has eliminated the need for retail outlets by allowing customers to order desktop and laptop computers on-line or over the phone. But what seals the deal is the 24/7 customer support system that allows Dell customers to work with trained customer service representatives and technicians to solve various kinds of technical and software issues. At the end of the day, the EC merchant will be judged on its ability to handle complaints promptly and effectively.

Google

Company founders Larry Page and Sergey Brin first met at Stanford University in 1995 when Page, 24, was visiting the campus as a graduate from the University of Michigan. Brin, 23, was among a group of students assigned to show him around. While they disagreed on many topics, they were in agreement on one of the toughest challenges facing the Internet at that time, namely, the ability to organize and retrieve information from massive amounts of data. Together, Page and Brin began work on a search engine called BackRub, named for its unique ability to analyze the "back links" pointing to a given website.[31] By 1997, BackRub had started to develop a reputation among the various computer technophiles who had seen it. In the meantime, Brin set up an office and the two began calling on potential investors who might be interested in licensing the developing search technology. One of those who showed an interest was Yahoo co-founder David Filo, who counseled them to grow the business themselves and make it scalable.

In September 1998, Google Inc. opened its door in Menlo Park, California. By then Google.com was still in a beta testing phase, but was answering 10,000 search queries per day. News media like *USA Today* and *PC Magazine* began to take notice of the newly emerging

234

search engine. In June 1999, Google announced that it had secured $25 million in funding from investment capital firms Sequoia Capital and Kleiner Perkins Caufield & Byers. The company moved to a new set of headquarters located in its current site in Mountain View, California. AOL and Netscape selected Google as their primary web search engine, which helped push traffic levels past 3 million queries per day.

The Launch of Key Word Searches

The launch of its key word search advertising program in 2001 provided the basic business model that would propel Google forward as a major communications company. In 2002, Google introduced a cost-per-click (CPC) pricing option that allows advertisers to pay for only those ads that are specifically queried by a user. This approach allows Google to target ad delivery based on the user's query. The ads are rank ordered in terms of relevance to the user's query. In principle, ads are supposed to reach only those people who actually want to see them, thus providing benefit to both users and advertisers.

Invention and Innovation

Over the years, Google has evolved a unique business culture. The company's headquarters, referred to as "the Googleplex," has an informal, highly charged atmosphere that encourages collegiality and innovation. Author Adam Lashinsky refers to it as "chaos by design":[32]

> The 1.3 million square foot headquarters is a mélange of two-story buildings full of festive cafeterias (yes, they're all free), crammed conference rooms and hallway bull sessions, all of it surrounded by sandy volleyball courts, youngsters whizzing by on motorized scooters . . . and anything goes spirit. It's a place where failure coexists with triumph, and ideas bubble up from lightly supervised engineers, none of whom worry too much about their projects ever making money.[33]

The core competency of Google's everyday endeavors is the search engine. Google researchers and staffers have steadily improved the search engine's capability, adding a variety of enhanced features, including the Google Directory, expanded language versions, key word searches, Gmail and Google Image. What information management tools the company lacked, it has acquired over time, including Picasa photo management, DoubleClick web ads and, more recently, YouTube on-line videos. In 2004, for example, Google acquired Keyhole Corporation, a digital and satellite image mapping company that provided satellite photo image capability. In time, that service would be transformed into Google Earth, which gives users a powerful new search tool to view 3D images across earth and the ability to tap a rich database of roads, businesses and many other points of interest. What distinguishes Google as a highly innovative company is its clarity of purpose and attention to detail. The company operates on the principle that information needs to be organized by analyzing the user's intention, what the key features and elements are that the user wants, and it then proceeds to reverse-engineer accordingly. Moreover, Google understands the power of synergy; that is, the add-on feature elements need to be complementary in purpose and scope.[34] Another important guiding principle is that Google employees are expected to spend 20 percent of their time on their own special projects. Any engineer within the company has the chance to create a new product or feature.

Strategic Challenges

INTELLECTUAL PROPERTY AND PRIVACY ISSUES

Google's stated goal, to "organize the world's information and make it universally available," has made it a lightning rod of criticism for various critics who are concerned about the company's business practices and services. As an example, the development of Google Book Search has led to copyright disputes with the Authors Guild and numerous publishers, given the company's stated aim to digitize millions of books. On another front, Google's continuing use of cookies and other information-gathering practices has led to concerns over privacy. A number of governments have raised concerns about the security risks posed by Google Earth's satellite imaging, which provides precise geographic details of buildings and towns. Finally, Google's cooperation with the governments of China, France and Germany to filter search results in accordance with regional laws and regulations has led to claims of censorship.

CLICK FRAUD

Click fraud has become a growing problem for major search engine companies like Google that rely on pay-per-click on-line advertising. Click fraud occurs when a person or computer software program imitates a legitimate user of the Internet by clicking on an ad for the purpose of generating an improper charge per click. What this does is to inflate the advertising bills for thousands of companies regardless of size and operation. The lure of pay-per-click on-line advertising is that the company pays only when a prospective customer clicks on the said ad. But what happens if people or a software program located in different parts of the world (that have no direct interest in the product) start hitting on the ads intentionally for the express purpose of running up the tab? Click fraud has become a serious problem for search engine companies, since it undermines the legitimacy of pay-per-click Internet advertising.[35] Critics point out that companies like Google and Yahoo are not doing enough to combat click fraud. Several Google advertisers, including Expedia.com, filed lawsuits against the company in 2006, claiming that up to 14–20 percent of the clicks on their bills were fraudulent or invalid. According to Brian Grow and Ben Elgin, "Google and Yahoo are grabbing billions of dollars once collected by traditional print and broadcast outlets, based partly on the assumption that clicks are a reliable, quantifiable measure of consumer interest that the older media simply can't match."[36]

Google Today

On August 19, 2004, Google made an initial public offering (IPO) of its stock to the general public on NASDAQ. The attraction for would-be investors is the belief that companies like Google represent the next generation in software development and information access.[37] According to Nielsen Media, Google is the most popular search engine on the web, with a 54 percent market share, ahead of Yahoo (23 percent) and MSN (13 percent). While the company's primary market is in the area of Internet search engine design, Google has begun to experiment with other markets, such as radio and print publications. On January 17, 2006, Google announced that it had purchased the radio advertising company dMarc, which will provide an automated system that allows companies to advertise on the radio. Google has also begun an experiment in selling advertisements from its advertisers in off-line newspapers and magazines. In October 2006, Google agreed to pay $1.65 billion in stock for YouTube, the video-sharing phenomenon that has given some breadth and depth to the principles of Web 2.0. There had been expressed interest in YouTube by virtually every major media and technology company that saw the value of public consumption and the estimated 100 million short videos being watched every day on that site.

Everyone from Viacom to Microsoft is under enormous pressure to have a major Internet presence. A year earlier, Rupert Murdoch's News Corporation spent $580 million to acquire MySpace.com. Google is expected to try to make money from YouTube by integrating the site with its search technology and its key word search advertising program. That said, the purchase of YouTube invites comparisons to the extraordinary valuations that were given to dozens of Silicon Valley companies during the height of the dotcom era of the late 1990s and early twenty-first century.[38]

Similarly, Google is investing in a future principle known as "cloud computing." Clouds are giant clusters of computers that house huge amounts of data that would be too big for regular computers to handle, such as analyzing enormous amounts of weather or geological data. Google cloud technology represents a network of hundreds of thousands of inexpensive servers linked together that could process information much faster than regular stand-alone computers. It would give smaller users the power of elite super-computers, which is presently available to a select number of government and university systems.[39] Already, other companies like Amazon.com are engaged in cloud computing by selling the power and analytic capability of their databases to smaller users.

Google, with a market value of $132 billion, can clearly afford the YouTube purchase and invest in cloud technology; but the question remains: How do you put a price tag on an unproven business? Therein lies Google's secret: the company's stated willingness to experiment and use existing tools and vast amounts of data to support promising ideas.

Strategic Challenges: Discussion

At the start of the twenty-first century, the Internet is being steadily woven into all aspects of work and leisure. The Internet has created a new business model that maximizes the potential for instantaneous communication to a worldwide customer base. EC has taken the principle of exchange efficiency to a whole new level in terms of retail trade and distribution. It has fundamentally changed how retail trade is conducted in terms of information gathering, marketing, production and distribution.

Intelligent Networking and Web 2.0

Web 2.0 represents the second generation of web-based communications and hosted services such as social networking, wikis and information blogs which aim to promote greater creativity and information sharing among users. The origins of the Web 2.0 concept date back to 2004 and the hosting of a media and technology conference co-hosted by Tim O'Reilly and John Battelle. Since then, the Web 2.0 concept has undergone a refining process in terms of its definition and meaning. It's important to understand what Web 2.0 is and is not. Web 2.0 is not an industry standard. And it's not a technical specification. Rather, Web 2.0 represents a new way of looking at the Internet and the possibilities for the future. Chief among them is using the Internet as a basic platform for information sharing and collaboration. This is especially important when it comes to electronic commerce and the advancement of new media.

New Media

The term *new media* is a relative phrase given that what's current in the field of media and telecommunications today can become quickly dated. That said, the Internet arguably serves as the unofficial demarcation point between old media and so-called new media. Since the early 1990s, we have witnessed the wholesale transformation of media and information technology, including developments in digital television and HD, on-line videogames, DVRs, cell phones and text messaging, iPods and the like. The term *new media* is built around the use of the Internet as the basis for delivering new and enhanced forms of information and entertainment. Central to this discussion are three important principles: convergence, permeability and virtual communication.

Convergence

In 1983, researcher Ithiel de Sola Pool characterized the joining together of two different technologies to create a third technology as a "convergence of modes."[40] The principle of convergence can be seen in the graphics display available on the Internet, including streaming video, MP3 file sharing and on-line videogames, to name only a few, where voice, data and video are combined to created an integrated whole. In the case of home entertainment systems, the emphasis is on multimedia systems, whereby components (and software) can be easily interfaced to create entirely new forms of media use and application. The television and computer monitor becomes a display vehicle for a variety of video and audio inputs, including broadcasting, cable television, IPTV and the Internet.

The main driving force behind convergence is the digitalization of media and information technology. Digital technology improves the quality and efficiency of switching, routing and storing of information. It increases the potential for manipulation and transformation of data.[41] In describing the merits of digital technology, MIT's Nicholas Negroponte differentiates between what he terms bits as against atoms:

> The best way to appreciate the merits and consequences of being digital is to reflect on the difference between bits and atoms. While we are undoubtedly in the information age, most information is delivered to us in the form of atoms: newspapers, magazines, and books. [In contrast] bits co-mingle effortlessly. They start to get mixed up and can be used and reused together or separately. The mixing of audio, video and data is called multimedia.[42]

Permeability

A second important element is the principle of permeability. The Internet is the quintessential example of intelligent networking. We operate from the premise that what gives the intelligent network its unique intelligence is the people and users of the system and the value-added contributions they bring to the system via critical gateway points. The critical gateway points are the various interface devices including desktop and laptop computers, PDAs, cellular phones, etc. Today, the Internet has grown exponentially in size and performance owing to the many contributions of its users, including improved website design, powerful search engines, unique information tools, and high-speed Internet access via cable modems and DSL technology. Together, they have greatly improved Internet navigation, organization and speed.

At the same time, permeability also means opening up the system to any number of unwanted influences and outcomes. From a systems perspective, the biological equivalent is the human body's susceptibility to various kinds of colds and viruses. What are some of the unintended consequences of intelligent networking to the person and organization? On one level, the problem translates into simple misinformation on the Internet. We see this routinely in the use of wikis, which allow regular users to submit volunteer entries to an Internet website based on their correct or incorrect understanding of a topic or issue: hence the success and sometimes occasional failure of websites like Wikipedia where entries can vary in terms of quality or understanding of the issue. At a deeper level, the problem of permeability can result in far more serious consequences like computer viruses, privacy invasion and Internet fraud.[43]

Virtual Communication

The term *virtual communication* can be used to describe the artificial space and network linkages connecting a disparate set of users using various forms of computer and communication technology. The communication, itself, can be both synchronous (real time) and asynchronous (different times). Virtual communication has also to do with the various kinds of on-line relationships that are formed as a result of using computer-mediated communication (i.e., electronic mail, Internet social networking, cell phone text messaging, etc.). Several researchers have examined the question of what distance and anonymity do to the communication process itself. In some cases, communication is somewhat inhibited owing to a lack of facial and verbal cues, while in other cases socioemotional content is in fact greatly increased. What is clear, however, is that computer-mediated language has created entirely new forms of shared meaning. Internet communication allows people to come together locally, nationally and internationally from the convenience of one's home, laptop or business. Such on-line relationships bring together people who

240

share a common interest. Nowhere is this more evident than in social networking websites like Facebook and MySpace. Facebook founder and designer Mark Zuckerberg would characterize Facebook as a mathematical construct that maps the real-life connections between people. Each person is a node radiating links to other people they know. What makes Facebook so compelling is that, as friends and acquaintances join Facebook, they become part of a larger social grid that matters to the individual. Since that person's friends are connected to other friends on the network, there is the opportunity to virtually expand one's circle of friends and acquaintances.[44]

Concluding Remarks

Today's information economy stands in marked contrast to some of the very assumptions and technology patterns of the past. Instead of time and business commerce being highly synchronized, today's working professional lives in a digital world of asynchronous and virtual communication that allows for information gathering and shopping on-line regardless of time zones, geographical borders and physical space. In addition, we are witnessing the demassification of media and entertainment products made possible by intelligent networking coupled with just-in-time manufacturing trends. For EC marketers, the steady shift from mass to micromarketing is being driven by a combination of technological change and strategic opportunity. Consumers can now interact directly with a manufacturer or service provider and thereby greatly reduce the role of the so-called middleman. We have entered the era of customization, whereby everything from MP3 music downloads to digital video recording has become increasingly available to us owing to the power of intelligent networking.

The Internet has been and will continue to be the all-important network engine that drives globalization forward. The Internet provides the basis for B2B, B2C and C2C forms of electronic commerce. It is also at the heart of supply chain management activities that enable today's large-scale organizations to operate on a global basis. If Gutenberg's printing press made reading more widely available to the masses[45] and television made the world a global village[46] then the Internet makes it possible for people, organizations and retail commerce to be more globally connected. The information economy has become a society of networks. We don't talk with people; we network with them.

10

TRANSNATIONAL MEDIA AND TELECOMMUNICATIONS

The Transnational Media Corporation

The transnational corporation is a nationally based company with overseas operations in two or more countries. One distinctive feature of the transnational corporation (TNC) is that strategic decision making and the allocation of resources are predicated upon economic goals and efficiencies with little regard to national boundaries. What distinguishes the transnational media corporation (TNMC) from other types of TNCs is that the principal commodity being sold is information and entertainment. It has become a salient feature of today's global economic landscape.[1]

The TNMC is the most powerful economic force for global media activity in the world today. As researchers Herman and McChesney point out, transnational media are a necessary component of global capitalism. Through a process of foreign direct investment, the TNMC actively promotes the use of advanced media and information technology on a worldwide basis. This chapter will consider the strategic rationale for why companies engage in transnational media ownership.

The TNMC: Assumptions and Misconceptions

During the past two decades, scholars and media critics alike have become increasingly suspicious of the better-known, high-profile media mergers. Such suspicions have given way to a number of misconceptions concerning the intentions of TNMCs and the people who run them. The first misconception concerning the TNMC is that such companies are faceless, monolithic business entities (i.e., Time Warner = Disney = Viacom). The real face of companies like Time Warner is its many divisions, including *Time* magazine, HBO, CNN, Time Warner Cable and AOL, to name only a few. As researchers Pilotta, Widman and Jasko point out, organizations (even large ones) are always human constructions; that is, they are made and transformed by individuals. The TNMC, like all companies, possesses its own distinct

242

culture which is embedded in its history, organizational philosophy and distinct approaches to business.[2]

The Sony Corporation, for example, is a company that was largely shaped and developed by its founders, Masaru Ibuka and Akio Morita. Together they formed a unique partnership that left an indelible imprint on Sony's world-wide business operations. For many years, all of Sony's top officials were Japanese, and strategic decision making occurred from the company's Tokyo headquarters. There was a sense of family and missionary zeal that was uniquely Japanese in approach. In his 1986 book *Made in Japan*, Akio Morita wrote: "The most important mission for a Japanese manager is to develop a healthy relationship with his employees, to create a family-like feeling with the corporation, a feeling that employees and managers share the same fate."[3]

Today, Sony is no longer the same company. The challenges of staying globally competitive have had a profound effect on Sony's organizational culture. The once family-like atmosphere of the past is no more. The vast majority of Sony's worldwide employees are not Japanese. They have not been part of the company's cultural network and history. The new Sony has steadily transformed itself into a transnational media corporation where more and more emphasis is being given to the value of local autonomy and individual performance. Sony has moved to a position where local manage-ment means finding the best person regardless of nationality. In April 2005, Sony for the first time in its corporate history promoted Welsh-born Howard Stringer, then president of Sony Corporation of America, to the position of chairman and CEO.

The second misconception is that such companies operate in most or all markets of the world. While today's TNMCs are indeed highly global in their approach to business, few companies operate in all markets of the world. Instead, the TNMC tends to operate in preferred markets, with an obvious preference (and familiarity) toward its own home market.[4] Bertels-mann AG is the largest European-based TNMC and ranks in the top seven worldwide. Bertelsmann is a TNMC that reflects the business philosophy and media interests of its founder, Reinhard Mohn, who believed in the importance of decentralization, a legacy that Mohn instilled in the company before his retirement in 1981. Thus a company like Bertelsmann AG describes its business philosophy as follows:

> Many years ago, Bertelsmann set as a strategic goal the establishment of an even balance among its businesses in Germany, other European countries and the U.S. We have succeeded in this area as well; each of these regions accounts for just under a third of overall revenues. A smaller portion of our business is being generated in Asia. That's why we truly consider ourselves a European American media company with German roots.[5]

The Globalization of Markets

The globalization of markets involves the full integration of transnational business, nation-states, and technologies operating at high speed. Globalization is being driven by a broad and powerful set of forces, including worldwide deregulation and privatization trends, advancements in new technology, market integration (such as the European Community, NAFTA, Mercosur, etc.) and the fall of communism. The basic requirements for all would-be players are free trade and a willingness to compete internationally. As Thomas Friedman points out, "Globalization has its own set of economic rules—rules that revolve around opening, deregulating and privatizing your company."[6]

The Rules of Free Market Trade

Today, there is only one economic system operating in the world. And that system is called free market capitalism. Whereas communism provided a safety net for inefficient business practices, free market capitalism rewards only those who create new and innovative products and services. It is admittedly a fast-paced and uncertain world. According to German political theorist Carl Schmitt, "The Cold War was a world of friends and enemies. The globalization world, by contrast, tends to turn all friends and enemies into competitors."[7] A basic tenet of free market trade is that the private sector is the primary engine of growth. It presupposes that the nation-state can maintain a low rate of inflation and keep prices stable. It further attempts to keep the size of government small and to achieve a balanced budget, if not a surplus. The rules of free market trade adhere to the principles of deregulation and privatization of business. At the domestic level, free market trade attempts to promote as much domestic competition as possible.[8] Free market trade means opening up one's banking and telecommunication systems to private ownership and competition and to provide a nation and its citizens with access to a wide variety of choices.

The Purpose of a Global Business Strategy

Most companies do not set out with an established plan for becoming a major international company. Rather, as a company's exports steadily increase, it establishes a foreign office to handle the sales and services of its products. In the beginning stages, the foreign office tends to be flexible and highly independent. As the firm gains experience, it may get involved in other facets of international business such as licensing and manufacturing abroad. Later, as pressures arise from various international operations, the company begins to recognize the need for a more comprehensive global strategy.[9] In sum, most companies develop a global business strategy through a process of gradual evolution rather than by deliberate choice.

244

Historically, the TNMC begins as a company that is especially strong in one or two areas. At the start of the 1980s, for example, Time Inc. (prior to its merger with Warner Communications) was principally in the business of magazine publishing and pay cable television, whereas News Corporation Ltd., parent company to Fox Television, was primarily a newspaper publisher. Today, both companies are transnational in scope and operation, with a highly diverse set of media products and services. Over time, the TNMC develops additional sets of core competencies. News Corporation, for example, has become the world's preeminent company in the business of direct broadcast satellite communication. News Corporation either fully owns or is a partial investor in five DBS services worldwide. DBS services account for an estimated 10 percent of the company's worldwide revenues.[10]

Table 10.1 identifies the seven leading TNMCs, including information pertaining to their country of origin and principal business operations.

Foreign Direct Investment

Foreign direct investment (FDI) refers to the ownership of a company in a foreign country. This includes the control of assets. As part of its commitment, the investing company will transfer some of its managerial, financial and technical expertise to the foreign owned company.[11] The decision to

Table 10.1 The Transnational Media Corporation

Companies	World Headquarters	Principal Business Operations
Bertelsmann AG	Germany	Book and record clubs, book publishing, magazines, and music and film entertainment.
NBC Universal	U.S.A.	Television and film entertainment, cable programming and theme parks.
News Corporation Ltd.	Australia/U.S.A.	Newspapers, magazines, television and film entertainment, and direct broadcast satellite.
Sony	Japan	Consumer electronics, videogame consoles, and software, music and film entertainment.
Time Warner	U.S.A.	Cable, magazines, publishing, music and film entertainment, and Internet service provision.
Viacom	U.S.A.	Television and film entertainment, cable programming, broadcast television, publishing, and videocassette and DVD rental and sale.
Walt Disney	U.S.A.	Theme parks, film entertainment, broadcasting, cable programming and consumer merchandise.

engage in FDI is based upon the profitability of the market, growth potential, regulatory climate and existing competitive situation.[12] The TNMC is arguably better able to invest in the development of new media products and services than are smaller, nationally based companies or government-supported industries. As I have pointed out in other research works, there are five reasons that help to explain why a company engages in FDI. They include: 1) proprietary assets and natural resources, 2) foreign market penetration, 3) research, production and distribution efficiencies, 4) overcoming regulatory barriers to entry and 5) empire building.[13]

Proprietary Assets and Natural Resources

Some TNCs invest abroad for the purpose of obtaining specific proprietary assets and natural resources. The ownership of talent or specialized expertise can be considered a type of proprietary asset. Sony Corporation's purchase of CBS records in 1988 and Columbia Pictures in 1989 enabled the company to become a formidable player in the field of music and entertainment. Rather than trying to create an altogether new company, Sony purchased proprietary assets in the form of exclusive contracts with some of the world's leading musicians and entertainers. In 2004, Sony applied the same strategy by acquiring Metro-Goldwyn-Mayer (MGM) Studios for $5.8 billion. Today, Sony holds the exclusive copyrights to various films that once belonged to Columbia Pictures and MGM Studios.

Foreign Market Penetration

Some TNMCs invest abroad for the purpose of entering a foreign market and serving it from that location. The market may exist or may have to be developed. The ability to buy an existing media property is the easiest and most direct method for market entry. This was the strategy employed by Bertelsmann AG when it entered the U.S. in 1986 and purchased Doubleday Publishing ($475 million) and RCA Records ($330 million). One year later, Bertelsmann consolidated its U.S. recording labels by forming the Bertelsmann Music Group (BMG), which is headquartered in New York City. Bertelsmann later added to its U.S. music holdings in 2002 by acquiring music downloading company Napster for $8 million. Today, the BMG music division is responsible for 24.4 percent of the company's worldwide revenues.

A variation on the direct-market-entry approach is for the TNMC to become an international contractor. The TNC will sometimes elect to license or franchise a special product or process rather than investing in costly plant and equipment.[14] The Walt Disney Company, for example, is able to successfully trade on its name worldwide. The formation of Tokyo Disney is based upon a limited partnership agreement between the company and the Oriental Land Company. The Walt Disney Company leases the company name and its characters in exchange for 10 percent of all gate fees and 5 percent from food and merchandise sales. Alternatively, one can operate as an international contractor. The establishment of Disneyland Paris (formerly Euro Disney), for example, is based on a limited partnership agreement that was signed in 1987 with the French government. The Walt Disney Company holds a 39 percent equity interest in Disneyland Paris and earns revenues based on gate receipts and merchandise as well as management consulting fees.

Research, Production and Distribution Efficiencies

The cost of research, production and labor is an important factor in the selection of foreign locations. Some countries offer significant advantages such as a well-trained workforce, lower labor costs, tax relief and technology infrastructure. Depending upon the country and/or technical facility, products and services can be produced for less cost and with greater efficiency. India, for example, is fast becoming an important engineering and manufacturing facility for many computer and telecommunications companies located in the U.S. Companies like Texas Instruments and Intel use India as a research and development hub for microprocessors and multimedia chips. Similarly, companies like IBM and Oracle use Indian IT engineers to develop new kinds of software applications. By some estimates, there are more information technology engineers in Bangalore, India (150,000), than in Silicon Valley (120,000). Research studies performed by Deloitte Research and the Gartner Group report that outsourcing and work performed in India have reduced costs to U.S. companies by an estimated 40 to 60 percent.[15]

Overcoming Regulatory Barriers to Entry

Some TNCs invest abroad for the purpose of entering into a market that is heavily tariffed. It is not uncommon for nations to engage in various protectionist policies designed to protect local industry. Such protectionist policies usually take the form of tariffs or import quotas. On October 3, 1989, the European Community (EC), in a meeting of the 12 nations' foreign ministers, adopted by a 10-to-2 vote the Television without Frontiers Directive. Specifically, EC Directive 89/552 was intended to promote European television and film production. The EC was concerned that the majority of broadcast air time be filled with European programming.[16] The plan called for imposing restrictions on the import of U.S. television programming and films.

The EC directive was initially viewed by many in the media field as a form of trade protectionism. In order to offset the effects of program quotas, the TNMC and second-tier television and film distributors adjusted to the EC directive by forming international partnerships or engaging in co-production ventures. By becoming a European company (or having a European affiliate), the TNMC was able to circumvent perceived regulatory barriers and exercise greater control over international television/film trade matters.[17]

Empire Building

Writers like Warren Bennis contend that the CEO is the person most responsible for shaping the beliefs, motivations and expectations for the organization as a whole.[18] The importance of the CEO is particularly evident when it comes to the formation of business strategy. For CEOs like Rupert Murdoch (News Corporation), Sumner Redstone (Viacom) and John Malone (Liberty Media), there is a certain amount of personal competitiveness and business gamesmanship that goes along with managing a major company. Success is measured in ways that go beyond straight profitability. A high premium is placed on successful deal making and new project ventures.

Today's generation of transnational media owners and CEOs are risk takers at the highest level, willing and able to spend billions of dollars in order to advance the cause of a new project venture. Viacom's Sumner Redstone, for example, is known for his aggressive leadership style and his tenacity as a negotiator. He is a fierce competitor. Redstone's competitive style can be seen in a comment he made in *Fortune* magazine:

> There are two or three of us who started with nothing. Ted Turner started with a half-bankrupt billboard company. Rupert Murdoch started with a little newspaper someplace in Australia. I was born in a tenement, my father became reasonably successful, and I started with two drive-in theaters before people knew what a drive-in theater was. . . . So I do share that sort of background with Rupert. People say I want to emulate him [Murdoch]. I don't want to emulate him. I'd like to beat him.[19]

The Risks Associated with FDI

The decision to invest in a foreign country can pose serious risks to the company operating abroad. The TNC is subject to the laws and regulations of the host country. It is also vulnerable to the host country's politics and business policies. What are the kinds of risks associated with FDI? There are the problems associated with political instability, including wars, revolutions and coups. Less dramatic, but equally important, are changes stemming from the election of socialist or nationalist governments that may prove hostile to private business and particularly to foreign-owned business.[20] Changes in labor conditions and wage requirements are also relevant factors in terms of a company's ability to do business abroad. Foreign governments may impose laws concerning taxes or currency convertibility and/or impose requirements involving technology transfer.

Alternatively, some countries may do too little, especially when it comes to such things as preserving intellectual property rights. FDI can only occur if the host country is perceived to be politically stable, if it provides sufficient economic investment opportunities and if its business regulations are considered reasonable. In light of such issues, the TNC will carefully consider the potential risks by doing what is called a country risk assessment before committing capital and resources.

Mergers and Acquisitions

The decades of the 1990s and early twenty-first century have witnessed an unprecedented number of international mergers and acquisitions that have brought about a major realignment of business players. Concerns for antitrust violations seem to be overshadowed by a general acceptance that such changes are inevitable in a global economy. The result has been a consolidation of players in all aspects of business, including banking, pharmaceuticals, aviation, media and telecommunications.[21] The communication industries, in particular, have taken full advantage of deregulatory trends to make ever larger combinations. Some of the more high-profile mergers and acquisitions include: Viacom's purchase of CBS for $37 billion (1999), America Online's merger with Time Warner for $162 billion (2001) and Comcast's $54-billion purchase of AT&T Broadband (2002), to name only a few. Mergers, acquisitions and strategic alliances represent different ways that companies can join together (or partner) to achieve increased market share, to diversify product line and/or to create greater efficiency of operation. The goal, simply put, is to possess the size and resources necessary in order to compete on a global playing field.

Mergers

In a merger transaction, two companies are combined into one company. The newly formed company assumes the assets and liabilities of both.[22] A clear example of a merger agreement was the joining together of Time Inc. and Warner Communications in March 1989 to form Time Warner Inc. Under the terms of the agreement, there was no cash purchase but rather an exchange of stock with an agreed-upon exchange ratio. The Time Warner board of directors would consist of 24 members, with equal representation from both sides of the merging parties. Although, technically, Time was acquiring Warner Communication, attorney Arthur Liman wrote at the time:

> The merger is a true combination of two great companies. For either company to be looked upon as anything but an equal partner in this transaction would sap that company of its vitality and destroy the

249

very benefits and synergy that the combination is intended to achieve.[23]

Similarly, in 2005 Sprint and Nextel Communications consummated a $36-billion merger agreement creating a combined wireless phone company with a customer base well positioned to challenge its two larger rivals, AT&T and Verizon. The Sprint Nextel combination is considered a merger of equals despite the fact that Nextel (and the Nextel network) has been absorbed into Sprint's overall network operation. Strategically, the two company's strengths fit very well with one another—Sprint is seen as a leader in wireless data communications and has a stronger presence in the consumer market, while Nextel has been the pioneer in the push-to-talk service and has its primary customer base among business customers.

Acquisitions

By contrast, an acquisition involves the purchase of one company by another company for the purpose of adding to (or enhancing) the acquiring firm's productive capacity. During an acquisition, one company acquires the operating assets of another company in exchange for cash, securities or a combination of both. A clear example of an acquisition was Viacom's 1999 decision to purchase CBS for $37 billion. For Viacom, the CBS purchase represented an opportunity to obtain a well-established television network as well as a company that owned Infinity Broadcasting, representing more than 1,600 U.S. radio stations. For its part, Viacom was home to several well-established cable network services, including MTV, Nickelodeon and Showtime. The purchase of CBS was expected to provide a steady distribution outlet for Viacom programs and to offer numerous cross-licensing agreements.[24]

Strategic Alliances

A strategic alliance is a business relationship in which two or more companies work to achieve a collective advantage. The strategic alliance can vary in its approach and design, ranging from a simple licensing agreement to the actual combining of physical resources.[25] As noted earlier, a good example of a strategic alliance can be seen in the form of the Walt Disney Company's licensing agreement with Tokyo Disneyland in Japan, which is privately owned by the Oriental Land Company. The Walt Disney Company licenses the operation, provides marketing support and collects royalties. In sum, mergers, acquisitions and strategic alliances are the most direct way for a company to expand and diversify into new product lines without having to undergo the problems associated with being a new start-up. Table 10.2 identifies the major mergers and acquisitions of media and telecommunication companies in the U.S. for the years 1997–2007.

Table 10.2 Major Mergers and Acquisitions: Media and Telecommunication Companies (1997–2007)

Alcatel	$11.6 billion purchase of Lucent Technologies (2006).
AT&T	$67.0 billion purchase of Bell South (2006).
Intelsat	$6.4 billion purchase of PanAmSat (2006).
SBC	$16.7 billion purchase of AT&T (2005).
Verizon	$6.7 billion purchase of MCI (2005).
Sprint	$36.0 billion merger with Nextel Communication (2005).
News Corporation	$6.1 billion purchase of DirecTV (2004).
NBC	$3.8 billion purchase of Vivendi/Universal (2004).
Comcast	$54.0 billion purchase of AT&T Broadband (2002).
Vivendi	$43.3 billion purchase of Seagram's (2001).
AOL	$162.0 billion purchase of Time Warner (2000).
Verizon	$52.8 billion purchase of GTE (2000).
Viacom	$37.0 billion purchase of CBS (2000).
SBC	$62.0 billion purchase of Ameritech (1999).
AT&T	$48.0 billion purchase of TCI Inc. (1998).
WorldCom	$36.5 billion purchase of MCI Com. (1997).

When Mergers and Acquisitions Fail

Not all mergers and acquisitions are successful. As companies feel the pressures of competition, they embrace a somewhat faulty assumption that increased size makes for a better company. Yet upon closer examination, it becomes clear that this is not always the case. Often, the combining of two major firms creates problems that no one could foresee. A failed merger or acquisition can be highly disruptive in terms of lost revenue, capital debt, duplication of effort and decreased job performance. The inevitable result is the elimination of staff and operations as well as the potential for bankruptcy. The effects on the support (or host) communities can be quite destructive.[26] There are four reasons that help to explain why mergers and acquisitions can sometimes fail. They include: 1) the lack of a compelling strategic rationale, 2) failure to perform due diligence, 3) post-merger planning and integration failures and 4) financing and the problems of excessive debt.[27]

The Lack of a Compelling Strategic Rationale

In the desire to be globally competitive, both companies go into the proposed merger with unrealistic expectations of complementary strengths and presumed synergies. The challenge going forward is to properly establish the correct price level (or valuation) of the targeted company.[28] Once negotiations are underway, there is sometimes undue pressure brought to bear to complete the deal. Unrestrained optimism regarding future performance can sometimes cloud critical judgment. The negotiation process suffers from what some observers call "winner's curse." The acquiring company often winds up paying too much for the acquisition. In the worst-case scenario, the very problems and issues that prompted consideration of a merger in the first place become further exacerbated once the merger is complete.

Failure to Perform Due Diligence

In the sometimes highly charged atmosphere of intense negotiations, the merging parties will sometimes fail to perform due diligence prior to the merger agreement. Both companies only later discover that the intended merger or acquisition may not accomplish the desired objectives.[29] The lack of due diligence can result in the acquiring company paying too much for the acquisition and/or later discovering hidden problems and costs. An example can be seen in AT&T's 1998 acquisition of TCI Cable for $48 billion. For AT&T, the merger agreement represented an opportunity to enter the unregulated business of cable television that gave the company direct connections into 33 million U.S. homes through TCI-owned and -affiliated cable systems. It was an intriguing strategy that earned AT&T respect from all quarters of the telecommunications field for its sheer breadth of vision. The plan, however, did not work out as originally conceived. First, the TCI plant and equipment was found be in less than satisfactory condition. Second, AT&T seriously underestimated the technical challenges and cost of rolling out new cable plant. Third and most importantly, AT&T was over-leveraged financially given its acquisition of TCI and Media One Cable, which made investors wary and put undue pressure on its stock price.[30] In October 2000, then CEO Michael Armstrong, reversed course and discontinued AT&T's original broadband strategy by dividing the company into four separate companies. In the final analysis, AT&T was unable to surmount the continuing decline in long-distance revenues coupled with the enormous costs of transforming TCI's cable operation into a state-of-the-art broadband network.[31] In 2001, AT&T agreed to sell its broadband division to Comcast Corporation for $54 billion.[32]

Post-Merger Planning and Integration Failures

If the proposed merger does not include an effective plan for combining divisions with similar products, the duplication of effort can be a source of friction rather than synergy. Turf wars erupt and reporting functions among managers become divisive. The problem becomes further complicated when there are significant differences in corporate culture. The post-merger difficulties surrounding AOL and Time Warner, for example, demonstrate the difficulty of joining two very different kinds of organizational cultures. AOL typified the high-paced and sometimes chaotic dotcom culture of the 1990s, whereas Time Warner demonstrated a more staid, buttoned-down approach to media management. There was an obvious suspicion and resistance that each of the merging parties brought to the agreement. The once-hoped-for synergies did not materialize, leaving the company with an unwieldy structure and bitter corporate infighting.

Financing and the Problem of Excessive Debt

In order to finance the merger or acquisition, some companies will assume major amounts of debt through short-term loans. If or when performance does not meet expectations, such companies may be unable to meet their loan obligations. The company may then be forced to sell off entire divisions in order to raise capital or, worse still, default on its payment altogether. Rupert Murdoch, president and CEO of News Corporation Ltd., is unique in his ability to structure debt and to obtain global financing. The Murdoch formula was to carefully build cash flow while borrowing aggressively. Throughout the early 1980s, Murdoch's excellent credit rating proved to be the essential ingredient to this formula. Each major purchase was expected to generate positive cash flow and thereby pay off what had been borrowed. Each successive purchase was expected to be bigger than the one before, thereby ensuring greater cash flow. In his desire to maintain control over his operations, Murdoch developed a special ability to manage debt at a higher level than most companies.

The problem with News Corporation's debt financing, however, reached crisis proportions in 1991 when the company was carrying an estimated debt of $8.3 billion. The problem was compounded by the significant cash drains from Fox Television and the BSkyB DBS service. All this came at a time when the business of mass media was enduring a worldwide economic recession. Murdoch was finally able to restructure the company's debt after several long and difficult meetings with some 146 investors. He nearly lost the company. Murdoch was able to obtain the necessary financing but not before the divestment of some important assets and an agreement to significantly pare down the company's debt load. In summarizing Murdoch's business activities and propensity for debt, the *Economist* magazine wrote, "Nobody exploited the booming media industry in the late 1980's better than Mr. Rupert Murdoch's News Corporation—and few borrowed more money to do it."[33]

Economic Concentration

In all areas of media and telecommunications, there has been a clear movement toward economic concentration. The increase in group and cross-media ownership is the direct result of TNMCs looking for ways to increase market share and promote greater internal efficiencies. The term *economic concentration* is used to describe the number of sellers within a given market. A market is said to be highly concentrated if it is dominated by a limited number of firms.[34] The fewer the number of product manufacturers or service providers, the higher the degree of concentration within a given market. This, in turn, can affect the degree of rivalry between competing firms in terms of product quality, diversity and cost. Moreover, highly concentrated markets exhibit strong barriers to entry for new competitors.

As researchers Alan Albarran and Bosina Miszerjewksi point out, there are two ways to examine the problem of economic concentration. The first way is to look at economic concentration in terms of single industry concentration.[35] How much does a single company dominate a specific area of media and telecommunications? Consider, for example, that Microsoft dominates the field of computer software and is responsible for over 80 percent of the world's PC desktop software. Similarly, News Corporation Ltd. is highly dominant in the area of direct broadcast satellites (British Sky Broadcasting, Star TV, DirecTV, etc.). The company controls over 70 percent of the world's market share in direct broadcast satellite television.

Cross-Media Ownership

The second way to look at economic concentration is in terms of cross-media ownership. How much does a single company control (or influence) multiple areas of media products and telecommunication services? The TNMC of the twenty-first century is distinguished by the sheer breadth of its media and telecommunication holdings, which can include a broadcast television network, select cable network services, cable television service operations, a major television or film studio, magazines and newspapers, a music production capability and a strong Internet presence. In addition, the TNMC can have a major presence in other signature related areas such as owning a theme park, a consumer electronics manufacturing capability, an e-commerce capability, a DBS service delivery capability, etc. Table 10.3 provides a brief sampling of seven major TNMCs in terms of their cross-media holdings.

Global Outsourcing

In recent years, a lot has been written about global outsourcing. The practice of global outsourcing involves moving or contracting some (or all) of a company's manufacturing or service operations to a foreign country. The primary reason for outsourcing is to take advantage of lower labor costs in a foreign country (i.e., FDI and production and distribution efficiencies). Outsourcing (or offshoring) has become a highly controversial issue when it involves large-scale job losses, companies closing factories and moving production facilities overseas. Nor is the problem confined to blue-collar workers and manufacturing jobs. The problem that once affected blue-collar workers only has begun to affect many white-collar workers as well. In recent years, service sector

Table 10.3 The Transnational Media Corporation: Select Examples of Feature Products and Services

Company	Broadcast Television	Cable Television	Television/Film Studios	Newspapers and Magazines	Signature Products and Services
Bertelsmann	RTL, Germany. VOX, Germany. M6, France. Five, Great Britain. Antena 3, Spain. RTL4, Netherlands.			Gruner & Jahr. *Stern* magazine. *Financial Times. Deutschland. GEO. Gala. Muy Interesante.*	Random House Publishing. Doubleday. Alfred A. Knopf. BMG Music, U.S.A.
NBC Universal	NBC Television. NBC television stations.	CNBC. MSNBC. USA— investment. Sci Fi— investment. Telemundo— investment.	Universal Studios.		Parks and resorts. Universal Studios, Hollywood, CA. Universal Studios, Orlando, FL.
News Corporation	Fox Broadcasting. Fox television stations. STAR TV.	Fox News. Fox Business Channel. Fox Sports Net. FX.	20th Century Fox.	*Sunday Times*, UK. *Sun*, UK. *News of the World*, UK. *Australian*, Australia. *New York Post*, U.S.	DirecTV DBS service. BSkyB DBS service. MySpace Internet service.
Sony			Sony Pictures. MGM Pictures.		Consumer electronics. PlayStation videogame systems.
Time Warner	CW Network— investment.	HBO. CNN. TNT. Cinemax.	Warner Bros.	*Time. People. Sports Illustrated. Fortune.*	Time Warner Cable. AOL Internet service.
Viacom	CBS Television.* CW Network— investment.	MTV. Nickelodeon. Showtime. BET. Spike TV.	Paramount.		Blockbuster video rental and sales.

(Continued Overleaf)

255

Table 10.3 Continued

Company	Broadcast Television	Cable Television	Television/Film Studios	Newspapers and Magazines	Signature Products and Services
Walt Disney	ABC Television.	ESPN. Disney Channel.	Walt Disney Pictures. Touchstone Pictures. Pixar Studios. Miramax.	ESPN the Magazine.	Parks and resorts. Disneyland, CA. Disney World, FL. Disneyland Paris. Hong Kong Disneyland. Tokyo Disney.

* In 2006, Viacom made the decision to officially separate its CBS Television network from its cable programming operations and to position it as a separate company.

companies, such as call centers and software companies, have laid off many American employees and contracted with companies in India and other countries to do call center and software work.

And why not? U.S. accounting firms will sometimes use accountants in India and the Philippines to prepare tax returns, paying those accountants $4,000 a year, compared with the $60,000 annual salaries earned by their American counterparts. Similarly, a chip designer in India with a Master's degree in electrical engineering and five years' experience often earns $12,000 a year. In contrast, a chip designer in the U.S. with similar credentials will earn $85,000 a year. The steady increase in outsourcing has been accelerated by other factors as well, including improved supply chain management and foreign manufacturing capability, better air transportation, improved logistics for shipping, overnight delivery, and highly efficient communication (i.e., e-mail, lower-cost international telephone calls and fax transmissions), which make it easier to work with foreign contractors. Moreover, advancements in desktop videoconferencing have made it easier for senior managers to maintain business relationships with contractors and executives in other countries.

The Origins of Outsourcing

The principle of outsourcing is by no means a new idea.[36] Starting in the 1960s and 1970s, some American textile and clothing companies began contracting out to producers in Asia to furnish some of the textiles and garments that had been previously manufactured in the U.S. For many companies, the main benefit was the lower labor costs in Asia, where factory workers often earned less than one-tenth the wages of comparable American factory workers. Outsourcing continued to accelerate throughout the 1980s, when U.S. companies began looking to Central and South America to accomplish some of the same manufacturing goals as well. It was during this time that outsourcing took on a new variation as giant retailers began creating private-label lines and moved clothing production from U.S. factories to low-wage factories abroad.

Many European clothing manufacturers began doing the same thing. It was only a matter of time before other American and European companies began outsourcing other types of product manufacturing, including auto parts, consumer electronics, etc. A major shift occurred when U.S. auto giants Ford, General Motors and Chrysler were not only outsourcing auto parts but also setting up entire assembly plants in foreign countries. They were soon followed by Toyota (Japan), Daimler Corporation (Germany), Nissan (Japan) and Volvo (Sweden), to name only a few.

Another important development in outsourcing took place in the late 1990s. American companies began to outsource not just products but information and communication services as well. Banks moved some call center operations, which handled customer questions, to places like Ireland, India, and other countries with English-speaking workers. Many telephone and computer companies followed suit, hiring firms in foreign countries to handle their call center operations. Even legal work was being outsourced, to the extent that overseas lawyers could research various laws, write basic contracts, and prepare the initial paperwork for patent filings.

The Challenges of Global Outsourcing

In a global economy, outsourcing is something of an inevitability. Defenders of the practice argue that outsourcing not only helps their companies lower costs, increase profits and stay competitive, but also benefits the domestic consumers by enabling companies to reduce the price of their goods and services. Outsourcing can also provide poorer nations with much-needed economic development, FDI and jobs. Not everyone agrees. Many workers and labor unions would argue that corporations that send manufacturing or services operations abroad are showing disloyalty to a nation's workforce, pushing down wages and hurting the national economy by eliminating jobs. Some economists further believe that outsourcing may prove to be a company's long-term undoing by indirectly promoting technology transfer, thus creating a situation where today's global partners may become tomorrow's future competitors. They warn that, if U.S. companies continue to move manufacturing and software development jobs to places like India and China, such outsourcing might eventually enable both countries (and their respective industries) to one day overtake American industry. Technology transfer under these circumstances would seriously undermine

U.S.-based technological leadership as well as the ability to create jobs and wealth.

Nike: A Case Study

Globalization and offshore manufacturing have fueled a major debate among human rights activists when it comes to the exploitation of workers in emerging foreign markets by promoting low wages and unsafe working conditions. Throughout the decade of the 1990s, Nike, the world's leading manufacturer of athletic shoes and clothing, found itself the target of repeated criticism for alleged abuses at its factories in Vietnam, Indonesia, China and Pakistan, including the unfair treatment of women and children.

Nike has been a corporate success story for more than three decades. Starting in the late 1970s, the Beaverton, Oregon, based company "began to capture the attention of runners and trend setting teenagers by selling a combination of good running shoes and street smart athleticism."[37] Nike went public in 1980 and by any objective measure has been a financial success story. The company's formula for success was simple. There would be no in-house production. All of the company's product manufacturing would be done offshore in lower-wage countries. According to Debora Spar:

> all product would be made by independent contracting factories, creating one of the world's first "virtual corporations"—a manufacturing firm with no physical assets. Then the money saved through outsourcing would be poured into marketing. In particular, [Phil] Knight [the founder of the company] focused from the start on celebrity endorsements using high profile athletes to establish an invincible brand identity around the Nike name. . . . Nike took the practice to new heights emblazoning the Nike Logo across athletes such as Michael Jordan and Tiger Woods, and letting their very celebrity represent the Nike image.[38]

Nike's success, however, was achieved on the backs of low-cost foreign labor. Nike first signed contracts with Japan but later shifted its supply base to firms in South Korea and Taiwan, where costs were lower and production reliable. In 1982, 86 percent of the Nike sneakers came from one of these two countries. But as South Korea and Taiwan became more prosperous and costs began to increase, Nike urged its suppliers to move their operations to new lower-cost regions. The company's foreign manufacturers readily complied by moving their plant and equipment to China and Indonesia. By 1991, Nike was able to produce its shoes at a cost that was 50 percent less than that of Taiwan and South Korea.[39]

In the beginning, Indonesia provided an ideal location for Nike. Wages were low, the workforce was highly manageable and the country had an authoritarian government that wanted the benefits of FDI. Slowly, all this began to change as a peculiar blend of labor unrest swept across the country. Strikes, which had been nonexistent in the 1980s, began to occur with greater frequency. In addition, Nike was the target of an outside agitator by the name of Jeff Ballinger, who had a deep-seated dislike for Nike and all that it stood for. It was Ballinger's belief that Nike and other such companies had an important obligation to treat their workers fairly. He was particularly concerned about the huge wage gap between workers in developed countries and those in developing countries. Ballinger's goal was to focus worldwide attention on the exploitation of third world factory workers by large U.S. companies.

Ballinger's strategy was very simple. He would use the power of Nike's marketing machine against the company itself. The Indonesian government was the first to respond, by raising the official minimum wage in January 1992. That same year, criticism and public awareness of Nike's offshore practices reached the covers of the mainstream U.S. press. In August 1992, *Harper's* magazine published a story with information supplied by Ballinger. What was particularly noteworthy about the story was the inclusion of a pay stub from an Indonesian factory worker and Michael Jordan's endorsement contract. The story highlighted the fact that, with the wage rates shown on the pay stub, it would take an Indonesian worker 44,492 years to make the equivalent of Jordan's endorsement contract. In July 1993, CBS News interviewed Indonesian workers who revealed that they were paid just 19 cents an hour. Women workers could only leave the company barracks on Sunday and needed a special letter of permission from management to do so.

How did Nike respond to such stories and charges? In the beginning, Nike simply ignored the problem. Later, Nike responded by arguing that labor conditions in the factories of its subcontractors were not its responsibility. The company could not and should not be held responsible for the actions of independent contractors. As Professor Keith Hearit points out, failing to own the problem is a classic tactical error in a crisis situation.[40]

The issue of foreign labor abuse was not unique to Nike. In 1996, American television talk host Kathie Lee Gifford found herself the target of human rights activists who claimed that a line of clothing that she endorsed was being manufactured by child labor in Honduras. Instead of denying the connection, Gifford tearfully and immediately rallied to the cause. While Nike had no direct involvement in the

Gifford story, the company nonetheless became the poster child for foreign worker exploitation.

And nothing drove home the point better than a July 1996 issue of *Life* magazine that featured a picture of a 12-year-old Pakistani boy stitching a Nike soccer ball with the swoosh logos clearly visible. In May 1997, Doonesbury, a highly popular U.S. comic strip, devoted a full week to Nike's labor issues. Nike was a company in trouble and the problem was not going away.

Throughout the decade of the 1990s, Nike's advertising campaigns have promoted a special blend of individualism and anti-authoritarianism. The irony of course is that the company's profits come from poorly paid workers who do not have unions and who live in countries ruled by autocratic regimes. But as the criticism has mounted, particularly from such mainstream publications as the *Wall Street Journal* and *Harper's* magazine, the company began to recognize that it was losing the public relations war. Nike had a serious image problem. As Ballinger clearly predicted, Nike's high-profile marketing machine could be turned on its head. And, for a company whose business is inextricably linked to image, this was an impossible situation. Starting in 2000, Nike began to reassess its offshore manufacturing facilities and subcontracts.

In subsequent years, Nike has taken the first in a series of steps to improve the working conditions for its offshore employees by running extensive training programs for its subcontractors and factory managers. The company has also become a co-founder of an international monitoring group called the Fair Labor Association (FLA). The FLA is a nonprofit organization composed of industry members, non-governmental organizations (NGOs) and colleges and universities whose goal is to improve working conditions in foreign factories by promoting adherence to international labor standards.

America Online and Time Warner: A Case Study

On January 10, 2000, America Online (AOL) the largest Internet service provider in the U.S., announced that it would purchase Time Warner Inc. for $162 billion. What was particularly unique about the deal was that AOL, with one-fifth of the revenue and 15 percent of the workforce of Time Warner, was planning to purchase the largest TNMC in the world. Such was the nature of Internet economics that allowed Wall Street to assign a monetary value to AOL well in excess of its actual value. What is clear, however, is that AOL president Steve Case recognized that his company was ultimately in a vulnerable position. Sooner or later, Wall Street would come to realize that AOL was an overvalued company with little substantive assets.

At the time, AOL had no major deals with cable companies for delivery. Cable modems were just beginning to emerge as the technology of choice for residential users wanting high-speed Internet access. Instead, AOL was dependent on local telephone lines and satellite delivery. Nor did AOL have any real content to speak of. In its role as America's premier Internet service provider (ISP), AOL pursued what Patricia Aufderheide describes as "walled gardens" business strategy, whereby the company attempted to turn users of the public Internet into customers of a proprietary environment.[41] The walled gardens strategy required AOL to control the user's first screen experience and to more or less direct the user to stay within the AOL overall framework. It made sense to a point, but in looking to the future AOL needed something more than a well-constructed first screen experience. Enter Time Warner, which was well positioned in both media content and high-speed cable delivery.

The proposed merger between AOL and Time Warner was promoted as the marriage of old media and new media. More specifically, AOL would try to position itself as the HBO of the Internet by featuring a number of value-added services like AOL news and sports, music downloads, instant messenger, dating services and AOL network security (virus protection), to name only a few. In principle, an AOL Time Warner combination would provide AOL with broadband distribution capability to Time Warner's 13 million cable households. AOL Time Warner cable subscribers would have faster Internet service as well as access to a wide variety of interactive and Internet software products. Both AOL and Time Warner's various magazines would be used to cross-promote each other's products.[42]

In retrospect, the AOL Time Warner merger may well be remembered as one of the worst mergers in U.S. corporate history. The first signs of trouble occurred in the aftermath of the dotcom crash beginning in March 2000. AOL, like most other Internet stocks, took an immediate hit. AOL's ad sales experienced a free fall, and subscriber rates flattened out. By 2001, AOL Time Warner stock was down 70 percent.[43] AOL's Robert Pittman was assigned the task of overseeing the post-merger integration. The economic downturn and subsequent loss of advertising had a strong negative impact on AOL's core business. AOL found itself financially weaker than it was a year earlier because of rising debt and a falling share price which left it without the financial means to pursue future deals. As an example, AOL was counting on future cable television deals to deliver on-line entertainment and news services. AOL Time Warner executives, in the meantime, angered big institutional investors by missing growth targets and spinning financial reports to make their performance look better than it was. Adding to the tension were new questions about AOL's accounting practices.[44] The AOL Time Warner merger suffered from a faulty strategic rationale as well as post-merger integration failures.

In the end, Time Warner CEO, Gerald Levin, bet the future of the company on the so-called marriage of old media and new media, leaving employees, investors and consumers questioning his judgment as well as having to sort through the unintended consequences of that action. In the aftermath of the AOL Time Warner merger, the company's new board has overseen a dramatic shake-up at the senior executive level, including Levin's retirement from the company and Pittman's forced resignation in July 2002.[45] In January 2003, Steve Case stepped down as co-CEO, claiming that he did not want to be a further distraction to the company. In their place, company directors installed Richard Parsons as chairman and CEO and two longtime Time Warner executives as his co-chief operating officers. Parsons was later succeeded by Jeffrey Bewkes.

In January 2003, AOL Time Warner reported a $99-billion loss from the previous year, making it the highest recorded loss in U.S. corporate history. Perhaps the most symbolic aspect of AOL Time Warner as a failed business strategy was the decision in September 2003 by the company's board of directors to change the name AOL Time Warner back to its original form, Time Warner Inc. In the aftermath of the AOL Time Warner debacle, the company has had to rethink its on-line strategy given advancements in cable modem and DSL technology. In June 2006, Time Warner announced that AOL would discontinue as a subscription service and adopt an advertiser-supported model more in line with that of such companies as Google and Yahoo.[46]

Strategic Challenges: Discussion

Global competition has engendered a new competitive spirit that cuts across nationalities and borders. A new form of economic Darwinism abounds, characterized by a belief that size and complementary strengths are crucial to business survival. As today's media and telecommunication companies continue to grow and expand, the challenges of staying globally competitive become increasingly difficult.[47] The relentless pursuit of profits and the fear of failure have made companies around the world vigilant in their attempts to right-size, reorganize and reengineer their business operations. Thus no company, large or small, remains unaffected by the intense drive to increase profits and decrease costs.

The strategic challenges faced by the TNMC are not unique to large, highly diverse media companies. Rather, the problems have to do with all companies that operate in an increasingly deregulated and privatized world of business. The real issue is not the size or number of today's TNMCs. Rather, it has to do with business priorities where the pursuit of profits can sometimes promote egregious forms of media violence and lower the standards of quality journalism.

The Deregulation Paradox

A basic tenet of free market competition is that the private sector is the primary engine of growth. Free market competition means opening one's banking and telecommunication systems to private ownership and competition and providing a nation and its citizens with access to a wide variety of choices.[48] In principle, deregulation is supposed to foster competition and thereby open markets to new service providers. The problem, however, is that complete and unfettered deregulation can sometimes create the very problem it was meant to solve, namely, a lack of competition. Instead of fostering an open marketplace of new players and competitors, too much consolidation can lead to fewer players and hence less competition. Researchers like Vincent Mosco call it the "mythology of telecommunications deregulation."[49] Other writers such as David Demers refer to it as the "great paradox of capitalism." I simply call it the deregulation paradox.[50] As Demers points out:

> The history of most industries in so-called free market economies is the history of the growth of oligopolies, where a few large companies eventually come to dominate. The first examples occurred during the late 1800s in the oil, steel and railroad industries. . . . Antitrust laws eventually were used to break up many of these companies but oligopolistic tendencies continue in these and most other industries.[51]

The communications industry is no exception. The events surrounding the collapse of Enron and WorldCom as well as the huge financial losses resulting from the AOL Time Warner merger caused a great deal of soul searching among those political representatives who have long championed the cause of deregulation such as Congressman Joe Barton (R-Tex.), who told *Business Week*, "We spent the last ten years breaking down walls between businesses, I think that's over."[52]

Diffusion of Authority

One of the more serious problems facing the public is that the TNMC has to a large degree become software ambivalent. In a free market economy, profitability and market potential are often the true test of whether a creative work makes it. The TNMC, given its diverse worldwide media activities, is often unwilling to impose professional (or ethical) restraints on the production of creative works regardless of whether such efforts are obscene or violent or result in the invasion of privacy. The failure to exercise critical judgment can sometimes lead to what Cohan describes as a diffusion of authority, whereby neither company nor person is fully aware of or takes responsibility for the actions of senior management.[53]

Critics argue that the TNMC needs to recognize its civic responsibility when it comes to the production of music and films that are highly sexist, violent and profane. Companies like Time Warner and News Corporation, for example, have come under increased scrutiny for their failure to exercise self-restraint when it comes to the marketing of select forms of hip hop music or tabloid, sensationalist journalism. In the area of journalism, the issue plays out in the crossing of the line between serious journalism and entertainment. Former CBS News anchor Walter Cronkite states the problem unequivocally:

> Will the journalism center hold in the changed economic environment of the future? In the last decade the networks have cut back news budgets while supporting the emergence of tabloid news shows, travesties of genuine news presentations. They bear the same relationship to the network news broadcasts as the *Enquirer* does to the *New York Times*.[54]

Concluding Remarks

What distinguishes the TNMC from other TNCs is that the principal article of trade is information and entertainment. It is a business mission that requires a greater degree of responsibility given the media's unique power to inform, persuade and entertain. What is clear, however, is that the pursuit of profits and organizational efficiency can sometimes blind senior management to exercising critical judgment when it comes to message content. A TNMC without a core business ethic is simply an organizational machine producing highly efficient products without considering the consequences. The direct fallout of such machine-like thinking is a diffusion of authority where neither company nor person takes responsibility for product quality and its potential impact on domestic and international audiences.

The problems cited become all the more complex at the international level. The TNMC possesses a level of power and influence that is second only to that of nation-states. Through a process of foreign direct investment, the TNMC actively promotes the use of advanced media and information technology. As a result, the geopolitical and cultural walls that once separated the nations of the earth are no longer sustainable. The resulting globalization of media activity has posed (and will continue to pose) a unique dilemma for many of today's host nations. On the one hand are the clear benefits of international free trade and the specific advantages that a TNMC offers, including jobs, investment capital, technology resources and tax revenue. On the other hand, the TNMC poses a set of unique challenges to host nations, including cultural trespass, challenges to political sovereignty, and privacy invasion. In the end, the goals of profitability and political sovereignty should not be considered mutually exclusive, but they do require a level of mutual cooperation and respect between the TNMC and the host nation. Both the host nation and the TNMC have a shared responsibility to create a system of globalization that is both desirable and sustainable.

Part 2

MANAGEMENT AND PLANNING STRATEGIES

11

TELECOMMUNICATIONS MANAGEMENT

Introduction

The field of media and telecommunications is a fast-paced and high-pressured environment. It is a world that is highly competitive, where success is measured in rating points, market share and sales volume. The clear lines and historical boundaries that once separated the fields of broadcasting, cable and telephony are becoming less distinct. A natural convergence of industries and information technologies is blurring those distinctions. Today's manager is faced with a different set of industry players and issues than was the case in past years.

What Do Managers Do?

Managing is a set of processes that ensure the smooth running of an organization. Managers give direction to their organization by providing leadership and deciding how to use people and resources to accomplish select goals and tasks.[1] To that end, the manager sets the tone for the work environment. In the best sense, a manager strives to create a positive and supportive environment where people feel free to do the best work possible.

Let us consider what it is that managers do. Being a manager involves six primary responsibilities. They include: 1) planning, 2) organizing, 3) leading, 4) staffing, 5) controlling and 6) communicating.

Planning

Planning defines where the organization wants to be in the future and how to get there. Planning requires the ability to set goals for the organization as well as defining tasks and use of resources needed to attain them. Goals and objectives are the end result of a planned set of activities. They state what is to be accomplished and when. The achievement of such goals and objectives should be measurable; for example:

1   to achieve over 10 percent annual growth in revenues
2   to achieve over 40 percent market leadership in the area of _____
3   to achieve greater productivity and efficiency in _____
4   to achieve technological leadership in _____
5   to implement a new technology or service in _____

Understanding the Organizational Mission

All planning has to occur within the context of the organization's mission. An organization's mission is the reason or purpose for the organization's existence. A well-conceived mission statement defines the fundamental unique purpose that sets a company apart from other firms of its type and defines where the company wants to be in the next five to ten years. Planning is very much tied to strategy (see Chapter 2). Strategy formulation is an ongoing process that should combine successful practices of the past with fresh and innovative approaches to the future (see Chapter 15). In most organizations, the mid-level manager is not the person who is responsible for strategy formulation. Rather, it is his/her responsibility to translate corporate strategy into action.

Also relevant to this discussion is the principle of *core competency*. A company's core competency is something the organization does especially well in comparison to its competitors. As an example, the Walt Disney Company's core competency is in the area of children's media/entertainment software. In his annual report to stockholders, former Walt Disney president and CEO Michael Eisner underscored the importance of core competency when he wrote:

> As always, we see ourselves primarily as entertainers, providers of programs these new media will need. . . . We remind ourselves always that it is the software that is important, the software that we continue to produce in the form of Disney animated classics, live action movies, TV series and specials, animated cartoons and Disney channel offerings.[2]

Organizing

Good organizational skills are necessary at all levels of management, but they are especially important for the mid-level manager who serves as the liaison between senior management and the department or staff that he/she supervises. Organizing speaks to the issue of how to implement short- and long-term goals as well as overseeing routine day-to-day operations.

Authority and Responsibility

Authority is the formal and legitimate right of a manager to make decisions, assign tasks and allocate resources to achieve organizational outcomes.

Managers exercise authority because of the positions they hold. In a cable television environment, for example, the general manager exercises formal authority by coordinating the responsibilities of the sales, marketing and technical staffs and assigning tasks accordingly. Managers can also exercise informal authority when they advise, recommend and counsel a staff person.

Establishing Priorities

All managers find themselves to a greater or lesser extent faced with the challenge of trying to balance routine office responsibilities (e.g., phone calls, e-mails, answering requests for information, etc.) with the need to complete organizational goals and project tasks. In order to successfully organize, the manager must be good at establishing priorities. To that end, effective managers exercise good time management skills, setting aside time to complete organizational goals and project tasks.

Hyrum Smith, a leading authority on time management and author of *The Franklin Day Planner*, suggests that one of the great time wasters is working for an organization that has shifting priorities. Management in an effort to respond quickly to emerging problems and opportunities shifts the energies of the organization from one priority to another. This becomes a form of management by crisis.[3] This kind of work environment can be very frustrating to working professionals, who never feel a sense of completion to the work they do. Instead, managers and staff feel as though they are getting pushed and pulled from one issue to the next. In such cases, the lack of clear priorities (and sense of completion) can be highly destabilizing to an organization.

Leading

A successful manager should exercise good leadership qualities. Leading means directing and motivating a group of employees (or staff) to move beyond their normal comfort zones and to reach for higher levels of performance. Leadership is not a stand-alone act but rather an ongoing relationship between those who purport to lead and those who follow. As we note in Chapter 14, a transformational leader is someone who motivates a group of people to accomplish more than was originally expected.

Vision

Leadership also means helping to instill a shared sense of vision. Highly successful leaders are able to communicate their vision throughout the organization and energize employees into action. Vision presupposes the ability to think conceptually (and long-term) and provide one's organization (or department) with the necessary strategies and tools in order to get there. The manager must be able to articulate the vision in a meaningful way and to mobilize his/her staff to achieve a defined set of outcomes. According to author John Kotter, "leadership defines what the future should look like, aligns people with that vision, and inspires them to make it happen."[4]

Motivation: Translating Vision into Action

Communication about the purpose and direction of the organization must be shared between (and among) people at all levels of the organization. For a mid-level manager, motivation is a very practical issue. The success of any proposed strategy is largely dependent upon the degree to which employees feel motivated to contribute in a meaningful way. Although the strategy (or its basic direction) may come from the top, successful implementation needs to happen at all levels of the organization.

Staffing

Today's manager has to be concerned with the staffing functions of an organization, that is, recruitment, training and evaluation. It is the responsibility of the manager to review and approve all personnel matters such as hiring and termination, wage and compensation levels, training and development, etc. It is also the responsibility of the manager to ensure that the organization is in compliance with all federal labor guidelines such as equal employment opportunity (EEO) and affirmative action requirements. In addition, the manager may be required to negotiate with labor unions on specific matters pertaining to employment practices (e.g., health, safety violations, etc.).

Recruitment

Recruitment has to do with the process of determining the staffing needs of an organization. To that end, the manager has to write the job description, advertise and interview potential candidates for new or replacement position openings. The manager will typically exercise one of two basic strategies when it comes to filling such positions. For starters, many organizations require that new position listings be posted within the organization first before going outside. This is referred to as internal recruitment. The easiest and most direct way of recruiting internally is through internal job postings on the company's website, newsletters, electronic mail, etc. Internal recruitment serves the dual purpose of advancing existing employees while keeping recruiting costs down.

Alternatively, the manager may elect to recruit outside the organization as well. We refer to this as external recruitment. Depending upon the position and the skills being sought, the manager may choose to advertise on the company's website as well as trade publications such as *Broadcasting & Cable,*

Telephony, Telecommunications Cablevision Multichannel News and *Information Week*. Advertising in a trade publication can be an effective way to advertise when the organization is looking for someone with specialized training such as a broadcast engineer, telecommunications network specialist, etc. In addition the manager may choose to utilize the website listings of professional trade associations such as the National Cable and Telecommunications Association (NCTA), the National Association of Broadcasters (NAB), and the United States Telecommunications Association (USTA), to name only a few. Another good source of employees is employment agencies, as well as university and college placement centers. Last, the classified section of the local newspaper is the simplest and most direct way to advertise for those positions that require general administrative or clerical skills.

Once the manager has identified a list of candidates, he/she arranges for a set of interviews to be conducted between the candidate and the company. For the applicant, the interview provides an opportunity to visit the facility and meet the manager(s) as well as prospective coworkers. In addition, the candidate learns more about the job tasks and responsibilities. For the manager, the interview provides an opportunity to assess the skill level and expertise of the potential candidate. Thus good interviewing skills become an essential element in making good hires. Finally, the manager is responsible for describing the terms and conditions of employment. This includes negotiating the salary and explaining benefits.

Orientation and Training

Orientation is the process of familiarizing new employees with the procedures and operations of the organization. Orientation should occur during the first several days of employment. Orientation is intended to familiarize the new hire with the specific assignments (or procedures) of a particular job as well as general information about the organization (e.g., health care benefits, sick leave, vacation, etc.). The level of orientation depends on the organization and the position.

The manager is also responsible for making sure that new employees have the proper training for a new job assignment. As an example, a new hire may be unfamiliar with the computer software that the organization uses, and the manager may send the person down to information technology (IT) for a series of training sessions. Job training can also occur offsite where an employee is sent to a specialized training program (or course) which is conducted by professional training groups. These kinds of courses are highly specialized and represent a significant financial commitment on the part of the organization towards the new employee.

Evaluation

The manager is responsible for conducting performance reviews. Depending upon the organization, the evaluation can be informal, where the manager or supervisor gives occasional feedback and suggestions for improvement, to a highly formalized review process. The performance review fulfills a twofold purpose. First, it allows the manager to identify the areas where an employee is particularly strong. The performance review provides an opportunity to praise an employee for a job well done by giving him/her appropriate rewards in the form of raises, merit pay and promotions. Second, the performance review allows the employer to give the employee suggestions on ways to improve job performance. For some employees, the performance review can be a difficult and challenging time. It is for this reason that the manager should dedicate a sufficient amount of time to conduct a proper evaluation.

Controlling

Organizational control can be defined as the process by which managers determine whether the organization (or department) is meeting a set of pre-determined goals, established targets or standards of performance. To that end, managers will use a variety of tracking tools (or measures) in order to obtain an accurate knowledge of organizational (or departmental) performance. Depending upon the kind of information being sought, such measures can include revenue statements, sales data by product line or geography, budget allocation, production output, quality control measures, etc. The information must be timely and unbiased. The reported data enables the manager to assess performance and take whatever corrective actions are necessary in order to ensure that the organization (or department) is on track in terms of meeting future goals and standards of performance.

Organizational control breaks down into five criteria. They include: 1) defining the objectives to be measured, 2) establishing standards of performance, 3) measuring actual performance, 4) comparing actual performance with the prescribed standard and 5) taking corrective action if needed. (See Chapter 2.)

Communicating

Managers spend at least 80 percent of every working day in direct communication with others. The communication process permeates every aspect of the manager's job. The manager is routinely communicating information to his/her superiors and subordinates through face-to-face meetings, e-mail, telephone calls and reports. In addition, the manager routinely engages in external communication with the general public.

Downward Communication

Downward communication refers to the messages and information being sent from senior (or mid-level) management to subordinates. One of the important responsibilities for any manager is to communicate information to employees. The manager must routinely convey information that may affect a person's ability to do his/her job properly. Such information may encompass a wide variety of topics, including:

1   implementation of goals and strategies;
2   task assignments and rationale;
3   changes in employee benefits;
4   performance feedback;
5   requests for information.

Upward Communication

Upward communication includes messages that flow from employees (and mid-level managers) upward through the organization. Mid-level managers serve as liaisons between the people they supervise and senior management. The ability to create clear lines of communication is an essential element for any organization. Employees need to be able to air grievances when a problem is emerging (or where something is not working). Part of the manager's responsibility is to represent departmental or staff needs upward. In addition, the manager is responsible for communicating other kinds of information, including:

1   staffing problems and issues;
2   suggestions for improvements;
3   performance reports;
4   grievances and disputes;
5   financial and other forms of tracking data.

External Communication

The manager fulfills a variety of roles when it comes to meeting with the general public. External communication involves those activities whereby the manager communicates outside the formal structures of the organization. The kinds of external communication are quite diverse. External communication can include everything from resolving a dispute with a dissatisfied customer to making a formal presentation at an industry conference. The following are just a few of the kinds of activities that involve external communication:

1   resolving a dispute with a dissatisfied customer;
2   performing a public relations role on behalf of your organization, such as supporting a United Ways campaign;
3   meeting with a client or vendor;
4   meeting with members of the media;
5   making a presentation in a public forum such as a conference, trade show, etc.

The Foundation of Management Theory

The practice of management has undergone a steady evolution that can trace its beginnings to the factory system of the 1800s. The first British and later American factories required a system of organization that necessitated managers formally organizing labor and resources. During the industrial age, managers found themselves having to address a variety of issues such as organizing complex manufacturing processes, training employees (many of them non-English-speaking immigrants) and supervising product output.

The years spanning 1880 to 1920 were a period of tremendous upheaval as America confronted the harsh realities associated with the industrial age, including unsafe working conditions, long hours, abusive child labor practices and unfair compensation for work performed. As a consequence, managers found themselves facing an altogether different problem on the factory floor, namely, labor dissatisfaction and strikes. In time, the formation of American labor unions as well as the passage of the Sherman Antitrust Act (1890) brought about a slow, steady reform of American industry. It was against the backdrop of the industrial age that the first management writers sought to find ways to achieve a balance between the need for increased productivity on the factory floor and recognition of the importance of satisfaction in the workplace.

As we consider the evolution of management theory, we discover that the field can be divided into five distinct perspectives, including:

1   the classical perspective;
2   the human relations perspective;
3   the management science perspective;
4   the modern management perspective,
5   the organizational performance perspective.

The use of the word *perspective* suggests a particular lens or way of looking at things. What it is important to remember, however, is that each perspective attempts to focus on different aspects of the management process. The writers, researchers and consultants presented in the next several pages share the common goal of trying to explicate how to make business organizations better and more efficient.

The Classical Perspective

The classical perspective is most closely associated with the industrial age, when much of the world's economy shifted from agriculture to industry. The industrial revolution was marked by a strong emphasis on cost efficiency, productivity and maximization of output. The industrial age reflected a management attitude that biggest was best and more was better. The classical perspective contains three separate but related subfields, including: 1) scientific management, 2) administrative management and 3) bureaucratic management.

Scientific Management

The scientific management approach is most closely associated with the work of Frederick W. Taylor (1856–1915), who was a mechanical engineer by trade. Taylor was concerned with finding ways to optimize employee performance. According to Taylor, labor productivity could best be achieved through scientifically determined management practices, thus earning him the title of "father of scientific management."[5] Taylor believed that managers are best suited for thinking, planning and administration, while workers are best suited for laboring. Taylor also believed that there is one best way to do a job. This approach can be seen in his work for the Bethlehem Steel Company, where he examined ways to improve the unloading of iron ore from rail cars and the reloading of finished steel. Taylor calculated that, with the proper tools, correct movements and sequencing, each man was capable of loading 47.5 tons of steel per day as compared to the usual 12.5 tons.

It is not surprising that Taylor was later vilified by American labor for his penchant for efficiency. Different writers have suggested that the purpose of Taylor's time–motion studies was to make workers interchangeable, like standardized parts—devoid of individuality and humanity.[6] This may be an overly critical assessment of Taylor's work. What is clear, however, is that Taylor was concerned with maximizing organizational output. It was Taylor's belief that, the more productive a person was on the job, the happier the person was in general. According to Taylor, financial incentives were the best motivators in achieving higher levels of productivity. In sum, well-paid productive people benefit both themselves and the organization. Some of Taylor's scientific management principles can still be seen today in those organizations that utilize time–motion studies (or simulation) for the purpose of achieving precision output. As an example, time–motion simulation forms the basis for today's computer-aided design (CAD) and manufacturing technologies.

Administrative Management

Henri Fayol (1841–1925) was a French mining executive who looked to the entire organization as the basis for achieving greater organizational efficiency. Fayol was among the first writers to recognize management as a process. His book *General and Industrial Management* was highly prescriptive in nature and describes how an organization ought to be run.[7] According to Fayol, an effective organization should be highly structured, with a clear set of guidelines outlining the tasks and responsibilities for both managers and workers. In his book, Fayol proposes five elements of management that describe what managers do. They include planning, organizing, command (assigning tasks), coordination and control. In addition, he identifies 14 principles designed to make an organization run smoothly (Table 11.1).

Fayol takes a highly rational view of the work environment. A clear structure and presentation of ideas facilitate a smooth-running organization—in

Table 11.1 Fayol's 14 Principles of Management (Adapted)

Principle	Explanation (Paraphrased)
Division of work	Work should be divided according to specialty.
Authority and responsibility	Managers exercise the right to give orders and can expect that employees are compliant.
Discipline	Employees are expected to be respectful and obedient.
Unity of command	The assignment of tasks and responsibilities should come from one supervisor.
Unity of direction	Those groups of activities that are similar in nature should be under the direction of one person.
Subordination of personal interest	The personal interests of a single employee give way to the larger concerns of the organization.
Remuneration of personnel	Wages should be fair and equitable and, to the extent possible, satisfactory to both employer and employee.
Centralization	Each organization should centralize its efforts in order to maximize employee skills and efficiency.
Scalar chain	There is a natural line of authority that goes from top to bottom (i.e., the so-called chain of command).
Order	Material and human resources should be co-located in order to create maximum efficiency.
Equity	Managers should be fair and equitable in their treatment of employees.
Tenure stability	Give employees sufficient time in order to learn a task and perform it well.
Initiative	It is essential that managers be given the freedom and power to develop and implement plans.
Esprit de corp	It is important to promote a spirit of collegiality among personnel.

sum, everything in its proper place. According to Fayol, employees are financially motivated and should be rewarded for their work with appropriate salary and benefits. Workers, for their part, should sublimate their personal interests for the goals of the organization.

Bureaucratic Management

The principles of bureaucratic management can trace their origins to the writings of German sociologist Max Weber (1864–1920), who was concerned with organizational structure. Unlike Fayol, who was highly prescriptive, Weber is more scholarly in approach and proposes the bureaucratic model as a way to describe the ideal functioning organization.[8] Weber's ideas are premised on the belief that structure is paramount. For Weber, the bureaucratic organization should operate through a well-defined hierarchy. This hierarchy is supported by a clear division of labor. In addition, the hierarchy should be highly centralized, with important decision making and power resting at the top.

Weber also emphasizes the importance of strict discipline; that is, organizations should function according to a set of well-defined policies and procedures. Such policies and procedures give an organization continuity. To that end, an organization based on rational authority is more efficient and adaptable to change, since formal structures and procedures are sustainable over time and are not dependent on the behaviors of individual people who may enter or leave an organization.

It is unfortunate that the word *bureaucracy* evokes a negative connotation in today's society. The word *bureaucracy* suggests a highly inflexible organization that adheres to countless rules and regulations. While Weber's principles may be partly responsible for some of the worst features of organizational bureaucracy, he can also be credited for having promoted the cause of standards in the workplace. The principle of standardization can be seen in such things as a standard pay scale for employees and standard operating procedures in military, hospital and business environments, as well as standards for quality control in production and manufacturing.

The Human Relations Perspective

Starting in the 1930s and 1940s, there began a move away from the classical perspective of management toward what became known as the human relations (or behavioral) school of management. Writers like Mary Parker Follett (1868–1933) and Chester I. Barnard (1886–1961) rejected the assumption that workers were principally motivated by economic considerations. Instead, both writers emphasized the importance of understanding human behaviors, needs and attitudes in the workplace.

The Hawthorne Studies

From 1924 to 1933, a number of research investigations were conducted at the Western Electric manufacturing plant in Hawthorne, Illinois. This set of investigations was conducted by Harvard University psychologist Elton Mayo (1898–1974) and a team of researchers. Mayo and his research team were interested in how changes in the physical work environment might affect worker productivity. Mayo and his group conducted all but one of the research investigations.

The illumination studies (the only investigation not conducted by Mayo) examined the impact of illumination (or lighting levels) on worker productivity. In this study, two groups of workers were isolated. The experimental group worked under varying levels of lighting, whereas the control group worked under normal lighting conditions. The initial findings concluded no significant difference in worker productivity between the two groups. It was at this point that Mayo and his team became centrally involved and expanded the Hawthorne studies to include other parts of the Western Electric plant. After more than a year and a half of study, the researchers concluded:

> that social satisfactions arising out of human association in work were more important determinants of work behavior in general and output in particular than were any of the physical or economic aspects of the work situation to which the attention had originally been limited.[9]

In other words, worker productivity was directly tied to social considerations and the added attention shown by the researchers and plant supervisors.[10] These preliminary findings were later borne out by additional studies conducted at the Hawthorne plant. The Hawthorne studies represented a major turning point in management theory by underscoring the importance of human relations and job satisfaction in the workplace. In addition, these studies illustrate the significance of informal and group communication in organizational settings.[11]

Maslow's Hierarchy of Needs

Another important contribution to the human relations perspective was Abraham Maslow (1908–1970), who formulated a series of theories pertaining to human motivation. Maslow proposed that human beings are motivated by a series of needs. These needs can be illustrated in a hierarchical order. Maslow's hierarchy consists of five levels of needs (Table 11.2).[12] The first three categories are considered lower-order needs, whereas the remaining two are referred to as higher-level needs. Self-actualization is the highest-level need and refers to the idea of becoming more fully realized or reaching one's highest potential.

Table 11.2 Maslow's Hierarchy of Needs

Need Level	Description
5 Self-actualization	Becoming fully realized or reaching one's highest potential.
4 Esteem	The desire of individuals to feel a sense of accomplishment.
3 Affiliation	Experiencing a strong sense of friendship or love for a person or group.
2 Safety	Living or working in a safe physical environment.
1 Physiological	Fulfilling basic physical needs such as food, water, shelter and sensory gratification.

In principle, a person will move through one or more of the categories of Maslow's hierarchy. Maslow, himself, was the first to point out that not all people have the same needs or work their way through the entire hierarchy. The significance of Maslow's hierarchy lies in its revelations concerning human motivation. What this means for managers is a recognition that individual employees are motivated by different things.

Herzberg's Motivation–Hygiene Theory

Frederick Herzberg (1923–2000) was a noted psychologist who became one of the most influential names in business management. Herzberg was concerned with human motivation issues. Herzberg's training as a clinical psychologist led him to consider what are the motivating factors that cause a person to be satisfied with his/her work. Throughout the late 1950s and early 1960s, Herzberg developed a set of theories, most notably the motivation–hygiene theory, as a way to explain worker motivation and job satisfaction.

Herzberg argued that the individual is positioned between two sets of forces. The first set of forces are the hygiene factors. The hygiene factors are extrinsic (external) and describe the person's relationship to the environment.[13] Hygiene factors typically include company policy, administration, salary, interpersonal relationships, working conditions, etc. Such factors are important but do not necessarily contribute to positive attitudes toward work. The second set of forces are the motivators. The motivators are intrinsic (internal) and serve as the real determiners of job satisfaction. They include such things as achievement, recognition, the work itself, responsibility and advancement.

McGregor's Theory X and Theory Y

One of the best examples of the human relations perspective can be seen in the writings of industrial psychologist Douglas McGregor (1906–1964).

McGregor was a professor at the Massachusetts Institute of Technology who examined the working beliefs of managers and their approach to motivating workers. Specifically, McGregor was interested in the following questions:

1   Are people (workers) generally motivated?
2   If given the opportunity, will people (workers) assume responsibility to complete a certain work task or will they look for shortcuts?
3   What kind of management style is necessary in order to ensure successful completion of a job or task assignment?

In his book entitled *The Human Side of Enterprise*, McGregor sets out to answer these questions by presenting two divergent sets of theories regarding management attitudes toward workers which he calls Theory X and Theory Y. Both Theory X and Theory Y make certain assumptions about human (worker) motivation.[14] They represent diametrically opposite points of view.

Theory X

Theory X presumes that workers are basically dull and lazy. They do not like to work and must be told what to do and are rewarded accordingly. According to Theory X:

1   By nature, most people find work not to their liking.
2   By nature, most people do not want to assume responsibility and would rather have someone tell them what to do.
3   Workers are generally uncreative and have nothing meaningful to contribute to the organization.
4   Workers are likely to feel motivated when their basic need to survive is threatened. Thus an important concern for such people is job security.
5   Workers must be watched very closely or they will slack off.

In sum, Theory X workers do not like work and are unwilling to assume responsibility for fear of making a mistake or being blamed. When a problem occurs, they are quick to point the blame in another direction and say "It wasn't my fault." Theory X workers require strict control and oversight. Finally, Theory X recognizes the use of fear and coercion as a motivating force.

Theory Y

Theory Y takes the opposite point of view. Theory Y states that people genuinely enjoy work when they are properly motivated:

1   People enjoy work since it involves many of the same elements as play.

2 In order to achieve organizational goals, the person must feel that the goals' attainment is within his/her control.

3 Most people are creative and have something to contribute to the organization.

4 True motivation is as much a psychological factor as it is physical.

5 Workers can perform effectively if management understands the things that motivate them (i.e., incentives, rewards, etc.).

In sum, workers essentially enjoy the work they do and will perform creatively and optimally if given a reasonable challenge. Moreover, Theory Y workers must believe that the organizational goal or set of tasks can be accomplished. According to McGregor, the truth about worker motivation probably lies somewhere in the middle. McGregor sees management as typically fostering one or the other kind of environment. The outcome tends to be a self-fulfilling prophecy (i.e., if you treat a worker like a child, he/she will act that way). Conversely, if you treat a worker with respect and empower him/her to do high-quality work, one can reasonably expect successful outcomes.

Ouchi's Theory Z

William Ouchi (1943–) closely observed the work of McGregor and steadily evolved a synthesis of both theories in what he later termed Theory Z. Ouchi's intention was to compare and contrast U.S. management practices with those of Japan. Theory Z speaks to the issue of how Japanese companies use their human resources in ways that are significantly different from American companies.[15] It was Ouchi's belief that U.S. business could learn a lot from its Japanese counterparts.

In his writing, Ouchi compares American organizations (Type A) with Japanese organizations (Type J). Some of the major differences can be seen with how both cultures address such things as organizational decision making, advancement and promotion, and general employment practices. As an example, Japanese organizations tend to emphasize consensus building and collective decision making, whereas American companies exhibit individual decision making. Such differences, in fact, reflect how both sets of workers see their organizations respectively. Japanese workers exhibit a more collective responsibility toward the company and its general welfare, whereas American workers tend to be more individualistic in their relationship to a corporate employer.

Ouchi is clear in pointing out that American organizations should not transform themselves into Japanese companies. This is neither practical nor realistic given the differences in culture between the two countries. Instead, Ouchi offers a series of principles that extol some of the unique benefits of the Japanese approach to business. Theory Z, for example, emphasizes the importance of training and development and taking the long-term view towards one's employees. This is reflected in the fact that Japanese companies tend to promote lifetime employment of workers, whereas American companies see the relationship as more short-term in nature. It should be remembered that Theory Z was written in 1981 at a time when Japan was experiencing its bubble economy and international exports were at an all-time high. The issue of lifetime employment is beginning to change in light of international competition. Today's Japanese companies, by contrast, are no longer able to make the same kind of commitment to their employees as might have been true in past years.

The Management Science Perspective

World War II represented a major turning point in terms of challenging existing management practices. During World War II, groups of scientists, mathematicians and efficiency experts were brought together to solve the problems of war production. Both the U.S. and Great Britain organized operational research teams for the express purpose of solving military problems. The challenge before them was how to manufacture and transport large amounts of materials, including transport vehicles, heavy weapons and support items (i.e., clothing, blankets and food) for soldiers in the field. The lessons of modern global warfare proved to be an important training ground by teaching future managers the basic principles of how to organize people and resources quickly and efficiently.

Operations Management

Out of this experience emerged the management science perspective that utilizes mathematics, statistical modeling and other quantitative techniques for purposes of planning and problem solving. In today's work setting, operations management specializes in the physical production of goods and services. Some of the more commonly used approaches to operations management include forecasting, inventory control, linear and nonlinear programming, queuing theory, scheduling and breakeven analysis.

As an example, queuing theory uses mathematics to calculate how to provide services that will minimize customer waiting time. Queuing theory is a standard procedure used by the nation's telephone companies in order to analyze traffic patterns in a voice and data network. When designing or upgrading a network, the phone company must determine the number of circuits necessary in order to accommodate periods of heavy load. The number and cost of circuits must be measured against a predetermined set of average use patterns and designed accordingly.[16] Operations management is central to the application of quality control methods such as Six Sigma, which is designed to produce outputs within highly demanding specifications (see Chapter 15).

284

Computer-Aided Design and Manufacturing

In today's work setting, operations management has been transformed through the use of computer-aided design and manufacturing. Both sets of tools emphasize the importance of visual representation and simulation. Computer-aided design (CAD) enables engineers to design and draft products in three dimensions using color and shading. CAD provides realistic simulations of how a design might appear before it is manufactured. It is used for the making of: 1) blueprints, 2) schematic diagrams, 3) elevation drawings and 4) multilayer drawings, etc. CAD systems have special features that give great precision to drawings so they are always properly scaled and accurate for production.[17]

Computer-aided manufacturing (CAM) allows the product manager and engineer to design the optimum manufacturing process for a product. As an example, the manufacturers of a new kind of optical fiber may want to test light-flow patterns, dispersion effects, heat-resistant tolerances, etc. before going into final production. In sum, with CAM, a computer can be made to:

1   simulate any manufacturing step—such as circuitry board design and assembly required for a new laptop computer or cell phone;
2   troubleshoot potential problems that may be encountered in the assembly process;
3   record how manufacturing equipment is to be set up and will eventually be used to guide computer-controlled manufacturing;
4   simulate potential problems that may be encountered external to the design and manufacturing process—such as signal attenuation tests, stress and wear, heat resistance, etc.

The Modern Management Perspective

Both the classical and human relations perspectives share the common goal of productivity. However, they differ significantly in terms of how to achieve that goal. The classical perspective emphasizes the importance of hierarchical structure and worker efficiency, whereas the human relations perspective emphasizes the importance of understanding worker motivation. The modern management perspective is not so much one perspective as multiple perspectives that look at different aspects of the management process. We will consider three kinds of perspectives that are highly representative of today's management thinking. They include: 1) management by objectives, 2) total quality management and 3) reengineering theory. While each perspective focuses on a different aspect of the management process, the perspectives share the common goal of making today's organizations better and more efficient.

Management by Objectives

The principles of management by objectives (MBO) are larger than the writings of any one individual. However, author Peter Drucker (1909–2005) popularized the term to the general public when he published *Management: Tasks, Responsibilities, Practices* in 1973. Peter Drucker was a writer, professor and adviser to senior executives for more than 50 years and published some 39 books on the subject of business and organizational leadership.

The principle of MBO involves the establishment of clearly defined short-term and long-term goals and developing procedures for accomplishing them.[18] To that end, managers and professional staff come together to help define a set of departmental (or project) goals and to implement a set of procedures accordingly. There are four basic steps in the design and implementation of an MBO plan: 1) establishing goals, 2) designing an action plan, 3) progress reviews and 4) evaluation.

Establishing Goals

An MBO plan starts with a recognition that certain organizational goals (or procedures) are in need of improvement. They might include such things as the need to: 1) increase profitability, 2) improve product quality or 3) introduce new products and services. The goals should be jointly derived and mutually agreed upon by various members of the organization. In addition, the goals should be attainable within a realistic time period. MBO is time consuming to implement and requires strong commitment on the part of management as well as the working staff.

Designing an Action Plan

Designing an action plan involves developing a course of action. In order to successfully implement a plan, senior managers define areas of responsibility and establish objectives for the different departments within the organization. There is a strong sense of charting, that is, progressive evaluation of organizational goals and worker performance.

Progress Reviews

The organization should periodically review the action plan to ensure that it is working properly. The periodic review allows managers to determine whether the action plan is working or if some kind of corrective action is needed. The action plan will sometimes need to be revised, factoring in such things as changes in the internal or external work environment or recognizing the need for special equipment (computers, etc.) that would greatly assist the organization in meeting its stated goals.

Evaluation

The final step in the MBO process is evaluation. The evaluation step allows management to determine whether organizational and departmental goals have been met. This step provides an important learning tool for future strategic planning efforts. The organization should reinforce good performance with appropriate praise, rewards, compensation, etc. The successful implementation of MBO is not without its problems. First and foremost is the issue of creating unrealistic and/or inappropriate goals. If the goals are not clear or require significant organizational resources, the implementation can prove to be a major distraction to the organization. A related problem is that some organizations become overly preoccupied with charting and paperwork, thereby making the progress review stage inflexible and unable to deal with a fast-changing work environment.

Total Quality Management

Total quality management (TQM) represents an approach to management whereby the entire organization is fully engaged to deliver quality products and services to its customers. The principles of total quality management date back to the 1940s to the work of American business consultants W. Edwards Deming and Joseph Juran, who were involved in helping to resurrect Japanese industry in the aftermath of World War II. Out of that experience and subsequent writings emerged the principles of total quality management.[19] As researcher Alan Albarran points out, the popularity of TQM in the U.S. emerged during the 1970s and early 1980s when American business was suffering from a perception of declining quality. Accordingly, TQM embraces quality and continuous improvement as fundamental to organizational goals. Says Alan Albarran:

> In TQM, managers combine strategic approaches to deliver the best products and services by continuously improving every part of the operation.[20]

There are four important elements that characterize TQM in action. They include: 1) employee involvement, 2) focus on the customer, 3) benchmarking and 4) continuous improvement.[21]

Employee Involvement

TQM embraces quality as a fundamental corporate goal. To that end, TQM requires company-wide participation in quality control. Workers must be trained, involved and empowered. Employee involvement in key decision making helps promote a sense of ownership in the outcome. In other words, once employees are personally involved and have a stake in the outcome, the organization is no longer just a place to work and get paid. An example of employee involvement can be seen in the case of Toyota Corporation, where men and women on the shop floor are given the authority to shut down car assembly when and if they spot a problem that can interfere with production output and quality. Moreover, they are encouraged to provide suggestions that will aid in the process of car assembly.

Focus on the Customer

One of the underlying principles of TQM requires that everyone should be considered a customer. To that end, customers fall into two basic categories, external and internal. External customers are those people including suppliers and buyers who interface with the organization from the outside. Internal customers are the various people and departments within an organization that depend on each other for materials and logistical support. As an example, the marketing department is a customer of printing services, and thus every effort should be made to provide excellent service.

Benchmarking

Benchmarking takes into consideration the idea that one can and should learn from the competition. The competition, for example, may have a superior product, service or work process. Benchmarking presupposes the ability to find out how others do things and then tries to imitate or improve upon it.[22] Through research and field trips by teams of workers, companies compare their products and business practices with those of the competition and make the appropriate changes when needed.

Continuous Improvement

TQM focuses on the importance of continuous improvement. TQM recognizes that there are few quick-fix solutions to problems. Rather, TQM emphasizes the importance of continuous improvement as the basis for producing long-term results. Everyone within the organization from senior management to the worker on the floor has a responsibility to improve product and service quality. Continuous improvement means that the organization benefits from the ongoing commitment to steadily improve products and procedures.

Reengineering

A number of management scholars have contributed to the principles of reengineering over the years. Authors Michael Hammer and James Champy, however, popularized the term to the general public when they published *Reengineering the Corporation: A Manifesto for Business Revolution* in 1993. Since then, the term *reengineering* has become part of the corporate lexicon of terms whenever an organization should decide to reorganize, downsize or fundamentally reshape its business operations.

The decision to reengineer usually comes about at a time when a company is faced with major competitive threats or recognizes that its operations are costly and inefficient. Hammer and Champy state the question very simply: "If I was recreating this company today, given what I know and given current technology, what would it look like?"[23] Reengineering often means starting over. It means throwing out old assumptions about how things were done in the past and developing new procedures and solutions.

According to Michael Hammer, reengineering represents a fundamental rethinking (or radical redesign) of business process intended to bring about dramatic improvements in organizational performance."[24] Improvements in performance can be measured in several ways, including reduced costs, greater speed and efficiency, improved customer service, etc. In order to accomplish such goals, reengineering presupposes the ability to rethink key business processes and a willingness to abandon old or outmoded ways of doing business. While the specifics of reengineering will vary from one organization to the next, there are certain features that are typical of a reengineered process. Examples include:

- creating cross-functional teams;
- streamlining the business process;
- designing multiple versions of a business process;
- sharing information and resources.

Creating Cross-Functional Teams

One of the basic tenets of reengineering is that you organize around key business processes which may be handled by a small, cross-functional work team rather than by rigidly defined organizational hierarchies or departments. A cross-functional team consists of members from various departments within the organization. They meet regularly as a group to solve ongoing problems of mutual interest.

Streamlining the Business Process

Reengineering presupposes the ability to identify customer needs and then designing a process and aligning people to meet those needs. A routine request for information, for example, should not be handed off among five different departments. Instead, the request should be handled by one person who is given the proper resources and authority to handle such requests. That person now performs the whole process and also serves as the single point of contact for the customer.

Customized Solutions to a Business Process

The traditional industrial model presumes that a factory's output is maximized when large quantities of a product can be produced identically for the least cost (e.g., standardized car assembly, etc.). The principle of standardization is still a critical element of today's manufacturing environment. Under a reengineering scenario, however, standardization gives way to customized solutions to a business process. This principle becomes especially important in the field of computer and telecommunications where issues pertaining to media programming and networking require unique solutions to customer needs. We have entered the generation of customized programming where consumers create for themselves music playlists on their iPods or line up their television viewing experience via their TiVo digital video recorder.

Sharing Information and Resources

In years past, large organizations tended to compartmentalize information. It was not uncommon to find that several divisions within an organization might create their own separate databases. The information was often duplicative and seldom shared between departments. The duplication of effort was both costly and inefficient. Today, computer and communication technology plays an ever important role in helping to fundamentally reengineer a business processes. Today, the emphasis is on the sharing of information resources across divisional lines, thus promoting greater efficiency in product manufacturing, marketing and distribution. A good example of this can be seen in the use of corporate intranets, discussed in Chapter 9, which allows organizational users to access a variety of information that is designed exclusively for internal use.

The Organizational Performance Perspective

Tom Peters and Robert Waterman

In Search of Excellence, by Tom Peters and Robert Waterman, was published in 1982 and became one of the first in a series of popular works that looked at the issue of organizational performance. The book examines the central question— what makes some companies truly excellent? Prior to the book's publication, Peters and Waterman were both consultants at the San Francisco office of business consulting firm McKinsey & Company. Peters and Waterman examined 43 of *Fortune* 500's top-performing companies. They started with a list of 62 of the best-performing McKinsey clients and then applied performance measures to separate out what they thought to be the weaker companies.[25]

Peters and Waterman developed eight common themes which they argued were responsible for companies exhibiting business excellence. In a later interview, Tom Peters acknowledged that one motivation for doing the research was to disprove the heavily systemized philosophy and practices of Peter Drucker and former U.S. Secretary of State Robert McNamara (who was a former business professor at Harvard and one-time president of Ford Corporation). According to Peters and Waterman, highly successful companies exhibit eight common themes.

- a bias for action—active decision making (i.e., "getting on with it");[26]
- autonomy and entrepreneurship—fostering innovation and nurturing "champions";
- being close to the customer—learning from the customers served by the business;[27]
- productivity through people—treating all members of the business organization as a contributing source of quality;
- promoting a hands-on, value-driven business philosophy that guides everyday practice;
- a stick-to-the-knitting formula; that is, stay with the business that you know;[28]
- simple form, lean staff—some of the best companies have minimal HQ staff;
- simultaneous loose–tight properties—excellent companies encourage autonomy on the shop floor and, at the same time, exhibit a strong organizational culture and values.

In 1982, *In Search of Excellence* did a great job for the time in identifying the critical elements necessary for ensuring business success. Critics point to the fact that the book may have lost some of its relevancy given today's global business environment. Moreover, writers like Jim Collins would probably disagree with Peters and Waterman's philosophy of sticking with the business you know. In a 2001 interview, Peters acknowledged that, were he to write *In Search of Excellence* today, he would not alter the eight major themes but would add to the list, including ideas pertaining to innovation, speed, turnaround time, etc.

Michael Porter

Michael Porter is a professor of management and business strategy at the Harvard Business School. Porter is considered a leading authority on the subject of business strategy, and his work serves as a foundation for many of today's university business courses on strategy. Porter's first major strategy book, entitled *Competitive Strategy: Techniques for Analyzing Industries and Competitors*, was published in 1980 and republished multiple times since then and has been translated into 19 languages. One of the important features of this book is the discussion concerning competitive forces. According to

Porter, there are five competitive forces that influence a company's competitive position. They include:

- threat of new entrants;
- intensity of rivalry among competing firms;
- threat of product substitutes;
- bargaining power of a firm's customers;
- bargaining power of a firm's suppliers.

Threat of New Entrants

The threat of new entrants refers to new or potential players that offer competitive products and services. Often, the new entrant develops a narrow niche strategy and looks to find ways to innovate in terms of product design or cost. Examples might include Skype, a telephone service that offers low-cost telephone service using VOIP technology.[29]

Intensity of Rivalry among Competing Firms

This refers to the business strategies and actions of one's competitors. The competition may have designed a better product or service. An example is the development of Microsoft's Xbox videogame system as a distinct competitive threat to the once highly dominant Sony PlayStation videogame system.[30]

Threat of Product Substitutes

There is no such thing as a static market. Changes in technology design or methods of distribution may affect the long-term viability of one's product or service.[31] An example is satellite television as a multichannel alternative to cable TV. Similarly, the ongoing development of telephone-based IPTV represents an altogether different product substitute to cable television. Similarly, the development of the Apple iPod has all but eliminated portable compact disc technology.

Bargaining Power of a Firm's Customers

Buyers can affect an industry through their ability to force down prices, bargain for higher quality and play competitors against each other. Buyers exercise important power when and if changing suppliers costs very little in time or money spent. Also, the power of a buyer becomes especially important if the product is perceived as standard or undifferentiated. This can be seen with commodity products such as television sets where buyers can exercise tremendous choice in terms of the product.[32]

Bargaining Power of a Firm's Suppliers

As Porter notes, suppliers can affect an industry though their ability to raise prices or reduce the availability of purchased goods or services. A supplier (or supplier group) is especially powerful if the supplier industry is dominated by a few companies that sell to many potential buyers. Equally important, a supplier (or supplier group) is powerful if the product or service is unique and/or where a comparable substitute is not readily available.[33] This can be seen with the National Football League (NFL) and its ability to negotiate sports rights packages with broadcast and cable programmers.

Michael Porter's second major book, *Competitive Advantage: Creating and Sustaining Superior Performance,* was published in 1985 and is considered one of the seminal works on the subject of business strategy. *Competitive Advantage* is a particularly important work on the subject of business excellence, since it provides the reader with a framework for understanding the strategies involved in enabling companies to achieve superior performance. We begin by understanding that a competitive business strategy is the comprehensive master plan used by an organization in order to achieve superior business performance.

According to Porter, there are three basic ways to implement a competitive business strategy, including: 1) cost leadership, 2) differentiation strategy and 3) focus (or narrow niche strategy). Cost leadership strategy is the ability to produce a product or service at lower cost and more efficiently than one's competitors. The goal for the firm is to become the low-cost producer in its industry.[34] Examples might include Wal-Mart, Alamo Rent A Car and Southwest Airlines, all of which emphasize low price. Differentiation strategy represents the ability to provide unique or superior value to the buyer in terms of product quality and/or special features. Says Porter, "in a differentiation strategy, a firm seeks to be unique in its industry along some dimensions that are widely valued by buyers."[35] Examples might include: DirecTV satellite television, Sony PlayStation 3 videogame system, and cable television's Home Box Office pay television service. Each of the said examples is trying to distinguish itself from the competition according to product quality and special features. The last competitive business strategy is focus. Focus (or narrow niche strategy) involves targeting a particular demographic or interest group and serving that niche cluster. Cable television provides some useful examples, including the Disney Channel (children's programming), MTV (youth and adult rock music entertainment), Black Entertainment Television (African American youth and adult entertainment and news) and the Christian Broadcast Network (Christian television programming).

Value Chain Analysis

The importance of value is essential to any discussion concerning an organization's internal capabilities and resources. Value chain analysis represents a template (or set of criteria) that an organization can use to promote strengths and efficiencies in the production and distribution of goods and services. According to researcher Lucy Küng, the purpose of value chain analysis is to identify and evaluate a firm's resources and capabilities. By studying their primary and support activities, firms better understand their cost structure and the activities in which they can create and capture value. Primary activities are directly involved in the flow of the product to customers (e.g., inbound logistics, operations, outbound logistics, marketing and sales and service). Support activities are used to support primary activities (e.g., firm infrastructure, human resource management, technology development and procurement).[36] In order to create competitive advantage, the firm must be able to 1) perform an activity in a manner that is superior to the performance of one's competitors and 2) perform a value-creating activity that is significantly different from one's competitors. Sometimes this means that a company will have to reconfigure or reengineer parts of the value chain (or process) in ways that are unique.[37] As an example, Amazon.com reconfigured the business of retail book sales by developing an EC model of sales and distribution.

Jim Collins

In 2001, author Jim Collins published *Good to Great*, which explored the question: What makes good companies great? Second, are there certain identifiable characteristics and business processes that enable companies to sustain greatness over time? Collins and his team of researchers began their analysis by sorting through a list of 1,435 companies and looking for those that made substantial improvements in their performance over time. They finally settled on 11 highly diverse companies that became the subject of their book. Collins identifies seven major precepts that form the basis for *Good to Great*. They include:

- Level 5 leadership;
- first who, then what;
- confront the brutal facts;
- the hedgehog concept;
- a culture of discipline;
- technology accelerators;
- the flywheel and the doom loop.

According to Collins, great leaders are not necessarily high-profile individuals with big personalities. Rather, great leaders (or what he terms Level 5 leaders) are self-effacing, displaying a curious blend of personal humility with a strong, professional will to get things done. Collins is quick to point out that celebrity leaders are too often more concerned with their own reputation than they are for establishing and securing the company's future success.

Collins argues that great organizational leadership begins by having a senior executive (or Level 5 leader) who identifies the right people for the right jobs and likewise determines who is not the right fit for the organization or position. According to Collins, the Level 5 leader begins by getting the "right people on the bus, the wrong people off the bus and the right people in the right seats."[38] In sum, not just people but having the right people is your most important asset. The issue of "confronting the brutal facts" speaks to the issue of environmental scanning, that is, having the honesty and discipline to determine the truth of your situation no matter what the circumstances. In order to do so, the organization must be able to lead with questions, not answers, and to conduct autopsies without blame.[39]

Collins believes that mere competence in an area can be a trap. Just because you've been doing something well for a long time doesn't necessarily mean you should be doing it in the future. The hedgehog simplifies a complex world around a simple unifying concept of greatness. In short, what are the necessary elements in order to transition from good to great? According to Collins, there are three intersecting circles that enable an organization to go from good to great. They include:

- What are you deeply passionate about?
- What can you be the best in the world at?
- What drives your economic engine?

Great companies display a culture of discipline. Successful outcomes depend on building a culture of highly disciplined people who are both knowledgeable and steady in their approach to product and process development. A culture of discipline evokes a kind of duality. On the one hand, working professionals have to adhere to a consistent, structured environment. On the other hand, it gives people tremendous opportunity and freedom to create within the parameters of that system.[40] According to Collins, great companies approach technology with thoughtfulness and creativity. They tend to avoid technology fads or technology for technology's sake. Instead, the technology applications are designed to fit within the hedgehog concept, that is, directly focused on accelerating momentum.

Finally, successful outcomes and transformations often appear dramatic to those observing from the outside. Such companies make it look easy. Collins coins the phrase "the flywheel and the doom loop" to explain that, no matter how dramatic the end result, the good-to-great transformations never happen overnight. There is no single moment or defining action. Rather, great companies are the result of a cumulative process of highly disciplined people contributing their best efforts going forward.[41]

12

TELECOMMUNICATIONS AND FINANCIAL MANAGEMENT

Ron Rizzuto, University of Denver, and
Mike Wirth, University of Tennessee

Introduction

Why should one study telecommunications finance? As you will see in this chapter, a good understanding of finance will help you: 1) understand the financial operations of the company you work for, 2) understand the financial strengths and weaknesses of your company and identify possible strategic changes that may be necessary and 3) understand how the investment community measures the financial performance of your company.

The purpose of this chapter is to provide an overview of telecommunications finance. The chapter includes:

1   a primer on accounting, with a "how to" on reading financial statements;
2   a tutorial on key financial ratios for interpreting financial performance; and
3   a primer on Wall Street terms, institutions and methods for evaluating media and telecommunication companies.

What Is Accounting?

Accounting provides a financial history of an organization. This history, like any other, tells the reader what has happened in the past. The main difference with this history is that it's mostly numbers with limited narrative. Understanding a company's financial history is important to those with management responsibilities as well as to those individuals (like shareholders) who are external to the firm.

The management of the firm needs this history to understand the overall performance of the company. This understanding helps managers determine how the firm's actual performance measures up to its budgeted targets. Knowledge of what is working and what needs fixing in the organization allows management to prepare plans for the next period (or budget cycle). Accounting provides a company's management with a "rear-view mirror." It tells where the company has been, where it is now and, through financial analysis, what changes are needed in order to plan for the future.

Financial Reporting to External Communities

A company's financial history also helps management focus on measures of financial performance that are critical to various external communities. Every corporation has external constituents with which it must communicate. If the firm is a public company (i.e., traded on a stock exchange), it must report its financial results both quarterly (10Q reports) and annually (10K reports) to the Securities and Exchange Commission (SEC) as well as to its shareholders. Shareholders are both individual investors and large investment groups that own stock in the company.

If the company has borrowed money, it must report its financial performance quarterly (and quite often monthly) to its lenders. In the case of media and telecommunication companies, they may also have to provide regulators like the Federal Communications Commission (FCC) and state public utility commissions with copies of their financial statements. Accountants prepare the financial history of a firm, particularly that of public companies, according to a set of rules called Generally Accepted Accounting Principles (GAAP). GAAP is a set of reporting standards that are currently the responsibility of the Financial Accounting Standards Board (FASB)[1] and the Securities and Exchange Commission. The objective of GAAP is to provide a set of rules for preparing financial statements so that the financial position of the company and the results of its operation are presented as fairly, consistently and accurately as possible. The major parts of a company's financial performance can be found in three kinds of financial statements: the income statement, the balance sheet and the statement of cash flows. In the next sections of this chapter, we will consider the purpose (and key components) of each of these statements.

Income Statement

A company's income (or profit and loss) statement measures the firm's famous "bottom line." In short, the income statement measures the amount of profit generated by the firm during a specified period of time. This information can be broken down quarterly or annually. The income statement is important because it tells managers and shareholders whether the firm is making money from the goods and services it has sold to its customers.

An income statement is generally broken down into two parts: revenues and expenses. The difference between revenues and expenses is the profit or loss for that period.

Revenues

Revenues refer to money coming into an organization. In a media and telecommunications environment, such revenue sources can include:

- advertising sales: national, regional, local;
- sale of facilities (i.e., production and graphics capability);
- network compensation if applicable;
- cable subscriber fees;
- money derived from home shopping network sales;
- high-speed Internet access fees;
- pay television (and pay-per-view) fees;
- telephone subscriber fees;
- telephone add-on features (i.e., voicemail, text messaging, etc.);
- home maintenance and security fees.

Expenses

Expenses refer to money being paid out by the organization. In a media and telecommunications environment, such expense items can include:

- salaries and wages;
- health benefits to employees;
- program expenses, license fees and newswire service fees;
- marketing expenses, advertising and promotion;
- sales expenses, travel and lodging, and client entertainment;
- plant and facilities (building operations and logistical support);
- equipment costs (broadcast studio equipment, satellite transponder lease fees, computer and networking expenses, etc.);
- maintenance and repair costs;
- charitable contributions.

Table 12.1 illustrates a sample income statement for television station KWLX-TV for the year 200X. Station KWLX's income statement begins with revenues, that is, with the dollars generated from the sale of advertising and other services. Some companies report revenues only as a one-line-item entry. Other firms, like KWLX-TV, provide a breakdown of revenues according to the type of product or service sold (i.e., national, regional or local advertising, network compensation, etc.).

Station KWLX-TV's Revenues

Station KWLX-TV achieved total revenue of $4,655,400 based on revenues generated from three sources: national and regional spot advertising

Table 12.1 KWLX-TV: Income Statement for Year Ending December 31, 200X

	$
Revenue:	
National/regional spot advertising	2,444,200
Local advertising	1,662,100
Network compensation	549,100
Total revenue	$4,655,400
Expenses:	
Technical	378,100
Programming	1,233,000
Selling expenses	358,600
General and administrative	870,400
Depreciation	407,400
Total operating expenses	3,247,500
Operating income	1,407,900
Interest	(401,600)
Taxes	(483,000)
Net income (earnings after taxes)	$523,300
Earnings per share	$5.23

($2,444,200), local advertising ($1,662,100) and network compensation ($549,100).

Station KWLX-TV's Expenses

The next category of entries on an income statement is operating expenses. These are the costs associated with providing products and services to the consumer. Station KWLX-TV's total operating expenses equaled $3,247,500. This was based on the following set of expenses:

- *Technical:* In this case, station KWLX-TV combined the salaries of the professional staff as well as video and editing production costs.
- *Programming:* This is the cost of purchasing and producing all programs aired by the station (i.e., syndicated programming, news programming, etc.).
- *Selling expenses:* These represent the expenses incurred in selling advertising, including travel and lodging expenses, entertainment and commissions to sales personnel.
- *General and administrative:* This category of expenses includes such things as mortgage payments, office expenses, telephone and salaries of administrative personnel.
- *Depreciation:* Station KWLX-TV, like all organizations, has a need to cost out the value of a capital asset over its estimated useful life. In the case of

a television station, capital assets would include: cameras, editing suites, towers, satellite dishes, etc. For example, if a satellite dish costs $25,000 and has a useful life of five years, then the accountants would spread the $25,000 cost over a five-year period. They might apportion $5,000 in cost for each year.[2] Accountants refer to this as depreciating the cost.

Operating Income

Operating income tells us the difference in dollar amount between total revenue and total operating expenses. As Table 12.1 illustrates, we take total revenue, $4,655,400, and subtract total operating expenses, $3,247,500, which leads us to a line item on the income statement called operating income, which for Station KWLX is $1,407,900.

Non-Operating Expenses

The next category of items on the income statement is non-operating expenses (i.e., interest and taxes). Interest expenses are the sum of all the interest a firm has paid on loans that have been outstanding during that time period. Interest expenses include only the interest portion of payments made. They do not include any principal repayments.[3] Income taxes include federal, state and/or local taxes on income. Such non-operating expenses are designated with brackets around them. Interest and taxes are the only non-operating expenses shown on KWLX's income statement.[4]

Net Income (or the Bottom Line)

The famous "bottom line" on the income statement is net income or earnings after taxes. Net income is the amount of profit the firm has made during the period. As Table 12.1 illustrates, KWLX-TV had a net income (or profit) of $523,300.

Earnings per Share

Income statements, particularly for publicly traded companies, also include a final item termed *earnings per share*. This figure is computed by dividing net income by the number of shares outstanding.[5] This earnings-per-share value simply represents the firm's profits on the basis of a share of stock. As you will see later in the chapter, this ratio is used by the external financial community.

Income Statements and the Principle of Zeroing Out

After an income statement is released, the statement gets zeroed out at the end of the period. In other words, after the year is over and profits are

determined, the income statement is closed out. The income statement is set
to zero in order to begin to capture the values for the next period. Any profits
that are produced are either paid out to shareholders in the form of dividends
or reinvested in the business.

Consolidated Income Statement

As part of their annual report to stockholders, most companies will provide a
consolidated income statement, which is a summary of the company's financial performance in terms of listing the key financial indicators, such as
revenues, operating income and net income. Consolidated income statements
will often provide a comparison of financial performance for the year under
review as well as the previous year (and/or previous four years). Table 12.2
provides a consolidated income statement for Verizon Inc. In 2005, the company achieved revenues of $75.112 billion, with an operating income of
$14.814 billion and a net income of $7.397 billion.

Table 12.2 Verizon: Consolidated Income Statement (in million dollars)

Results of Operations	2005	2004	2003	2002	2001
Operating revenues	75,112	71,283	67,468	67,056	66,513
Operating income	14,814	13,117	7,407	14,877	11,402
Income before discontinued operations, extraordinary items and cumulative effect of accounting change	7,397	7,261	3,460	4,591	545
Per common share—basic	2.67	2.62	1.26	1.68	0.20
Per common share—diluted	2.65	2.59	1.25	1.67	0.20
Net income	7,397	7,831	3,077	4,079	389
Net income available to common shareowners	7,397	7,831	3,077	4,079	389
Per common share—basic	2.67	2.83	1.12	1.49	0.14
Per common share—diluted	2.65	2.79	1.12	1.49	0.14
Cash dividends declared per common share	1.62	1.54	1.54	1.54	1.54
Financial position:					
Total assets	168,130	165,958	165,968	167,468	170,795
Long-term debt	31,869	35,674	39,413	44,003	44,873
Employee benefit obligations	18,819	17,941	16,754	15,392	11,895
Minority interest	26,754	25,053	24,348	24,057	21,915
Shareowners' investment	39,680	37,560	33,466	32,616	32,539

Source: Verizon Corporation, "Consolidated Income Statement," Available at: http://investor.veri-
zon.com/financial/annual/2005/financials03.html (retrieved March 12, 2006).

Balance Sheet

The balance sheet is a statement that reports the firm's financial position at a point in time. The balance sheet provides a snapshot of what a company owns (assets) and what are its outstanding debts (or liabilities). The review point is typically at the end of a business quarter or calendar year. In addition, the balance sheet provides a statement regarding owners' equity, that is, the value (or net worth) of the organization. It is the amount by which assets exceed liabilities. For a corporation, owners' equity is often referred to as stockholders' equity. Owners' equity is the cumulative result of business transactions that have occurred throughout the life of the organization leading up to the current review point.

What Does the Information Reveal?

A balance sheet is a useful statement because it provides management and shareholders with answers to such questions as:

- What assets does the company own?
- How much money has the company borrowed to finance its assets?
- Have lenders or shareholders put up the majority of the money to finance the company's assets?
- What are the company's short-term and long-term debts?
- What is the present value (or worth) of the company at the time period under review?

Assets

Assets refer to the value of what the organization owns. Assets are typically broken down according to current, fixed and other:

- *current:* includes cash on hand, bank accounts, accounts receivable, value of supplies, etc.;
- *fixed:* building, land, equipment facilities (i.e., transmitters, studio equipment, computers, etc.);
- *other:* financial investments and intangibles (e.g., FCC license).

Liabilities

Liabilities reflect the organization's short-term and long-term debt (i.e., what it owes). Liabilities are typically broken down according to current and fixed liabilities:

- *current:* money owed for supplies, services, taxes, commissions, music license fees, employee benefits, etc.;
- *fixed:* the unpaid balance on bonds, mortgages and other long-term debt.

Table 12.3 provides an example of a balance sheet for station KWLX-TV. The top section of the balance sheet is the asset section, which indicates what the company owns. The most liquid assets (i.e., those most easily converted into cash) are listed first. The second section of the balance sheet tells the reader what the firm owes (i.e., liabilities), along with the firm's net worth (i.e., equity).

Station KWLX-TV's Assets

Cash is the first asset item listed since it is the most liquid (i.e., easiest to convert to cash) of all assets. If a firm has cash invested in savings accounts, certificates of deposit or other short-term interest-bearing securities, the cash category may be labeled "Cash and cash equivalents." In our example, KWLX-TV has $488,900 in cash.

Next on the list of assets is accounts receivable. This is what customers owe station KWLX-TV as a result of credit sales. In KWLX's case, customers owe $1,303,500.

Table 12.3 KWLX-TV: Balance Sheet for Year Ending December 31, 200X

	$
Assets:	
Cash	488,900
Accounts receivable	1,303,500
Programming rights	244,400
Total current assets	2,036,800
Buildings and equipment	3,095,900
Land	228,200
Net fixed assets	3,324,100
Total assets	$5,360,900
Liabilities:	
Accounts payable	977,800
Sales commissions payable	146,700
Notes payable	896,200
Total current liabilities	2,020,700
Long-term debt	2,036,900
Total liabilities	4,057,600
Common stock	500,000
Retained earnings	803,300
Total equity	1,303,300
Total liabilities and equity	$5,360,900

Programming rights are the next asset item for broadcasters. For a television station, these are the licenses and rights to broadcast various types of syndicated programs which have been purchased by the station.[6] The first three lines on the asset side of KWLX's balance sheet are summed up under the heading "Total current assets." These are assets which will be used up or converted to cash in less than one year. The total current assets for station KWLX is $2,036,800.

The fixed (or long-term) assets follow next on the balance sheet. These consist of buildings and equipment, as well as land. These are tangible or physical assets that are recorded on the basis of their historical cost. In other words, they are valued at what it cost the business to originally purchase them, not at what they may be worth now.[7]

The last line of the asset section of the balance sheet is "Total assets," which is a summation of KWLX's entire set of assets. In this example, station KWLX has total assets worth $5,360,900.

Station KWLX-TV's Liabilities

Liabilities and equity make up the other section of the balance sheet. The liability entries (what station KWLX owes) appear first. Liabilities, just like assets, are listed in decreasing order of liquidity. All liabilities requiring payment within one year are categorized on the balance sheet as "Total current liabilities." Table 12.3 contains three current liability categories: accounts payable, sales commissions payable and notes payable.

The first entry, accounts payable, is what a company owes its vendors and suppliers. As Table 12.3 illustrates, KWLX owes $977,800. Sales commissions payable are commissions that KWLX owes its sales staff (i.e., money that has yet to be paid), which is equal to $146,700. Notes payable are next. Typically these are short-term interest-bearing loans (or bank loans), which for KWLX are equal to $896,200. The total current liabilities for station KWLX are $2,020,700.

Long-term debt comes next. This is borrowed money that will need to be repaid more than one year from the date of the balance sheet. In KWLX's case, there is only one long-term debt entry—$2,036,900. Total liabilities are a summation of current liabilities and long-term debt. In the case of station KWLX, $4,057,600 represents the total set of claims creditors have against KWLX's assets.

Equity

As mentioned earlier, the balance sheet provides the reader with an understanding of the firm's equity, that is, the present value (or net worth) of the owners of the organization. Owners' equity or stockholders' equity is the cumulative result of business transactions that have occurred throughout the life of the organization leading up to the current review point. We arrive at this figure through the simple formula of:

Assets − Liabilities = Equity (or A − L = E)

The equity section of the balance sheet typically includes two types of entries, that is, money that shareholders have invested in the firm (common stock) and profits the company has reinvested in itself (i.e., retained earnings) rather than paying it out to shareholders in the form of dividends. KWLX has total equity of $1,303,300. Of this amount, $500,000 was invested by shareholders and $803,300 was reinvested profits.

Consolidated Balance Statement

As part of their annual report to stockholders, most companies will provide a consolidated balance statement, which is a summary of the company's financial performance in terms of listing the key financial indicators, including company assets, liabilities and stockholders' (or owners') equity. Table 12.4 provides a consolidated balance statement for Microsoft Inc. for the year 2006. In 2006, Microsoft claimed combined total assets of $69.597 billion. The company claimed total liabilities of $29.493 billion and stockholders' equity of $40.104 billion.

Statement of Cash Flows

The statement of cash flows represents a summarized view of the company's checkbook. The primary function of this statement is to track the inflow and outflow of cash from the business. The statement of cash flows is important because it provides answers to such questions as:

- Was the cash flow generated through operations positive or negative? In sum, did more cash come in than go out?
- How much cash was invested to grow the business?
- How much cash from external financing was required?
- Where did the external financing come from?

The statement of cash flows in Table 12.5 is quite representative of what is used by today's media and telecommunications companies. The statement of cash flows can be divided into four parts, including:

1 cash flows from operating activities;
2 cash flows from investing activities;
3 cash flows from financing activities;
4 increase or decrease in cash and cash equivalents.

Table 12.4 Microsoft: Consolidated Balance Statement (in million dollars)

	June 30, 2006	June 30, 2005
Assets:		
Current assets:		
Cash and equivalents	6,714	4,851
Short-term investments (including securities pledged as collateral	27,447	32,900
Total cash and short-term investments	34,161	37,751
Accounts receivable, net of allowance for doubtful accounts of $142 and $171	9,316	7,180
Inventories, net	1,478	491
Deferred income taxes	1,940	1,701
Other	2,115	1,614
Total current assets	49,010	48,737
Property and equipment, net	3,044	2,346
Equity and other investments	9,232	11,004
Goodwill	3,866	3,309
Intangible assets, net	539	499
Deferred income taxes	2,611	3,621
Other long-term assets	1,295	1,299
Total assets	$69,597	$70,815
Liabilities and stockholders' equity:		
Current liabilities:		
Accounts payable	2,909	2,086
Accrued compensation	1,938	1,662
Income taxes	1,557	2,020
Short-term unearned revenue	9,138	7,502
Securities lending payable	3,117	–
Other	3,783	3,607
Total current liabilities	22,442	16,877
Long-term unearned revenue	1,764	1,665
Other long-term liabilities	5,287	4,158
Commitments and contingencies		
Stockholders' equity:		
Common stock and paid-in capital—shares authorized 24,000; outstanding 10,062 and 10,710	59,005	60,413
Retained earnings (deficit), including accumulated other comprehensive income of $1,119 and $1,426	(18,901)	(12,298)
Total stockholders' equity	40,104	48,115
Total liabilities and stockholders' equity	$69,597	$70,815

Source: Microsoft Corporation, "2006 Financial Review," Available at: http://www.microsoft.com/msft/reports/ar06/flashversion/10k_fr_bal.html (retrieved April 1, 2007).

Table 12.5 KWLX-TV: Statement of Cash Flows for Year Ending December 31, 200X

	$
Cash flows from operating activities:	
Net income	523,300
Depreciation and amortization	407,400
Changes in accounts receivable	(203,500)
Changes in programming rights	(34,000)
Changes in accounts payable	27,800
Changes in sales commission payable	11,700
Net cash provided by operating activities (OCF)	732,700
Cash flows from investing activities:	
Purchase of property and equipment	(100,000)
Sales of property and equipment	–
Net cash used in investing activities (ICF)	(100,000)
Cash flows from financing activities:	
Proceeds from borrowings	–
Repayment of debt	(200,000)
Dividends	(100,000)
Proceeds from stock issuance	–
Purchase of company stock	–
Net cash provided by financing activities (FCF)	(300,000)
Increase (decrease) in cash and cash equivalents (OCF + ICF + FCF)	332,700
Cash and cash equivalents, beginning of year	156,200
Cash and cash equivalents, end of year	488,900

The rule for the statement of cash flows is very simple: Cash inflows are shown as positive figures, whereas cash outflows are shown as negatives (in parentheses). The increase (or decrease) in cash and cash equivalents plus the beginning cash balance equals the ending balance.

Cash Flows from Operating Activities (OCF)

This section tracks all the cash flows in the day-to-day running of a business. It includes collections from customers and all expenses paid out in cash, including salaries, selling, programming and interest expenses, and taxes. If the company is generating positive cash flow from operations, the business is said to be "cash flowing" or "operating above breakeven." If it is operating in a negative situation, then the company will have to rely on external financing sources in order to keep the business solvent. In Table 12.5, station KWLX's net cash provided by operating activities (OCF) is $732,700. It's not uncommon for media and telecom start-up companies to exhibit negative cash flow from operations during the early stages of their development.

Cash Flows from Investing Activities (ICF)

This section refers to the cash spent to buy property, equipment and other businesses. The amount of investing cash flows indicates how much the company is investing in activities that will grow the business. Since this section of the cash flow statement is all about growth, it will generally be negative. The only time it will be positive is when the company is selling assets. In Table 12.5, Station KWLX's net cash used in investing activities (ICF) is negative $100,000.

Cash Flows from Financing Activities (FCF)

This section refers to cash coming in from (or going out to) lenders and investors. The money coming in typically includes loans from banks and stock sales to investors. The money going out includes loan repayments, dividend payments and stock repurchases. As noted above, if a company is not generating positive operating cash flow (OCF) and/or is making substantial investments in plant and equipment, then the firm is in all likelihood relying heavily on external financing to fund its businesses.[8] The cash flows from financing activities (or FCF) would therefore be positive. By contrast, companies with strong positive OCF (i.e., "cash cows") and limited reinvestment relative to their operations will have negative FCFs. These firms typically pay large dividends to shareholders, repay their loans and engage in stock repurchase programs. In Table 12.5, station KWLX's net cash provided by financing activities is negative $300,000.

Increase or Decrease in Cash and Cash Equivalents

This is the summation of the statement of cash flows. In other words, it is all the cash received by the firm minus all the cash paid out. The number is computed by adding OCF, ICF and FCF. In Table 12.5, the increase in cash and cash equivalents for station KWLX is $332,700.

Clearly, if the figure is negative, the firm has reduced its cash and cash equivalents during the period. The greater the negative value, the faster the cash "burn rate" for the company. As an example, Internet start-up companies are notorious for having a high cash "burn rate." What is most important, however, is the cash and cash equivalents end-of-the-year figure. This bottom-line figure tells managers and shareholders whether or not the operations are "cash flowing" or paying their way. In Table 12.5, the cash and cash equivalents end-of-the-year figure for Station KWLX is $488,900.

Interpreting Financial Performance

Before beginning a discussion on financial performance, it is useful to understand that today's media and telecommunication companies operate at one of three stages in a financial life cycle. The three phases include: 1) the infancy stage, 2) the growth stage and 3) the maturity stage. The key difference among the three financial stages is their level of profitability. The traditional accounting definition of profitability is net income (i.e., revenues minus all expenses).

The Infancy Stage

New company start-ups are typically in a financial infancy stage. Such companies are focused on building their network infrastructure, as well as on growing their customer base. For these companies, profitability is not really the issue. They are focused on establishing themselves in the marketplace and growing their market share. Companies like Sirius (a satellite radio service provider) and MySpace (an Internet content provider) are examples of companies in their financial infancy. These firms are referred to as Phase 1 companies.

The Growth Stage

Companies that are in a financial growth phase are well established in the marketplace, but are not necessarily profitable. Such companies are growing and expanding and generating considerable expense in terms of developing infrastructure and building audiences. The combination of expenses and interest loan payments often eliminates earnings performance. Companies like Apple iTunes and Verizon's FiOS direct-to-home television service will require high capitalization before seeing a return on investment. These firms are referred to as Phase 2 companies.

EBITDA

Firms in the infancy and financial growth phase define profitability as earnings before interest, taxes, depreciation and amortization (EBITDA). EBITDA is also referred to as operating cash flow. Since Phase 1 and 2 firms are not generating earnings, the traditional measures of profitability (i.e., net profit margin and return on equity) are not useful indicators of profitability. As a result, these firms have adopted the EBITDA margin as their indicator of financial performance:

$$\text{EBITDA margin} = \frac{\text{EBITDA}}{\text{Total revenue}}$$

In principle, the higher the ratio becomes, the more profitable the firm.

309

Similarly, firms with negative EBITDA are identified by a negative margin value. A lower negative ratio indicates a company that is steadily improving (or moving toward) profitability. As an example, Apple iTunes might have an EBITDA margin of 29.3 percent, whereas Sirius Radio might have a negative margin of −36.2 percent.

The Maturity Stage

Companies that are financially mature generate net income. They define profitability in terms of net income, earnings per share and net income growth. Such companies as AT&T and Verizon are considered financially mature. Similarly, the major television networks (i.e., ABC, CBS, NBC and Fox) would also be considered financially mature companies. These firms are referred to as Phase 3 companies.

Someone who is trying to understand the financial performance of a media or telecommunications firm must understand where the company is in its financial life cycle. As will be discussed later, the measures of profitability and security market performance vary depending on where the firm is in its financial life cycle.

Profitability Ratios

In this next section, we will consider a few of the key measures for interpreting financial performance. Although there are several ways to measure financial performance, two of the most important methods are to look at profitability ratios, including net profit margin and return on equity. Profitability ratios are especially important for analyzing the financial performance of Phase 3 companies.

Net Profit Margin

This measures how much of each dollar generated in revenue ends up as profit. The higher this figure, the better. The formula for calculating net profit margin is:

$$\text{Net profit margin} = \frac{\text{Net income}}{\text{Total revenue}}$$

Return on Equity

This measures the rate of return that a firm earns on each dollar of equity invested by its shareholders. Clearly, the higher the value, the more successful are the shareholders. The formula for calculating return on equity is:

$$\text{Return on equity} = \frac{\text{Net income}}{\text{Total stockholders' equity}}$$

Segment Disclosures

One of the important tools for understanding how a media or telecommunications company has performed can be seen in different kinds of segment disclosures. The goal is to understand how a company has performed over a one- to five-year time period according to such baseline measurements as revenue or net income comparisons, product line contributions to overall revenue, product line contributions in percentages, and product line contributions according to geographic location.

The various graphs and illustrations depicting this information are used by senior management for purposes of strategic planning and analysis. Some of the same information and graphic illustrations are included in the company's annual report to its stockholders.

Revenues and Net Income Comparison

This kind of segment disclosure allows the reader to understand how a company has performed over a two- to five-year time period. The value of such graphic illustrations is to highlight whether a company's growth trend has been good, poor, consistent or erratic. Figure 12.1 provides a comparison of Walt Disney's revenue and net incomes spanning a four-year time period,

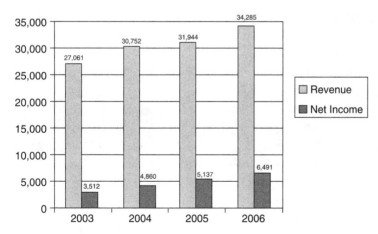

Figure 12.1 The Walt Disney Company: Revenue and Net Income, 2003–2006 (in million dollars).

Source: Walt Disney Corporation, "Financial Highlights," Available at: http://corporate.disney.go.com/investors/annual_reports/2006/int/fh.html (retrieved March 12, 2006).

for the years 2003–2006. In 2006, the Walt Disney Company realized a revenue of $34.285 billion and a net income of $6.491 billion.

Revenues by Division (or Product Line)

The value of this kind of segment disclosure is that it allows the reader to understand how a company has performed according to the main divisions (or product line areas) that make up the organization. It illustrates those areas of the company that are dominant, as well as pointing out potential imbalances in terms of how the company generates revenues. Figure 12.2 provides a breakdown of Walt Disney's contributing revenues according to its four major divisions for the years 2003–2006. During the four-year time span, media networks, including ABC Television and ESPN cable sports programming, have contributed the most to the company's overall growth, followed by the company's Disney World and Disneyland parks and resorts division.

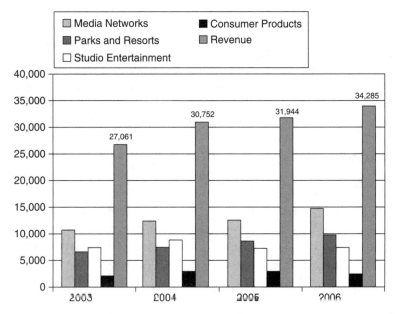

Figure 12.2 The Walt Disney Company: Revenue by Major Division, 2003–2006 (in million dollars).

Source: Walt Disney Corporation, "Financial Highlights," Available at: http://corporate.disney.go.com/investors/annual_reports/2006/int/fh.html (retrieved March 12, 2006).

Percentage Contributions by Division (or Product Line)

This kind of segment disclosure allows the reader to understand the percentage contribution by division or product line to a company's yearly revenue performance. As before, it illustrates those areas of the company that are performing well, while pointing out potential imbalances in terms of how the company generates revenues. It should be pointed out that too much dependency on one area of the company puts the company at risk, lest there be a downturn in that particular market or segment. Figure 12.3 provides a breakdown of Comcast Corporation's financial performance for 2006 according to percentage contributions by major product line. Figure 12.4 provides a breakdown of Sony Corporation's financial performance for 2006 according to percentage of sales and operating revenue. The diagram is accompanied by a brief business description of each division.

Wall Street Primer

Financial Market Overview

Companies need money (capital) to execute their business plans. Most telecommunication companies' capital needs are greater than their internal sources of capital (i.e., reinvested profits). As a consequence, telecommunication companies need to locate lenders (or investors) who have excess funds.

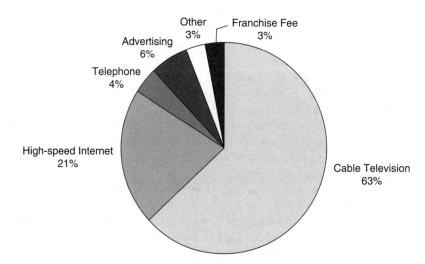

Figure 12.3 Comcast Corporation: Percentage Contributions to Overall Revenue by Major Division, 2006.

Source: Comcast Corporation, "Year End 2006 Results," Available at: http://media.corporate-ir.net/media_files/irol/11/118591/Earnings_4Q06/q406.htm (retrieved March 12, 2006).

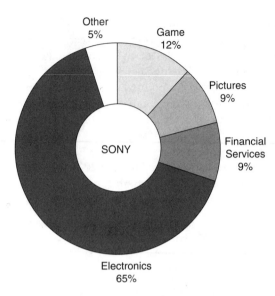

Other 5%

Game 12%

Pictures 9%

SONY

Financial Services 9%

Electronics 65%

Electronics: comprises audio, video, televisions, information and communications equipment, semiconductors and other products.

Game: encompasses videogame consoles and software businesses.

Pictures: encompasses motion pictures, television programming and related businesses.

Financial: comprises business activities involving life insurance, banking, finance, etc.

Other: comprises a number of different business activities, including Sony Music Entertainment (Japan), a joint business partnership with Bertelsmann AG (Sony BMG Music Entertainment) and Sony Network Services.

Figure 12.4 Sony Corporation: Percentage of Sales and Operating Revenue by Major Division, 2006.

Source: Sony Corporation, "2006 Financial Highlights," Available at: http://www.sony.net/SonyInfo/IR/financial/highlight/index.html (retrieved March 12, 2006).

The financial markets are the mechanism that brings lenders and borrowers together.[9]

The financial markets, as the name suggests, are a multitude of individual markets. Each market deals with a different type of investment instrument (i.e., stocks, corporate bonds, mortgages, etc.). Likewise, each market connects different types of lenders and borrowers. Generally, markets that deal with instruments having maturity in excess of one year are referred to as the capital markets. Financial markets with instruments with maturities of less than one year are called money markets.

Lenders (investors) may participate directly with a borrower in the financial markets by buying a direct investment in the company in the form of securities (i.e., stocks and bonds). Alternatively, lenders (investors) may participate indirectly in the financial markets by buying the securities of financial intermediaries (i.e., commercial banks, insurance companies, pension funds, market funds, credit unions, etc.). The financial institutions then purchase the direct securities of the borrower organizations. As a consequence of this process of intermediation of savings, the financial markets include both institutional and individual investors.

Some telecommunication companies are owned by the public; that is, their shares are traded on a stock exchange, allowing stockholders to sell the shares they own or to buy additional shares whenever they like.[10] In contrast, many telecommunication firms are privately owned. There is no public market for the shares of private companies. As a result, these shareholders cannot increase or decrease their ownership without special buy/sell agreements with the principals of the company. Although the pros and cons of being a public company are beyond the scope of this chapter, it is clear that a primary reason for becoming a public company is the ability to raise significant amounts of capital to fund major growth projects.

The Stock Market and Common Stocks

The common stock of public companies is traded on one or more of the major U.S. or international stock exchanges. Typically, however, most firms are traded on only one stock exchange. There are two basic types of stock markets. They include:

1   *Organized stock exchanges:* These include the New York Stock Exchange (NYSE), as well as several regional exchanges (i.e., Pacific, Chicago, Philadelphia, and Boston stock exchanges); the Tokyo Stock Exchange (Japan); the London Stock Exchanges (U.K.), the Hang Seng (Hong Kong), etc.
2   *Over-the-counter market:* This stock exchange is a virtual market that relies heavily on telephone and computer trading as opposed to a physical marketplace like one of the organized exchanges. Examples include NASDAQ (U.S.A.), LIFFE (U.K.), SIMEX (Singapore) and SFE (Australia).

NASDAQ

Frequently, stocks traded in the over-the-counter market are said to be traded on the National Association of Security Dealers Automated Quotation system (NASDAQ). NASDAQ is the computerized trading market used by the brokers and dealers who make up the over-the-counter market.

Quotations from the various stock markets appear daily in the newspapers. Examples of stock quotations appearing in daily newspapers are listed in Table 12.6. As Table 12.6 illustrates, the stock values are quoted on a per-share basis. The first column (YTD % Change) gives the percentage change in the stock for the year to date. The next column (Stock) lists the name of the company, and the third column provides the stock's ticker symbol. The dividend yield column reports the dividends for the past four quarters as a percentage of the current stock price. For AT&T, the dividend yield is 3.6 percent. Price earnings (P/E) ratio follows dividend yield. The P/E is the closing price divided by the company's earnings for the previous four

Table 12.6 Sample Stock Quotations for Selected Telecommunication Firms Listed on NYSE and NASDAQ

	YTD % Change	Stock	Symbol	Dividend Yield	P/E	Last	Net Change
NYSE	10.3	AT&T	T	3.6	21	39.43	0.26
	−9.5	Time Warner	TWX	1.1	13	19.72	−0.13
	0.1	Viacom A	VIA	−	35	41.06	0.49
	0.2	Viacom B	VIAB	−	−	41.11	0.45
	1.8	Verizon	VZ	4.3	18	37.92	0.35
NASDAQ	−8.0	Comcast A	CMCSA	−	32	25.95	0.09
	14.2	EchoStar	DISH	−	32	43.43	0.56
	10.4	Liberty Media Inter- active A	LINTA	−	−	23.82	−0.24
	12.9	Liberty Media Capital A	LCAPA	−	−	110.59	1.32
	−6.7	Microsoft	MSFT	1.4	24	27.87	0.12

quarters. The final two columns indicate the closing stock price and the net change from the prior trading day. For AT&T, the closing price was $39.43, and the change from the previous day was $0.26.

The quotations for the firms listed in Table 12.6 are secondary market listings (i.e., the market for shares that are already outstanding). The quotations represent the price paid by investors trading shares among themselves. The company itself does not receive any funds from the secondary marketplace.

A firm receives cash from the sale of stock only during a public offering process when the company initially goes public (i.e., an initial public offering or IPO). For example, in August 2004, Google went public at $85 per share. At the time of the IPO, Google received $85 for each share that was sold to the public.[11]

Voting Shares

Sometimes firms have different classes of stock that allow a greater number of votes per share than the traditional one vote to one share. Class B shares have greater voting rights than Class A. The primary reason for having Class B type shares is to help defend the company against hostile takeovers by concentrating the voting shares in the hands of "friendly shareholders." As illustrated in Table 12.6, Viacom has both Class A and Class B shares outstanding.

Tracking Stock

A recent trend in the telecommunication industry is for companies to create a tracking stock. A tracking stock is a mechanism whereby shareholders can concentrate their ownership of a firm in only one part of the company's operation as opposed to the entire entity. The primary benefit of a tracking stock from a company's perspective is to allow a high-performing subsidiary company (within a complex corporate structure) to grow and garner investment value without being hampered by the financial performance of sister companies. For example, as illustrated in Table 12.6, Liberty Media Corporation has its Liberty Interactive Group tracking stock that tracks its interests in QVC, Provide Commerce, IAC/Interactive Corporation and Expedia, while its Liberty Capital group tracking stock includes Liberty's interest in Starz Entertainment, News Corporation and Time Warner.[12]

Debt Securities

A significant portion of the financing of telecommunication companies is borrowed money. Commercial banks have historically been among the primary lenders to commercial enterprises, particularly cable television companies. Although the terms vary by borrowing and type of loan, commercial bank loans are generally short- or intermediate-term (i.e., six months to ten years) and are floating-rate loans. The interest rate is variable as opposed to being fixed.

Some telecommunication companies, particularly those that are mid-sized or large, borrow funds directly from institutional investors (e.g., pension funds, insurance companies, etc.). These loans may be fixed or floating rate-type instruments. Mid-sized and larger telecommunication firms may also utilize the public bond markets to issue corporate notes and bonds. Typically, corporate notes have maturities of seven to ten years, whereas bonds have maturities in excess of ten years.

Corporate Bonds

Frequently, corporate bonds are fixed-rate instruments. Corporate bonds are often rated by bond rating agencies like Moody's and Standard & Poor's (S&P). As Table 12.7 illustrates, the highest-rated bonds carry Moody's (Aaa) or S&P's (AAA) rating respectively. Bonds rated by Moody's as Ba or B and S&P as BB or B are often referred to as "junk bonds" or high-yield bonds. The primary difference between high-quality and junk bonds has to do with the level of investment risk. Junk bond firms are more highly leveraged; that is, the firm is carrying a high debt-to-cash-flow ratio. Junk bond firms also have much lower interest coverage ratios than so-called high-quality bonds.

Table 12.7 Moody's and Standard & Poor's Ratings

	High Quality			Investment Grade	Junk Bonds			
					Substandard		Speculative	
Moody's	Aaa	Aa	A	Baa	Ba	B	Caa	C
Standard & Poor's	AAA	AA	A	BBB	BB	B	CCC	D

Note: Both rating agencies use modifiers for bonds within a category as well. For example, Moody's uses a 1, 2 or 3 designation, with 1 being the strongest and 3 the weakest (i.e., A1 is a stronger credit rating as compared to A3). Standard & Poor's uses a + and − system (i.e., A+ is a stronger credit rating than A−).

In the past, many telecommunication firms in their infancy (or start-up) stage used the junk bond market as a major source of funding.

Summary

This chapter examines three aspects of telecommunication finance. They include: 1) an accounting primer, which looks at the basics of reading financial statements, 2) the interpreting of financial performance, and 3) a Wall Street primer, which provides an overview of the investment community.

Accounting Primer

Accounting represents the financial history of the firm. It tells the reader what has happened financially to a company during a specified period of time. The management of the firm needs this history in order to understand the overall financial performance of the company. In addition, this financial history helps management focus on measures of financial performance which are critical for purposes of strategic planning as well as providing relevant information to external constituents such as stockholders and bondholders.

The income statement is a statement that measures the firm's famous bottom line. The income statement is important because it tells managers and shareholders whether the firm is making money from the goods and services it has sold to the public. The income statement begins with revenues and then includes operating expenses (i.e., technical costs, administrative and selling expenses, etc.). Operating income is the difference between revenues and operating expenses. Non-operating expenses and income (i.e., interest income and income taxes, etc.) are subtracted from operating income to determine "net income."

The balance sheet is a statement that reports the financial position of a company at a point in time. This statement provides a snapshot of what the company owns (assets) and what it must pay out (liabilities). The balance sheet helps provide the reader with an understanding of the historical value of the operation (broadcast station, cable operation or telecommunications company) at a certain point in time. We call this owners' equity or net worth. We arrive at this figure through the simple formula of:

Assets − Liabilities = Equity or (A − L = E)

A company's statement of cash flows represents a summarized view of the firm's checkbook. It reports a firm's cash inflows and outflows. This statement indicates such things as whether the company generated sufficient cash flow from operations to pay its operating expenses, how much cash was invested to grow the business, and the sources of external financing. This statement is divided into three sections, including cash flows from: 1) operating activities, 2) investing activities and 3) financing activities. The addition of these three sections explains the change in the firm's cash position for the period.

Interpreting Financial Performance

A key part of understanding a company's financial performance is to recognize the financial life cycle stage in which the firm is operating. The three stages are: 1) the infancy stage, 2) the growth stage and 3) the maturity stage. During the infancy stage, a company is focused on building its network and infrastructures and growing its customer base. During the growth stage, companies are well established in the marketplace, but are not necessarily profitable. Such companies are growing and expanding and generating considerable expense in terms of developing infrastructure and building audiences. Companies that are financially mature generate net income. They define profitability in terms of net income, earnings per share and net income growth.

Although there are several ways to measure financial performance, among the more important methods are two profitability ratios: net profit margin and return on equity. Profitability ratios are especially important for analyzing the financial performance of Phase 3 companies. One of the important tools for understanding how a media or telecommunications company has performed can be seen by examining different kinds of segment disclosures, including revenue and net income comparisons, product line and/or percentage contributions to overall revenue, etc.

Wall Street Primer

The common stocks of public companies are traded on one or more of the stock exchanges. There are two basic types of stock markets: 1) organized exchanges like the New York Stock Exchange and the London Stock Exchange and 2) over-the-counter markets like NASDAQ. Sometimes firms have different classes of stock (Class A and Class B) that allow a greater number of votes per share. The primary reason for having higher voting shares for Class B shares is to help protect the firm from an unfriendly take-over. A recent trend in the telecommunications industry is for firms to create a "tracking stock." A tracking stock is a mechanism whereby shareholders can concentrate their ownership of a firm in only part of the company's operation as opposed to the entire entity. Historically, telecommunication companies have used a significant amount of debt to finance their operations. Commercial banks have traditionally been among the primary lenders to the industry. Mid-sized and larger telecommunication firms may also utilize the public bond markets to issue corporate notes and bonds. Typically, corporate notes have maturities of seven to ten years, whereas bonds have maturities in excess of ten years. Frequently, corporate bonds are fixed-rate instruments. Corporate bonds are often rated by bond rating agencies like Moody's and Standard & Poor's (S&P).

13

TELECOMMUNICATIONS MARKETING

Heidi Hennink-Kaminski, University of North Carolina at Chapel Hill

Introduction

Telecommunications is one of the most dynamic and complex industries in the world. The tremendous growth of information and entertainment products has dramatically changed the communication landscape. Today's consumers are faced with innumerable choices. Increased competition in the fields of media and telecommunications has created a highly competitive and crowded marketplace. The ability to succeed in an ever-changing field like media and telecommunications requires strong marketing skills.

What Is Marketing?

Marketing involves understanding what consumers want and what motivates them to buy and designing the optimum product or service to meet those needs. To that end, marketing involves the creative design, promotion, sale and distribution of products and services to the marketplace. It requires selling the right product (or service) at the right price, at the right place, using the right promotional tools. Collectively, these four elements are referred to as the "Four Ps" of marketing, or the *marketing mix.*[1]

Marketing also requires the ability to build and sustain valued customer relationships over time. Telecommunication companies such as cable operators are continually in the business of attracting new customers and preserving the ongoing relationship with existing ones. In short, marketing requires more than simply making the first-time sale. It's about keeping customers so satisfied that they will not turn to another company's products or services to meet their needs. In the field of media and telecommunications, understanding and responding to the consumer are essential against a backdrop of audience fragmentation and increased consumer choice. Preserving the valued relationship with an existing customer is critical.

The Marketing Plan

A successful marketing plan identifies the product, service or idea that the company will sell to consumers and the strategies and tactics it will employ to do so profitably, including product development, distribution, pricing and promotion. The marketing plan outlines specific and measurable marketing objectives. Central to the discussion is whether the company is trying to introduce an altogether new product or service or whether the goal is to increase market share within an existing market. There are four steps to a basic marketing plan. They include: 1) situation analysis, 2) marketing strategy, 3) marketing mix, and 4) customer relationship management. This can be seen in Figure 13.1.

1. Situation Analysis

The situation analysis provides the research foundation that is used to help advance a future marketing strategy as well as refine an existing one. The analysis is typically ongoing and subject to change as the company continues to monitor both internal and external factors affecting the company's business and marketing environment. The purpose of the situation analysis is to understand the strategic challenges facing a company and the problems and opportunities associated with those ongoing changes. The situation analysis consists of two basic parts: a consumer analysis and a market analysis.

Consumer Analysis

Fundamentally, marketers needs to understand the reasons and motivations that prompt consumers to watch the television programs that they view and to select the product brands that they use. Moreover, the marketer needs to understand the process that consumers go through when making such decisions. To that end, the marketer is interested in answering the following questions:

- Who are the consumers and what do they have in common?
- How do they use the said product or service?
- What motivates them to buy or use a product or service?
- What do we know about the consumers' general lifestyle?

The answers to these questions provide insight about how to create products and services that satisfy consumer needs and wants, as well as how and where to best communicate to them. This is especially important in the field of media and telecommunications, where television programs and advertisements are extremely expensive to produce. Television programmers will typically introduce a pilot episode with a target audience in mind in order to test the audience's reactions and feedback before fully developing the said program into a series. Similarly, advertisers test ad concepts with select focus groups in order to better understand how they interpret and respond to the message. Ensuring that a television program will attract the right target audience or that an advertisement will resonate with consumers is more important than ever given the volatility of today's media environment. The public has access to an unprecedented number of entertainment and information choices, including the ability to avoid commercials by using digital video recorders (DVRs).

The marketing professional has access to a number of different kinds of research reports. The following are some of the more common categories of syndicated research, including demographic, psychographic, product usage and media usage reports.

Demographic and Product Usage Reports

Product usage reports are important because they define product users within certain categories in terms of demographics, degree of product/brand usage and brand loyalty. These reports are more likely to be used for marketing telecommunications products and services rather than to guide programming decisions. *Simmons Study of Media and Markets*, published by the Simmons Market Research Bureau (SMRB), and *Mediamark Reporter*, published by Mediamark Research and Intelligence (MRI) are the two major syndicated sources of product usage information. Each year both services report on the usage of products, brands and services among 40,000 adults in more than 800 categories by age, gender, education, occupation, geographic location, race, income and media usage. These reports help describe current consumers based on common characteristics, which helps guide the selection of a target market. Media planners and buyers also use these reports to gain insight into how members of their target market use different media and where advertisements might best reach them.

Psychographic Reports

The demographic information provided in the product usage and audience ratings reports discussed above are often not enough for fully understanding the consumer and what guides their decision making. Psychographic research looks at the psychology of buying and what motivates consumers to behave the way they do. Specifically, it looks at the psychological make-up of the consumer in terms of personality, motivation and attitude, as well as lifestyle elements. Psychographic research can be helpful in differentiating among target audiences with similar demographic characteristics. VALS™ and Scarborough Research represent two of the better-known psychographic research companies frequently used in media and telecommunications.

VALS (VALUES AND LIFESTYLE PROGRAM)

VALS is a psychographic-based research product developed by SRI International and owned by SRI Consulting Business Intelligence.[2] The VALS research approach starts by dividing U.S. adult consumers into one of eight segments based on personality traits that drive their purchasing behavior. The eight personality traits are a blend of what motivates consumers to purchase different products and services and how it reflects personal and professional identity, factoring in such crucial elements as income, education, energy level and willingness to take risks. Generally speaking, marketers use VALS for four purposes: 1) to identify the best target markets, 2) to predict the shopping interests of potential target groups, 3) to determine the best ways to communicate with the target group in terms of brand positioning and media selection and 4) to gain insight into why the target market acts the way it does. Broadcasters, for their part, use VALS to understand and develop programming strategies that will resonate with their viewing audiences, as well as to guide promotional strategies on how to draw audiences to those programs.

SCARBOROUGH RESEARCH

Scarborough Research is a joint venture between Arbitron and VNU Media measurement. It surveys more than 200,000 adults nationwide in 80 demographic market areas (DMAs) about their shopping patterns, lifestyle and media habits.[3] Data is gathered using telephone interviews, self-administered questionnaires and television diaries and released twice a year. The consumer feedback helps media companies and advertising agencies better identify target markets and determine where to best reach consumers within those markets, better understand the marketplace, distinguish between brands and monitor competitors.

Scarborough provides information about lifestyle behaviors (e.g., leisure activities, sports attendance), shopping preferences (e.g., stores shopped, brand preferences), product usage (e.g., telephone, prepaid phone cards, wireless/cellular phone), and media usage for television, cable, radio, Internet, Yellow Pages, magazines, newspapers and outdoor advertising. Scarborough also provides multicultural studies that focus on Hispanic and African American consumers.

Geo-Demographic Reports

Geo-demographic research is based on the idea that people who live near one another tend to exhibit similar lifestyle characteristics. In other words, birds of a feather flock together. Research shows that people tend to seek out neighborhoods that are compatible with their lifestyles and that the character of a neighborhood tends to persist over time once it is established. These reports typically coincide with census data. Marketers use geo-demographic research to identify, locate and determine how best to reach their target market.

PRIZM

PRIZM is a lifestyle segmentation research product developed by Claritas, Inc.[4] PRIZM stands for Potential Rating Index for Zip Markets and provides information about consumers at the zip code level. PRIZM defines every micro-neighborhood in the U.S. into one of 66 neighborhood types based on social rank (income, employment, education), household composition (i.e., age, sex, family type), mobility (i.e., length of residency, auto ownership), ethnicity (i.e., race, foreign birth, ancestry, language), urbanization, and housing (i.e., owner/renter, home values, number of stories). These 66 groups are then clustered into 14 larger social groups.

Table 13.1, for example, showcases PRIZM's "Urban Uptown" social group and the five neighborhood segments associated with that group. The

Table 13.1 PRIZM-NE Urban Uptown Social Group

04. Young Digerati—Young Digerati are the nation's tech–savvy singles and couples living in fashionable neighborhoods on the urban fringe. Affluent, highly educated and ethnically mixed, Young Digerati communities are typically filled with trendy apartments and condos, fitness clubs and clothing boutiques, casual restaurants and all types of bars–from juice to coffee to microbrew.

07. Money and Brains—The residents of Money & Brains seem to have it all: high incomes, advanced degrees and sophisticated tastes to match their credentials. Many of these citydwellers–predominantly white with a high concentration of Asian Americans–are married couples with few children who live in fashionable homes on small, manicured lots.

16. Bohemian Mix—A collection of young, mobile urbanites, Bohemian Mix represents the nation's most liberal lifestyles. Its residents are a progressive mix of young singles and couples, students and professionals, Hispanics, Asians, African–Americans and whites. In their funky rowhouses and apartments, Bohemian Mixers are the early adopters who are quick to check out the latest movie, nightclub, laptop and microbrew.

26. The Cosmopolitans—These immigrants and descendants of multi–cultural backgrounds in multi-racial, multi-lingual neighborhoods typify the American Dream. Married couples, with and without children, as well as single parents are affluent from working hard at multiple trades and public service jobs. They have big families, which is unusual for social group U1.

29. American Dreams—American Dreams is a living example of how ethnically diverse the nation has become: more than half the residents are Hispanic, Asian or African-American. In these multilingual neighborhoods–one in ten speaks a language other than English–middle-aged immigrants and their children live in middle-class comfort.

Source: Claritas, Inc. (PRIZM NE/Urban Uptown: Available at: http://www.claritas.com/claritas/Default.jsp?ci=3&si=4&pn=prizmne_segmentsρoupU)

five segments in Urban Uptown are home to the nation's wealthiest urban consumers. Members of this social group tend to be affluent to middle-class, college educated and ethnically diverse, with above-average concentrations of Asian and Hispanic Americans. Although this group is diverse in terms of housing styles and family sizes, residents share an upscale urban perspective that's reflected in their marketplace choices. Urban Uptown consumers tend to frequent the arts, shop at exclusive retailers, drive luxury imports, travel abroad and spend heavily on computer and wireless technology. The Urban Uptown group consists of the following segments: Young Digerati, Money and Brains, Bohemian Mix, the Cosmopolitans, and American Dreams.

Market Analysis

The situation analysis also includes a market analysis, that is, a strategic assessment of the external factors that can affect the performance of a company's products and services. This effort is in keeping with the principles of external scanning discussed in Chapter 2. As part of the strategic analysis, the company is concerned with the following types of questions:

- What is the general economic climate? Is it conducive to promoting and advancing the said company's products and services?
- What has been the overall sales performance of the said company's products and services during the past three years? How do they stack up against the competition?
- What social, cultural or technological changes are impacting consumer use and/or the company's ability to market? (See SWOT model, Chapter 2.)

In sum, a company must understand the dynamics of the marketplace as well as the relative strengths of what the competition is doing in order to be successful. While this is true of any business, it is particularly important in the field of media and telecommunications, where sudden innovations and changes can have a dramatic impact on the marketplace. For example, peer-to-peer file sharing and the rise of MP3 players have transformed the music industry and pose a significant challenge to the future of traditional music sales and delivery. Similarly, video rental companies such as Blockbuster face increased competition from PPV cable television and direct-mail DVD companies such as Netflix. The situation analysis typically concludes with a summation of the critical issues facing the company. (See the Appendix to this chapter.)

2. Marketing Strategy

The marketing strategy represents the approach (or blueprint) by which the company hopes to achieve strong sales performance and develop good customer relationships. A sound marketing strategy requires a well-defined target market and a focus on consumer needs. When developing a marketing strategy, the company should be concerned with three primary issues: selecting the target market, product positioning and building brand equity.

Selecting the Target Market

It is virtually impossible for a company to serve all consumers in a market. As a result, companies must decide which consumers offer up the best potential. To do so, a company engages in market segmentation, that is, the process of dividing the overall market into smaller segments (or clusters) based on demographic, psychographic, geographic and behavioral factors. The idea is to identify a homogeneous group of consumers with similar characteristics such as age, income, lifestyle, and tastes and preferences. The information gathered for the consumer analysis plays a vital role here. The company then decides which segment(s) to target and makes subsequent product design, distribution, pricing and promotion decisions that coincide with that target market.

Companies have several options when identifying a target market. The number and types of target markets a company decides to serve depend on a number of factors, including budget, personnel, competitive landscape and type of product or service. Regardless, the target market must be substantial enough to generate a reasonable profit and accessible through a variety of marketing communication channels.[5] The target market is typically defined by several criteria, including demographics, psychographics, and product usage (heavy, medium, light).

Product Positioning

Once the target markets have been selected the company must decide how to position the product or service in the mind of the consumer. Product positioning refers to how a product or service is differentiated from the competition. According to Michael Porter, "in a differentiation strategy, a firm seeks to be unique in its industry along some dimensions that are widely valued by buyers."[6] Examples might include: satellite television (DirecTV), premium pay television services (HBO), music innovation (Apple iTunes) and cable sports programming (ESPN). Each of the said examples is trying to distinguish itself from the competition according to product quality and special features.

Consider, for example, different cable networks that offer round-the-clock news programming, including CNN, Fox News and CNBC. CNN has positioned itself as the world's leader in news coverage, providing "News you can trust." Its news coverage is more global and has the look and feel of a news magazine. Alternatively, Fox News has positioned itself as a more conservative, "proAmerican news organization," evidenced by the U.S. flag fluttering in the background. Its slogan reads: "We Report, You Decide." Finally, CNBC has positioned itself as the cable news leader for the business community and uses the slogan "First in Business Worldwide."

Another example can be found in the cellular telephone industry. Nextel has positioned itself as having the world's largest push-to-talk mobile network and has adopted the slogan "Stay Connected." Verizon Wireless emphasizes the strength and dependability of its network as "richer, deeper, broader," and "We never stop working for you." Alternatively, AT&T (formerly Cingular) has positioned itself as having the network with the fewest dropped calls. In sum, product positioning reflects the decisions that companies make in determining how their products and services are going to be positioned in relationship to the competition.

Building Brand Equity

Building brand equity (or brand management) goes hand in hand with product differentiation. The brand exists in consumers' minds as a perceptual map of values, thoughts and feelings they associate with that brand. Brand management (or branding) focuses on developing and maintaining a set of attributes and values which elicit a certain level of expectation on the part of the consumer. Consider, for example, the kind of expectations that are generated when consumers observe names like Apple, Disney and Sony, to name only a few.

The consistent use of a brand name, symbol or logo makes the brand instantly recognizable and elicits certain rational and emotional associations in the consumer's mind. From a marketer's perspective, a positive brand image will facilitate customer loyalty, create pricing advantage, and become a useful segmentation tool. For the consumer, brand value and connection have been built over time through a number of contact points. Moreover, brands are enduring; once a consumer knows a brand, it is not easily forgotten.[7] Brands also say something about product quality and transferability. If the consumer likes the Disney theme park experience (brand), for example, he/she is a strong candidate for trying other Disney products, such as the Disney Channel (cable television) or Disney water cruises.

Table 13.2 represents the 30 most highly valued global brands as determined by Interbrand and *Business Week* for 2006.[8] Brand value is an estimate of how much the brand is likely to earn in the future.[9] Twelve of these brands are associated with the fields of media and telecommunications.

As marketing specialists David Aaker and Erich Joachimsthaler point out, brand equity is a strategic asset that can be the basis of competitive advantage and long-term profitability.[10] Thus the marketing plan must do more than manage how brand images are communicated. It must guarantee that the company consistently delivers on the brand promise associated with the product or service, by meeting or exceeding consumer expectations.

Table 13.2 The 30 Most Valued Global Brands of 2006

Rank	Brand	Country of Origin	Sector	2006 Brand Value ($m)
1	Coca-Cola	U.S.	Beverages	67,000
2	Microsoft	U.S.	Computer software	56,926
3	IBM	U.S.	Computer services	56,201
4	GE	U.S.	Diversified	48,907
5	Intel	U.S.	Computer hardware	32,319
6	Nokia	Finland	Telecom equipment	30,131
7	Toyota	Japan	Automotive	27,941
8	Disney	U.S.	Media/entertainment	27,848
9	McDonald's	U.S.	Restaurants	27,501
10	Mercedes	Germany	Automotive	21,795
11	Citi	U.S.	Financial services	21,458
12	Marlboro	U.S.	Tobacco	21,350
13	Hewlett-Packard	U.S.	Computer hardware	20,458
14	American Express	U.S.	Financial services	19,641
15	BMW	Germany	Automotive	19,617
16	Gillette	U.S.	Personal care	19,579
17	Louis Vuitton	France	Luxury	17,606
18	Cisco	U.S.	Computer services	17,532
19	Honda	Japan	Automotive	17,049
20	Samsung	South Korea	Consumer electronics	16,169
21	Merrill Lynch	U.S.	Financial services	13,001
22	Pepsi	U.S.	Beverages	12,690
23	Nescafé	Switzerland	Beverages	12,507
24	Google	U.S.	Internet services	12,376
25	Dell	U.S.	Computer hardware	12,256
26	Sony	Japan	Consumer electronics	11,695
27	Budweiser	U.S.	Alcohol	11,662
28	HSBC	U.K.	Financial services	11,622
29	Oracle	U.S.	Computer software	11,459
30	Ford	U.S.	Automotive	11,056

Sources: Interbrand and *Business Week*, "Best Global Brands 2006," Available at: http://www.ourfishbowl.com/images/surveys/BGB06Report_072706.pdf.

3. The Marketing Mix (Four Ps)

Once marketers have selected the target market, decided on a positioning strategy and determined marketing objectives, it is time to decide on the proper marketing mix. The marketing mix is a set of tools a company uses to create demand among customers. As mentioned earlier, we refer to this as the four Ps: product, price, place (distribution) and promotion.

Product

Product development is concerned with developing the right combination of features and benefits produced at the right cost that gives value to the customer. Product development involves decisions about design, styling, features and packaging. The situation analysis is central to the discussion since it gives the marketer important insights about what consumers want as well as a strategic analysis of what the competition is currently doing. The goal of product design is to create products or services with a competitive advantage. This can include introducing altogether new products and services to market or providing enhancements on existing ones by developing new features and applications. Innovation (and innovative thinking) plays a critical role in product development (see Chapter 15).

For broadcasters and cable programmers, the ongoing challenge is to create new and innovative programming. Sometimes success comes in the form of an altogether new programming format, such as CBS's *Survivor*. But sometimes success is realized by innovating on an existing format. Take, for example, the program *American Idol* by Fox Television. The program has been an astounding success not because it represents a new or unique programming idea but simply because of the way it is packaged and presented (i.e., the talent show concept has been around for decades).

Packaging speaks to the issue of how the product or service is presented to the consumer. Packaging involves both product design and aesthetics. The package is an important part of any marketing strategy and can often be the deciding factor in whether a product is successful. As an example, a cellular telephone must fulfill its primary objective as a voice communication device. At the same time, it must be attractive and fun to use. Consider, for example, Motorola's RAZR super-slim cell phone, which has won numerous design awards for its sleek look.

Price

Marketers must also determine what price to charge for a given product or service. The issue of pricing represents a critical issue. There are a host of factors to consider, including the need to cover the costs associated with product development, marketing and distribution. In addition, the marketer must determine what consumers are realistically willing to pay for the said product or service while remaining competitive vis-à-vis the competition. A company, for example, may decide to position its product or service as the low-cost alternative. This is often the case for parity products, that is, goods and services for which there is no discernible difference. This can be seen in such things as cellular telephone plans in which local and long-distance coverage may be the same or similar. As a result, companies like AT&T, Verizon, Sprint Nextel and T-Mobile compete on the basis of price and select service features.

Alternatively, products that are highly distinguishable (i.e., with strong brand identity) may command a higher price than the competition. Apple Computer, for example, has done an excellent job of positioning its desktop and laptop products as intuitive, user friendly and forward thinking. As a result, Apple has a reputation for being highly innovative and is able to command higher prices for its products as compared to its PC-based rivals.[11] Another pricing strategy is to bundle several products or services together and offer the package at a reduced price. As an example, cable operators like Comcast, Time Warner and Cox Cable bundle their cable television, Internet and telephone services into a discounted package (i.e., a so-called triple play of services) in markets where they are competing with telephone companies for broadband delivery and telephone service.

Place (Distribution)

Marketers must also determine marketing channels by which the product or service will be made available to consumers. Oftentimes, these marketing channels are made up of several steps and include other partners who play a role in getting the product or service into the hands of the consumer. There are three basic types of marketing channels: direct, indirect, and multi-channel distribution.[12] Some companies utilize a direct marketing channel to the consumer. Product distribution can be made available on-line via the Internet (i.e., B2C) or the telephone and/or through mail catalogues. This can be seen with such products as Dell and Gateway computers, L.L. Bean and Eddie Bauer retail clothing, etc. (see Chapter 9).

Other companies prefer to use indirect (or second-party) marketing channels, employing the assistance of retail outlets to distribute products and services. Paramount Studios, for example, relies on department stores and superstores such as Target and Wal-Mart, as well as large specialty stores like Circuit City and Best Buy, to distribute its television and film software products. Increasingly, more and more companies are engaging in multi-channel distribution, that is, a combination of marketing channels to reach potential customers. For example, music companies like Sony/BMG and Warner Brothers Records rely on a combination of traditional music outlets, department stores and superstores, as well as EC outlets like Amazon.com and Apple iTunes. The strategic lesson learned from companies like Dell Computers, Apple iTunes and Netflix is that many kinds of retail products do not have to be offered in a bricks-and-mortar (i.e., traditional retail) format. Rather, such products and services can be effectively distributed via the Internet in combination with direct mail delivery.

Promotion

The final element of the marketing mix is promotion. According to Sylvia Chan-Olmsted, the goal of promotion is to attract new customers and retain existing ones. The challenge for the marketer is to select the right mix of promotion strategies and advertising media in order to successfully reach the desired audience.[13] Promotion involves decisions about the best methods for communicating information to the desired audience in terms of what, when and where. Promotion goals will vary depending on the specific needs of the organization. They can include such things as creating product or service awareness, encouraging trial use, promoting brand switching, correcting false impressions, increasing product use and building brand preference or loyalty.

Today, marketers have a number of promotional tools available to them. We refer to this as the *promotional mix*. As Table 13.3 illustrates, the number of ways to promote a product or service has greatly expanded beyond the traditional advertising and direct sales promotion strategies of the past. What it is important to remember is that not all products and services are the same. They need to be marketed differently. To that end, companies must select the best combination of promotional tools and carefully coordinate them to deliver a clear, consistent and compelling message. This is known as *integrated marketing communication* (IMC), and it is critical to building brand equity.[14]

One of the newest approaches to the principle of promotional mix is viral marketing, which is a technique that leverages the Internet and existing social networks to increase brand awareness and generate media coverage. It involves creating a website and an e-mail message or funny video clip so compelling that customers will want to pass it along to their friends.[15]

Promoting Media and Telecommunications

Broadcast and cable programmers, for example, recognize the need to attract viewers by placing paid advertisements for their programs on their own

Table 13.3 Elements of the Promotional Mix

Advertising
Consumer sales promotion
Trade promotion
Marketing public relations
Sponsorship
Direct/relationship marketing
Branded entertainment
Product placement
Personal selling
Product licensing
Viral marketing

station or cable channel and competing broadcast or cable channels, as well as on the Internet, radio and billboards. In addition, publicists representing the networks may arrange for the actors from the program to be interviewed on television programs like the *Jay Leno Show, Oprah* and *Good Morning America* or by radio personalities and newspaper or magazine reporters. The movie industry operates similarly, employing advertising and public relations initiatives to create awareness and stimulate demand. The promotional mix typically changes once the movie shifts into rental or retail distribution, expanding to include sales promotion and direct marketing initiatives. These media companies employ a number of promotional tools to accomplish their marketing communication objectives. For example, Comcast may engage in television and radio advertising to create awareness of its ability to provide high-speed Internet access. It might also initiate a direct marketing campaign toward existing customers via the Internet or traditional mail by offering them an incentive to try its high-speed Internet service at a discounted rate for a period of time. Similarly, cellular phone companies may engage in both advertising and sales promotion activities to encourage consumers to switch networks by offering special discounted contract rates or by offering free (or discounted) phones as part of the overall package.

One of the main challenges for today's marketer is the fact that consumers are faced with an abundance of media choices. This creates both a problem and an opportunity. On the one hand, marketers have the obvious challenge of cutting through the noise and clutter of competing promotional messages. The problem is further exacerbated by the wide-scale diffusion of new recording technologies such as DVRs which makes commercial avoidance that much easier. On the other hand, marketers are now availing themselves of the opportunity to engage in personal marketing approaches using such things as the Internet to refine and tailor personalized messages.

4. Customer Relationship Management

The fourth part of the marketing plan is customer relationship management. As mentioned earlier in the chapter, marketing involves building and sustaining valued customer relationships over time. To that end, an effective marketing plan must go beyond how to attract new customers and address how the company plans to preserve and develop existing customer relationships. This is particularly important in the fields of media and telecommunications, where consumers have an abundance of choices and the competition is fierce.

Lifetime Customer Value

Strategic marketing places an emphasis on building longer-term relationships with customers rather than on individual transactions and short-term sales. As a result, marketers focus on what is called lifetime customer value (LCV). The concept of LCV was first developed by direct and catalogue marketers who wanted to understand the potential for new customer revenue based on existing relationships. It recognizes that some existing customers will continue to purchase products or services in the future while others will not, owing to factors including competition.[16]

Retaining and growing customers over time are important for two reasons. First, many marketing experts suggest that it costs five to ten times more to acquire new customers than it does to preserve existing customer relationships. So building on one's current customer base makes good financial sense.[17] Second, having a set of satisfied customers creates the opportunity to *cross-sell* additional products and services, as well as *up-selling*, that is, selling products and services with higher profit margins. For example, Cox Cable engages in cross-selling when it markets Internet and telephone services to its current cable customers. Similarly, Amazon.com has expanded the types of products it sells beyond books to include music, videos and clothing apparel. Verizon engages in up-selling when it markets text-messaging packages to existing cellular customers, a service which costs very little to provide.

Building and Managing Customer Relationships

Marketing experts Gary Armstrong and Philip Kotler define customer relationship management (CRM) as "the overall process of building and maintaining profitable customer relationships by delivering superior customer value and satisfaction."[18] To that end, a company must accomplish three things: deliver value, satisfy customers and build in mechanisms for customer loyalty and retention.

Customer Value

A company must first acquire a customer. This requires that the company create and promote a program, product or service that the consumer perceives as more valuable than that of the competition, underscoring the importance of selecting the right marketing mix (or four Ps) for the target market.

Customer Satisfaction

Once it has selected the said product or service, the company must ensure that the product or service meets, or preferably exceeds, the expectations of the customer. This involves fulfilling the brand promise articulated in the marketing strategy and communicated through marketing communication activities. Armstrong and Kotler talk about the importance of creating customer delight, that is, exceeding expectations by delivering more than one promise.[19] Such delight often results in consumer advocacy, where customers talk favorably about the company, make purchase recommendations to others, wear logos or icons on apparel, or make some other type of public statement about their enthusiasm or support.[20]

Customer Loyalty and Retention

Creating customer value and satisfaction is central to the principle of creating an ongoing relationship with the customer. Successful customer relationship management requires that the company develop formal strategies for building loyalty and retaining customers. Traditionally this has involved capturing, storing and analyzing detailed information about customers and using that information to manage future interactions with customers. Today it's about using that information to create an emotional relationship with the customer that moves beyond rational preference, often using personalized communication tools such as the Internet.

Sources of Marketing Information

A comprehensive understanding of the customer is vital to a company's ability to attract and retain more profitable customers over time. Effective customer relationship marketing begins with a good database of information, including demographic, psychographic and behavioral data about customers or prospects. Collectively, this information can be used to:

- identify the most profitable customers to target;
- identify where and how to reach those customers most effectively;
- personalize and tailor marketing offers and communication messages to the individual.

Companies typically have a wealth of data available to them. Some of this information is proprietary and stored in internal databases. For example, Verizon wireless maintains a database on its existing customers that includes a history of phone purchases, service contracts, credit information, interactions with customer service representatives, responses to satisfaction surveys, and visits to the website. As noted earlier, companies also rely on syndicated market research to better understand consumers in general and to evaluate the performance of specific communication vehicles. Telecommunication companies can overlay this information with their proprietary data to sharpen consumer insights, while media companies often rely on these reports in the absence of specific transactional information about individual customers.

Relationship Marketing Strategies

Customer retention is central to the principles of CRM based on the belief that deeper points of contact between the company and the customer will foster customer loyalty as well as increase new business opportunities. Long-term customer retention presupposes three important elements: customer interaction, personalization and retention.

Customer Interaction

Companies interested in LCV seek to increase the level of personalized service and experiences for the customer across all points of contact. In addition to traditional communication channels such as toll-free numbers, the Internet has proven to be a highly effective method for providing personalized customer service. Dell Computers, for example, introduced on-line chat support when it realized that many customers experienced long wait times when using the toll-free number for assistance. Other websites feature discussion groups or chat rooms where customers can interact with each other and the company on a variety of issues, such as addressing spyware or privacy issues.[21] Many companies also customize their website content based on information about the individual customer. This is the underlying marketing strategy and advertising appeal of such websites as MySpace and YouTube.

Personalization

As discussed in Chapter 9, the Internet plays an increasingly important role in the marketing environment and has contributed to the shift from mass to micromarketing. One of the unique attributes of the Internet is the computer's ability to track a user's on-line activity, thereby providing an unprecedented opportunity to monitor individual queries and transactions. Companies interact with the customer on-line to learn about specific interests, and customers have the ability to volunteer feedback. This ongoing interaction allows companies to personalize product and service offerings, thus adding value to the customer. Such interaction takes personalized communication to a whole new level by giving marketers the opportunity to tailor messages at the individual level (i.e., micromarketing), thus adding value to the customer. For example, Amazon.com suggests certain books or music based on prior purchases when customers return to the site. Similarly, a visitor to iVillage, an on-line community website, encounters advertisements, promotions and editorial articles tailored specifically to the user based on his/her demographic, psychographic and behavioral data.[22]

Retention

The goal of retention marketing is to prevent product or brand switching. In a field like cable television, maintaining customer loyalty is an absolute must. Retention marketing is designed to prevent existing customers from switching or canceling their service. There are a number of ways that a company can engage in retention marketing. One such strategy is to design rewards programs whereby customers are given value-added extras, such as an upgrade or free night's hotel lodging by enrolling with Starwood Hotels' Preferred Guest or Hilton Hotels' HHonors programs. Similarly, airlines have their frequent-flyer packages, such as Northwest's World Perks and Delta's SkyMiles programs. The opposite approach is to erect financial barriers that discourages brand switching. For example, cellular telephone companies typically require customers to sign two-year contracts, including termination fees if customers change providers before the contract's expiration date. A third strategy is bundling, mentioned earlier, whereby companies like cable operators will offer their customers a combined package of cable television, high-speed Internet and telephone service at a discounted price.

Discussion

Marketing involves understanding what consumers want and what motivates them to buy and designing the optimum product or service to meet those needs.[23] In turn, that product or service must be promoted to the target audience in a manner that effectively communicates its superior value. This represents a formidable challenge in the fields of media and telecommunications, where consumers face a broad array of information and entertainment choices.

How do consumers choose among the various product and service offerings? The goal of marketing is to help shape consumer expectations about the value and satisfaction they will derive from making one selection over another. Satisfied customers buy again and tell others about their experiences. Dissatisfied customers often switch to competitors and criticize the product to others.

This chapter outlined the four basic steps to developing a successful marketing plan: conducting a situation analysis, developing a marketing strategy, determining the marketing mix (product, price, distribution and promotion) and managing customer relationships. In summary, successful marketers must attract, preserve and grow target customers by delivering superior customer value over time.

Appendix: More about Marketing Research

Marketing research plays an important role in developing the marketing plan. It can help marketers better understand consumer preferences and purchase behavior, assess market share and potential, and measure the effectiveness of pricing, distribution and promotional strategies.

Secondary and Primary Data

Marketing research includes gathering secondary and/or primary data. Secondary data is information that already exists somewhere. It includes some of the reports discussed in the chapter, such as PRIZM, Scarborough and Mediamark Research (MRI). Researchers often start by looking at secondary data because it often can be obtained more quickly and less expensively than data obtained by conducting new research. However, secondary data may not answer a specific question that the marketer has, creating the need to collect primary data for a specific purpose. As an example, a television network can examine the Nielsen ratings to see how a program is performing among the target audience. However, the ratings do not provide information about what the audience likes or doesn't like about the program. As a result, the network may commission a series of focus group studies where members of the target audience are assembled to watch the program and discuss it.

Quantitative and Qualitative Research

In general, there are two kinds of approaches to marketing research: quantitative and qualitative. Quantitative research emphasizes precise, numerical measurement of consumers and their behaviors, typically expressed in terms of "how many" or "how much." This research usually involves some type of survey or audit, including telephone surveys, mall intercepts or panel-based ratings data such as Nielsen's. Information is typically gathered from a sample of people and the results are then projected to a larger population, e.g., the percentage of women between the ages of 18 and 34 who tuned in to *Grey's Anatomy* between 8:00 and 8:30 P.M. on a given Thursday evening or the number of unique visitors per day on the website of a local radio station. (See Chapter 3.)

Conversely, qualitative research seeks the meanings and motivations behind opinions and behaviors rather than providing exact numerical measures. This research typically involves the examination and subjective interpretation of the actions, words and ideas expressed by the consumer during an interview or in a focus group or in written diaries. Qualitative research is typically expressed from the perspective of the individual and is not meant to be projected to a larger group of people. However, it can provide important consumer insights and is often used in conjunction with quantitative research to develop the marketing strategy. It is particularly useful for evaluating product and program concepts, ads and campaigns. For example, a cellular company may show a focus group a rough cut of a television ad for a new campaign. The focus group would comprise six to ten members of the target market who would comment on what they thought the ad communicated and how it made them feel. This information would then be used to create a final version of the advertisement. Alternatively, a company developing a new website may observe how members of its target audience interact with the website and then interview them about their reactions to that experience.

14

LEADERSHIP AND
CHANGE MANAGEMENT

*Rod Rightmire, Indiana University, and
Richard Gershon, Western Michigan University*

Introduction

Leadership—yes, it differs from management, but the important fact about leadership is that it is integral to, and essential for, effective management. In his book *On Becoming a Leader*, author Warren Bennis writes, "Managers do things right—leaders do the right things."[1] That sounds like a cliché, doesn't it? But think about it. You are the news director at Channel 13 and the manager in you demands the best possible six o'clock news every night of the week. Do it right—be a good manager. But the leader in you needs to be asking, "How can we improve the quality of our news effort? How can we combat Channel 6's effort to overtake us in the next ratings book?" That's leadership, and it should be coming from that same news director who is concerned about getting it right each night. In sum, effective management is a melding, if you will, of leadership and management.

Leadership Defined

Leadership is a process that involves influence and the art of directing people within an organization to achieve a clearly defined set of goals and outcomes. Successful leaders know what they want to accomplish in terms of organizational outcomes. As Peter Northouse writes:

> Leadership involves influence; it is concerned with how the leader affects followers. Influence is the sine qua non of leadership. Without influence, leadership does not exist. . . . Leadership includes attention to goals. This means that leadership has to do with directing a group of individuals toward accomplishing some task or end.[2]

One of the central arguments in this chapter is that leadership is not a stand-alone act, but rather an ongoing relationship between those who purport to lead and those who follow. One of the early discussions involving the principles of leadership comes from James MacGregor Burns in his 1978 seminal text, *Leadership*. Burns draws a distinction between what he calls *transactional* leadership and *transformational* leadership. According to Burns:

> [Transactional leadership] occurs when one person takes the initiative in making contact with others for the purpose of an exchange of valued things. . . . Contrast this with [transformational leadership]. Such leadership occurs when one or more persons engage with others in such a way that leaders and followers raise one another to higher levels of motivation and morality.[3]

Transactional Leadership

Transactional leadership refers to the various kinds of exchange that occur between leaders and followers. Often the exchange is tied to a system of rewards and punishments. As an example, a politician engages in transactional leadership when he/she promises voters an increase in jobs or improvements in the local school in exchange for being elected. Similarly, managers who offer promotions to employees who surpass their monthly sales goals are exhibiting a kind of transactional leadership.

How does transactional leadership apply in the real world of cable television sales? Let's consider a sales department in a cable programming service where a conscientious sales manager is trying to create an environment where the sales force will be more productive. In the first instance, the sales manager's approach is to motivate his team with the tried and true contest—sales person of the month/the year/the decade. You get the picture. But consider the implications. There is undoubtedly, among the group, one sales person who can win the contest by simply renewing some of the existing major accounts. In contrast is the new kid on the block with a phone book or an Internet list serve. He/she is faced with the prospect of doing a lot of cold calling or mass e-mailings. Motivated or demotivated? One winner and a whole lot of losers. . . . Will such an approach result in increased sales for that sales department? Does such an approach demonstrate good leadership on the part of the sales manager?

Let's contrast this with a different kind of leadership approach. In the second instance, the sales manager reached out to her staff in a way in which everyone felt they had a chance to win, and that would positively affect the entire sales department. The second sales manager found a very simple but effective solution: not one contest winner, but several. She gave an award for most new business for the likes of the new kid on the block, another for the largest increase over the last month, one for best new sales person and, of course, one for most business. This is transactional leadership at its best, but done in a way that leads to an increase in the effectiveness of the whole department.[4]

Another important consideration in transactional leadership is the perceived value of that which is being exchanged. A different sales manager was concerned that his contest garnered very little enthusiasm from his staff. When asked about the prize, he indicated it was an opportunity to select merchandise from a catalog. After all, he did a lot of shopping for clothes and sporting goods from the catalog. It's not hard to imagine the blank expression on everyone's face. The sales manager could not understand why his staff was not very enthusiastic about the opportunity to pick something from a catalogue. But, more importantly, he didn't know what to do about it. A suggestion was finally made that he ask the sales people what they would like to have as a form of recognition. The answer was surprisingly very simple. They wanted a glass plaque with an inscription. And they wanted to use the remaining money to cover a light evening on the town. They wanted to go dancing. Most of the sales force was young and they wanted to have fun. In transactional leadership, it becomes important that the leader and one's constituents agree on the value of the exchange.

Transformational Leadership

Transformational leadership raises the dynamics of organizational performance to a whole new level. A transformational leader can be described as someone who motivates a group of people to accomplish more than was originally expected. The leader must inspire the members of his/her organization to become actively involved in the accomplishment of a larger set of goals and initiatives. History is filled with examples of transformational leaders, including Mohandas Gandhi, Martin Luther King and Nelson Mandela, to name only a few. Their followers willingly subjected themselves to police brutality, went to jail and, in some cases, gave up their lives because they believed in a cause greater than themselves. At the same time, transformational leadership is not strictly the province of social activists, politicians and artists. Rather, the application of transformational leadership can be found at every level of an organization.

According to Bernard Bass, the transformational leader exhibits three critical elements. They include:

1 raising a person's level of awareness, that is, to become more conscious about the long-term goals of the organization or cause;
2 getting a person to transcend his/her own self-interest for the sake of the organization or cause;
3 altering a person's needs and wants in support of the organization or cause.[5]

Charismatic Leadership

In recent years, a lot of attention has been given to the subject of charismatic leadership. In 1976, Robert House examined the question of charismatic leadership by looking at different personality features that make up the charismatic leader.[6] According to House, the charismatic leader is someone who is confident, tends to dominate in group situations and has a strong desire to influence the general conversation. In addition, the charismatic leader tends to serve as a role model for others. Charismatic leaders promote a kind of belief system that they expect their constituents to follow.[7] Northouse cites the example of Mohandas Gandhi, who preached nonviolence and was an exemplary role model of civil disobedience. This is evidenced in one of Gandhi's more often quoted phrases, "Be the change you want to see in the world."

The challenge for the charismatic leader is not to outshine the teaching itself. Sometimes, the charismatic leader calls too much attention to himself/herself at the expense of guiding and managing the organization.[8] As Jim Collins points out, great leaders (or what he calls Level 5 leaders) embody a paradoxical mix of personal humility and professional will. "They are ambitious to be sure, but ambitious first and foremost for the company and not themselves."[9] Similarly, Joseph Badaracco makes the point that the most effective leaders are rarely public heroes. These men and women are seldom high-profile champions of causes. Rather, they lead their respective organizations "patiently, carefully and incrementally."[10] Charisma alone is no substitute for effective leadership.

Putting Leadership into Practice

We have tried to define leadership. But what does it take to put leadership into practice? Are there certain identifiable characteristics that make some leaders truly great in comparison to their peers? Over the years, numerous management writers, political figures and athletes have attempted to answer this question by offering their own perspective on the "right stuff" of leadership. In this section, we consider five important characteristics that help to explain what it takes to be an effective leader. They include:

1   vision;
2   effective communication;
3   alignment;
4   trust and integrity;
5   a willingness to take risks.

Vision

The word *vision* suggests something grand or mystical. But, for most organizations, vision is simply a clear plan (or strategy) that is designed to achieve a successful outcome. In his book *Leading Change*, author John Kotter suggests that a leader's strategic vision should convey a picture of what the future will look like, as well as appealing to the long-term interests of organizational members, customers and others who have a stake in the enterprise.[11] The leader may be asked to take an underperforming company and turn it around or take a successful organization and institute needed changes in order to make it progressively better. The situations and tasks may vary. What is most important, however, is that the transformative leader instills a sense of mission to the task at hand and obtains commitment to achieve new or untried goals. An effective leader must have vision, that is, the willingness to think conceptually and articulate a view of the future.

David Sarnoff and RCA

A good example from the past was David Sarnoff at RCA. His idea of the "radio music box" led to the first mass production of radios. As a result, he was promoted to general manager of RCA and a few years later to president of the company at the age of 39. His efforts also led to the formation of the NBC radio network in 1926. The same NBC would later become the NBC television network in 1948. David Sarnoff would also be instrumental in promoting the adoption of electronic television, as well as advancing industry support for NBC's color standard.

When *Wisdom* magazine published a special edition entitled "The Universe of David Sarnoff," it printed congratulatory letters from four presidents of the United States: Herbert Hoover, Franklin Roosevelt, Harry Truman and Dwight Eisenhower. President Roosevelt said, in part:

> I congratulate David Sarnoff personally for his splendid leadership. His organization throughout the years has created new wonders and brought into being new services in all phases of radio activity for the benefit of the American people and people everywhere.[12]

Bill Gates and Microsoft Corporation

William (Bill) H. Gates is chairman and co-founder of Microsoft Corporation, the worldwide leader in computer desktop software and solutions. Microsoft employs more than 71,000 people in 103 countries and regions. In 1973, Gates entered Harvard University as a freshman, and lived down the hall from Steve Ballmer, Microsoft's current chief executive officer. While at Harvard, Gates developed a version of the programming language BASIC for the first microcomputer—the MITS Altair. In his junior year, Gates left Harvard to devote his time to Microsoft, a company he had begun in 1975 with his childhood friend Paul Allen.

From the beginning, Gates understood the importance of personal computing and what it could mean for business and residential users.[13] Further, Gates and his team from Microsoft recognized that the future of personal computing would lie in software development and not hardware, a mistake that would prove costly to companies like IBM and Hewlett-Packard. Gates's foresight and his vision for personal computing have been central to the success of Microsoft. Under Gates's leadership, Microsoft has created what has become the de facto standard for business software in the area of desktop and laptop computing.

Effective Communication

Once the vision has had a chance to resonate, it must be communicated forcefully and effectively. Such communication happens at all levels of the organization. As John Kotter writes:

> the real power of a vision is unleashed only when most of those involved in an enterprise or activity have a common understanding of its goals and direction. That shared sense of a desirable future can help motivate and coordinate the kinds of actions that create transformations.[14]

Effective communication skills require the ability to articulate the vision and organizational strategy in a meaningful way and to mobilize one's staff to focus on a set of goals and outcomes. Simply laying out the organizational strategy via a memo or e-mail is not enough. The leader must also be an educator. According to John Gardner, "Leaders teach. . . . Teaching and leading are distinguishable occupations, but every great leader is clearly teaching—and every great teacher is leading."[15]

Effective communication also requires the leader to possess good listening skills. Hearing is not the same thing as listening. Good listening skills require the ability to stay present when someone is speaking and giving the person your full, undivided attention. Avoid being the person who has a quick answer (or solution) for every question posed. Very often, the person who knocks on your door is not necessarily looking for answers, but simply wants to be heard. In sum, a successful leader understands the value of good communication skills both as a presenter and as a listener.

Alignment

The success of any major project or undertaking requires a high degree of buy-in from those members of the organization who will be responsible for implementing the proposed strategy. We call this alignment. In its simplest form, alignment means teamwork, that is, a willingness to pull together for the good of the project or organization. Alignment means getting the entire organization moving forward in the same direction. The leader plays an important role by articulating a clear vision and by creating a productive and supportive work environment. To that end, developing alignment requires good communication and consensus-building skills. According to S. Donley Ritchey, retired CEO of Lucky Stores, Inc.:

> A real essential for effective leadership is that you can't force people to do very much. They have to want to, and most times I think they want to if they respect the individual who is out front, if they have confidence that the person has some sort of vision for the company. . . . I don't have any flashes of brilliance of how you teach somebody to be a leader, but I know you can't lead unless somebody's willing to follow.[16]

A Word about Motivation

Closely tied to the principle of alignment is the issue of motivation. As S. Donley Ritchey points out, the leader cannot force someone to do good work. Motivation is indeed a subtle process that comes from within. However, the leader does have an important role to play in establishing the proper work environment in which members of an organization feel motivated to accomplish their best. Let's consider some of the ways in which leaders motivate others by setting the right tone:

1 *Recognizing good work when it is performed:* This can include public recognition in the form of a plaque or public display. Or it can include dinner for two at a favorite restaurant or a similar-type reward. It can also be as simple as a handshake or compliment for a job well done.

2 *Making the work environment of satisfying place to come to work:* Many of today's companies provide their employees with an exercise facility, food and coffee dispensaries, day care or greater flextime in determining one's schedule.

3 *Promotion and advancement:* A good leader recognizes the value of promoting good employees by giving them the opportunity to take on greater responsibility. Sometimes, this is accompanied by a pay raise and/or change in title.

While each work situation is different, an effective leader needs to create the kind of atmosphere where people feel appreciated, confident and a strong sense of accomplishment. According to John Gardner, "a leader must recognize the needs of followers or constituents, help them see how those needs can be met, and give them confidence that they can accomplish that result through their own efforts."[17]

Ivan Seidenberg and Verizon

One of the best examples of corporate alignment can be seen in the work of Ivan Seidenberg, president and CEO of Verizon Communications. Seidenberg started his career in telecommunications some 30 years ago as a cable splicer's assistant. In 2000, as chief executive of Bell Atlantic, he combined his operations with independent telephone company GTE to form Verizon Communications. Seidenberg is widely seen as a CEO with a unique vision of the telecom world, in part because he literally knows the business from the ground up and has seen its evolutionary cycle from many vantage points. Today, Seidenberg is considered one of the most powerful and politically savvy of the big telecom corporate players. He has positioned Verizon to be a full-service provider of wired and wireless telephony, high-speed Internet access and distributor of multichannel television to the home using the uniquely designed IPTV format. As a leader, Seidenberg has a personal touch that inspires intense loyalty.

Richard Wiley and the FCC

Over the years, there have been a number of FCC commissioners who have worked hard to advance the cause of a new communication or information technology. One such person was Richard Wiley, who demonstrated a remarkable ability to bring people together and build alignment involving highly complex issues. While chairman of the FCC, Wiley proved to be an excellent public servant and developed a reputation for building consensus among divergent groups of people. When he left the Commission, Richard Wiley established the highly successful law firm of Wiley Rein and Fielding.

In the late 1980s, Richard Wiley was selected as chairman of the FCC's Advisory Committee on High Definition Television. The challenges were enormous given the complexity of the issues, including equipment standards, manufacturing requirements, frequency allocation, and the cost of implementation by the nation's broadcast stations. Building industry consensus involving the future of HDTV would be a formidable task. More to the point, he would have to build alignment, where none could be found. Throughout the proceedings, it was not uncommon to hear such comments as: "I may disagree with him, but I know he will be fair." That said, Richard

Wiley and his committee were responsible for setting into motion the set of standards that would result in present-day high-definition television.

Trust and Integrity

If the leader cannot be trusted, the ability to lead is compromised. Is there anything more important than trust? An instructor has proof that a student has cheated on an exam; a person finds out that a spouse is having an affair; a manager discovers that an employee has falsified accounting records. In each instance there will be consequences. The student may fail; the marriage may end in divorce; the company may become the target of a government investigation. A violation of trust will have a profound and lasting effect. Nothing is more important to a company than its reputation in the marketplace.

Effective leadership starts by creating a climate of trust. The leader should lead by example and create a positive and safe work environment. What are some of the issues that often undermine trust? Let's explore three: 1) inconsistency, 2) not maintaining a confidence and 3) gossip.

Consistency is the ability to convey the same message (good or bad) to those who would seek information from you. A clear, consistent style goes a long way in generating trust. Consistency also has to do with making sure that people really hear what you're saying. To that end, say what you mean and mean what you say. Second, learn to maintain a confidence once it's given. All it takes is for one person to believe that the confidence that he/she shared with you has been broken. After that, the team or group of subordinates will avoid telling you anything that is important or personal. And third, avoid gossiping about someone who is not present. This is sometimes difficult, since a person may come to you in confidence for the express purpose of talking about someone else in the organization. Such conversations are unavoidable. Speaking before a class at Indiana University, the late Clark Pollock, former president of Nationwide Communications, said: "We come into the world, and we leave the world, with only two things of importance—our word and our good name."

A Willingness to Take Risks

Individuals manage risk every day of their lives. We purchase car insurance to minimize the financial risk of having an accident. We accept a new job, knowing that there is a certain amount of risk in making a change. As mid-level managers, we assume a level of risk whenever we hire a new person. The business leader's risk, however, is quite different. The business leader assumes a high degree of professional risk when it comes to initiating a major merger or acquisition or backs the introduction of an altogether new product or service. Strategic decision making at that level involves a high degree of risk and may result in failure. The financial stakes can be enormous. Consider,

348

for example, Time Warner's CEO, Jerry Levin, and his decision to merge with Internet service provider AOL at a cost of $162 billion.

Rupert Murdoch and News Corporation

In 1985, Australian media owner Rupert Murdoch entered the U.S. market with the purchase of seven television stations from Metromedia Inc. for $2 billion. The purchase of the seven Metromedia stations allowed News Corporation the ability to lay the foundation for what would become the future Fox television network. A year later, News Corporation Ltd. bought 20th Century Fox for $1.55 billion. The start-up of Fox Television defied the conventional wisdom of the day: specifically, that there was no room for a fourth television network in the U.S. It would take several years and several billion dollars in losses before Fox would achieve profitability. A few years later, Murdoch was willing to test the waters again, with the 1989 launch of Britain's first direct broadcast satellite (DBS) service, called Sky Television. The start-up of Sky Television (later to be called British Sky Broadcasting— BSkyB) was done at a time well before the technology had proven itself in the marketplace. In time, BSkyB would become the preeminent European DBS service provider, but not before sustaining an estimated $1.2 billion in losses between the years 1989 and 1993. In summarizing Rupert Murdoch's business activities throughout the 1980s, *The Economist* wrote: "Nobody exploited the booming media industry in the late 1980's better than Mr. Rupert Murdoch's News Corporation—and few borrowed more money to do it."[18]

Ted Turner and CNN

An excellent example of risk taking can be seen with the start-up of the Cable News Network. Prior to the advent of CNN in 1980, the American public was basically exposed to three television network news services. There was no precedent for a 24-hour television news service, let alone on cable television. On June 1, 1980, CNN was officially launched, providing news all the time. Ted Turner, president and founder of CNN, stated at the time: "I'm going to do news like the world has never seen before."[19] In the beginning, CNN struggled as a start-up news organization. It was dismissed by other news organizations as the "chicken noodle network." Moreover, providing 24-hour continuous news coverage was a huge financial challenge. In time, CNN would assert its legitimacy as a news organization. Among its many television news coups was its handling of the Space Shuttle *Challenger* disaster, special coverage of the abortive democratic revolution in China, for which it received a Peabody Award, and its coverage of the Persian Gulf War. CNN has multiple worldwide additions and has established itself as a highly respected international television news service. Some years later, reflecting back on the success of CNN, Turner noted: "It was a gamble. Everything's a gamble. You know, the sun could fall out of the sky tomorrow. The plane could crash. The lights could go out. You know life is a gamble."[20]

Followership

The leader must have someone to lead. Or, as John Gardner says, the leader needs constituents. Followership deals with effective upward management. The manager at every level of an organization must develop procedures, behaviors and initiatives which result in effective upward management. According to Warren Bennis, "The longer I study effective leaders, the more I am persuaded of the underappreciated importance of effective followers."[21] Similarly, John Gardner remarks, "In a sense, leadership is conferred by followers."[22]

Anyone who has ever worked on a television news set knows that there's more to directing than simply framing the next shot or having the video news insert ready to roll at a precise moment. If the director can get his/her production crew to buy into the concept of "program," the entire production staff will be looking for ways to make the newscast better. The camera operator will be looking for a shot the director hasn't considered; the technical director will suggest a new visual effect. The program will be qualitatively better and the audience and the advertiser will respond accordingly. What is the difference? The difference in quality is the result of a director (or leader) who cares enough to create an environment in which the production staff wants to achieve the best possible outcome. In the end, the director creates a strong sense of teamwork, where everyone feels a part of something greater than themselves.

How followers (or members of the team) respond is critical not only to the welfare of the organization (or project mission) but to their personal and professional development as future leaders. The experience gained at one level of management provides the foundation in preparing that person for the next level of management responsibility within the organization. Indeed, it is impossible to be a leader without first learning how to be a good constituent. So what does it take to be an effective constituent? Let's consider four important attributes. They include the ability to:

1   take responsibility;
2   communicate openly;
3   translate vision into action;
4   balance priorities and get the job done.

Take Responsibility

Effective followership requires the manager and his/her support team to take responsibility for an assignment (or problem) when it is given to them. The effective leader owns the problem and does not look to deflect it to someone else. As former president Harry Truman once said, "The buck stops here." Taking responsibility is the sign of a true professional. This is where you establish your credibility whether as a skilled athlete leading a sports team in a comeback situation in the final two minutes of a game or as a telecommunications professional who has to lead a technical team into action in order to offset a major network power failure. Managing in a high-tech environment means having the ability to say cool under pressure. The combination of the right technical skill coupled with the ability to develop fast and efficient solutions to an emerging problem soon makes you the go-to person whenever such situations arise.

Communicate Openly

An effective manager keeps the senior administration fully informed with reliable information. At the same time, the same manager keeps his/her own department or professional staff equally informed. As any experienced manager can tell you, there are few secrets in any organization, particularly in a media and telecommunications environment. The problem is that a lack of reliable information often breeds uncertainty, insecurity and rumors. Most people want to know what is happening. Just as the manager needs to be kept informed, so do the members of an organizational team. Constituents are remarkably adept at dealing with problems, even bad news.

We recall one instance of an advertising agency staff who knew they were not going to receive Christmas bonuses because rumor had it that the agency was in financial trouble. There was even some talk among the staff that the agency might have to close. When management realized the magnitude of the problem, they called a meeting to indicate that, indeed, there would be no Christmas bonuses that year—but that the company would have no trouble surviving. While the information was not good news, the facts were not as bad as the rumors suggested. It's about openness. Constituents need to know the bad news as well as the good.

Translate Vision into Action

The mid-level manager is often the person responsible for translating the senior administration's vision into action. As mentioned in Chapter 2, strategies often fail because they aren't executed well.[23] Strategy implementation is the process by which strategies are effectively put into practice. One of the difficult challenges is that everyone agrees to the plan, but no one is responsible for results. This is where effective followership comes into play. It is the project or mid-level manager who must execute on the details. He/she is ultimately responsible for making sure that the job gets done. Translating vision into action involves five things:

351

- communicating the goals and objectives of senior management;
- assembling the project team in order to carry a proposed strategy or programmatic change;
- establishing the proper budget where appropriate;
- setting up the time frame for implementation;
- working through the operational support issues necessary in order to get the job done (i.e., scheduling issues, technical and equipment support, etc.).

Balance Priorities and Get the Job Done

Planning is about staying organized and balancing priorities. And, more importantly, it's making sure that the job gets done. Most senior and mid-level managers are working on a number of projects at the same time. At issue is the fact that the mid-level manager must balance these tasks against the day-to-day routine assignments of writing reports, doing personnel evaluations, meeting with vendors, etc. Add to this mixture the unexpected brush fires such as a major equipment failure, an unexpected call from the news media or a senior manager wanting a piece of information in two hours' time and you get the world of day-to-day management. The mid-level manager typically reports to a senior-level executive as well as being responsible for supervising a departmental staff. He/she must routinely try to navigate two sets of constituents whose issues are quite different. At the end of the day, the mid-level manager is responsible for making sure that the job gets done.

The Challenges of Being a Leader

Managers are routinely faced with organizational challenges that test their leadership skills on a day-to-day basis. The issues can range in size and complexity from employees missing a project deadline to highly destructive organizational conflict. Each situation is unique and requires good managerial insight. Let's consider some of the routine work challenges of a constituent that can sometimes test a manager's leadership skills. They include:

- destructive conflict;
- not getting the job done;
- problem transfer;
- putting the manager in a corner.

Destructive Conflict

Conflict and differences of opinion are a natural part of any organizational setting and it should not be assumed that they are necessarily bad. In fact, just the opposite may be true. A spirited discussion can provide fresh and creative solutions to an otherwise difficult problem. The general manager who assembles a group of "yes persons" for department heads is on the fast track toward mediocrity. The key to such discussion is that it be constructive. That said, if one or more members of a project team cannot get along, it creates a tension that becomes slowly corrosive to the well-being of the entire organization. Over time, team members avoid wanting to attend departmental or project meetings. Organizational conflict can occur for other reasons as well. Sometimes, it may be as simple (or complex) as one group of constituents who are uncomfortable with another group member because of his/her working style. The person may be loud and obnoxious. Sometimes organizational conflict is more subtle and may be due to a person's race, ethnicity or sexual orientation. A woman who is openly gay, for example, may make the work environment challenging for a segment of employees whose religious and social views are more conservative in nature. In the end, no organization can tolerate destructive conflict. The manager himself/herself has to navigate these differences and find common meeting points.

Not Getting the Job Done

All too often, followers simply fail to get the job done. Author Hyrum Smith suggests that, when people use the phrase "I've been too busy," what they are really saying is that they have a different set of priorities.[24] The follower has to be aware of the manager's set of priorities. To do otherwise is to be a poor constituent. At issue is the fact that, when a job goes unfinished, someone else has to step in and finish the assignment. If no one else is available, the manager may have to put aside what he/she is doing to complete the task. In the final analysis, it is the manager who is ultimately responsible for ensuring that a major project or assignment gets completed within the organization. Are there times when a constituent cannot realistically finish the said project or task assignment? Yes! However, building a strong track record of proven performance goes a long way in reassuring the manager that the occasional missed deadline is an exception and not the rule.

Problem Transfer

In a classic *Harvard Business Review* article entitled "Management Time: Who's Got the Monkey?," writers William Oncken and Donald Wass discuss the issue of time management and the problems associated with constituents who fail to take responsibility.[25] Rather than taking responsibility for solving a problem, the subordinate is only too willing to transfer that responsibility to his/her superior. The authors use the analogy of a monkey, meant to symbolize responsibility, and on whose back that monkey belongs. Oncken and Wass would argue that problem transfer begins the moment a monkey successfully executes a leap from the back of a subordinate to the back of a superior and does not end until the monkey is returned to its proper owner. The bottom line is that good constituents should not transfer their responsibilities to the manager.

Putting the Manager in a Corner

Good managers do not allow themselves to be put in a corner. What this means is having a constituent say something like "Either you do this or I quit" or a similar ultimatum. Being an effective constituent recognizes the value of providing one's boss with viable options, not ultimatums. Delivering an ultimatum to one's boss is rarely a positive or productive way for a constituent to deal with a problem. One corporate manager who was consulted for this book said that an ultimatum is usually a sign of a mismatch between two people. The reason for the poor fit could be either the boss or the employee. The result, however, is that an ultimatum is probably going to be synonymous with a resignation. Providing options is more constructive than delivering ultimatums. The advice to the constituent who is inclined to give an ultimatum is: "Do whatever you want. Just be prepared to accept the most serious consequences for your actions." In the final analysis, bosses, not constituents, conduct showdowns.

Leadership Ethics

As noted earlier, a scandal involving corporate misconduct such as the falsification of an earnings report can have a devastating effect on the company's standing and reputation in the marketplace. The lack of investor confidence can translate into billions of dollars in lowered stock value and the loss of working capital. In the worst-case scenario, it can lead to the eventual demise of the company itself. During the 2000–2001 time period, falling markets and accounting scandals tarnished the once iconic image of the chief executive officer (CEO) as business leader. The self-dealing that characterized a handful of CEOs fostered public resentment and called into question a system that would allow a handful of senior-level executives to enrich themselves at the public's expense. At issue were the excesses of a few senior-level executives who pursued personal enrichment schemes and cashed out millions in stock options while employees were losing their jobs and life savings. This reality overturned several decades of conventional wisdom about the value of self-regulation.[26] As the following case study shows, deregulated markets do many things well. But they are sometimes not effective at policing themselves.[27]

WorldCom

Starting in the mid-1990s, the Mississippi-based WorldCom corporation quickly rose to become the number two long-distance telephone carrier in the U.S. Along the way, the company used its soaring stock to make 70 acquisitions, including a hostile takeover of MCI in 1998. MCI was at that time a company more than three times the size of WorldCom. The combination of WorldCom's UUNET network and MCI's Internet backbone made the company the largest carrier of Internet traffic in the world. Beginning in 2002, WorldCom experienced a stunning reversal of fortune. WorldCom became the focus of intense scrutiny by regulators and law enforcement officials after the public disclosure that WorldCom had improperly overstated its earnings by $3.8 billion in 2001 and the first quarter of 2002.[28] It was the largest accounting fraud in U.S. corporate history. The number subsequently grew to $11 billion. A U.S. Congressional investigation into the WorldCom affair revealed that WorldCom's accounting department under the direction of chief financial officer (CFO) Scott D. Sullivan had manipulated the company's financial record keeping in order to paper over multibillion-dollar losses. It was done with the intention of propping up WorldCom's deteriorating financial standing on Wall Street.[29]

It isn't clear why WorldCom's misstatements weren't caught immediately by its outside auditors. The answer, in part, can be explained by the accounting firm responsible for its financial audit, Arthur Andersen, the same company that was responsible for the Enron debacle and the shredding of documents. The firm signed off on WorldCom's financial statements. Arthur Andersen later issued a statement that CFO Sullivan had been deceptive in his financial reporting to the company's auditors. What ultimately brought about the accounting disclosure was the work of the company's internal auditing department headed up by Cynthia Cooper. On June 20, Cooper and a member of the WorldCom internal audit team went to Washington to meet with WorldCom's audit committee representing the company's board of directors. At the meeting, Cooper presented her findings. Sullivan was asked to resign and was later fired. Afterwards, WorldCom made public its findings regarding the accounting fraud. CFO Scott Sullivan and accounting director Buford Yates were indicted in August 2002 by U.S. federal prosecutors for fraud and misrepresentation. In 2005, Sullivan pleaded guilty to conspiracy, securities fraud and making false financial filings. He would later testify that he took CEO Bernard Ebbers's insistence that the company "hit its numbers" as a directive to commit accounting fraud.[30] Sullivan was sentenced to five years in prison.

WorldCom would subsequently file for Chapter 11 bankruptcy protection. The company's newly appointed board of directors hired the law firm of Wilmer, Cutler & Pickering to conduct an internal investigation of the company's past activities. Among the committee's many findings was that WorldCom's leadership failures began at the top. CEO Bernard Ebbers "created the pressure that led to the fraud":

> He demanded the results he had promised, and he appeared to scorn the procedures (and people) that should have been a check on misreporting. When efforts were made to establish a corporate Code of Conduct, Ebbers reportedly described it as a "colossal waste of time." He showed little respect for the role lawyers played with respect to corporate governance matters within the Company. While we have heard numerous accounts of Ebbers' demand for results—on occasion emotional, insulting, and with express reference to the personal financial harm he faced if the stock price declined—we have heard none in which he demanded or rewarded ethical business practices.[31]

In March 2005, Ebbers was convicted on nine counts for his part in the $11-billion accounting fraud at WorldCom. He was sentenced to 25 years in prison.[32]

In the aftermath of the accounting disclosure, WorldCom filed for bankruptcy, and the fallout has been significant. WorldCom discharged 17,000 of its employees (or 28 percent of the company's workforce). The company saw its stock plummet from a one-time high of $64.50 per share to stock that traded at 83 cents per share. Company employees lost their jobs as well as much of their retirement savings which was tied up in WorldCom stock. The company's bondholders and other creditors also suffered heavy losses. At the time, WorldCom was carrying $32 billion in debt.[33] As the company's financial standing quickly deteriorated, WorldCom's assets proved to be worth far less than its $32-billion debt owing to the softness of the telecommunications market. In the meantime, the California public employees' retirement system, the largest state pension fund in the U.S., sued WorldCom to regain some $580 million in losses resulting from the accounting disclosures. As part of its Chapter 11 reorganization plan, WorldCom renamed itself MCI. In January 2006, Verizon Communications acquired MCI at a cost of $6.8 billion.

Discussion: Managing in a Time of Change

In 2001, author Jim Collins published *Good to Great*, which explored the question: What makes good companies great? Are there certain identifiable characteristics and business processes that enable companies to sustain greatness over time? According to Collins, great leaders are not necessarily high-profile individuals with big personalities. He is quick to point out that leadership skill is not abut charisma. Celebrity leaders are too often more concerned with their own reputation than they are for establishing and securing the company's future success. Instead, great leaders (or Level 5 leaders) are oftentimes self-effacing, displaying a curious blend of personal humility and a strong, professional will to get things done.

Collins argues that effective organizational leadership begins by developing a culture of discipline. Successful outcomes depend on building a culture of highly disciplined people who are both knowledgeable and steady in their approach to product development and innovation. A culture of discipline evokes a kind of paradox. On the one hand, working professionals have to adhere to a consistent, structured environment. On the other, it gives people tremendous opportunity and freedom to create within the parameters of that system.[34] Therein lies the possibility for sustained growth as well as the potential to advance innovative change.

Today's media and telecommunications environment is characterized by change. The Bureau of Labor reports that people in their twenties change jobs every 18 months. The challenge for today's business leader is how to work with change, that is, to make it a point of organizational strength rather than something to be avoided. Throughout this book, we've discussed the kinds of external and internal pressures that can affect an organization, including changes in the competitive marketplace, changes in technology, changes in global competition and changes in the organization's management structure, to name only a few. In short, there is no such thing as a steady, predictable work environment. In order to compete in the new world of work, the successful manager must be able to exhibit strong leadership skill while staying flexible in the face of corporate turbulence and international business pressures. Put another way, successful managers must be ready and able to adapt to a variety of changing situations. Change is a natural process and not something to be feared. Great companies, like great leaders, stay disciplined while remaining flexible.

15

INNOVATION AND TECHNOLOGY MANAGEMENT

Introduction

The lessons of business history have taught us that there is no such thing as a static market. There are no guarantees of continued business success for a company in a particular market segment. In 1942, Joseph Schumpeter introduced the principle of "creative destruction" as a way to describe the disruptive process that accompanies the work of the entrepreneur and the consequences of innovation. In time, companies that once revolutionized and dominated select markets give way to rivals that are able to introduce improved product designs, offer substitute products and services and/or lower manufacturing costs.[1] The net consequences of creative destruction can be significant, including the ceding of market leadership, the discontinuation of an existing product and the potential loss of jobs.[2]

Today, the competitive landscape has become ever more challenging. Global competition has engendered a new competitive spirit that cuts across countries and companies alike. No company large or small remains unaffected by the desire to increase profits and decrease costs. Therefore, all companies are faced with the same basic question, namely, what are the best methods for staying competitive over time? In a word, "innovation." The term *innovation* can mean different things depending on its use. Innovation can mean the gradual improvement to an existing product or service. But innovation can also mean introducing an entirely new product or service concept to the marketplace.

Why Is Innovation Important?

Innovation is important because it creates a long-term lasting advantage for a company or organization.[3] It allows a business to develop and improve on its existing product line as well as preparing the groundwork for the future. Consider, for example, the impact that cellular telephony has had on traditional wireline telephone service. Starting in the early 1990s, cell phones offered the value proposition to consumers of mobility and convenience. But that was only the beginning. In time, cell phones would provide lasting advantage to cell phone manufacturers and carriers alike by providing consumers with text messaging, photo imaging and more recently MP3 file sharing and music playback capability.

Innovation is also important because it offers up the opportunity to meet untapped customer demands. Sometimes, the issue is not about harnessing so-called breakthrough technologies. Rather, innovation (and innovative thinking) is about finding new ways to improve upon existing technologies and services. Consider, for example, the dramatic growth of cell phone technology among developing nations located in Southeast Asia, Latin America and Eastern Europe. The deployment of cellular telephone systems is proving to be faster and more cost-effective than building (or reconstructing) traditional telephone systems. This is especially true in those regions of the world with poor wireline infrastructure. In urban areas, cellular telephone deployment eliminates the challenges of implementing physical wireline systems that require the negotiation of rights-of-way clearance between carriers and cities, as well as the arduous task of stringing wire on buildings and houses and cutting up city streets. Developing countries account for a major portion of all wireless subscribers.

Innovative thinking comes into play when it comes to the challenges of deploying cell phone technology among rural residents living inside developing nations. Nokia Corporation, for example, created a specially designed dustproof keypad for those countries with dry, arid living conditions and harsh winds.[4] Nokia learned some important lessons about technology diffusion as well. In India, for example, Nokia estimates that there are some 90,000 points of sale for its phones, ranging from modern stores to makeshift kiosks. That makes it difficult to control how Nokia products are displayed and sold. The solution for Nokia was to outfit a fleet of blue Nokia-branded vans that travel the countryside to show people how to use cellular telephones and get the maximum value from them. Along the way, the Nokia team learned that many rural residents form buying clubs, pooling their money to buy handsets one at a time until everyone has one.[5]

Highly successful companies are those that are willing to experiment and not rest on their past success. The goal of highly innovative companies is to make innovation a sustainable, repeatable process. This chapter will examine the importance of innovation (and innovative thinking) to the long-term success of today's media and telecommunications companies. Specifically, it will address two important questions. First, why do good companies fail to remain innovative over time? Second, what are the best methods for initiating innovative change within an organization? The arguments presented in this chapter are theory based and supported by case-study evidence. An important point to remember is that even the best-managed companies are susceptible to innovation failure.

What Is Innovation?

Everett Rogers defines innovation as "an idea, practice or object that is perceived as new by an individual."[6] In principle, there are two kinds of innovation, namely, sustaining technologies versus disruptive technologies.[7] According to author Clayton Christensen, a sustaining technology has to do with product improvement and performance. The goal is to improve on an existing technology by adding new and enhanced feature elements. A computer manufacturer, for example, is routinely looking to improve on basic design elements like speed and throughput, processing power and graphics display. In short, a sustaining innovation targets demanding high-end customers with better performance than what was previously available.[8]

In contrast, a disruptive (or breakthrough) technology represents an altogether different approach to an existing product design and process. A disruptive technology redefines the playing field by introducing to the marketplace a unique value proposition.[9] Authors W. Chan Kim and Renée Mauborgne in a series of articles for the *Harvard Business Review* introduce the term *value innovation* as a way of describing how successful businesses capture uncontested market space and thereby make competition irrelevant.[10]

A good example of this can be seen in the area of electronic commerce (EC). eBay Inc., for example, is an American Internet company that holds online auctions and shopping, allowing people and businesses to buy and sell goods and services worldwide. eBay has sometimes been described as the world's largest garage sale. Auctions on eBay include: art and antiques, automotive, business and industrial, crafts, collectibles, fashion, jewelry, photography, travel, toys and tickets, as well as many other items that are listed, bought and sold. Today, there are over 212 million registered eBay buyers and sellers worldwide.[11] At the start of the twenty-first century, EC has created a new business model that maximizes the potential for instantaneous communication to a worldwide customer base. More importantly, EC companies like eBay have redefined the competitive landscape by offering consumers a unique value proposition. There is no going backward.

In the field of business and technology, innovation breaks down into three subset areas. They include: 1) product innovation, 2) process innovation and 3) business model innovation. Some of today's more creative companies are innovating in all three areas.

Product Innovation

Product innovation refers to the complex process of bringing new products and services to market as well improving (or enhancing) existing ones. Select examples of media and telecommunications product innovation can be seen in Table 15.1.

Table 15.1 Select Examples of Media and Telecommunications Product Innovation

---

Sony and Philips: the compact disc (CD).
Google: search engines and electronic mapping.
Apple: iPod portable music playback device.
Microsoft: desktop software and enhancements.
Walt Disney: theme parks and resorts.
Home Box Office: premium television and film.
Verizon, FiOS: telephone-based IPTV television service.

Sony and Philips: The Compact Disc

In the early 1960s, the general junction laser was developed at MIT's Lincoln Labs and later improved at Bell Research Labs. But it was Sony and the Philips Corporation that would refine the idea into the modern compact disc (CD). In 1975, the optical and audio teams at both Sony and Philips began collaborating on the digital recording of information on to a laser disc. Sony president Norio Ohga, a former student of music, was enamored with the possibilities of digital recording. He designated a small group of Sony engineers to give the laser disc top priority. In the spring of 1976, the team of audio engineers proudly presented Ohga with an audio laser disc 30 centimeters wide (approximately the size of an LP record). It was capable of providing the listener with 13 hours and 20 minutes of digital sound. As author John Nathan wrote, "For their pains, they received a withering lecture on the folly of engineering for its own sake and the importance of developing a business sense."[12]

In the meantime, Philips audio division in Eindhoeven, Holland, was busy at work on its own version of the optical laser disc. From August 1979 to June 1980, both companies saw the value of collaboration as teams of engineers would alternate site visits to both sets of laboratories in Tokyo and Eindhoeven. At a June meeting of the Digital Audio Disc conference, both Sony and Philips presented a set of recommended standards. In the weeks and months that followed, both Sony and Philips engineers worked together toward refining the CD player.

Demonstrations of the CD were being made worldwide in preparation for the planned launch of the CD in October 1982. Norio Ohga, for his part, was convinced that CDs would eventually replace records, given the technology's superior sound quality. That said, however, Ohga recognized that the development of the CD would meet with fierce resistance from many in the recording industry (including even some at CBS Records) who felt threatened by CD technology. It should be noted that, in 1968, Sony had entered into a joint partnership with CBS records to form CBS/Sony records. That partnership would prove vital in promoting the cause of CD technology.

361

In one such product demonstration, executives stood up in an auditorium in Athens, Greece, and demonstrated their resistance to business change by chanting "The truth is in the groove. The truth is in the groove."[13] To them, the CD format was an unproven technology made by hardware people who knew nothing about the software side of the business. Worse still, the conversion to a CD format would require enormous sums of money while possibly destabilizing the entire music industry.

On August 31, 1982, an announcement was made in Tokyo that four companies, including Sony, CBS, Philips and Polygram, had jointly developed the world's first CD system. In time, the Sony/Philips CD became the de facto standard throughout the industry. By 1986, CDs had topped 45 million titles annually, overtaking records to become the principal recording format. CD technology would ultimately redefine the field of recording technology and spawn a whole host of new inventions, including the portable CD music stereo, the digital video disc (DVD) and the CD-based videogame console. For Sony, CD technology would prove invaluable for a soon-to-be-launched videogame system called PlayStation.

Process Innovation

Today, innovation is about much more than developing new products. It is about reinventing business processes and building entirely new markets that meet untapped customer needs. Innovation is also about taking corporate organizations built for efficiency and rewiring them for creativity and growth. Process innovation is about finding new and better ways for conducting one's business. As such, process innovators are "obsessive problem solvers." Central to this discussion are the principles set forth in various kinds of performance improvement strategies, including total quality management (TQM), Six Sigma, value stream analysis and lean process management. Total quality management (TQM) is the oldest and perhaps best known of the said performance improvement strategies. The principles of total quality management date back to the 1940s to the work of American business consultants W. Edwards Deming and Joseph Juran, who were involved in helping to resurrect Japanese industry in the aftermath of World War II. Out of that experience and subsequent writings emerged the principles of total quality management. TQM represents an approach to management and operations whereby the entire organization is fully engaged to deliver quality products and services to its customers. TQM embraces quality and continuous improvement as fundamental organizational goals. To that end, TQM requires company-wide participation in quality control issues.[14] (See Chapter 11.)

In 1986, Bill Smith at Motorola Corporation developed a set of process improvement strategies known as Six Sigma. The goal of Six Sigma is to systematically improve processes by eliminating defects. Six Sigma was greatly influenced by the six preceding decades of quality improvement methodologies, starting with TQM. Six Sigma asserts that manufacturing and business processes can be measured, analyzed and controlled and that continuous efforts to reduce variation in process outputs are key to improving product quality. The term *Six Sigma* refers to a highly capable process designed to produce outputs within highly demanding specifications.[15] The principles of Six Sigma are especially important to companies engaged in the manufacture of high-end computer and communications equipment.

In sum, successful process innovation is about finding new methods for improving the design and operations of one's business. Process innovation presupposes a constant refining and improvement process that leads to the goal of improved product quality and customer service. Select examples of media and telecommunications process innovation can be seen in Table 15.2.

Dell Computers

The company known as Dell Computers was established by Michael Dell in 1984 and has grown to become one of the world's preeminent manufacturers of desktop and laptop computers. Dell builds computers to customer order and specification using just-in-time manufacturing techniques. The company has built its reputation on direct sales delivery to the end consumer combined with strong customer support.

Michael Dell started out as a pre-med student at the University of Texas. Dell soon became fascinated by computers and created a small niche in the assembly and sale of PCs (and PC components) out of his dormitory room. Dell bought excess supplies at cost from IBM dealers, which allowed him to resell the components at 10–15 percent below the regular retail price. He then began to assemble and sell PC clones by purchasing retailers' surplus stock at cost and then upgrading the units with video cards, hard disks and

Table 15.2 Select Examples of Media and Telecommunications Process Innovation

Dell Computers	Creating a highly successful business model utilizing just-in-time manufacturing techniques as well as direct-to-home sales capability and delivery.
Sony	Has pioneered manufacturing innovation by giving workers on the floor greater responsibility for improving product quality and performance.
HBO	The delivery of television via satellite to cable operating systems gave rise to the principle of cable television networking, including such companies as HBO, CNN, MTV, ESPN, Disney, etc.
HTML language code	Developed by Tim Berners-Lee of CERN; made possible hypertext linking and gave rise to the WWW Internet concept.
Pixar Studios	Has pioneered the development of computer-generated cartoon animation.

memory. He then sold the newly assembled IBM clones at 40 percent below the cost of an IBM PC.[16] By April 1984, with sales reaching $80,000 a month, Dell dropped out of the university and formed a company called PCs Limited. The ability to sell directly to the end user at a discounted price proved to be a winning formula, and by the end of 1986 sales had reached $33 million. PCs Limited was renamed Dell Computers in 1987, and the company soon opened its first set of international offices.

From 1990 to 1993, Dell experimented with distributing through retailers in hopes of faster growth, but soon realized that such methods were less profitable and refocused on direct sales. By 1996, Internet sales had taken off and the company realized that computer-savvy individuals preferred the convenience of custom-ordering what they wanted directly from Dell and having it delivered to their door. During this time, Dell had become master innovators, using two important processes. The first process was customization using a just-in-time manufacturing capability. Dell Computers would build computers to customer order and specification, thereby eliminating excess inventory and the need for storage. The second important process was direct-to-consumer sales delivery, thus avoiding costly investment in retail store infrastructure. It was a process model that other computer manufacturers would soon adopt.

Today, Dell has an international workforce of 35,000 employees located in 34 countries and three major regions of the world, including the Americas, Europe/Middle East and Asia Pacific. Each region has its own headquarters and its own assembly plants and supply network. Because of Dell's build-to-order philosophy, the company requires an excellent system of communication in order to meet customer demands and to ensure a ready supply of parts on hand to support various kinds of configuration requests.[17] Instead of producing all the necessary components itself, Dell contracts with other manufacturers to produce the parts. Dell does the complete final assembly, but is extremely dependent on outside sources and contractors. In more recent years, Dell has evolved a highly sophisticated supply chain management system that tracks information between and among suppliers, distributors and other key component players involved in product manufacturing and support (Figure 15.1).

In the past, Dell had assembled each computer using an assembly-line process in which a single individual would install a single component and the partly assembled PC was sent on to the next station. In 1997, Dell switched to a technique known as "cell manufacturing" by which a team of workers would work together to assemble an entire PC at a workstation (or cell).[18] This new technique resulted in a steep decline in assembly time and increased productivity per square foot of assembly space. The cell manufacturing production concept has been fully incorporated into the company's global-wide supply chain management system.

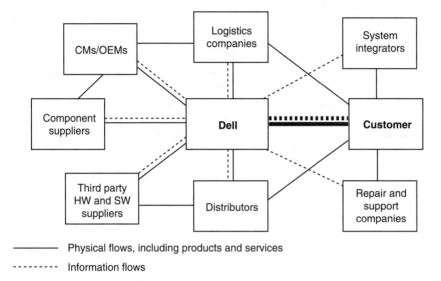

Physical flows, including products and services

Information flows

Figure 15.1 Dell's Inventory and Production Management System.

Source: Dell Inc.; Kenneth Kraemer and Jason Dedrick, "Dell Computer: Organization of a Global Production Network," Available at: http://www.crito.uci.edu (retrieved October 6, 2006).

Business Model Innovation

Business model innovation involves creating an altogether new approach for doing business. Business model innovation is transformative; that is, it redefines the competitive playing field by introducing an entirely new value proposition to the consumer. W. Chan Kim and Renée Mauborgne in a book entitled *Blue Ocean Strategy* reintroduce the term *value innovation* as a way of describing how successful businesses capture uncontested market space and thereby make competition irrelevant.[19] The metaphor of "ocean" refers to the marketplace. "Blue oceans" refers to untapped or uncontested markets which offer little or no competition for those companies prepared to swim the waters and design an altogether new product or service. According to the authors, blue ocean strategy represents an opportunity to create something different from everyone else (i.e., a new value proposition). In doing so, competition becomes irrelevant since no one has claimed that landscape by offering the said product or service. They cite the example of Cirque du Soleil, which redefined the business of circus entertainment by combining theatre, dance and circus artistry in a way that had never been done before. Select examples of media and telecommunications business model innovation can be seen in Table 15.3.

Table 15.3 Select Examples of Media and Telecommunications Business Model Innovation

HBO	Developing the principle of pay television services.
Apple	Creating iTunes, the first sustainable MP3 music downloading business.
eBay	Electronic auctioning on the Internet, creating the world's largest on-line marketplace.
News Corporation	Advancing the development of direct broadcast satellite television, BSkyB, STAR TV, DirecTV, etc.
Amazon	Creating a highly successful EC business model, Amazon.com, specializing in the delivery of books and other retail items.
Google	Advancing the development of key-word-search Internet advertising.

Apple

Steven Jobs is the co-founder and CEO of Apple and CEO of Pixar Entertainment. Pixar was acquired by the Walt Disney Company in 2006. Jobs is currently the largest Disney shareholder and a member of Disney's Board of Directors. Steve Jobs is considered a leading figure in both the computer and entertainment industries. Jobs' history in business has contributed greatly to the mythos of the quirky, individualistic Silicon Valley entrepreneur, emphasizing the importance of design while understanding the crucial role of innovation in making information and entertainment products more accessible to the public at large.[20]

Together with Apple co-founder Steve Wozniak, Jobs helped popularize the personal computer in the late 1970s. In 1976, when Jobs was twenty-one, he and his friend Steve Wozniak built the first Apple personal computer. The Apple computer transformed people's thinking about computers from a device that was used by big business to a small box that could be used by ordinary people. In the early 1980s, Jobs understood the commercial potential and importance of the mouse driven graphics user interface. The 1984 introduction of the Apple MacIntosh, with its simple-to-use graphics interface and mouse technology, challenged the prevailing thinking that computers were strictly the domain of IT professionals in white lab coats. The Apple MacIntosh could be used by small business and novice users alike.[21]

Jobs has long been criticized for his aggressive management style. After losing a power struggle with the board of directors in 1985, Jobs resigned from Apple and founded NeXT, a computer company specializing in the higher education and business markets. Apple Computers struggled for the next ten years and in 1996 bought NeXT for $402 million, thus bringing Jobs back to the company he founded. A year later, Jobs became Apple's interim CEO after the directors forced the resignation of then-CEO Gil

Amelio in a boardroom coup. Jobs immediately terminated a number of projects and focused on the importance of software development partnerships.

At the 1997 Macworld Expo, Steve Jobs announced that Apple would be entering into partnership with Microsoft. Included in this was a five-year commitment from Microsoft to release Microsoft Office for Macintosh as well a $150 million investment in Apple. It was also announced that Internet Explorer would be shipped as the default browser on the Macintosh.

In 1998, the iMac line of personal computers was introduced. The design team was lead by Jonathan Ive, who later served as the chief designer for the Apple iPod portable music carrier. The iMac had a new translucent blue plastic exterior, which proved a hit among consumers. More colors were added later. The iMac proved highly successful, and sold close to 800,000 units in its first five months. In 2001, the Mac OS X operating system based on Jobs' NeXT was introduced.

Later that same year, Steve Jobs, Jonathan Ive and the team from Apple were responsible for the development of the Apple iPod digital audio player. The iPod is an example of a blue ocean strategy that redefined the playing field of music recording and storage by enabling the device to record and store music using prevailing MP3 Internet technology and software. The iTunes on-line audio music store was introduced in April 2003 and sells individual songs at a cost of $0.99 The iTunes music service has introduced a different value proposition to the marketplace by fundamentally challenging some basic assumptions involving traditional music sales and retailing. Consumers can now personalize their music play lists and obtain any song they wish just by downloading it via the Internet.[22] The combination of the Apple iPod and iTunes media store have created the first sustainable music downloading business model of its kind. It qualifies as both a new business model innovation as well as a business process innovation since it successfully takes advantage of MP3 software distribution technology. In 2007, Apple in partnership with AT&T introduced the Apple iPhone which combines Apple's first widescreen iPod with mobile telephone capability. The combined device supports both Internet capability as well as video voicemail.

Why Companies Fail to Innovate

Authors Jim Collins and Jerry Porras, in the book *Built to Last*, make the argument that highly successful companies are those that are willing to experiment and not rest on their past success.[23] Over time, tastes, preference and technology change. Innovative companies keep abreast of such changes, anticipate them and make the necessary adjustments in strategy and new product development. The question may be asked: if strategic adjustment and innovation are such basic elements, why then don't more companies succeed at it? Researcher Clayton Christensen makes the argument that even the best-managed companies are susceptible to innovation failure. In fact, past success can sometimes become the very root cause of innovation failure going forward. Ironically, the decisions that lead to failure are made by executives who work for companies widely regarded as the best in their field.[24]

The Innovator's Dilemma

A central argument of this chapter is that even well-managed companies are sometimes susceptible to innovation failure. The main reason is that such companies are highly committed to serving their existing customers and are often unable (or unwilling) to take apart a highly successful business in favor of advancing unfamiliar and unproven new technologies and services. Clayton Christensen posits what he calls the *innovator's dilemma*, namely, that a company's very strengths (i.e., the ability to develop reliable suppliers, be responsive to customer needs and realize consistent profits) now become barriers to change and the agents of a company's potential decline. As Robert Birnbaum points out, "strength becomes weakness, and the same factors that initially drive a company's success become responsible for its ultimate failure."[25] Advancing new technologies and services requires expensive retooling and may produce results not initially seen as useful by the company's major customers. Such companies lose because they fail to invest in new product development and/or because they fail to notice small niche players that enter the market and are prepared to offer low-end customers good solutions at better value.[26] The anticipated profit margins in serving this group become hard to justify given the high cost of entry, not to mention the possible abandonment of an otherwise highly successful business. Therein lies the innovator's dilemma.

The Innovator's Dilemma and Product Life Cycle

Product life cycle theory was initially proposed by Raymond Vernon in the mid-1960s and explains the evolution of a product's development from the point of its introduction into the marketplace to its final stages of decline.[27] The theory of product life cycle has evolved over the years and has come to include a series of four stages, including: 1) introduction, 2) growth, 3) maturity and 4) decline. After a product or service is launched, it goes through the various stages of a life cycle and reaches a natural decline point.[28] The innovator's dilemma is to know when in the course of the product life cycle to innovate (Figure 15.2). The decision to innovate represents a strategic choice to phase out (or cannibalize) a mature product in favor of an untested one. The decision to innovate has to occur well before the product hits its decline phase in order to allow sufficient time for development. That means that the critical decision occurs right at the time when the product is mature and realizing its highest profits. The downside risk is that the

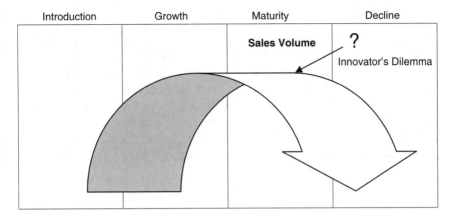

| Introduction | Growth | Maturity | Decline |

Sales Volume ?

Innovator's Dilemma

Figure 15.2 The Innovator's Dilemma and Product Life Cycle.

manufacturer may get it wrong and thereby destabilize an otherwise highly successful product line. Consider, for example, the 2006 launch of Microsoft's Vista operating software as a replacement to its predecessor, Windows XP operating software. Work on Vista began in 2001 under the code name Longhorn. The release of Windows Vista came more than five years after the introduction of Windows XP, thus making it the longest time span between two releases of Microsoft Windows. Vista has become the subject of a number of criticisms by various user groups.[29] As some critics have pointed out, Vista is hard to load and contains an array of features that can make desktop and laptop computers less stable and run more slowly.

The history of media and telecommunications is replete with examples of companies faced with the innovator's dilemma. It is worth noting that many companies that are highly regarded as innovative can momentarily lose their innovative edge only to rebound at a later time (e.g., IBM, Sony, Apple, Nintendo, etc.). In fact, few companies are able to remain consistently innovative across time. We now consider four reasons that help to explain why companies fail to innovate. They include:

- the tyranny of success;
- organizational culture;
- lengthy development times and poor coordination;
- a risk-averse culture.

The Tyranny of Success

Past success can sometimes make an organization very complacent; that is, it loses the sense of urgency to create new opportunities.[30] Author Jim Collins makes the point unequivocally when he writes "good is the enemy of great."[31] Companies, like people, can become easily satisfied with organizational routines. They become preoccupied with fine-tuning and making slight adjustments to an existing product line rather than preparing for the future. They are engaged in what MIT's Nicholas Negroponte describes as the problem of "incrementalism." Says Negroponte, "incrementalism is innovation's worst enemy."[32] The history of business is filled with examples of past companies like General Motors, IBM and Sears, to name only a few, where senior management failed to plan for the future. Such companies did not anticipate a time when a substitute product (or changing market conditions) might come along and dramatically alter the playing field.

IBM

Consider, for example, that IBM made its name and fortune in the development of mainframe computers. At the start of the 1980s, IBM recognized that the computing needs of the modern business organization were undergoing a major change. More and more, business computing was shifting away from the centralized mainframe towards the stand-alone desktop computer. Initially, IBM got it right with the development of the IBM PC. But the wild success of the IBM PC also began to undermine the company's core mainframe business. Instead of adjusting to the future, IBM became a victim to its own corporate bureaucracy and past success. The company was deriving less and less revenue from mainframe computers and no revenue from PCs either. According to author Paul Carroll, IBM executives actually saw most of the problems coming, both in PCs and in the rest of the business. They commissioned month-long task forces who correctly forecasted that changes in the marketplace would eventually harm IBM. Even with this knowledge, IBM's senior management could not bring themselves to fully prepare for the impending changes that were about to occur.

Organizational Culture

Organizational culture (or corporate culture) refers to the collection of beliefs, values and expectations shared by an organization's members and transmitted from one generation of employees to another. Organizational culture is deeply rooted and presupposes certain basic assumptions, attitudes and behaviors that are expected of all members of the work team. In the best sense, it provides strength and continuity to the organization over time. As researcher Edgar Schein points out, organizational cultures are relatively enduring and sometimes difficult to change.[33]

But what happens when organizational culture stands in the way of innovation? What happens when being tied to the past (and past practices) interferes with a company's ability to move forward? The combination of past success and an unbending adherence to management orthodoxy can seriously undermine a company's ability to step out of itself and plan for the future. Suddenly, creative thinking and the ability to float new ideas get caught up in a stifling bureaucracy. Consider, for example, that in 1984 AT&T possessed 90.1 percent of America's long-distance telephone market. In time, that lead would steadily decline to 40 percent.[34] Yet, despite the competitive and technological challenges, one of the most salient issues going forward was how to address the company's own internal culture.

The management at AT&T understood the external challenges. The problem was how to overcome the company's institutionalized bureaucracy. The culture was sometimes irreverently referred to as "carpetland." As journalist Leslie Cauley writes:

> Literally a century in the making, the culture was so omnipresent that it even had its own nickname: the Machine. It was an apt moniker. Almost impenetrable to outsiders, the Machine was a self perpetuating mechanism that was loath to change. . . . Process was a big part of the Machine's artistry. At AT&T's operational head-quarters in Basking Ridge, New Jersey, meetings could ramble on for weeks or even months. It was not uncommon for AT&T execs to have meetings to talk about meetings. Ditto for memos about memos. . . . The Machine steadfastly resisted change, and embraced those who did the same.[35]

In summary, talented employees who attempt to test the boundary waters of an organization's internal culture are met with such well-worn corporate phrases as "That's not the [AT&T or IBM] way" or "That's the way we've always done it around here." As Gary Hamel points out, "a lot of what passes for management wisdom is unquestioned dogma masquerading as unquestionable truth."[36]

Lengthy Development Times and Poor Coordination

The combination of changing technology and shifting consumer demands makes speed to market paramount today. Yet companies often can't organize themselves to move faster. Too often, companies that are highly compartmentalized can become immobilized when it comes to fast turnaround times, given the entrenchment of existing department and area silos. This, in turn, results in a lack of coordination that can seriously impair product innovation and development times. As *Business Week* noted in a 2006 survey, the number one obstacle to innovation is slow development times. According to the survey, respondents noted that the biggest challenge to product innovation was lengthy development times (32 percent) followed by a lack of coordination (28 percent).[37]

Lengthy development times and poor coordination are closely tied to the execution of strategy. The problem often starts with executive failure to properly articulate the goals of innovation change to the organization as a whole. This, in turn, leads to a lack of acceptance (or buy-in) from the mid-level managers and professional staff who are responsible for implementing the proposed changes. More specifically, there is a poor alignment of goals to actions. In his seminal work *Diffusion of Innovation*, Everett Rogers defines diffusion as "the process by which an innovation is communicated through certain channels over time among the members of a social system."[38] Rogers's definition contains four elements that are present in the diffusion process. They include: 1) innovations, 2) communication channels, 3) time and 4) members of a social system. For purposes of this discussion, communication channels (i.e., how information is presented and distributed) and time (the decision process and rate of adoption) are crucial to whether an organization's R&D team are fully engaged and sense the urgency in planning for change.

Risk-Averse Culture

Current businesses are understood and well established. A variety of commitments have been made in terms of people, manufacturing and marketing, production schedules, and contracts going forward. Such commitments to ongoing business activities have an established trajectory. There is a clear pattern of success that translates into customer clients, sales volume and public (and business) awareness for the work that has been accomplished to date. At the same time, forward-thinking companies recognize the need to develop new business opportunities. Playing it safe poses its own unique hazards. Even well-managed companies can suddenly find themselves outflanked by changing market conditions and/or the introduction of a substitute technology or service. Consider, for example, the impact that the Apple iPod had on the Sony Walkman portable music CD player.

Sony

Sony's co-founder Akio Morita was the quintessential marketer. He understood how to translate new and interesting technologies into usable products. Nowhere was this more evident than in the development of the original Sony Walkman portable music player in 1979. The Walkman created a totally new market for portable music systems. By combining the features of mobility and privacy, the Walkman contributed to an important change in consumer lifestyle. Throughout the decades of the 1980s and 1990s, portable music systems became commonplace and were found in places ranging from major urban subways to health and recreation facilities worldwide. For Sony, the Walkman was just one of many examples for a company internationally recognized for its innovation prowess. Inside Japan, Sony was considered the coolest company to work for.

And yet even Sony is not invulnerable to the innovator's dilemma and the problems associated with innovation failure. As illegal music downloads exploded in popularity in the late 1990s, Sony, like the rest of the music industry, was unable or unwilling to adapt to the changing technology environment. Sony's music and film divisions wanted to protect their intellectual property software from being stolen. Equally important, Sony's electronics division had a long history of building proprietary technology and didn't want to build devices that played MP3 music software. More specifically, Sony didn't want to cede its commitment to existing audio technology, most notably the Sony Walkman portable music CD player. After all, the Walkman had proven be a highly successful technology in the past and a steady source of revenue over the years (i.e., the innovator's dilemma).

Even as music fans illegally downloaded songs by the thousands onto their PCs, Sony was slow to react. Instead of addressing the MP3 market, Sony chose instead to build devices around its own MiniDisc technology. The introduction of the Apple iPod in 2001 was a watershed event in digital music.[39] The combination of the Apple iPod and the company's iTunes music store in April 2004 proved to be the quintessential example of a disruptive technology. It redefined the music industry. The irony, of course, was that Sony; arguably one of the most innovative media companies in the world, knew about the research and development work being done at Apple in the area of MP3 storage technology. Yet Sony was not prepared to move quickly enough to change strategy and preserve its control over the portable music market.

In sum, successful businesses (with an established customer base) find it hard to change. There are no guarantees of success when it comes to new project ventures. Not surprisingly, companies can become risk averse to change. As Rosabeth Moss Kanter writes, whenever something new is created, there is always going to be a high degree of uncertainty tied into the project. No one knows for certain what resources will be required, how the project will turn out and how it will be received:

> the newer it is, the more likely that there will be little or no precedent and no experience base to use to make useful forecasts. Timetables may prove unrealistic. Anticipated costs may be overrun. Furthermore, the final form of the product may look different from what was originally envisioned.[40]

Discussion

Lessons Learned—Strategies Going Forward

Strong innovative companies start by changing the culture of the organization. As Robert Hoff notes, "inspiration is fine, but above all, innovation is really a management process."[41] There are no shortcuts when it comes to innovation. Putting the right structures, people and processes in place should occur as a matter of course—not as an exception.[42] Not every innovative solution has to be a blockbuster. Sometimes, small incremental changes in the area of process innovation can make a big difference to an organization's bottom line. The Japanese auto industry uses the term *kaizen* to describe the principle of continuous improvement. Forward-thinking companies go beyond simply supporting research and development programs to creating a culture where everyone has a role to play in making the organization better.

Developing a Culture of Innovation

Companies, like people, can become easily satisfied with organizational routines that stand in the way of being innovative. Instead of blue ocean thinking, managers become preoccupied with fine-tuning and making slight adjustments to an existing product line rather than preparing for the future. Forward-thinking companies must be able to deconstruct management orthodoxy. Respect for past success is important. However, too much reliance on the past can make you risk averse. Instead, forward-thinking companies must create a culture of innovation, where experimentation and development mistakes are all part of the process of testing new boundaries. Accordingly, the CEO sets the tone by putting his/her full weight behind the need to be creative and make a difference in the overall performance of the organization.

The Value of Partnerships and Collaboration

One of the most important lessons executives have learned about innovation is that companies can no longer afford to go it alone. The traditional model of R&D is to create and manufacture products exclusively within the confines of one's own company. The basic logic is, if you want something done right, you've got to do it yourself. Researcher Henry Chesbrough challenges that basic assumption and makes the argument that the not-invented-here approach is no longer sustainable. Clearly, companies like Sony and Philips recognized this some years ago when they co-developed the compact disc.

Instead, companies should be drawing business partners and suppliers into so called *innovation networks*. According to Chesbrough, the idea behind open innovation is that there are simply too many good ideas available externally and held by people who don't work for your company. They simply cannot be ignored:

> Even the best companies with the most extensive internal capabilities have to take into consideration external knowledge and ideas when they think about innovation. So good ideas can come from outside as well as inside. And they can go to market not only inside your company, but also outside, through others.[43]

Open Communication and Keeping Everyone Involved

Once a major start-up project is underway, other division heads can sometimes become resentful that needed resources are being diverted from businesses with an established track record to support what appears to be a speculative venture. Moreover, they perceive privileges and rewards are being given to the new project start-up that exceed what other established businesses are getting at the present time. Over time, there evolves an unspoken culture clash between those who are free to experiment (and have all the fun) and those who make all the money by providing reliability and growth.[44]

Innovators and start-up projects should not work in isolation if they want their ideas to catch on. There has to be a level of buy-in and support that cuts across divisional lines. Open communication will go a long way in building a coalition of supporters who will provide project support both during formal meetings and behind the scenes. There should never be a perception that the new start-up group is off doing its own thing. Rather, everyone should have a stake in the outcome.[45]

Keep the Project Review Process Flexible

Another important lesson is that overly tight performance review measures can strangle innovation. There is a tendency among well-established companies to apply the same performance review metrics to new project start-ups, thus weakening the venture before it has the opportunity to get some traction. Too much emphasis on traditional performance metrics like return on investment (ROI) or risk tolerance at the early stage of development can kill a good project before it gets off the ground. Traditional demographic research (and market segmentation data) reflects information that is currently available, but it cannot accurately forecast what customers want and would be willing to pay for.[46] It cannot fully consider blue ocean opportunities, since there is no basis of analysis and comparison. In sum, strict controls have their place, but flexibility goes a long way in ensuring that promising projects have the possibility to see the light of day.

The Value of Customer and New Employee Insights

What is the value of one good idea or suggestion? No one knows better than one's customers what they want in terms of improved product or service performance. Taking time to understand the day-to-day behavior activities of one's customers in their daily work routine can go a long way in helping to understand the kinds of special features and benefits that may be of interest to them in the long term. The principle of engaging one's customers goes beyond the focus group to the point where the sales associate and researcher try to determine the essential tools (and habits) that drive the customer's work-day engine. Other important insights can come from both mid-level and new employees who may have been with the organization less than two years. An invitation for them to attend an upper-level staff meeting can sometimes provide a fresh perspective on the challenges faced by the organization. They may provide some new and innovative solutions to a problem.

The lessons of business history have taught us that there is no such thing as a static market. There are no guarantees of continued business success for a company in a particular market segment. Over time, tastes, preference and technology change. Innovative companies keep abreast of such changes, anticipate them and make the necessary adjustments in strategy and new product development. The irony, of course, is that even the best-managed companies are susceptible to innovation failure. Specifically, a company's very strengths and ongoing success can lay the groundwork for its eventual decline. This occurs at a time when the company is realizing some of its highest success (i.e., the innovator's dilemma). There is also the element of risk when attempting to develop a new product or service. The solution, therefore, is to develop a culture of innovation where risk and experimentation are supported. Failure is also part of the process. If innovation can be likened to a sports team, there is no such thing as a perfect 30–0 season. Rather, innovation is about putting together a winning record (perhaps 26–4) and making innovation (like games) a sustainable, repeatable process.

NOTES

1 TELECOMMUNICATIONS ECONOMICS I: PRINCIPLES OF MARKET STRUCTURE, SUPPLY AND PRICING AND BUSINESS CONDUCT

1 Joseph Turow, *Media Systems in Society* (New York: Longman, 1992), 10.
2 John M. Lavine and Daniel B. Wackman, *Managing Media Organizations* (New York: Longman, 1988), 14–15.
3 Throughout parts of Europe and Asia, broadcasting, telephone and mail delivery are often combined under the auspices of a central government organizing entity referred to as a ministry of post, telephone and telegraph (PT&T).
4 The question is sometimes raised: what about cable television? Cable television has not traditionally performed as a common carrier given the fact that one does not typically lease their facilities. Rather, a cable operator packages entertainment and information content for a subscription fee. That said, however, the role of cable operators is beginning to change. As we will see in later chapters, cable operators are becoming increasingly involved in the delivery of telephone services.
5 Robert Picard, *Media Economics: Concepts and Issues* (Newbury Park, CA: Sage, 1989), 8, 14.
6 Steven Wildman, "Paradigms and Analytical Frameworks in Modern Economics," in A. Albarran, M. Wirth and S. Chan-Olmsted (eds.), *Handbook of Media Management and Economics* (Mahwah, NJ: Lawrence Erlbaum, 2005), 72–76.
7 David Aaker, *Managing Brand Equity: Capitalizing on the Value of a Brand Name* (New York: Free Press, 1991).
8 Alan Albarran, *Media Economics*, 2nd ed. (Ames, IA: Iowa State University Press, 2002), 31.
9 Richard Gershon, *The Transnational Media Corporation: Global Messages and Free Market Competition* (Mahwah, NJ: Lawrence Erlbaum, 1997), 203.
10 Albarran, *Media Economics*, 17–19.
11 Eric W. Rothenbuhler and John M. Streck, "The Economics of the Music Industry," in A. Alexander, J. Owers and R. Carveth (eds.), *Media Economics*, 2nd. ed. (Mahwah, NJ: Lawrence Erlbaum, 1998), 213–214.
12 Thomas F. Baldwin, D. Steven McVoy and Charles Steinfield, *Convergence: Integrating Media, Information and Communication* (Thousand Oaks, CA: Sage, 1996), 128–131.
13 International Olympic Committee, "Evolution of Broadcast Rights Fees," Available at: http://www.olympic.org/uk/organisation/facts/revenue/broadcast_uk.asp (retrieved August 17, 2005).

14 Chris Isidore, "Got to Have Friends," *CNN Money*, January 21, 2004, Available at: http://money.cnn.com/2004/01/20/news/companies/last_friends/ (retrieved August 18, 2005).

15 "Free market economics" is a term generally used to describe a market in which the economic forces of supply and demand have the full opportunity to alter the price for a product or service. Such competition is completely unfettered.

16 J. Juran, *Juran on Planning for Quality* (Cambridge, MA: Productivity Press, 1988).

17 B. Brocka and S. Brocka, *Quality Management: Implementing the Best Ideas of the Masters* (Burr Ridge, IL: Irwin, 1992).

18 G.T. Fairhurst, "Echoes of the Vision: When the Rest of the Organization Talks Total Quality," *Management Communication Quarterly*, 6 (1993): 334.

19 Thomas Peters and Robert Waterman, *In Search of Excellence: Lessons from America's Best Run Companies* (New York: Harper & Row, 1982).

20 Jim Collins, *Good to Great* (New York: HarperCollins, 2001).

21 Ibid., 13.

22 Ibid., 164–188.

23 Bill Capodagli and Lynne Jackson, *The Disney Way: Harnessing the Management Secrets of Disney in Your Company* (New York: McGraw-Hill, 1999), 36–37.

24 Lorri L. McGough, "Definitive Disney," *Association Management* (March 1992): 87–88.

25 Cable Television Report and Order, 52 F.C.C., F.2d 1 (1975).

26 Home Box Office v. F.C.C., F.2d 9 (1978).

27 Home Box Office v. F.C.C., F.2d 9 (1978) at 28.

28 Richard Gershon, "Pay Cable Television: A Regulatory History," *Communications and the Law*, 12(2) (June 1990): 18–20.

29 The U.S. Congress passed the Sherman Antitrust Act in 1890. This law has two main parts. The first prohibits "every contract, combination in the form of a trust or otherwise, or conspiracy" that limits competition. The second part of the law prohibits monopolization (or attempts to monopolize), specifying penalties for violators. Moreover, people or firms injured by a violation of the Sherman Act are allowed to sue for damages.

30 By 1890, the Standard Oil Trust had become the foremost petroleum refining and marketing combination in the U.S. Its monopoly over the industry could not be disputed. Standard Oil controlled 90 percent of the U.S. market for refined petroleum products.

31 The Clayton Act grew out of the well-publicized Standard Oil and American Tobacco cases of 1911. The Clayton Act was passed in 1914 in order to address four types of potentially anticompetitive business practices: price discrimination, mergers, exclusive dealing and tying arrangements and interlocking directorates.

32 In 1897, the U.S. Supreme Court in U.S. v. Trans-Missouri Freight Association established the principle that collusive agreements among competing firms to restrict output and fix prices were illegal and that direct evidence is sufficient to determine illegality. Since then, the Supreme Court has consistently ruled that collusive agreements among competing firms to restrict output and fix prices are illegal in principle and not just applicable to a specific case. See U.S. v. Trans-Missouri Freight Association, 166 U.S. 290 (1897).

33 Organization of the Petroleum Exporting Countries, Available at: http://www.opec.org/home/ (retrieved August 10, 2005).

34 Dinkar Ayilavarapu, "OPEC in the Line of Fire," *Asia Times*, October 1, 2002, Available at: http://www.globalpolicy.org/security/oil/2003/0128opec.htm (retrieved August 10, 2005).

35 "Going after Gates," *Business Week*, November 3, 1997, 34.
36 United States District Court for the District of Columbia v. Microsoft, Inc., Civil Action No. 98–1232 (TPJ).
37 "Microsoft Enjoys Monopoly Power," *Time*, November 15, 1999, 61–65.

2 TELECOMMUNICATIONS AND STRATEGIC PLANNING

1   Richard Gershon, "Issues in Transnational Media Management," in A. Albarran, M. Wirth and S. Chan-Olmsted (eds.), *Handbook of Media Management and Economics* (Mahwah, NJ: Lawrence Erlbaum, 2005), 203–228.
2   Richard Gershon, *Telecommunications Management: Industry Structures and Planning Strategies* (Mahwah, NJ: Lawrence Erlbaum, 2001), 305.
3   Richard Gershon, "The Transnational Media Corporation: Environmental Scanning and Strategy Formulation," *Journal of Media Economics*, 13(2) (2000): 81–101.
4   Thomas Wheelen and J. David Hunger, *Strategic Management and Business Policy* (Reading, MA: Addison Wesley Longman, 1998), 52–67.
5   Henry Mintzberg, "Planning on the Left Side and Managing on the Right," *Harvard Business Review*, July–August (1976): 56.
6   There are numerous strategic planning models, but most can be reduced to the essential elements found in the strengths, weaknesses, opportunities and threats (SWOT) model as a way to illustrate the environmental scanning process. The SWOT model is part of the design school of strategic management that seeks to attain a match between an organization's external opportunities and internal capabilities.
7   Telecommunications Act of 1996 (P.L. No. 104, 110 Stat. 56), section 204 (codified at 47 U.S.C. § 309(k)(1)).
8   Barbara Cherry, "Regulatory and Political Influences on Media Management and Economics," in A. Albarran, M. Wirth and S. Chan-Olmsted (eds.), *Handbook of Media Management and Economics* (Mahwah, NJ: Lawrence Erlbaum, 2005), 91–111.
9   Charles Hill, *International Business* (New York: McGraw- Hill, 2000), 278.
10 "RIAA Anti Piracy," Available at: http://www.riaa.com/issues/piracy/default.asp (retrieved September 15, 2005).
11 Ibid.
12 Richard Daft, *Management*, 4th ed. (New York: Harcourt Brace, 1997), 249.
13 Clayton Christensen, *The Innovator's Dilemma* (Boston, MA: Harvard Business School Press, 1997), XV–XVII.
14 "Reinhard Mohn," *The Nation*, June 12, 1989, 810.
15 *Bertelsmann AG 1998 Annual Report*, Available at: http://www.bertelsmann.de/english/ geschber98/ (retrieved September 15, 2005), 3.
16 Terrence Deal and Allan Kennedy, *Corporate Cultures: The Rites and Rituals of Corporate Life* (Reading, MA: Addison Wesley, 1982).
17 Richard Gershon and Tsutomu Kanayama, "The Sony Corporation: A Case Study in Transnational Media Management," *International Journal on Media Management*, 4 (2002): 44–56.
18 A. Morita, M. Shimomura and E. Reingold, *Made in Japan* (New York: E.P. Dutton, 1986).
19 See Lucy Küng, *Strategic Management in the Media* (London: Sage, 2008), 18–24, and Sylvia Chan-Olmsted, *Competitive Strategy for Media Firms* (Mahwah, NJ: Lawrence Erlbaum, 2006), 24.
20 Michael Porter, *On Competition* (Boston, MA: Harvard Business School Press, 1998).

21 John Nathan, *Sony: The Private Life* (Boston, MA: Houghton Mifflin, 1999).
22 "Jack Welch on being number one or two," Available at: http://www.oligopolywatch.com/2003/11/08.html (retrieved December 21, 2005).
23 Michael E. Porter, *Competitive Advantage: Creating and Sustaining Superior Performance* (New York: Free Press, 1985).
24 Ibid., 12–16.
25 Larry Bossidy and Ram Charran, *Execution: The Discipline of Getting Things Done* (New York: Crown Business, 2002), 22.
26 Peter Drucker, *The Practice of Management* (New York: Harper & Row, 1954).
27 Jim Collins, *Good to Great* (New York: Harper Business, 2001), 41–45.
28 Ibid., 54.
29 Ibid., 88.
30 "In the Zone," *Business Week*, October 17, 2005, 70.
31 "The Entertainment Glut," *Business Week*, February 16, 1998, 88–90.

3 BROADCAST TELEVISION

1 Motion Picture Association, *U.S. Entertainment Industry: 2006 Market Statistics* (Encino, CA: MPA Worldwide Market Research, 2006), 35. Available at: http://www.mpaa.org/USEntertainmentIndustryMarketStats.pdf (retrieved August 8, 2007).
2 Ibid., 27.
3 Ibid., 41.
4 John Vivian, *The Media of Mass Communication*, 7th ed. (Boston, MA: Pearson, 2006), 182.
5 Bruce Owen and Steven Wildman, *Video Economics* (Boston, MA: Harvard University Press, 1992), 3–4.
6 Syndication is the licensing of a television or film product by a program distributor to an affiliate or independent broadcast station on an exclusive basis, that is, one station per market.
7 "NBC Sells $900 Mln of Ads for Turin Olympics, Forecasts Profit," Available at: http://quote.bloomberg.com/apps/news?pid=10000103&sid=aRL3V9ZiTr Ns&refer=news_index (retrieved February 13, 2006).
8 Owen and Wildman, *Video Economics*, 26–27.
9 Discussions concerning the establishment of noncommercial "educational" radio (and later television) date back to early developments in radio communication starting in 1925. In 1967, the Carnegie Commission on Educational Television issued a report calling for the establishment of a corporation for public television. As Head and Sterling point out, "the commission used the word public rather than educational to disassociate itself from what many regarded as the somber and static image projected by the existing educational television services." See Sydney W. Head and Christopher H. Sterling, *Broadcasting in America*, 6th ed. (Boston, MA: Houghton Mifflin, 1990) 353–354.
10 Ibid., 256.
11 "The Public Broadcasting Service: An Overview," Available at: http://www.pbs.org/aboutpbs/aboutpbs_corp.html (retrieved August 18, 2007).
12 George Rodman, *Mass Media in a Changing World* (Boston, MA: McGraw-Hill, 2006), 274–275.
13 "The Public Broadcasting Service: An Overview."
14 Rodman, *Mass Media in a Changing World*, 416–417.
15 "Special Report: 100 Leading National Advertisers Supplement," *Advertising Age*, Available at: http://www.adage.com/images/random/lna2005.pdf (retrieved February 10, 2006).

16 Susan Tyler Eastman and Douglas Ferguson, *Media Programming: Strategies and Practices*, 8th ed. (Boston, MA: Thomson Wadsworth, 2009), 3.

17 This material is based on a series of presentations given at the 2007 Business and Diversity Conference, sponsored by the Walt Disney Company in cooperation with the International Radio and Television Society, Burbank, CA, August 14–16, 2007.

18 John von Sooten, "Domestic Syndication," in Susan Tyler Eastman (ed.), *Broadcast/Cable Programming* (Belmont, CA: Wadsworth Publishing, 1993), 86–88.

19 Raymond Carroll and Donald Davis, *Electronic Media Programming* (New York: McGraw-Hill, 1993), 18.

20 Ibid., 18.

21 Barry Sherman, *Telecommunications Management* (New York: McGraw-Hill, 1995), 389.

22 Why sampling works: A properly selected sample represents the larger whole (or universe). The laws of chance or probability predict that a random selection of a small sample (usually households) from a large population will make that sample representative—within a predictable degree of accuracy of the entire population. In addition, major characteristics of the population as a whole will appear in such a sample in about the same proportion as their distribution throughout the entire population.

23 Daniel Kimmel, *The Fourth Network* (Chicago, IL: Ivan R. Dee, 2004).

24 "Ten Years from Wannabe to Big Four," *Broadcasting and Cable*, September 22, 1997, 37.

25 "$3B Deal Puts TV Guide in Murdoch Fold," *Boston Herald*, August 8, 1988.

26 "Murdoch, Turner: A Study in Contrasts," *Washington Post*, September 7, 1986, D3–D5.

27 William Shawcross, *Murdoch* (New York: Simon & Schuster, 1992), 62–76.

28 Home Box Office v. Federal Communication Commission, 567 F. 2d (D.C. Cir. 1977). Cert. denied, 434 U.S. 829 (1977).

29 Ithiel de Sola Pool, *Technologies of Freedom* (Cambridge, MA: Harvard University Press, 1983), 50.

30 A 60-minute television program takes 8 to 20 minutes to download using a high-speed connection. In contrast, it usually takes ten months to a year for a completed television season to become available on DVD for rental or purchase.

31 "Apple Releases Video iPod, May Change TV Rules," Available at: http://www.usatoday.com/tech/products/gear/computing/2005-10-12-imac-remote_x.htm (retrieved May 13, 2006).

32 "PVR," Available at: http://www.webopedia.com/TERM/P/PVR.html (retrieved May 12, 2006).

33 Dolby Digital, formerly known as AC-3, is a digital audio coding technique that reduces the amount of data needed to produce high-quality sound. Dolby Digital takes advantage of how the human ear processes sound. By reducing or masking noise, it reduces the amount of data to one-tenth of the data on a compact disk (CD).

34 Plasma televisions contain a mixture of neon and xenon gas that fills the small space between two sheets of glass. When this mixture is stimulated by electrical current, the process creates a vibrant picture. LCD screens tend to be smaller than plasma and projection HDTVs. They are thin (about 2 inches thick) and lightweight, so they can be hung on a wall. Their display is bright and crisp, and they have a wide viewing angle.

35 WIMAX (Worldwide Interoperability for Microwave Access) provides wireless capability that enables users to connect to the Internet. It has a much broader

range, and can connect entire neighborhoods, regions or cities with wireless Internet.

36 "The Entertainment Glut," *Business Week*, February 16, 1998, 90.

4 CABLE TELEVISION

1 Another important community was Lansford, Pennsylvania, located about 70 miles northwest from Philadelphia. In the late 1940s, television reception from the three major networks was all but nonexistent. A radio and TV dealer by the name of Bob Tarlton helped install the first set of twin lead wires from neighboring Summit Hill into Lansford, thus making it possible for several of the local bars and apartments to benefit from the clearer reception. Tarlton saw the business potential of a community antenna TV system. Shortly thereafter, he put together a group of local investors and founded Panther Valley Television. See Patrick Parsons and Robert Frieden, *The Cable and Satellite Television Industries* (Boston, MA: Allyn & Bacon, 1998), 30–31.

2 Brian Lockman and Dan Sarvey, *Pioneers of Cable Television* (Jefferson, NC: McFarland & Company, 2005), 9–24.

3 Patrick Parsons, "Two Tales of a City," *Journal of Broadcasting and Electronic Media*, 40(3) (1996): 354–365.

4 Parsons and Frieden, *The Cable and Satellite Television Industries*, 29.

5 The Service Electric Cable TV system was owned by John Walson, the same cable entrepreneur who had started the first system in Mahanoy City, Pennsylvania. At the time, he was the largest cable operator in the state of Pennsylvania and the twelfth largest in the U.S. See Lockman and Sarvey, *Pioneers of Cable Television*, 21.

6 Home Box Office, Inc., *HBO: The First Ten Years* (New York: HBO Inc., 1982), 12.

7 Richard Gershon, *Telecommunications Management: Industry Structures and Planning Strategies* (Mahwah, NJ: Lawrence Erlbaum & Associates, 2001), 60.

8 Richard Gershon and Michael Wirth, "Home Box Office: The Emergence of Pay Cable Television," in Robert Picard (ed.), *The Cable Networks Handbook* (Riverside, CA: Carpelan Press, 1993), 114–122.

9 Paul Kagan, Remarks contained in the *Pay TV Guide: Editor's Pay TV Handbook* (New York: HBO, 1984).

10 CableLabs, "Cable System Primer," Available at: http://www.cablelabs.com/news/primers/cable_system_primer.html (retrieved April 10, 2008).

11 Retransmission consent is an option granted to U.S. television stations as part of the Cable Communications Policy Act of 1992, which grants local (or area) television stations "must carry" rights (i.e., the cable operator must carry the station on the system) or they may elect cash payment (or the equivalent). Typically, small stations like a religious channel will elect must-carry status knowing that the station will be given a guaranteed slot on the cable system. In contrast, a television station will instead elect must-carry payment (or the equivalent) knowing that the station is too high-profile not to be carried on the cable system. The cable operator, however, can refuse to pay the said broadcast station. In lieu of cash compensation, the broadcast station or parent company (e.g., Viacom, Disney, etc.) may work out an agreement whereby the cable operator agrees to carry additional forms of broadcast or cable television programming on the system.

12 Cable Communications Policy Act of 1984, 47 U.S.C. (1984).

13 National Cable and Telecommunications Association, "Industry Statistics," Available at: http://www.ncta.com/ContentView.aspx?contentId=66 (retrieved September 5, 2007).

NOTES

14 The years 1950 and 1951 saw the advent of two types of pay television experiments, including Skiatron's "Subscribervision" and International Telemeter's "Telemeter" system. The Subscribervision system required the use of plastic punch cards, which were purchased in advance of the showing. The viewer would simply insert the plastic punch cards into the television set. This activated a decoder device that would translate the over-the-air signal into a usable picture. The Skiatron system was first tested by WOR-TV in New York City in 1950. The Telemeter system was more in keeping with a PPV approach—a difficult marketing concept even then. The Telemeter system required the user to insert money into a coin box that was attached to the television set. Station KTLA-TV in Los Angeles served as the first test site. See Gershon, "Pay Cable Television, A Regulatory History," 4–5.

15 National Cable and Telecommunications Association, "Premium Cable Units," Available at: http://www.ncta.com/ContentView.aspx?contentId=67 (retrieved September 10, 2007).

16 Plasma televisions contain a mixture of neon and xenon gas that fills the small space between two sheets of glass. When this mixture is stimulated by electrical current, the process creates a vibrant picture. LCD screens tend to be smaller than plasma and projection HDTVs. They are thin (about 2 inches thick) and lightweight, so they can be hung on a wall. Their display is bright and crisp and, like plasma, they have a wide viewing angle.

17 Leslie Ellis, *Definitive Broadband: Next Generation* (New York: Lundwall Communications, 2005), 26.

18 Unlike the situation with DSL service, cable modem subscribers share a connection. This presents a security issue, as well as speed issues, since the bandwidth is shared between a number of users.

19 National Cable and Telecommunications Association, "Cable Modem Penetration Rate," Available at: http://www.ncta.com/images/BbandAvail_Web.gif (retrieved March 17, 2006).

20 VOIP converts the voice signal from the user's telephone set into a digital signal that is sent over the Internet. The signal is reconverted into a regular voice signal at the back end, thus making it possible to use a regular telephone set. The use of IP as a generic platform to support both voice and data communication offers up some important price advantages when compared to traditional telephony.

21 "About QVC," Available at: http://www.qvc.com/asp/frameset.asp?nest=/main-hqwel.html&dd=/nav/navhqwel.html&cm_re=HP-_-INFO-_-COMMUNITY FORUM&qic (retrieved May 4, 2006).

22 Cable Communications Policy Act of 1984, 47 U.S.C. § 622(b) 1984.

23 Nicholas Miller, "The 1992 Cable Act: New Rules for Franchise Regulation and Renewal," presentation given at the NATOA 1993 Training Seminar, Covington, KY, April 26–27, 1993.

24 Ibid.

25 Robert M. Ogles, "Music Television (MTV)," in Robert Picard (ed.), *The Cable Networks Handbook* (Riverside, CA: Carpelan Press, 1993), 137–143.

26 Megan Mullen, *The Rise of Cable Programming in the United States* (Austin, TX: University of Texas Press, 2003), 172–173.

27 "Sumner's Gemstone," *Forbes*, February 21, 2000, 105–111.

28 Ibid.

29 Tom Lowry, "Can MTV Stay Cool?," *Business Week*, February 20, 2006, 50–60.

30 "Barton Voices Support for National Cable Franchising," Available at: http://www.tvweek.com/news.cms?newsId=9463 (retrieved February 28, 2006).

31 "Barton Gives Bells 10 Years," http://www.informationweek.com/internet/showArticle.jhtml?articleID=179103510&pgno=2 (retrieved February 28, 2006).
32 John Eggerton, "House Would Grant 10-Year National Franchise," Available at: http://www.broadcastingcable.com/article/CA6319469.html?display=Breaking+News (retrieved March 27, 2006).
33 Ibid.
34 Leslie Cauley, "How We Pay for Cable May Be about to Change," *USA Today*, Available at: http://www.usatoday.com/money/industries/technology/2006-03-01-ala-carte-cable_x.htm (retrieved March 27, 2006).
35 Leslie Cauley, "FCC Puts A La Carte on the Menu," *USA Today*, September 11, 2007, 1B.
36 "FCC 'A La Carte' Report Says Consumers' Cable Bills Could Be Cut by 13 Percent," US Newswire, Available at: http://releases.usnewswire.com/GetRelease.asp?id=60771 (retrieved February 2, 2006).
37 Federal Communications Commission, "12th Annual Report to Congress on Video Competition," Available at: http://hraunfoss.fcc.gov/edocs_public/attachmatch/DOC-263763A1.pdf (retrieved May 5, 2006).
38 Leslie Cauley, "Telecoms' Quest for Customers Leads to IPTV," *USA Today*, Available at: http://www.usatoday.com/money/industries/telecom/2005-08-16-telecoms-iptv_x.htm (retrieved April 24, 2006).
39 Brian Roberts, "Comments on the Future of the Cable Television Industry," given at the opening plenary session of the 2006 NCTA Cable Industry Conference, Atlanta, GA, April 10, 2006.
40 Section 304, Telecommunications Act of 1996.
41 Cable companies are required to separate two key features of a standard set-top box: navigation and security. In principle, any navigation system (i.e., a set-top box that tunes and displays a cable feed) should be able to interface with any cable provider's security system.
42 "FCC: Dual Carriage Will Last Three Years," Available at: http://www.multichannel.com/index.asp?layout=article&articleid=CA6478706 (retrieved September 16, 2007).
43 Rouzbeh Yassini, *Planet Broadband* (Indianapolis, IN: Cisco Press, 2004), 4.

5 TELECOMMUNICATIONS ECONOMICS II: PRINCIPLES OF PUBLIC UTILITIES, COMMON CARRIERS AND INFORMATION CARRIAGE

1 Martin Bronfenbrenner, Werner Sichel and Wayland Gardner, *Economics*, 3rd ed. (Boston, MA: Houghton Mifflin, 1990), 600, 833.
2 See Munn v. Illinois, 94 U.S. 113 (1877). The U.S. Supreme Court upheld regulation of prices charged by grain elevators.
3 see City of Los Angeles v. Preferred Communications, Inc., 476 U.S. 488, 12 Media L. Rep. 2244 (1986).
4 See United States v. American Telephone & Telegraph Company, Western Electric Company, Inc., and Bell Telephone Laboratories, Inc., U.S. District Court (D.C. Cir. 1974), Civil Action No. 74–1698, Civil Action No. 82–0192 ("Modification of Final Judgment," 1982).
5 Ithiel de Sola Pool, *Technologies of Freedom* (Cambridge, MA: Harvard, 1983), 75–107.
6 Robert Loube, "Price Cap Regulation: Problems and Solutions," *Land Economics*, 71(3) (1995): 286–298.

7 Thomas Friedman, *The Lexus and the Olive Tree* (New York: Farrar, Straus & Giroux, 1999).

8 Ira W. Lieberman, "Privatization: The Theme of the 1990's," *Columbia Journal of World Business*, 28(1) (1993): 10–11.

9 Trudy Bell, "The Decision to Divest: Incredible or Inevitable," *IEEE Spectrum*, November 1985, 46.

10 Robert Britt Horwitz, "For Whom the Bell Tolls: Causes and Consequences of the AT&T Divestiture," *Critical Studies in Mass Communication*, 3 (1986): 119–154.

11 Sony Corporation, Inc., *Genryu: Sony Challenges 1946–1968* (Tokyo, Japan: Sony Inc., 1988).

12 Bell, "The Decision to Divest: Incredible or Inevitable," 46–47.

13 The FCC undertook a review of its microwave policy towards the private use of microwave facilities. Because the decision involved the allocation of frequencies above 890 MHz, the proceeding became known as the Above 890 decision. See In the Matter of Allocation of Frequencies in the Bands above 890 Mc, 27 F.C.C. 359 (1959), recon. denied, 29 F.C.C. 825 (1960).

14 Kevin Wilson, *Deregulating Telecommunications* (Boston, MA: Rowman & Littlefield, 2000).

15 Daniel Gross, "William McGowan and MCI: A New World of Telecommunications," *Forbes: Greatest Business Stories of All Time* (New York: John Wiley & Sons, 1996), 284–297.

16 Gerald Brock, *The Telecommunications Industry: The Dynamics of Market Structure* (Cambridge, MA: Harvard University Press, 1981), 218.

17 Starting in 1913, the U.S. Justice Department initiated the first phase of an antitrust lawsuit against AT&T resulting from AT&T's attempt to acquire rival telegraph carrier Western Union. After some tense negotiation, AT&T and the Justice Department reached an out-of court settlement known as the Kingsbury Agreement. The agreement established AT&T as a government-sanctioned monopoly. In return, AT&T agreed to divest its controlling interest in Western Union and allow non-competing independent telephone companies to interconnect with the AT&T long-distance network.

18 See In Re Applications of Microwave Communications Inc., 18 FCC 2d 953 (1969).

19 Bro Uttal, "How to Deregulate AT&T," *Fortune*, November 30, 1981, 73.

20 In the late 1970s, the FCC set out to examine this issue by initiating a series of three Computer inquiries that would examine the difference between basic transmission service and enhanced network services. In 1980, the FCC issued its now famous Computer II Decision, which opened the way for new and enhanced telecommunication products and services.

21 Bell, "The Decision to Divest: Incredible or Inevitable," 46–47.

22 Christopher Sterling, Phyllis Bernt and Martin Weiss, *Shaping American Telecommunications* (Mahwah, NJ: Lawrence Erlbaum, 2006), 145–177.

23 Charles L. Brown, "Recasting the Bell System," *Columbia Journal of World Business*, 18(1) (1983): 5–7.

24 "Did It Make Sense to Break Up AT&T?," *Business Week*, December 4, 1984, 86–87.

25 See United States v. American Telephone & Telegraph Company, Western Electric Company, Inc., and Bell Telephone Laboratories, Inc., U.S. District Court (D.C. Cir. 1974), Civil Action No. 74–1698, Civil Action No. 82–0192 ("Modification of Final Judgment," 1982).

26 "Did It Make Sense to Break Up AT&T?," 86–87.

27 Sterling, Bernt and Weiss, *Shaping American Telecommunications*, 157–159.

6 TELEPHONY

1   In a standard telephone, the transmitter contains a sensitive diaphragm which will either compress or expand, causing resistance to the current to increase or decrease. Such variations in resistance cause modulation of the electric current. The modulated current (which corresponds to the human voice) is then transmitted to the receiver at the other end. See Regis Bates and Donald Gregory, *Voice and Data Communications Handbook* (New York: McGraw-Hill, 1998), 56–57.

2   The receiver is composed of a permanent magnet (and wire coils wrapped around it) and a diaphragm. The permanent magnet exerts a constant pull on the diaphragm, thus keeping it in a stationary position. The wire coil is continuously reacting to the modulated current coming from the transmitter. It creates a fluctuating magnetic field. This constant motion (or vibration) of the diaphragm is responsible for changing the electrical waves back into sound waves.

3   Bates and Gregory, *Voice and Data Communications Handbook*, 55–57.

4   Steven Shepard, *Telecom Crash Course* (New York: McGraw-Hill, 2002), 145.

5   The advantages of a star topology include: fault isolation and the ease of bypassing and repairing faulty terminals. The disadvantage is that the star topology requires more cable than other topologies in order to interconnect all stations.

6   Nortel Corporation, *Telephony 101: An Introduction to the Public Network* (Mississaugua, Ontario: Northern Telecom, 1994), 39–40.

7   David Atkin and Tuen-yu-Lau, "Local and Long Distance Telephony," in August Grant and Jennifer Meadows (eds.), *Communication Technology Update*, 8th ed. (Boston, MA: Focal Press, 2002), 243.

8   Under the terms of the MFJ, equal access was designed to ensure that all long-distance carriers were to be treated equally in terms of numbering plans, quality of service and price. As an example, consumers wishing to select MCI as their IXC should not have to dial additional numbers to get MCI as a long-distance carrier. Nor should MCI pay more or less than AT&T in order to interface with the LEC. Equal access is accomplished through a software program in the switching system called "Dial 1." A consumer should be able to access the designated IXC by dialing the number 1 followed by the called party's ten-digit telephone number. The designated IXC and access code are preprogrammed into the LEC's main switch for purposes of direct distance dialing.

9   Douglas Sicker, "The End of Federalism in Telecommunication Regulations?," *Northwestern Journal of Technology and Intellectual Property*, 3(2) (2005), Available at: http://www.law.northwestern.edu/journals/njtip/v3/n2/3/.

10 The basic digital circuit in the PSTN is a 64-kilobits-per-second channel, originally designed by Bell Labs, called a "DS0" or Digital Signal 0. To carry a typical phone call from a calling party to a called party, the audio sound is digitized at an 0 Khz sample rate using 8-bit pulse code modulation. The call is then transmitted from one end to another via telephone exchanges. The call is switched using the SS7 signaling protocol between the telephone exchanges.

11 P.J. Louis, *Telecommunications Internetworking* (New York: McGraw-Hill, 2000), 132.

12 Ibid.

13 The SS7 protocols were developed by AT&T starting in 1975 and adopted as a worldwide standard by the ITU in 1981. SS7 was designed to replace Signaling

System No. 5 and Signaling System No. 6, both of which used in-band signaling methods. See Guy Redmill, "An Introduction to SS7," Available at: http://www.c7.com/ss7/whitepapers/brooktrout_into_to_ss7.pdf.

14 The problem of bending light around corners was overcome by John Tyndall, a British physicist who in 1870 demonstrated how light could be guided through a bend in a stream of water. The concept would lead to the development of optical fiber in the late 1960s.

15 Light pulses move easily down the fiber optic line because of a principle known as total internal reflection. The principle of total internal reflection states that, when the angle of incidence exceeds a critical value, light cannot get out of the glass; instead, the light bounces back in.

16 It is worth noting that optical fibers do not transmit all wavelengths of light with the same efficiency. The attenuation of light signals is much higher for visible light (wavelengths of 400–700 nm) than for light in the near infrared region (wavelengths from 700 to 1,600 nm).

17 Optical fiber size is measured in terms of the diameter of both the core and cladding denoted in microns (um). It is expressed as a ratio between the core and the cladding.

18 While there are several available commercial sizes, the current multimode fiber that is most typically used is a 62.5-micron core with a 125-micron outer cladding (or 62.5/125 um).

19 SONET (Synchronous Optical Network) is a standard for optical transport formulated by the Exchange Carriers Standards Association for the American National Standards Institute (ANSI), which sets industry standards in the U.S. for telecommunications and other industries. SONET defines optical carrier levels and electrically equivalent synchronous transports signals for fiber optic-based transmission. See Uyless Black, *Emerging Communications Technologies*, 2nd ed. (Upper Saddle River, NJ: Prentice Hall, 1997), 251–255.

20 Bates and Gregory, *Voice and Data Communications Handbook*, 879.

21 The DSL Forum is a consortium of approximately 200 leading industry players covering telecommunications, equipment, computing, networking and service provider companies. See DSL Forum, Available at: http://www.dslforum.org/ (retrieved October 3, 2007).

22 VOIP Market to Hit $4 Billion by 2010: Report," Available at: http://www.networkingpipeline.com/showArticle.jhtml?articleID=166400972 (retrieved 12 May 2006).

23 Ibid.

24 Ed Gubbins, "FTTH Con: U.S. FTTH Connections Top 2 Million," Available at: http://telephonyonline.com/ (retrieved October 5, 2007).

25 "FTTH 2007 Europe," Available at: http://www.telecommagazine.com/news-globe/article.asp?HH_ID=AR_2838 (retrieved October 5, 2007).

26 "Barton Voices Support for National Cable Franchising," Available at: http://www.tvweek.com/news.cms?newsId=9463 (retrieved February 28, 2006).

27 "Barton Gives Bells 10 Years," Available at: http://www.informationweek.com/internet/showArticle.jhtml?articleID=179103510&pgno=2 (retrieved February 28, 2006).

28 Texas, Indiana, Kansas and South Carolina already have signed into law a state approval process. Virginia passed a variation that speeds up the local approval process by setting deadlines. Similar bills are pending in Pennsylvania, California, Iowa, Michigan, Minnesota, New Jersey, Tennessee, North Carolina and Louisiana. Connecticut recently ruled that AT&T doesn't need franchises for its service on any level.

29 Robert Frieden, "Revenge of the Bellheads: Handicapping the Odds for a Tiered and Branded Internet," Paper available at: http://papers.ssrn.com/sol3/cf_dev/AbsByAuth.cfm?per_id=102928 (retrieved March 4, 2006).

30 Kim Hart and Sara Kehaulani Goo, "Tech Faceoff: Net Neutrality, In the Eye of the Beholder," Available at: http://www.washingtonpost.com/wp-dyn/content/article/2006/07/01/AR2006070100138.html (retrieved July 7, 2006).

31 "Stopping the Big Giveaway," Available at: http://www.savetheinternet.com/blog/2006/06/30/stopping-the-big-giveaway-by-john-kerry/?rss=feed (retrieved July 11, 2006).

7 SATELLITE COMMUNICATION

1 Patrick Parsons and Robert Frieden, *The Cable and Satellite Television Industries* (Boston, MA: Allyn & Bacon, 1998), 91–93.

2 Dennis Roddy, *Satellite Communications*, 2nd ed. (New York: McGraw-Hill, 1998), 164–169.

3 Satellites can drift along a longitudinal plane. These maneuvers are termed east–west station keeping maneuvers. Satellites operating at 4/6 GHz band must be kept within +/−0.1 degree of the designated longitude. Satellites operating at 12/14 GHz band must be kept within +/−0.05 degree of the designated longitude. Satellites can also drift along a latitudinal plane. These maneuvers are termed north–south station keeping maneuvers. Countering the drift requires more fuel than the east–west station keeping maneuvers. The north–south station keeping tolerances are the same as those for east–west station keeping.

4 Richard Gershon and Michael Wirth, "Home Box Office," in Robert Picard (ed.), *The Cable Networks Handbook* (Riverside, CA: Carpelan Press, 1993), 115–117.

5 DirecTV, "Investor Relations," Available at: http://phx.corporate-ir.net/phoenix.zhtml?c=127160&p=irol-homeprofile (retrieved July 8, 2006).

6 EchoStar, "About Us," Available at: http://www.dishnetwork.com/content/aboutus/company_profile/index.shtml (retrieved July 8, 2006).

7 Futron, "Satellite Manufacturing: Production Cycles and Time to Market," White Paper, May 2004, Available at: http://www.futron.com/pdf/Production_Schedule_White_Paper.pdf (retrieved July 7, 2006).

8 Satellite Industry Association, "State of the Satellite Industry Report," Available at: http://www.sia.org/PDF/2007StateofSatelliteIndustryReport.pdf (retrieved October 22, 2007).

9 Bruce Elbert, *The Satellite Communication Applications Handbook* (Boston, MA: Artech House, 1997), 421–436.

10 Michael Mirabito and Barbara Morgenstern, *The New Communication Technologies*, 5th ed. (Boston, MA: Focal Press, 2004).

11 William Rogers, Neil Armstrong, David Anderson et al., *Report of the Presidential Commission on the Space Shuttle Challenger Accident* (Washington, D.C.: U.S. Government Printing Office, 1986). See also Columbia Accident Investigation Board complete report, Available at: http://caib.nasa.gov/.

12 The U.S. Space Shuttle was the world's first reusable piloted spacecraft. It was designed as a multipurpose vehicle capable of conducting scientific experiments as well as deploying satellites into low earth orbit. While the Space Shuttle proved successful in the deployment of satellites, its complex design and refurbishing delays led to a number of setbacks. The Space Shuttle *Challenger* flew nine successful missions before a major disaster occurred in

January 1986. The entire crew was lost in what became the most devastating tragedy in NASA's history. In the aftermath of the Space Shuttle *Challenger* disaster and a report released by a presidential investigatory commission, President Ronald Reagan announced that NASA would withdraw from the business of launching commercial satellites. According to the report, NASA's overly ambitious launch schedule contributed to the Space Shuttle *Challenger*'s disaster. The nation's reliance on the Shuttle as its principal space launch capability created a relentless pressure on NASA to increase the flight rate (p. 201). Such pressures played a role in the decision to launch the *Challenger* despite adverse weather conditions. On February 1, 2003, the Space Shuttle *Columbia*, completing its twenty-eighth mission, disintegrated about 15 minutes before its scheduled landing at the Kennedy Space Center in Florida. All seven members of the crew were killed. The destruction of the Space Shuttle *Columbia* all but eliminated NASA from the commercial satellite launch business.

13 Arianespace is a commercial launch services leader, holding more than 50 percent of the world market for satellites to geostationary transfer orbit (GTO). Created as a commercial space transportation company in 1980, Arianespace has signed contracts for more than 265 satellite payloads.

14 A rocket must be controlled very precisely to deliver a satellite into the desired orbit. An inertial guidance system (IGS) inside the rocket makes this control possible. The IGS determines a rocket's exact location and orientation by precisely measuring all of the accelerations the rocket experiences, using gyroscopes and accelerometers. The IGS knows exactly where the rocket was at launch and it knows the different points of acceleration the rocket experiences during flight. In turn, the IGS can calculate the rocket's position and orientation in space.

15 "Launch Insurance," Available at: http://www.britinsurance.com/Products/Aerospace (retrieved July 10, 2006).

16 "Commercial Space and Launch Insurance," Available at: http://ast.faa.gov/files/pdf/q42002.pdf (retrieved July 10, 2006).

17 David Whalen, "Communications Satellites: Making the Global Village Possible," Available at: http://www.hq.nasa.gov/office/pao/History/satcomhistory.html (retrieved May 19, 2005).

18 Richard Gershon, "Intelsat: Global Cooperation in an Era of Deregulation," *Telecommunications Policy*, 14(3) (1990): 249–259.

19 Kenneth Katkin, "Universal Global Interconnection after INTELSAT," paper presented at the 30th Telecommunications Policy Research Conference, Washington, D.C., September 29, 2002.

20 Gershon, "Intelsat: Global Cooperation in an Era of Deregulation," 249.

21 Daya Kishan Thussu, "Lost In Space," *Foreign Policy*, 124 (May/June 2001): 70–71.

22 Gershon, "Intelsat: Global Cooperation in an Era of Deregulation," 255.

23 Sean Murphy, "Privatization of INTELSAT," *American Journal of International Law*, 95(4) (October 2001): 894.

24 Katkin, "Universal Global Interconnection after INTELSAT," 17.

25 "Top 20 Fixed Satellite Operators, 2004," Available at: http://www.space.com/spacenews/top20_satellite_2004.html (retrieved May 23, 2005).

26 Gregory Twachtman, "Intelsat Closing Raising Some Eyebrows," *Satellite News*, February 7, 2005, 6.

27 Intelsat, "Intelsat Completes Acquisition of PanAmSat," Press Release, Available at: http://www.intelsat.com/pdf/press_releases/2006/20060703.pdf (retrieved August 3, 2006).

8 CELLULAR AND WIRELESS COMMUNICATION

1   Richard Gershon, "Cellular Telephony," in D.H. Johnston (ed.), *Encyclopedia of International Media and Communications*, Vol. 1 (San Diego, CA: Academic Press, 2003), 175–188.

2   Science, Technology and Economic Development, SRI Policy Division, "Chapter 4: The Cellular Telephone," Available at: http://images.google.com/imgres-?imgurl=http://www.sri.com/policy/csted/reports/sandt/techin2/ch4img-4.gif&imgrefurl=http://www.sri.com/policy/csted/reports/sandt/techin2/chp4.html&h=312&w=312&sz=4&hl=en&start=4&tbnid=wEYyFLl5wOaKzM:&tbnh=117&tbnw=117&prev=/images%3Fq%3Dcell% 2Bsplitting%2Band% 2Bsectoring%26gbv%3D2%26svnum%3D10%26hl%3Den%26sa%3DG (retrieved October 27, 2007).

3   Ran Wei, "Wireless Telephony," in August Grant and Jennifer Meadows (eds.), *Communication Technology Update*, 10th ed. (Burlington, MA: Focal Press, 2006), 311–324.

4   Gershon, "Cellular Telephony," 175–188.

5   Thomas Farley and Mark van der Hoek, "Cellular Telephone Basics," Available at: http://www.privateline.com/mt_cellbasics/index.html (retrieved August 8, 2006).

6   CTIA—The Wireless Association, "Wireless Quick Facts," Available at: http://www.ctia.org/media/industry_info/index.cfm/AID/10323 (retrieved October 25, 2007).

7   The principle of frequency reuse is not unique to the business of cellular telephony. Radio and television stations effectively share the same block of frequencies across the U.S., with enough space in between to avoid co-channel interference.

8   Tom Farley and Mark van der Hoek, "Cell and Sector Terminology," Available at: http://images.google.com/imgres?imgurl=http://www.privateline.com/Cellbasics/sevencellcluster.gif&imgrefurl=http://www.privateline.com/Cellbasics/Cellbasics02.html&h=209&w=204&sz=3&hl=en&start=6&um=1&tbnid=8sGRro5GSZqlsM:&tbnh=106&tbnw=103&prev=/images%3Fq%3Dseven %2Bcell%2Bclusters%26svnum%3D10%26um%3D1%26hl%3Den%26sa %3DN (retrieved October 27, 2007).

9   Uyless Black, *Emerging Communications Technologies* (Upper Saddle River, NJ: Prentice Hall, 1997), 298–301.

10   Regis Bates and Donald Gregory, *Voice and Data Communications Handbook* (New York: McGraw-Hill, 1998), 740–745.

11   International Engineering Consortium, "Cellular Communications," Available at: http://www.iec.org/online/tutorials/cell_comm/topic05.html (retrieved December 5, 2007).

12   For example, a TDMA-based digital system can carry three times as many calls as an analog system. Digital cellular also improves the quality and efficiency of switching, routing and storing of information. It increases the potential for manipulation and transformation of voice and data. This becomes especially important when it comes to Internet access and cell phone image processing.

13   International Engineering Consortium, "Cellular Communications, Digital Systems," Available at: http://www.iec.org/online/tutorials/cell_comm/topic06.html (retrieved December 5, 2007).

14   In many communication systems, the cost of the communication channels represents a large percentage of the total cost of the system. The channels, therefore, must be shared as much as possible to ensure that their capacity is fully utilized. Multiplexing is a technique for combining more than one signal on a channel at

the same time (i.e., the multiple encoding of information signals on to a single communication's line).

15 In reality, only one person is actually using the channel at any given moment, but he/she uses it only for short bursts. He/she then gives up the channel momentarily to allow the other users to have their turn. This is very similar to how a computer with just one processor can seem to run multiple applications simultaneously.

16 Consider, for example, a TDMA channel that is 30 KHz wide and 6.7 milliseconds long and is split into three time slots. Each conversation gets the radio for one-third of the time. This is possible because the voice data has been digitized and compressed so that it takes up significantly less transmission space. TDMA is the access method used in the U.S. by the Electronics Industry Alliance and the Telecommunications Industry Association for Interim Standard 54 (IS-54) and Interim Standard 136 (IS-136). TDMA systems operate in both the 800 MHz (IS-54) and 1900 MHz (IS-136) frequency bands.

17 "Code Division Multiple Access," Available at: http://en.wikipedia.org/wiki/CDMA (retrieved December 10, 2007).

18 CTIA—The Wireless Association, "Wireless Quick Facts."

19 International Telecommunications Union, "Key Statistics and Analysis," Available at: http://www.itu.int/ITU-D/ict/statistics/ict/index.html (retrieved December 20, 2007).

20 In the U.K. alone, the Blair government generated an estimated $33 billion from the sale of spectrum space. Germany was able to raise $45 billion from spectrum auction sales. Other European finance ministers soon followed. In the end, the auction system may have propped national coffers but it was a major financial drain to Europe's various wireless carriers, which found themselves paying exorbitant fees for a resource and technology that was several years into the future.

21 "Move over 3G: Here Comes 4G," *Economist*, Available at: http://www.economist.com/business/displayStory.cfm?story_id=1816742 (retrieved June 10, 2006).

22 Many of the early 3G phone designs had delivery speeds of 9.6 Kbps. In principle, 3G phones need to achieve Internet delivery speeds comparable to today's DSL and cable modem networks. Today's 3G data rates don't come close to the speeds delivered by the aforementioned broadband networks.

23 The 700 MHz spectrum became available as a result of the government-mandated digital TV transition. The availability of new spectrum space results from television broadcasters moving from their former analog signal assignments to a new digital format and set of assigned frequencies which requires substantially less spectrum space. Spectrum bidders for this auction included a wide variety of media and telecom companies like Google, Verizon Wireless, Microsoft and AT&T.

24 V. Jung and H.J. Warnecke, *Handbook for Telecommunications* (Berlin, Germany: Springer, 1998), 123.

25 The Bluetooth electronic protocol is named after Harold "Bluetooth" Gormson, who was a former Danish king, born around 910.

26 The WiMAX Forum, "Mobile WiMAX, the Best Personal Broadband Experience," June 2006, Available at: http://www.wimaxforum.org/home/ (retrieved October 28, 2007).

9 THE INTERNET AND ELECTRONIC COMMERCE

1 Michael Mirabito and Barbara Morgenstern, *The New Communication Technologies*, 5th ed. (Boston, MA: Focal Press, 2004), 231.

2 See Everett Rogers, *Diffusion of Innovations*, 4th ed. (New York: Free Press, 1995); Ithiel de Sola Pool, *Technologies of Freedom* (Cambridge, MA: Harvard University Press, 1983).
3 Rogers, *Diffusion of Innovations*, 412.
4 R Fidler, *Mediamorphosis* (Thousand Oaks, CA: Pine Forge Press, 1997).
5 Thomas Friedman, *The World Is Flat* (New York: Farrar, Straus & Giroux, 2005).
6 "A Way out of the Web Maze," *Business Week*, February 24, 1997, 95.
7 "Now It's Your Web," *Business Week*, October 5, 1998, 166.
8 David Aaker, *Managing Brand Equity: Capitalizing on the Value of a Brand Name* (New York: Free Press, 1991).
9 Alan Albarran, *Management of Electronic Media*, 2nd ed. (Belmont, CA: Wadsworth, 2002).
10 Louisa Ha, "Enhanced Television Strategy Models: A Study of TV Websites," *Internet Research: Electronic Networking Applications and Policy*, 12(3) (2002): 235–247.
11 B. Hurst, "Add Value Not Gimmicks with ETV," *Marketing News*, July 10, 2005, 37.
12 Louisa Ha and Sylvia Chan-Olmsted, "Enhanced TV as Brand Extension: TV Viewers' Perception of Enhanced TV Features and TV Commerce on Broadcast Networks' Websites," *International Journal of Media Management*, 3(4) (2001): 202–213.
13 Ibid., 210.
14 Ithiel de Sola Pool, *Technologies without Boundaries* (Cambridge, MA: Harvard University Press, 1990).
15 Philip Napoli, "The Audience Product and the New Media Environment: Implications for the Economics of Media Industries," *International Journal of Media Management*, 3 (2001): 66–73.
16 Sylvia Chan-Olmsted, "Marketing Mass Media on the World Wide Web," in Alan Albarran and David Goff (eds.), *Understanding the Web: Social, Political and Economic Dimensions of the Internet* (Ames, IA: Iowa State University Press, 2000), 112.
17 Steven Heyer, "Keynote Remarks," presentation given at the *Advertising Age* Madison and Vine Conference, Beverly Hills, CA, 2003.
18 A central ad server is a computer server that stores advertisements and delivers them to website visitors. Ad servers come in two variations: local ad servers and remote (or third-party) ad servers. Local ad servers are typically run by a single publisher and serve ads to that publisher's domains, allowing fine-grained creative, formatting and content control by that publisher. Remote ad servers can serve ads across domains owned by multiple publishers. They deliver the ads from one central source so that advertisers and publishers can track the distribution of their online advertisements, and have one location for controlling the rotation and distribution of their advertisements across the web.
19 Pop ups tend to be highly popular and arguably the crudest form of Internet advertising. Some critics have likened pop-ups to a nightclub hawker trying to entice someone into a bar or cafe. Pornographic websites are among the most common users of pop-up ads. Some particularly vicious types of pop-up ads are programmed to hijack the user's Internet session. These forms of pop-ups sometimes spawn multiple windows and, as each window is closed, it activates a code that spawns another window, sometimes indefinitely. This action is referred to as a Java trap or a spam cascade.
20 T.L. Stanley, "Eat That, Subservient Chicken: OfficeMax Site Draws 36M," *Advertising Age*, January 29, 2007, 4, 35.

21 Louise Story, "Facebook Is Marketing Your Brand Preferences with Your Permission," *New York Times*, November 7, 2007, 28.

22 Brooke Capps, "How to Succeed in Second Life," *Advertising Age*, May 28, 2007, 6.

23 J.M. Tarn, D. Yen and M. Beaumont, "Exploring the Rationales for ERP and SCM Integration," *Industrial Management and Data Systems*, 102(1) (2002): 26–34.

24 M. O'Hara-Devereaux and R. Johansen, *Globalwork* (San Francisco, CA: Jossey-Bass, 1994); G. Huber, "A Theory of the Effects of Advanced Information Technologies on Organizational Design, Intelligence and Decisionmaking," *Academy of Management Review*, 15 (1990): 195–204.

25 Eli M. Noam, *Interconnecting the Network of Networks* (Cambridge, MA: MIT Press, 2001); de Sola Pool, *Technologies without Boundaries*; John Naisbitt, *Megatrends* (New York: Warner Books, 1982).

26 Richard Gershon, "Intelligent Networking and the Information Economy," in K. Lewandowski (ed.), *The Annual Review of Communications*, Vol. 57 (Chicago, IL: International Engineering Consortium, 2004), 611–622.

27 S. Zheng, D. Yen and J.M. Tarn, "The New Spectrum of the Cross-enterprise Solution: The Integration of Supply Chain Management and Enterprise Resource Planning Systems," *Journal of Computer Information Systems*, 41(2) (2000): 84–93.

28 G. Dredden and J. Bergdolt, "Enterprise Resource Planning," *Air Force Journal of Logistics*, 31(2) (2007): 48–52.

29 Joel Goldhar and David Lei, "The Shape of 21st Century Global Manufacturing," *Journal of Business Strategy*, March/April 1991, 38.

30 Zheng, Yen and Tarn, "The New Spectrum of the Cross-enterprise Solution."

31 "Google Corporate History," Available at: http://www.google.com/corporate/history.html (retrieved June 5, 2007).

32 Adam Lashinsky, "Chaos by Design," *Fortune*, October 2, 2006, 86–96.

33 Ibid., 88.

34 Bala Iyer and Thomas Davenport, "Reverse Engineering Google's Innovation Machine," *Harvard Business Review*, April 2008, 60.

35 "Click Fraud," *Business Week*, October 2, 2006, 44–57.

36 Ibid.

37 "Googling for Gold," *Business Week*, December 5, 2005, 61–68.

38 Andrew Ross Sorkin, "Dot-Com Boom Echoed in Deal to Buy YouTube," Available at: http://www.nytimes.com/2006/10/10/technology/10deal.html?ex=1161748800&en=e3al718713927ead&ei=5070 (retrieved October 10, 2006).

39 "Google and the Wisdom of Clouds," *Business Week*, December 4, 2007, 49–55.

40 de Sola Pool, *Technologies of Freedom*, 23.

41 Lucy Kung, *Strategic Management in the Media* (London: Sage, 2008), 92–97.

42 Nicholas Negroponte, *Being Digital* (New York: Vintage, 1995), 18.

43 Richard A. Gershon, "Intelligent Networking and the Information Economy," in K. Lewandowski (ed.), *Annual Review of Communications*, Vol. 57 (Chicago, IL: International Engineering Consortium, 2004), 611–622.

44 Steven Levy, "Facebook Grows Up," *Newsweek*, August 27, 2007, 41–45.

45 Irving Fang, *A History of Mass Communication: Six Information Revolutions* (Boston, MA: Focal Press, 1997).

46 Marshall McLuhan, *Understanding Media: The Extensions of Man* (New York: McGraw-Hill, 1964).

10 TRANSNATIONAL MEDIA AND TELECOMMUNICATIONS

1 See Richard Gershon, "Issues in Transnational Media Management," in A. Albarran, M. Wirth and S. Chan-Olmsted (eds.), *Handbook of Media Management and Economics* (Mahwah, NJ: Lawrence Erlbaum, 2006), 203–228; David Demers, *Global Media: Menace or Messiah?* (Cresskill, NJ: Hampton Press, 1999); Alan Albarran and Sylvia Chan-Olmsted (eds.), *Global Media Economics* (Ames, IA: Iowa State University Press, 1998); Edward Herman and Robert McChesney, *The Global Media: The New Missionaries of Corporate Capitalism* (London: Cassell, 1997); Richard Gershon, *The Transnational Media Corporation: Global Messages and Free Market Competition* (Mahwah NJ: Lawrence Erlbaum, 1997).

2 J. Pilotta, T. Widman and S. Jasko, "Meaning and Action in the Organizational Setting: An Interpretive Approach," in *Communication Yearbook*, Vol. 12 (New York: Sage, 1988): 310–334.

3 A. Morita, M. Shimomura and E.M. Reingold, *Made in Japan* (New York: E.P. Dutton, 1986), 130.

4 See Richard Gershon, "The Transnational Media Corporation and the Economics of Global Competition," in Yahya R. Kamalipour (ed.), *Global Communication*, 2nd ed. (Belmont, CA: Wadsworth, 2007), 52; Gershon, "Issues in Transnational Media Management," 204.

5 Bertelsmann, Inc., *1998 Annual Report* (New York: Bertelsmann, Inc., 1998), 3.

6 Thomas Friedman, *The Lexus and the Olive Tree* (New York: Farrar, Straus & Giroux, 1999), 8.

7 Ibid., 11.

8 "The New Economy," *Business Week*, January 31, 2000, 74–92.

9 Gershon, "Issues in Transnational Media Management"; S. Robock and K. Simmonds, *International Business and Multinational Enterprises*, 4th ed. (Homewood, IL: Irwin, 1989).

10 "News Corporation 2006 Annual Report," Available at: http://www.newscorp.com/Report2006/AR2006.pdf, p. 48 (retrieved December 15, 2006).

11 R. Grosse and D. Kujawa, *International Business: Theory and Application* (Homewood, IL: Irwin, 1988).

12 J. Behrman and R. Grosse, *International Business and Governments: Issues and Institutions* (Columbia, SC: University of South Carolina Press, 1990); Grosse and Kujawa, *International Business: Theory and Application*.

13 R. Gershon, "The Transnational Media Corporation: Environmental Scanning and Strategy Formulation," *Journal of Media Economics*, 13 (2000): 81–101.

14 Grosse and Kujawa, *International Business: Theory and Application*, 87–93.

15 "The Rise of India," *Business Week*, December 8, 2003, 66–76.

16 Fred Cate, *The European Broadcasting Directive*, Communication Committee Monograph Series (Washington, D.C.: American Bar Association, 1990); Deirdre Mueller, *Europe in the Media* (Mahwah, NJ: Lawrence Erlbaum, 2003), 10–34.

17 Barry Litman, *The Motion Picture Industry* (Boston, MA: Allyn & Bacon, 1998).

18 Warren Bennis, *Leaders and Visions: Orchestrating the Corporate Culture* (New York: Conference Board, 1986).

19 "There's No Business like Show Business," *Fortune*, June 22, 1998, 104.

20 D. Ball and W.H. McCulloch, *International Business: The Challenge of Global Competition*, 6th ed. (Chicago, IL: Irwin, 1996).

21 See Herbert Howard, "Television Station Ownership in the United States," *Journalism Communication Monographs* 8(1) (2006): 3–78; Benjamin Compaine and Douglas Gomery, *Who Owns the Media?*, 3rd ed. (Mahwah, NJ: Lawrence Erlbaum, 2000).

22 Gary Ozanich and Michael Wirth, "Mergers and Acquisitions: A Communications Industry Overview," in A. Alexander, J. Owers and R. Carveth (eds.), *Media Economics: Theory and Practice*, 2nd ed. (Mahwah, NJ: Lawrence Erlbaum, 1998).

23 Richard Clurman, *To the End of Time* (New York: Simon & Schuster, 1992), 189.

24 "CBS," *Business Week*, April 5, 1999, 75–82.

25 Sylvia Chan-Olmsted, "The Strategic Alliances of Broadcasting, Cable Television and Telephone Services," *Journal of Media Economics*, 11(3) (1998): 33–46.

26 Bruce Wasserstein, *Big Deal: The Battle for Control of America's Leading Corporations* (New York: Warner Books, 1998), 149–150.

27 Gershon, *The Transnational Media Corporation*, 5–8.

28 Ozanich and Wirth, "Mergers and Acquisitions: A Communications Industry Overview."

29 Wasserstein, *Big Deal: The Battle for Control of America's Leading Corporations*, 144–154; "The Case against Mergers," *Business Week*, October 30, 1995, 122–126.

30 See Leslie Cauley, *End of the Line: The Rise and Fall of AT&T* (New York: Free Press, 2005); Mark Robichaux, *Cable Cowboy: John Malone and the Rise of the Modern Cable Business* (Hoboken, NJ: John Wiley & Sons, 2003).

31 "Armstrong's Vision of AT&T Cable Empire Unravels on the Ground," *Wall Street Journal*, October 8, 2000, 1, A-11.

32 Joseph DiStefano, *Comcasted* (Philadelphia, PA: Camino Books, 2005), 147–158.

33 "Murdoch's Kingdom," *Economist*, August 7, 1990, 62.

34 Alan Albarran and Bosina Miszerjewksi, "Media Concentration in the U.S. and European Union: A Comparative Analysis," paper presented at the 6th World Media Economics Conference, Montreal, Canada, May 12, 2004.

35 Ibid.

36 Before World War II (1939–1945), the U.S. economy was largely self-sufficient, producing the great majority of what the country needed in terms of food, steel, housing, communications and automobiles. The principle of outsourcing first begins with the development of international trade following World War II. The U.S. was the primary engine that promoted the cause of international trade, including a reduction in tariffs on various imported goods. It was done with the goal of promoting economic recovery for both war-torn Europe and Asia. In the 1950s, U.S. presidents Harry Truman and Dwight Eisenhower worked hard to rebuild Japan's economy, starting with its textile industry. As Japan continued to rebuild, the U.S. began importing textile products from Japan and later South Korea, Hong Kong, Taiwan and the Philippines. One reason that textiles proved to be the starting point is that such items are easy to produce.

37 Debora Spar, *Hitting the Wall: Nike and International Labor Practices*, Harvard Business School Case Study Series, 9–700–047, September 6, 2002, 1–23.

38 Ibid., 2.

39 Mark Clifford, "Pain in Pussan," *Far Eastern Economic Review*, April 2, 1992, 50.

40 Keith Hearit, *Crisis Management by Apology: Corporate Response to Allegations of Wrongdoing* (Mahwah NJ: Lawrence Erlbaum, 2006).

41 Pat Aufderheide, "Competition and Commons: The Public Interest in and after the AOL–Time Warner Merger," *Journal of Broadcasting and Electronic Media*, 46(4) (2002): 515–531.

42 Gail Faulhaber, "Network Effects and Merger Analysis: Instant Messaging and the AOL Time Warner Case," *Telecommunications Policy*, 26 (2002): 311–333.

43 "AOL, You've Got Misery," *Business Week*, April 8, 2002, 58–59.

44 "Failed Effort to Coordinate Ads Signals Deeper Woes at AOL," *Wall Street Journal*, July 18, 2002, 1, A6.

45 Nina Munk, *Fools Rush In: Steve Case, Jerry Levin and the Unmaking of AOL Time Warner* (New York: HarperCollins, 2004).
46 "AOL Flips Business, Offers Service for Free," *Information Week*, Available at: http://informationweek.com/internet/showArticle.jhtml?articleID=191601667 (retrieved January 25, 2007).
47 John Dimmick, *Media Competition and Coexistence: The Theory of Niche* (Mahwah, NJ: Lawrence Erlbaum, 2003).
48 Thomas Friedman, *The World Is Flat* (New York: Farrar, Straus & Giroux, 2005).
49 Vincent Mosco, "The Mythology of Telecommunications Deregulation," *Journal of Communication*, 40 (1990): 36–49.
50 See Gershon, "The Transnational Media Corporation and the Economics of Global Competition," 67; Gershon, "Issues in Transnational Media Management," 219.
51 See David Demers, *Global Media Newsletter*, 2(1) (2000): 1; Demers, *Global Media: Menace or Messiah?*.
52 "The Enron Scandal," *Business Week Online*, Available at: http://www.businessweek.com/magazine/content/02_04/b3767711.htm (retrieved January 28, 2002).
53 J. Cohan, "I Didn't Know and I Was Only Doing My Job: Has Corporate Ethics Governance Careened Out of Control?," *Journal of Business Ethics*, 40 (2002): 275–299.
54 Walter Cronkite, *A Reporter's Life* (New York: Alfred A. Knopf, 1996), 375.

11 TELECOMMUNICATIONS MANAGEMENT

1 Peter Drucker, *Management: Tasks, Responsibilities, Practices* (New York: Harper & Row, 1973).
2 Walt Disney Company, *1993 Annual Report to Stockholders* (Burbank, CA: Walt Disney Co., 1993), 4.
3 Hyrum W. Smith, *The 10 Natural Laws of Successful Time and Life Management* (New York: Warner Books, 1994), 34–35.
4 John P. Kotter, *Leading Change* (Boston, MA: Harvard Press, 1996), 25.
5 Charles Wrege and Ann Stoka, "Cooke Creates a Classic: The Story behind F.W. Taylor's Principles of Scientific Management," *Academy of Management Review*, October 1978, 736–749.
6 Howard Zinn, *The 20th Century: A People's History of the United States* (New York: HarperCollins, 1980), 34–35.
7 Henri Fayol, *General and Industrial Management*, trans. Constance Storrs (London: Pitman, 1949).
8 Max Weber, *Max Weber: The Theory of Social and Economic Organization*, trans. and ed. Talcott Parsons and A.M. Henderson (New York: Free Press, 1947).
9 A. Carey, The Hawthorne Studies: A Radical Criticism, *American Sociological Review*, 32 (1967): 404.
10 Among social science researchers, the term *Hawthorne effect* has come to mean the effects of personal influence that research investigators can have on the problem (or people) being investigated.
11 Katherine Miller, *Organizational Communication: Approaches and Processes* (Belmont, CA: Wadsworth, 1995), 44–47.
12 Abraham Maslow, *Motivation and Personality* (New York: Harper & Row, 1954).
13 Frederick Herzberg, *Work and the Nature of Man* (New York: Thomas Y. Crowd Co., 1966).

14 Douglas McGregor, *The Human Side of Enterprise* (New York: McGraw-Hill, 1960).
15 William G. Ouchi, *Theory Z* (New York: Avon Books, 1981).
16 Telephone traffic engineers must routinely balance two competing objectives. Ideally, the traffic engineer must design the telephone network with sufficient resources to switch and route every call that is placed. At the same time, given that network telephone traffic patterns vary significantly according to time of the day and select days of the week and year, meeting the ideal of providing maximum capacity in all situations would be wasteful and cost prohibitive.
17 As an example, an architect is asked to submit a set of preliminary drawings as part of a bid to win a new construction job. The accuracy of the design and the cost projections will make the difference to whether the contract is won. And from the architect's standpoint, the original design is, after all, a program stored on a computer hard drive, CD or flash memory card that can be reused or changed later on.
18 Richard Daft, *Management*, 4th ed. (New York: Harcourt Brace, 1997), 224–225.
19 W. Edwards Deming, *Out of the Crisis* (Cambridge, MA: MIT Press, 1982).
20 Alan Albarran, *Management of Electronic Media*, 2nd ed. (Belmont, CA: Wadsworth, 2002), 88–89.
21 Daft, *Management*, 60–61.
22 The Xerox Corporation defines benchmarking as "the continuous process of measuring products, services and practices against the toughest competitors or those companies recognized as industry leaders." See Howard Rothman, "You Need Not Be Big to Benchmark," *Nation's Business*, December 1992, 64–65.
23 Michael Hammer and James Champy, *Reengineering the Corporation: A Manifesto for Business Revolution* (New York: Harper Business, 1993), 31.
24 Michael Hammer and Steven Stanton, *The Reengineering Revolution: A Handbook* (New York: Harper Business, 1995), 3.
25 Tom Peters, *In Search of Excellence*, Available at: http://www.businessballs.com/tompetersinsearchofexcellence.htm (retrieved January 25, 2007).
26 Tom Peters and Robert Waterman, *In Search of Excellence: Lessons from America's Best Run Companies* (New York: Warner Books, 1982), 119–155.
27 Ibid., 156–199.
28 Ibid., 292–305.
29 Michael Porter, *Competitive Strategy: Techniques for Analyzing Industries and Competitors* (New York: Free Press, 1980), 7–17.
30 Ibid., 17–22.
31 Ibid., 23–24.
32 Ibid., 24–27.
33 Ibid., 27–29.
34 Michael E. Porter, *Competitive Advantage: Creating and Sustaining Superior Performance* (New York: Free Press, 1985), 12.
35 Ibid., 14.
36 Lucy Küng, *Strategic Management in the Media* (London: Sage, 2008), 18–24.
37 Porter, *Competitive Advantage*, 64–67, 130–132, 166–169.
38 Jim Collins, *Good to Great* (New York: Harper Business, 2001), 63.
39 Ibid., 88.
40 Ibid., 142–143.
41 Ibid., 186–187.

12 TELECOMMUNICATIONS AND FINANCIAL MANAGEMENT

1 FASB is an accounting body that began in 1973 as a successor to the Accounting Principles Board. FASB issues Statements of Financial Accounting Standards that establish GAAP rules.

2 This example assumes the firm is using straight-line depreciation. With this method, the capital cost is apportioned evenly over the useful life of the asset. Accelerated methods of depreciation allow for more rapid depreciation of capital assets.

3 Sometimes firms have accrued interest expenses and have not made actual payments. Accrued interest recognizes that a company owes a lender interest but the actual cash payments have not been made. The interest expense line item includes both actual interest payments and accrued interest expenses.

4 By comparison, other companies are likely to have such items as interest income (i.e., income from the investment of excess cash in interest-bearing securities).

5 The actual earnings-per-share calculation is based on the weighted average shares of stock outstanding during the year, not on the shares outstanding at the end of the year.

6 Programming rights are often included in both the current asset and fixed asset portion of the balance sheet. Current programming rights would be those programs that will be "aired" in the current year. The non-current ones would be rights to air programming in future years. The accounting profession has a GAAP rule that governs the allocation (i.e., amortization) of programming rights.

7 The original cost of the assets is also reduced by accumulated depreciation. Accumulated depreciation is the sum of all of the cost of the assets that has been allocated to prior years' depreciation expense. Land does not get depreciated, only buildings and equipment.

8 Firms that have a significant amount of cash can support themselves by reducing their cash balance, as opposed to relying on external sources of cash.

9 The term *borrowers* is used generically to mean corporations seeking funds. The funds might be lent, or they might be invested in the firm as equity.

10 There are some public stocks that are thinly traded; that is, the number of shares traded on a daily basis is small. Hence, there is less liquidity in these stocks, so a shareholder cannot sell his/her stocks without having a significant impact on the stock price.

11 Google did not receive exactly $85. This figure was reduced by fees paid to the investment bankers who underwrote the offering.

12 Liberty Media has agreements pending whereby it will exchange its News Corporation investment for an equity stake in DirecTV and it will receive ownership of the Atlanta Braves for its Time Warner investment.

13 TELECOMMUNICATIONS MARKETING

1 Gary Armstrong and Philip Kotler, *Marketing: An Introduction*, 7th ed. (Upper Saddle River, NJ: Pearson Prentice Hall, 2005).

2 Available at: http://www.sric-bi.com/VALS (retrieved December 18, 2006).

3 Scarborough Research, Available at: http://www.scarborough.com (retrieved December 15, 2006).

4 Claritas PRIZM NE, Available at: http://www.claritas.com/claritas/ Default.jsp?ci=3&si=4&pn=prizmne.

5 Donald E. Parente, *Advertising Campaign Strategy: A Guide to Marketing Communications*, 4th ed. (Canada: Thomson South-Western, 2006), 104–105.

6 Michael E. Porter, *Competitive Advantage: Creating and Sustaining Superior Performance* (New York: Free Press, 1985), 14.
7 Peter Mihailovic and Leslie de Chernatony, "The Era of Brand Culling—Time for a Global Rethink?," *Journal of Brand Management*, 2(5) (1995): 308–315.
8 "Best Global Brands Report 2006," Available at: http://www.interbrand.com/best_brands_2006.asp (retrieved December 20, 2006).
9 Brand value estimate is based on three things, including a forecast of current and future revenues attributable to the branded products, a measure of how the brand influences consumer demand at the point of purchase, and a benchmark of the brand's ability to secure ongoing customer demand and sustain future earnings.
10 David Aaker and Erich Joachimsthaler, *Brand Leadership, 2000* (New York: Free Press, 2000), 9.
11 "How to Milk an Apple," *Business Week*, February 3, 2003, 44.
12 Armstrong and Kotler, *Marketing: An Introduction*, 337.
13 Sylvia Chan-Olmsted, "Telecommunication Marketing," in Richard Gershon, *Telecommunications Management: Industry Structures and Planning Strategies* (Mahwah, NJ: Lawrence Erlbaum, 2001), 295.
14 Esther Thorson and Jeri Moore, *Integrated Communication: Synergy of Persuasive Voices* (Mahwah, NJ: Lawrence Erlbaum, 1996).
15 The main strength of viral marketing is its ability to reach a large number of interested people at a low cost. Its success depends on a high pass-along rate from person to person. Notable examples include the website featuring Burger King's Subservient Chicken; *The Ring Two* movie promotion that directed people to www.she-is-here.com, a website where users shared their unexplainable experience with the dreaded tape; and the promotion by the movie studio of the Blair Witch Project as a real-life documentary.
16 Don Schultz and Heidi Schultz, *IMC—The Next Generation: Five Steps for Delivering Value and Measuring Returns Using Marketing Communication* (Boston, MA: McGraw-Hill, 2004), 269–277.
17 Frederick Reichheld, *The Loyalty Effect* (Princeton, NJ: Harvard Business Press, 1996).
18 Armstrong and Kotler, *Marketing: An Introduction*, 16.
19 Ibid., 17.
20 Schultz and Schultz, *IMC—The Next Generation*.
21 Kenneth Clow and Donald Baack, *Integrated Advertising, Promotion and Marketing Communications*, 2nd ed. (Upper Saddle River, NJ: Pearson Prentice Hall, 2004), 454.
22 Schultz and Schultz, *IMC—The Next Generation*, 118–123.
23 Chan-Olmsted, "Telecommunication Marketing."

14 LEADERSHIP AND CHANGE MANAGEMENT

1 Warren Bennis, *On Becoming a Leader* (Reading, MA: Addison-Wesley, 1989), 45.
2 Peter Northouse, *Leadership Theory and Practice*, 3rd ed. (Thousand Oaks, CA: Sage, 2004), 3.
3 James MacGregor Burns, *Leadership* (New York: Harper & Row, 1978), 19–20.
4 Credit for this idea goes to former sales manager Jeff Cash when he was at station WCMH-TV in Columbus, Ohio.
5 Bernard M. Bass, *Leadership and Performance beyond Expectations* (New York: Free Press, 1985), 20.
6 Robert J. House, "A 1976 Theory of Charismatic Leadership," in J.G. Hunt

and L.L. Larson (eds.), *Leadership: The Cutting Edge* (Carbondale, IL: Southern Illinois University Press, 1976), 189–207.

7 Northouse, *Leadership Theory and Practice*, 171.
8 Jim Collins, *Good to Great* (New York: HarperCollins, 2001), 72–73.
9 Ibid., 39.
10 Joseph Badaracco, *Leading Quietly* (Boston, MA: Harvard Business School Press, 2002), 1.
11 John P. Kotter, *Leading Change* (Boston, MA: Harvard Press, 1996), 71–72.
12 "Tribute to David Sarnoff," *Wisdom: The Magazine of Knowledge and Education* (ed. Leon Gutterman), 3(22) (1958): Inside Cover.
13 "Bill Gates," Available at: http://www.microsoft.com/presspass/exec/billg/bio.mspx (retrieved June 28, 2007).
14 Kotter, *Leading Change*, 85.
15 John W. Gardner, *On Leadership* (New York: Free Press, 1990), 18.
16 Bennis, *On Becoming a Leader*, 58.
17 Gardner, *On Leadership*, 184.
18 "Murdoch's Kingdom," *Economist*, August 18, 1990, 62.
19 Hank Whittemore, *CNN: The Inside Story* (Boston, MA: Little, Brown, 1990), 1.
20 Ibid., 153.
21 Warren Bennis, "Followers Make Good Leaders Good," *New York Times*, December 31, 1989, 33.
22 Gardner, *On Leadership*, 24.
23 Larry Bossidy and Ram Charran, *Execution: The Discipline of Getting Things Done* (New York: Crown Business, 2002), 22.
24 Hyrum W. Smith, *The 10 Natural Laws of Successful Time and Life Management* (New York: Warner Books, 1994), 28.
25 William Oncken and Donald Wass, "Management Time: Who's Got the Monkey?," *Harvard Business Review*, Classic Reprint, 1999, first published in November/December 1974, 1–8.
26 Robert Kuttner, "Today's Markets Need New Rules," *Business Week*, July 29, 2002, 26.
27 Ibid.
28 "Congress Begins WorldCom Investigation," *Wall Street Journal*, June 28, 2002, A3, A9.
29 WorldCom's finance department in 2001 had categorized billions of dollars as capital expenditures; that is, the company's routine operating costs could be stretched forward several years into the future. So-called capital expenditures were in fact regular telephone connection fees that WorldCom paid local telephone companies for completing long-distance calls. These kinds of expenditures are not considered capital outlays, but routine operating costs that should normally be reconciled at the close of each fiscal year. This accounting maneuver allowed WorldCom to translate a $662 million loss into a $2.4 billion profit in 2001.
30 "Lies, Damned Lies and Scott Sullivan," Available at: http://www.forbes.com/business/2005/02/17/cx_sr_0217ebbers.html (retrieved February 17, 2005).
31 The Special Investigative Committee of the Board of Directors of WorldCom, Inc. Available at: http://www.edgar-online.com/bin/irsec/finSys_main.asp-?dcn=0000931763–03–001862&x=126&y=27 (retrieved June 10, 2003).
32 "Ebbers Gets 25 Years," CNNMoney.com, Available at: http://money.cnn.com/2005/07/13/news/newsmakers/ebbers_sentence/ (retrieved July 13, 2005).
33 "Woe Is WorldCom," *Business Week*, May 6, 2002, 86–90.
34 Collins, *Good to Great*, 142–143.

15 INNOVATION AND TECHNOLOGY MANAGEMENT

1 Joseph Schumpeter, *Capitalism, Socialism and Democracy* (New York: Harper & Row, 1942).
2 Creative destruction occurs when something new and innovative replaces something that is older. A good example of this is the effect that personal computers had on mainframe computers. In this case, entrepreneurs created one of the most important technology advancements of the twentieth century.
3 Gary Hamel, "The What, Why and How of Management Innovation," *Harvard Business Review*, February 2006, 74.
4 "Most Innovative Companies," *Business Week*, May 14, 2007, 60.
5 Ibid.
6 Everett Rogers, *Diffusion of Innovation*, 4th ed. (New York: Free Press, 1995), 11.
7 Clayton Christensen, *The Innovator's Dilemma* (Boston, MA: Harvard Business School Press, 1997), XV–XVII.
8 Clayton Christensen, *The Innovator's Solution* (Boston, MA: Harvard Business School Press, 2003), 34.
9 The principle of disruptive technology owes its aegis to the work of Joseph Schumpeter, who argued that innovation leads to the gales of "creative destruction" as new innovations cause old ideas, technologies and skills to become obsolete. In Schumpeter's view, creative destruction, however difficult and challenging, leads to continuous progress moving forward. A good example of this is the impact that personal computers had on mainframe computers.
10 W. Chan Kim and Renée Mauborgne, "Value Innovation: The Strategic Logic of High Growth," *Harvard Business Review*, 82(7) (2004): 172–180.
11 The Bid Floor, "eBay Facts, Growth Statistics and FAQ's," Available at: http://www.thebidfloor.com/ebay_facts.htm (retrieved May 28, 2007).
12 John Nathan, *Sony: The Private Life* (New York: Houghton Mifflin, 1999), 138.
13 Ibid., 143.
14 Everyone within the organization from senior management to the worker on the floor has a responsibility to improve product and service quality. Second, TQM emphasizes the importance of continuous improvement as the basis for producing long-term results. Continuous improvement means that the organization benefits from the ongoing commitment to steadily improve products and procedures. See Richard Daft, *Management*, 4th ed. (New York: Harcourt Brace, 1988), 60–61.
15 In particular, processes that operate with Six Sigma quality produce at defect levels below 3.4 defects per (one) million opportunities (DPMO). Six Sigma's implicit goal is to improve all processes to that level of quality or better. See Peter Pande, Robert Neuman and Roland Cavanagh, *The Six Sigma Way* (New York: McGraw-Hill, 2000).
16 Arthur Thompson and A.J. Strickland, "Dell Computer Corporation," Available at: http://www.mhhe.com/business/management/thompson/11e/case/dell.html (retrieved October 6, 2006).
17 Kenneth Kraemer and Jason Dedrick, "Dell Computer: Organization of a Global Production Network," Available at: http://www.crito.uci.edu (retrieved October 6, 2006).
18 Thompson and Strickland, "Dell Computer Corporation."
19 W. Chan Kim and Renée Mauborgne, *Blue Ocean Strategy* (Boston, MA: Harvard Business School Press, 2005).
20 "Executive Profile, Steve Jobs," Available at: http://investing.businessweek.com/businessweek/research/stocks/people/person.asp?personId=340149&symbol=AAPL (retrieved March 14, 2008).

21 Jeffrey Young and William Simon, *iCon: Steve Jobs* (Hoboken, NJ: John Wiley & Sons, 2005), 58–98.
22 Ibid., 275–298.
23 Jim Collins and Jerry Porras, *Built to Last* (New York: HarperCollins, 1994).
24 Christensen, *The Innovator's Dilemma*, xii–xiii.
25 Robert Birnbaum, review of *The Innovator's Dilemma*, Available at: http://www.aaup.org/AAUP/pubsres/academe/2005/JF/BR/birn.htm (retrieved September 12, 2007).
26 Christensen, *The Innovator's Dilemma*, xii–xiii.
27 See Raymond Vernon, "International Investment and International Trade in the Product Cycle," *Quarterly Journal of Economics*, LXXX (1966): 190–207; Louis Wells, "A Product Life Cycle for International Trade?," *Journal of Marketing*, 32(3) (1968): 1–6.
28 During the maturity stage the product or service is well established. Production costs are low and there is less need for advertising. In addition, the market has become more competitive, with several new entrants offering alternative products and services. The decline stage represents just that: a decline in sales volume. This can be due to product saturation within the market (everyone who needs a TV set has bought one), technological obsolescence (VCRs) or the availability of a new product substitute (iPod).
29 Microsoft's Vista operating system software has proven controversial since it enforces new forms of digital rights management aimed at restricting the copying of protected digital media.
30 Michael Tushman and Charles O'Reilly, *Winning through Innovation* (Boston, MA: Harvard Business School Press, 1997), 1–16.
31 Jim Collins, *Good to Great* (New York: HarperCollins, 2001), 1, 16.
32 Nicholas Negroponte, "Incrementalism Is Innovation's Worst Enemy," *Wired*, April 1995, 188.
33 Edgar Schein, *Organizational Culture and Leadership* (San Francisco, CA: Jossey Bass, 1985), 8–12.
34 David Kirkpatrick, "Could AT&T Rule the World?," *Fortune*, May 17, 1993, 55–66.
35 Leslie Cauley, *End of the Line: The Rise and Fall of AT&T* (New York: Free Press, 2005), 116–117.
36 Hamel, "The What, Why and How of Management Innovation," 74.
37 "The World's Most Innovative Companies," *Business Week*, April 24, 2006, 68.
38 Rogers, *Diffusion of Innovation*, 5.
39 "Apple Music Event 2001—The First Ever iPod Introduction," Available at: http://www.youtube.com/watch?v=kN0SVBCJqLs (retrieved November 12, 2007).
40 Rosabeth Moss Kanter, *When Giants Learn to Dance* (New York: Simon & Schuster, 1989), 217.
41 Robert Hoff, "Building an Idea Factory," *Business Week*, 11 October 2004, 194.
42 Jena McGregor, "Most Innovative Companies," *Business Week*, May 14, 2007, 60.
43 "Most Innovative Companies," 60.
44 Rosabeth Moss Kanter, "Innovation: The Classic Traps," *Harvard Business Review*, November 2006, 73–83.
45 Ibid., 79.
46 Christensen, *The Innovator's Solution*, 73–100.

PEOPLE INDEX

Aaker, David 224, 328
Albarran, Alan 224, 254, 287
Allan, Paul 345
Armstrong, Gary 334
Armstrong, Michael 252
Åsdal, C.G. 195
Aufderheide, Pat 261

Badaracco, Joseph 343
Ballinger, Jeff 259–260
Ballmer, Steve 344
Barton, Joe 263
Bass, Bernard 342
Battelle, John 238
Baxter, William 136
Bell, Trudy 134
Bennis, Warren 248, 340, 350
Bergdolt, J. 231
Bernard, Chester I. 279
Bernt, Phyllis 136
Bewkes, Jeff 262
Birnbaum, Robert 367–368
Biondi, Frank 89
Bochco, Steven 55
Bossidy, Larry 39
Brin, Sergey 234
Brown, Charles 135
Burns, James MacGregor 341

Cannell, Steven 55
Caroll, Paul 370
Carroll, Ray 75, 77
Case, Steve 260, 262
Cauley, Leslie 371
Champy, James 288–289
Chan, Chin Bong 93–94
Chan-Olmsted, Sylvia 225–226
Charran, Ram 39

Chesbrough, Henry 374
Christensen, Clayton 360, 367–368
Cohan, J. 264
Collins, Jim 17, 44, 294–295, 343, 357, 367, 369
Cooper, Cynthia 355
Cronkite, Walter 264

Davies, Donald 148
Davis, Donald 75, 77
Deal, Terrence 31
Dell, Michael 363–364
Demers, Dave 263
Deming, W. Edwards 17, 287, 362
Disney, Walt 31
Dredden, G. 231
Drucker, Peter 286, 291

Eastman, Susan Tyler 65
Ebbers, Bernard 167, 355–356
Eisenhower, Dwight 344
Eisner, Michael 270
Elgin, Ben 237
Ellinghouse, William 133

Fairhurst, Gail 17
Fayol, Henry 278–279
Ferguson, Doug 65
Follett, Mary Parker 279
Fowler, Mark 95
Frieden, Robert 91, 171
Friedman, Thomas 244

Gandhi, Mohandas 342–343
Gardner, John 345, 347, 350
Gates, Bill xvi, 344–345
Gershon, Richard 92, 246, 340
Gifford, Kathy Lee 259

Goldhar, Joel 232
Green, Harold H. 135
Grow, Brian 237

Ha, Louisa 224–225
Hamel, Gary 371
Hammer, Michael 288–289
Hartenstein, Eddie 181
Hearit, Keith 259
Hennink-Kaminski, Heidi 321
Herman, Edward 242
Herzberg, Frederick 281
Heyer, Steven 225
Hoff, Robert 373
Hoover, Herbert 344
House, Robert 343
Hunger, J. David 25
Hunt, E.K. 193

Ibuka, Masaru 31, 243
Iger, Robert 86
Ive, Jonathan 367

Jasco, S. 242
Joachimsthaler, Erich 328
Jobs, Steve xiv, 366–367
Jordan, Michael 258–259
Juran Joseph 17, 287, 362

Kagan, Paul 92
Kanter, Rosabeth Moss 373
Kennedy, Allan 31
Kerry, John 172
Kim, W. Chan 360, 365
King, Martin Luther 342
Kleinrock, Leonard 148
Knight, Phil 258
Kotler, Philip 334
Kotter, John 272, 344–345
Küng, Lucy 294

Lashinski, Adam 235
Lauhren, J. 195
Lee, Charles R. 166
Lee, Tim Berners 217–218
Lei, David 232
Levin, Gerald 91, 262, 349
Liman, Arthur 249

Malone, John 248
Mandela, Nelson 342
Martin, Kevin 120
Mauborgne, Renee 360, 365

Mayo, Elton 280
McChesney, Robert 242
McGowan, William G. 167
McGrath, Judy 116
McGregor, Douglas 281–283
McNamara, Robert 291
McSlarrow, Kyle 116
Mintzberg, Henry 25
Miszerjewksi, Bozena 254
Mohn, Reinhard 30, 243
Morita, Akio 31–32, 243, 372
Mosco, Vincent 263
Murdoch, Rupert 81–84, 237, 248, 253, 349

Nathan, John 361
Negroponte, Nicholas 239, 370
Noble, Dan 193
Northhouse, Peter 340, 343

Ohga, Norio 361
Oncken, William 353
O'Reilly, Tim 238
Ouchi, William 283
Owen, Bruce 51, 56

Page, Larry 234
Paley, William 31
Parsons, Ed 91
Parsons, Patrick 91
Parsons, Richard 262
Perry, Rick 170
Peters, Tom 17, 290–291
Picard, Robert 6
Pilotta, J. 242
Pittman, Robert 261–262
Pollock, Clark 348
Poole, Ithiel de Sola 85, 225, 239
Poras, Jerry 367
Porter, Michael 33, 291–293, 327

Reagan, Ronald 95, 129, 191
Redstone, Sumner 115, 248
Rightmire, Rod 340
Ring, D.H. 193
Ritchie, S. Donley 346
Rizzuto, Ron 296
Rogers, Everett 218, 360, 372
Roosevelt, Franklin 344

Saffo, Paul 218

Sarnoff, David 344
Saunders, George 135
Schein, Edgar 370
Schmitt, Carl 244
Schumpeter, Joseph 358
Seidenberg, Ivan 166–167, 347
Sherman, Barry 78
Smith, Bill 362
Smith, Hyrum 271, 353
Spar, Deborah 258
Sterling, Christopher 136
Stringer, Howard 32, 243
Sullivan, Scott 355

Taylor, Frederick W. 277
Trienens, Howard 135
Truman, Harry 344, 351
Turner, Ted 31, 181, 248, 349–350
Turow, Joseph 3,

Van der Hoek, Mark 196

Vernon, Raymond 368

Walson, John 90, 91
Wass, Donald 353
Waterman, Robert 17, 290–291
Weber, Max 279
Weiss, Martin 136
Welch, Jack 36
Wheelen, Thomas 25
Widman, T. 242
Wildman, Steven 51, 56
Wiley, Richard 347–348
Wirth, Michael 92, 296
Wolf, Dick 55
Woods, Tiger 258
Wozniak, Steve 366

Yates, Buford 355
Young, W.R. 193

Zuckerberg, Mark 241

COMPANY INDEX

ABC 7, 52–53, 56, 65, 68, 84–86, 95, 224, 310
Alamo 293
Alcatel 209, 251
Alltel 127
Amazon.com xiv, 29, 216, 220, 222, 225, 238, 331, 366
America On-Line (AOL) 222–223, 249, 251–252, 260–263
American Express 29
Apple xiv, 10–12, 29, 86, 102, 210, 214, 233, 309–310, 327–328, 331, 361, 366–367, 369, 372–373
Arabsat 127, 185
Arbitron 78, 324
Arianespace 188–189
AT&T xiv, 7, 26, 118, 127, 130–137, 139–140, 169–171, 175, 194, 249, 251–252, 310, 328, 330, 370–371

Bertelsmann 30, 31, 243, 245–246, 255
Bertelsmann Music Group (BMG) 246
Best Buy 331
Black Entertainment Television 39, 85, 97, 100, 293
Blockbuster Video 29, 229
Boeing 178, 184, 189
British Sky Broadcasting 253, 349

CB Network 100
CBS 7, 52–53, 58, 65, 84–85, 95, 224, 246, 249–251, 310, 330, 361–362
Charter 94–95
Christian Broadcast Network 293
Chrysler 257
Circuit City 331
Cirque du Soleil 365
Cisco 29, 94–95

Claritas 325–326
Clearwire Communications 213
CNBC 327–328
CNN 85, 92, 95–96, 100–101, 181, 242, 349–350
Comcast xiv, 9, 26, 94–95, 108, 130, 170–171, 249, 251–252, 313, 331
Cox Cable xiv, 26, 108, 130, 331
CW Network 53, 60

Daimler 257
Dell 29, 102, 220, 234, 331, 363–365
Deloitt Research 247
DirecTV 26, 118, 181–182, 327
Discovery channel 101
Dish Network (Echostar) 26, 118, 181–182
Disney 9, 18, 29, 37, 44–48, 52, 55, 56, 86, 102, 242, 245–246, 250, 255, 270, 311–312, 328, 361
Disney Channel 96, 293, 328
Dreamworks 102

eBay 220–222, 233, 360, 366
Enron 263, 355
ESPN 29, 45–46, 85, 92, 95–96, 100–101, 181, 224, 327
Eutelsat 185
Expedia 219

Federal Express 220
Ford 257
FOX 7, 52, 53, 81–84, 95, 224, 245, 253, 310, 349, 330
FOX News 327
Fujitsu 209

Gartner Group 247

Gateway 220, 331
General Electric 36
General Motors 257, 370
Globalstar 185
Google 29, 171, 218, 221–223, 228,
    234–238, 262, 316, 361, 366
Great Wall 189

HBO 8, 19, 85, 91–92, 95, 106, 175,
    180–181, 224, 242, 261, 293, 327,
    361, 363, 366
Hewlett Packard 345
History Channel 97
Home Shopping Network 105

IBM 247, 345, 362–363, 369–371
Inmarsat 185
Intel 9, 29, 247
Intelsat 127, 176–177, 190–192, 251
International Launch Services 189
International Telecommunications
    Union 146, 149, 187–188

Kagan Research 103, 105

Lands' End 220, 233
Lexis Nexis 221
LG 208
Liberty Media 248, 317
L.L. Bean 233, 331
Lockheed Martin 188–189
Loral Space & Communication 127, 185
Lucky Stores 346

McDonalds 35
MCI 133–134, 139, 167–168, 251,
    355–356
Mediamark Research and Intelligence
    323
Metro-Goldwyn-Mayer (MGM) Studios
    246
Microsoft xvi, 9, 22, 23, 29, 171, 224,
    237, 292, 306, 344–345, 361, 369
Mitsubishi 189
Motorola 27, 193, 208, 330, 362
MTV 38, 92, 95, 101, 114–116, 181,
    224, 250, 292

NASA 188
Nationwide Communications 348
NBC Universal 7, 9, 14, 15, 36, 52–53,
    55, 65, 68, 84–85, 95, 224, 245, 251,
    255, 310

Netflix xiv, 30, 326
News Corporation Ltd. 9, 37, 188, 237,
    245, 248, 251, 253, 255, 349, 366
Nielsen Media Research 51, 78–81,
    237
Nike 229, 258–260
Ningbo Bird 209
Nissan 257
Nokia 195, 208, 359
Nordsat 127, 185
NTT DoCoMo 205

Office Max 229
Oracle 247
Orbital 189

Palapa 127, 185
Panasonic 209
Pantech Curitel 209
Paramount 52, 55, 102
PayPal 234
Philips 361–362, 374
Pixar Studios 46, 363, 366
PSLV 189
Public Broadcasting Service (PBS)
    60–62, 95, 100, 224

QVC 105
Qwest 127, 139

Rand 148
RCA 175, 344

Samsung 208
SatMex 185
Scarborough Research 324
Sea Launch 189
Sears 220, 369
SES 127, 185
Showtime 250
Simmons Market Research Bureau
    323
Sirius Radio 127, 251–253
Sony 10, 29–31, 33–34, 102, 224, 243,
    245–246, 255, 292, 314, 328,
    361–363, 369, 372, 374
Sony BMG 331
Sony Ericsson 27, 208
Southwest Airlines 293
SpaceX 189
Sprint-Nextel 7, 127, 133, 250–251,
    328, 330
SRI Consulting Business 324

Stratos 185
Sun Microsystems 22

Target 220, 331
TCI 251–252
Telefonica 27
Telefutura 53–54
Telemundo 53–54, 100
TeleSat Canada 127, 185
Texas Instruments 247
Time Warner 10, 37, 108, 171, 242,
    245, 249, 251–253, 255, 260–263,
    331, 348
Time Warner Cable 242
T-Mobile 7, 127, 330
Toshiba 102
Toyota 288
Twentieth Century Fox 53, 55, 349

Univision 53–54, 100
UPS 220
USA Network 101, 181

Verizon 7, 26, 118, 127, 130, 139,
    165–170, 227, 251, 301, 309–310,
    330, 347, 356, 361
Verizon Wireless 127
Viacom 115, 237, 242, 245, 248, 255,
    316
VNU Media Measurement 324
Volvo 257
Vonage 157

Wal-Mart 13, 21, 293, 331
Warner Brothers Records 331
WebMD 221
Wiley, Rein and Fielding 347
Wilmer, Cutler and Pickering 356
WorldCom 167–168, 251, 263,
    355–356

XM Radio 182

Yahoo 171, 218, 221–223, 228, 237,
    262

SUBJECT INDEX

Advertisers 52, 62–65
  Advertising agency 62–63
  Broadcast advertising 63–65, 74
Anticompetitive behavior
AT&T divestiture, break up of 129,
  131–137, 139, 144
  Modification of Final Judgment 136

Branding, brand management 8,
  224–225, 328
Broadcast industry structure 52–65
  Advertisers 52, 62–65
  Independent stations 52, 59
  Network affiliate stations 52, 57
  Owned and operated stations (O&Os)
    57–58
  Program producers, distributors 52,
    55–56
  Public broadcasting 52, 60–62
  Station groups, group broadcaster 57
  Television networks 52, 53–55
    Network clearance 55
    Network compensation 59
Broadcast programming 65–70,
  Day parts 67
  Financial interest and syndication
    rules 54
  Negotiation 75–77
  Positioning and profitability 69
  Primetime 67
  Program development 65–66
  Program selection and scheduling
    66–69, 72
  Syndication 54, 56, 73–77
Broadcast station management 70–72
  Business 51, 71–72
  Engineering 71
  News 71

Responsibilities of general manager
  71–72
Research, Sales and marketing 70,
  77–78
  Cost per thousand 81
  Demographics 51–52
  Rate cards 78
  Ratings and shares 78–81
  Station representative (rep.) 74–75

Cable communications policy act, 1984
  96, 114, 129
Cable networking 91–92, 95, 97
Cable television 90–121, 180–181, 218,
  240, 321, 327, 331
  Business structure, 7, 9, 94, 96–97,
  Cable cards 119
  CATV, early history 86, 90, 91
  Customer service 98, 109–110
  Dual carriage ruling 120
  Franchise, franchise fees 110–114,
    116
  Hybrid fiber coaxial cable 93, 103
  Information services 102–105,
    120–121
    Cable modems, Internet access 103,
      121, 218, 240
    Cable telephony 103
    Home shopping 104–105
  Multiple system operator (MSO) 35,
    94, 95–96, 98–99, 108, 321, 331
  Narrowcasting 96, 225
  Pay cable television 100–101, 123
    Pay per view – video on demand
      101–102, 326
  Programming 96–98, 100–102, 107
  Responsibilities of cable manager
    99–100

Cable television – *Cont.*
  Sales and Marketing 98, 106–109
  System design, overview 92–94
Cellular telephony and wireless 12, 88,
    193–215
  3G Wireless 12, 207–208, 212, 214
  Base station 196, 198–201
  Bluetooth 211
  Business 206, 209–211
  Cell site 196
  Cell splitting 197–199
  Cellular geog. service area (CGSA)
    196–197
  Cellular telephone, Digital cell phone
    196, 202–203, 208–211
  Early history 193–195
  Frequency Reuse 193, 197
  Global system for mobile comm.
    (GSM) 204–208
  Mobile tel. switching office (MTSO)
    196, 198, 200–201
  Multiple access, principle of 203–205
    Fixed vs. demand assignment 203
    FDMA 203–204
    TDMA 204–205
    CDMA, W-CDMA 204–205,
    208
  Text messaging 210, 239
Common carriers 5, 127, 138
Compact disk (CD) 12–13, 28–30,
    361–362, 372
Computer aided design, manufacturing
    277
Core competency 29, 245, 270
Cross media ownership 37, 85, 253–254
Cross subsidization, price averaging
    127–128

Demographics 51, 375
Deregulation 95, 129–130, 244, 262,
    356
Deregulation paradox 263
Diffusion of authority 263, 301
Digital television xiii, 87–88
Digital video disks (DVD) 8, 29, 30, 37,
    56, 74, 102, 326, 362
Digital video recorder (DVR) xiii–xiv,
    84, 86–87, 158, 225, 239, 290
Direct broadcast satellite (DBS) 7, 14,
    118, 126, 175–176, 181–182,
    245, 253, 349
Diversification 35–36

Economic concentration 253–254
Economies of scale 13, 14
Electromagnetic spectrum 11, 12
Electronic commerce 12, 14, 219–221,
    233–234, 238, 241, 360
  Business to business (B2B) 220, 241
  Business to consumer (B2C) 220, 241
  Consumer to consumer (C2C)
    220–221, 241, 331
  Exchange efficiency 13, 233, 238
Elements of market structure 6
  Barriers to entry 8
    Absolute cost barriers 8
    Established leaders 9
    Scale economy barriers 9
  Buyer concentration 10
  Demand growth 10–11
  Product differentiation 8
  Seller concentration 7
    Monopoly 7
    Oligopoly 7
    Pure Competition 8
European community 247
Exclusive dealing – tying arrangements
    22, 23

Federal Communications
    Commission xiii, 12, 19, 54, 95,
    100, 149, 170, 193–194, 297,
    302 347
Fiber optic communication 11, 150–153
  SONET 139, 153–154
Financial management 296–320
  Assets and liabilities 302–305, 319
  Balance sheet 302–306, 318
  Corporate bonds 317–318, 320
  Depreciation 299–300
  EBITDA 309–310
  Equity, owners' equity 304–305
  Generally accepted accounting
    principles (GAAP) 297
  Income statement 297–301, 318
  Income projecting financial performance
    309–313, 319
  NASDAQ 315–316, 319
  Net income 300, 310–312
  Profitability ratios 296, 310–311
  Securities Exchange Commission
    (SEC) 297
  Segment disclosures 311–313
  Statement of cash flows 305–308, 319
  Stock Market 315–316, 319–320

Tracking stock 317, 320
Wall Street primer 313–320
High definition television (HDTV)
    87–88, 98, 100, 102, 105, 130,
    239, 347
Home Box Office v. FCC 19, 20, 85
Horizontal integration 35

Innovation 330, 358–376
    Business model 365–367
    Culture of innovation 373–374
    Partnerships and collaboration 374
    Process innovation 362–365
    Product innovation 360–362
    Why companies fail to innovate
        367–373
        Lengthy development times 371
        Organizational culture 370–371
        Risk averse culture 372–373
        Tyranny of success 369–370
    Innovator's dilemma 30, 368–369,
        373
Intellectual property 236, 249
    Music piracy 28, 29
Internet 11–12, 14, 22, 85, 130, 148,
    216–241, 331, 367
    ARPANet 148, 216–217
    Click fraud 236–237
    Hypertext mark up language (HTML)
        217–218, 221, 363
    Internet service providers (ISP)
        170–171, 261
    Marketing 223–229
        Advertising 226–228
        Banner ads. 227
        Key word search 228, 235
        Micromarketing, personalization
            219–220, 225–226, 290, 336
        Viral marketing 229, 332
    Net Neutrality 170–172
    Portals, search engines 221–223, 226
    Social networking 216, 222,
        228–229, 240
        Facebook 216, 222, 229, 237, 241
        My Space 216, 222, 229, 237, 241,
            309
        You Tube 222, 229, 237–238
    Television websites 224–225
    Web 2.0 238–239
Internet protocol television (IPTV) 7,
    118–119, 126, 155, 157–158,
    169–170, 347

iPhone 210, 214, 367
iPod xiv, 86, 102, 225, 239, 290,
    367, 372–373
iTunes xiv, 12, 171, 216, 233, 309–310,
    327, 331, 367

Just-in-time manufacturing 225, 232,
    364

Leadership
    Challenges 352–354
    Charismatic 343, 357
    Ethics 354–356
    Followership 350–352
    Level 5. 295, 343, 357
    Transactional 341–342
    Transformational 271, 341–342

Management (What do managers do?)
    269–276
    Communicating 274–276
    Controlling 274
    Leading 271–272
    Organizing 270–271
    Planning 269–270
    Staffing 272–274
Management theory 276–295
    Classical perspective 276–279
        Administrative management
            278–279
        Bureaucratic management 279
        Scientific Management 277
    Human relations perspective 276,
        279–284
        Hawthorne studies 280
        Hierarchy of needs theory
            280–281
        Motivation-hygiene theory 281
        Theory X & Y 281–283
        Theory Z 283–284
    Management science perspective 276,
        284–285
        Computer aided design and
            manufacturing 285
        Operations management 284
    Modern management perspective 276,
        285–290
        Management by objectives
            286–287
        Reengineering 288–290
        Total quality management 17,
            287–288

Management theory – *Cont.*
  Organizational performance
    perspective 276, 290–295
Management labor relations
Market conduct 16, 17
  Anticompetitive behavior 20, 21, 22
    Exclusive dealing and tying 22–23
    Predatory pricing 21
    Price fixing and collusion 20–21
  Attitudes – product quality 16–18
  Legislating against competition
    18–20
Marketing, marketing plan 322–339
  Customer relationship management
    322, 333–337
    Building customer relationships
      334–336
    Lifetime customer value 333–334
    Relationship marketing strategies
      336–337
  Marketing mix (Four Ps) 322,
    329–333
    Price 330–331
    Product 330
    Place 331
    Promotion 332–333
  Marketing strategy 326–329
    Product positioning 327–328
    Selecting target market 327
  Quantitative v. qualitative research
    338–339
  Situation analysis 322–326, 330
    Consumer analysis 322
    Demographic research 323, 327
    Geo-demographic research
      324–326
    Market research 326, 337–339
    Psychographic research 323, 327
Media mix 63
Media organizations 3
Mergers and acquisitions 249–252,
  260–262, 348
  Strategic alliances 250
Microeconomics 6
Motion Pictures Expert Group (MPEG)
  175
MP3 xv, 12, 203, 210, 216, 239, 241,
  326, 359, 367, 373
Munn v. Illinois 124

National Association of Broadcasters 19,
  273

National Association of Television
    Program Executives (NATPE) 74
National Cable & Telecommunications
    Association 97, 103–105,
    116–117, 169, 273
Natural monopolies 122, 126
New media 216, 239–241
  Convergence 239
  Permeability, principle of 240
  Virtual communication 240–241
Nordic Mobile Telephony (NMT) 195

Olympic Games 14–16
Organizational culture 30–31, 242–243,
  370–371
Organizational decisionmaking 31–32
OPEC 20

Personal computer 12, 22, 23, 130,
  344–345, 363–364, 366, 370
Post Telephone & Telegraph (PT&T) 127
Price cap regulation 129
Price fixing and collusion 20, 21
Privacy issues 236
Privatization 130–131, 244, 262
Product life cycle 30, 368–369
Production cycles 3
Program producers, distributors 52,
  55–56
Public broadcasting 52, 60–62
  Corporation for Public Broadcasting
    60
  Organization and financing 61–62
  Public Broadcasting Service (PBS)
    60–62
Public utilities 122–126
  Justification 125–126
  Problems with 126
  Regulation 123–124
    Public utility commissions 124,
    297

Radio Frequency Identification (RFID)
    tags 232
Rate of return regulation 128–129
Recording Industry Association of
    America (RIAA) 28
Retransmission consent 95, 97, 119

Satellite communication 13, 173
  Applications
    Broadcast TV 180

Cable television 180–181
  Mobile 183
  Satellite radio 182
  VSATs 176
  Business of 183–190
    Ground equipment 184–185
    Launch 183–184, 187–188
    Satellite carriers 183–186
    Satellite manufacturing 184–185
  Earth station 175, 178
  Footprint 175–176
  Geosynchronous orbit 173
  Global positioning satellites 183
  Spin and three axis stabilization
    177–178
  Telemetry, tracking and command
    179
  Transponder 174–175
Sherman Antitrust Act 20, 276
Six Sigma 284, 362–363
Small business consulting 159–165
Strategic planning 24
  Evaluation and control 24, 42–44,
    48–49
    Measuring performance 42, 43
    Taking corrective action 44
  Environmental scanning 24–34, 48
    External environment 25–29
    Internal environment 29–34
  Strategy Formulation 24, 34–39,
    48–49
    Competitive business strategy
      37–39
    Planning and growth strategies
      35–37
  Strategy Implementation 24, 39–42,
    48–49
Supply and pricing 11–12
Supply chain management 220–221,
    229–234, 364
  Enterprise resource management
    (ERP) 231–233
Swedish Telecommunications Adm.
    195
SWOT (Strengths, Weaknesses 25,
    48
  Opportunities and Threats Model)
Syndication 54, 56, 73–77
  Syndication contract features
    76–77

Tariffs and rates 128

Telecommunications Act, 1996 26
Telephony
  Business structure
  CLECs 139, 155
  DSL 138, 155–156, 218, 240,
    347
  Franchising policy issues 169–170
  Local access and transport area (LATA)
    144
  Local exchange carrier (LEC) also
      Incumbent LEC (ILEC) 138–140,
      144, 149, 155, 157–158,
      169–170
  Queuing theory 284
  Regional Bell operating companies
    139
  Switching and routing 141–149
    Class 5 telephone switch
      143–145
    Handset and box 140
    Local loop 141–142
    North America numbering plan
      149–150
    Packet switching 145–149,
      157–158
    SS7 146–147
    Star network configuration
      142–143
    Telephone number 149–150
    Touchtone 140–141
    T1-T4 (DS1-DS4) 153–154
Total quality management (TQM)
    17–18, 287–288, 362–363
Transnational media corporation 30, 32,
    37, 53, 242–265
  Assumptions and misconceptions
    242–243
  Foreign direct investment (FDI) 242,
    245–249, 257, 259, 264
    Risks associated with 248–249
  Global outsourcing, off shoring
    254–260
  Purpose of a global business strategy
    244–245
  Technology transfer 257

United States Telecommunications As.
    273
United States v. Microsoft 22, 23
Universal service 127, 131

Value chain analysis 33, 34, 293–294

Vertical integration 36–37, 44–48, 54

Voice over Internet protocol (VOIP) 27, 104, 138, 148, 155–157, 213

Wi-Fi 211–212

WIMAX 88, 212–214

Windowing 56

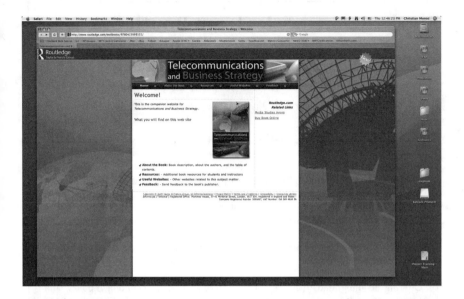

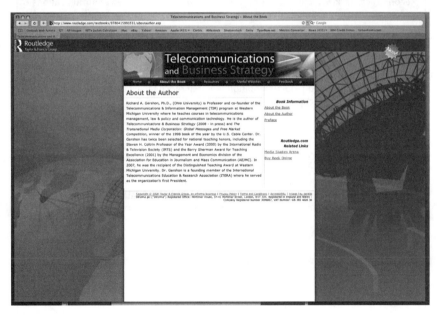

 Visit the companion website: www.routledge.com/textbooks/9780415993531

Related titles from Routledge

Shaping American Telecommunications
A History of Technology, Policy, and Economics

Christopher H. Sterling, Phyllis W. Bernt, and Martin B.H. Weiss

Shaping American Telecommunications examines the technical, regulatory, and economic forces that have shaped the development of American telecommunications services. This volume is both an introduction to the basic technical, economic, and regulatory principles underlying telecommunications, and a detailed account of major events that have marked development of the sector in the United States. Beginning with the introduction of the telegraph and continuing through to current developments in wireless and online services, authors Christopher H. Sterling, Phyllis W. Bernt, and Martin B.H. Weiss explain each stage of telecommunications development, examining the interplay among technical innovation, policy decisions, and regulatory developments.

Offering an integrated treatment of the interplay among technology, policy, and economics as key factors defining the development of the telecommunications sector in the United States, this volume also provides:

- background material to facilitate understanding of each sector;

- contexts for many so-called "new" issues, problems, and trends, demonstrating origins from years or decades in the past; and

- careful annotation, documentation, and reference tables to enable further research on the topics discussed.

This unique multidisciplinary approach provides a balanced view of U.S. telecommunications history, in context with relevant economic, legal, social, and technical analyses. As such, it is essential reading for advanced students in telecommunications needing to understand how the telecommunications industry and service developed to its current form. The volume will also serve as a supplemental text in courses on telecommunications regulation, and it will be of value to professionals in the field seeking context and background for their daily work.

ISBN 13 hbk 978–0–8058–2236–6

Available at all good bookshops
For ordering and further information please visit:
www.routledge.com